D1761023

Maynooth Research Guides for Irish Local History: Number 12

Exploring the history and heritage of Irish landscapes

Patrick J. Duffy

FOUR COURTS PRESS

Set in 10.5 pt on 12.5 pt Bembo by
Carrigboy Typesetting Services for
FOUR COURTS PRESS LTD
7 Malpas Street, Dublin 8
e-mail: info@four-courts-press.ie
www.four-courts-press.ie
and in North America by
FOUR COURTS PRESS
c/o ISBS, 920 N.E. 58th Avenue, Suite 300, Portland, OR 97213

© Patrick J. Duffy 2007

A catalogue record for this title
is available from the British Library.

ISBN 978–1–85182–965–1

All rights reserved. No part of this publication may be
reproduced, stored in or introduced into a retrieval system,
or transmitted, in any form or by any means (electronic,
mechanical, photocopying, recording or otherwise),
without the prior written permission of the
copyright owner.

SPECIAL ACKNOWLEDGMENT

AN
CHOMHAIRLE
OIDHREACHTA

THE
HERITAGE
COUNCIL

This publication was grant-aided by the Heritage Council
under the 2007 Publication Grant Scheme.

The author wishes to acknowledge financial assistance
from the NUIM Publications Fund.

Printed in England
by MPG Books Ltd, Bodmin, Cornwall.

Contents

Illustrations

Abbreviations

BT	British Telecom
CDB	Congested Districts Board
CIE	Córas Iompar Éireann
CoI	Church of Ireland
CSO	Central Statistics Office
DoE	Department of Environment
DPJ	*Dublin Penny Journal*
DS	Down Survey
ED (DED after 1898)	Electoral Division (District Electoral Division)
ESRC	Economic and Social Research Council (UK)
ESB	Electricity Supply Board
GAA	Gaelic Athletic Association
GIS	Geographical Information Systems
GMT	Greenwich Mean Time
GNR	Great Northern Railway
GPO	General Post Office
GS&WR	Great Southern and Western Railway
GSI	Geological Survey of Ireland
GSIHS	Group for the Study of Irish Historic Settlement
IFC	Irish Folklore Collection (see NFC)
IHS	*Irish Historical Studies*
IHTA	*Irish Historic Towns Atlas*
ILC	Irish Land Commission
IMC	Irish Manuscripts Commission
IUP	Irish University Press
JRSAI	*Journal of the Royal Society of Antiquaries of Ireland*
MGWR	Midland Great Western Railway
NAI	National Archives of Ireland
NFC	National Folklore Collection
NGI	National Gallery of Ireland
NI	Northern Ireland
NLI	National Library of Ireland
NUIM	National University of Ireland, Maynooth
OPW	Office of Public Works
OS	Ordnance Survey
OS*i*	Ordnance Survey Ireland
OS*ni*	Ordnance Survey Northern Ireland
PLU	Poor Law Union
PRONI	Public Record Office Northern Ireland

RDS	Royal Dublin Society
REO News	*Rural Electrification Organisation Newsletter*
RIA	Royal Irish Academy
R.I.A. Proc	*Royal Irish Academy Proceedings*
RIC	Royal Irish Constabulary
RSAI	Royal Society of Antiquaries of Ireland
RTÉ	Rádio Telefís Éireann
SMR	Sites and Monuments Record
TCD	Trinity College Dublin
TIBG	*Transactions of the Institute of British Geographers*
UAFP	Ulster American Folk Park
UFTM	Ulster Folk and Transport Museum
UAHS	Ulster Architectural Heritage Society
UCC	University College Cork
UJA	*Ulster Journal of Archaeology*
UK	United Kingdom

Acknowledgments

Thanks to Marian Lyons for her meticulous editorial advice, Ray Gillespie for his unstinting problem-solving skills, and Assumpta Duffy for her constant support.

Thanks for their help in myriad ways to Gerry Moran, Willie Nolan, Brian Dornan, Willie Smyth, Jacinta Prunty, Brendan Toal, Proinnsias Breathnach, Dennis Pringle, Brendan Bartley, Rob Kitchin, Rod Teck, Mary Kelly, Karen Keaveney, Mary O'Brien, Penny Woods, Gerry Lyne, Bill Crawford, Brian Turner, Trevor Parkhill, Brian Graham, Margaret Crawford, Brian Walker, Sophie Hillan, Myrtle Hill, Julie Anne Stevens, Paul Ferguson, Terry Dooley, Vincent Comerford, Seamas Ó Maitiú and Muirenn Duffy.

Thanks to staff in the National Library, National Gallery, Castlebar Library, Monaghan County Museum, PRONI, Russell Library Maynooth, the Ulster Museum, Land Valuation Office, ESB Archives, and Longleat Library.

I am especially grateful to Jim Keenan for his careful preparation of the illustrations, maps and diagrams.

In memory of Padraig Clerkin
who knew and loved his landscape and place in Monaghan
(1959–2006)

Preface

> The past is all about us, the past has made us what we are and the legacy of the past is the foundation of the problems of the future. What we have inherited from the past can weigh us down or inspire us … [1]

Unprecedented modification of the Irish landscape by new transport systems, suburban sprawl and scattered rural housing has resulted in a form of landscape trauma never before experienced in this country. Enormous material (and emotional) legacies are being irreversibly altered. Though there appears to be a growing interest in the heritages of landscape, environment and nature, in general young people, who are largely suburban in origin, are seldom seen exploring the landscape. It might be said that for many young people today, cyber worlds are more familiar than the local material landscape. The landscape is a most important fact in our lives. We live in it and move around in it: it is the daily context of our experience as human beings. More importantly, it was also the context of those who went before us and have signed it with the marks of their passage, not only the great monuments and buildings of distinction, but the ordinary everyday settlement landscapes of hedges, houses and placenames. The striking thing about our landscapes, therefore, is that for centuries there has been a steady procession through these spaces and places gradually adding to the sum of their parts today. We continue to alter the legacy, but government intervention and planning today have greater potential than ever before to control and influence future development and change in the landscape.

This study focuses chiefly on the history and heritage of our modern landscapes, which emerged in the past four or five hundred years. During this period most of the familiar lineaments of landscape were laid down.

---

1 Robert M. Newcomb, *Planning the past: historical landscape resources and recreation* (Folkestone, 1979), p. 18.

'Every real existence, except God, is local, and hence every event also of which we have any knowledge had its locality. The relation of place is thus one of the most constant principles of association in every science, and in every mind.'

James Bell, *A system of geography, popular and scientific or a physical, political and statistical account of the world and its various divisions* (Edinburgh and Dublin, 1847), 6 vol.

CHAPTER I

Introducing landscape

The green fields surrounding the white houses of Ballymenone contain history. Once they were cropped with spades and loys during long days of heavy toil, but now they have been given over to grass, and the farmer's life is easier. Once the fields along the bottom were flooded regularly, but now the Arney has been dredged, and the lowland hay is better. Once the grass of the upland fields was sparse, and it took three acres to support a cow, but now the grass has been thickened with fertilizers, and the cattle are healthier and more numerous … Life improves, and improvement comes of change, but change need not come from, or lead to, violent disruption.[1]

The past lives on in the landscape which surrounds us, even more than in documentary records. Landscape might be said to be produced in two senses, materially and metaphorically: materially, in the sense that the landscape is a legacy of past economic and social order; and metaphorically in the sense that it produces meanings which vary over time as different 'readings' or constructions are put on it. Landscape is very much an all-embracing, sometimes ambiguous term – originally derived from a generalised view or prospect, or a tract of inhabited land.

In the strict meaning of the word, landscape is the natural environment, acted upon and fashioned by the economic, cultural and social practices of humanity in the past. 'Our human landscape is our unwitting autobiography … our ordinary day-to-day qualities are exhibited for anybody who wants to find them and knows how to look for them.'[2] The French geographer, Vidal de la Blache, wrote about the personality of place reflected in the *pays locales* of France, where culture, history and environment were in rhyme, where a place resembles 'a medal struck in the likeness of a people'. He particularly emphasised the significance of ordinary landscapes and people, evoking a sense of place, identity and belonging reflected in local material landscapes and associated communities.[3] European landscape diversity has grown out of the way histories, social change and environmental variety have interacted to produce distinctive places and communities, that is, landscapes. The French historian Fernand Braudel's similar perspective on *la longue durée* is becoming popular again with a rising interest in the evolution of local as opposed to global landscapes.[4] Irish geographer Estyn Evans's ideas on habitat, heritage and history in

1 H. Glassie, *Passing the time: folklore and history of an Ulster community* (Dublin & Philadelphia, 1982), p. 429. **2** P.F. Lewis, 'Axioms for reading the landscape' in D. Meinig (ed.), *The interpretation of ordinary landscapes* (New York, 1979), p. 12. **3** P. Vidal de la Blache, *Tableau de la géographie de la France* (Paris 1903 and 1979). **4** See F. Braudel, *The identity of France*

Leabharlanna Fhine Gall

Ireland also belong to this school of landscape history with their focus on topographies of mountain, valley and bog, ecologies of plants and woodland, and the human imprint of settlement. Ireland too has its *pays* reflected in the existence of distinctive 'places' like the Burren, Muskerry, Corkaguiney, Decies, Bargy and Forth, Erris, Farney, the Fews, Lecale, and other localities like Joyce Country, Connemara, Gweedore, Inisowen, the Laggan, Mourne country, Glendalough and Glenmalure.

The historical study of landscape is concerned with origins and evolution over time, with incremental change and continuities through the centuries to the present day place which we know. The landscape's spatial order can be seen as the most up-to-date version of an ongoing quest for an 'optimal' landscape. There are economic costs (of pre-existing investment in an infrastructure of fields, roads and settlement) and social/emotional costs (in bonds of family, roots and belonging) underlying tensions for conservation and change. Evans has spoken of the stage of landscape never being cleared for the next act in the drama of historical change with the present being constrained by actions taken in earlier periods.[5] The shapes and morphologies of earlier landscape layouts persist, with many of the housing developments and communications networks today, for example, continuing to fit an eighteenth- and nineteenth-century infrastructure of roads and railways. Landscape as palimpsest (in which inscriptions from early periods endure to the present) is a metaphor for the kind of change that is most characteristic of landscapes: they are marked with layers upon layers of incremental changes – described by one writer as the scar tissue of earlier inscriptions. Therefore, this is one of the most distinctive characteristics of landscape – the legacies from different times in the past accumulating to form the present day landscape. Simon Schama's apposite landscape metaphor invokes the idea of horizons of history: 'the sum of our pasts, generation laid over generation, like the slow mould of the seasons, forms the compost of our future'.[6]

Because of this we can talk of ordinary vernacular landscapes as being particularly representative of past landscape order enduring in the present, reflecting traditional structures of landholding, ways of building or cultivating and harvesting, or indeed of slower ways of getting around in the past. In this sense the field patterns, hedgerow construction, the rural houses and farmyards, road and lane networks, and location of settlements, for example, reflect elements of much older ways of living. There is often a disjuncture between the inherited landscape legacy and the needs of a modern economy and life: its scale or morphology is outmoded perhaps, more appropriate in the age of horse-drawn machinery or carts, or manual labour. Up until approximately a century ago, it was a walking world for most people – and landscapes had evolved accordingly. Broad social and economic changes have impinged on forms of the inherited landscape in different places at

(London, 1988) and *The Mediterranean and the Mediterranean world of Phillip II* (London, 1972).
5 E. Estyn Evans, *The personality of Ireland: habitat heritage and history* (Cambridge, 1973), p. 70.
6 S. Schama, *Landscape and memory* (London, 1996), p. 574; see R. Muir, *Approaches to landscape*

different rates. Landscape conservation, however, is about retaining and maintaining worthwhile elements of these earlier phases such as obsolete and abandoned relict features which are emblematic of lost worlds.

Broadly speaking there are two approaches to studying landscape with an emphasis on the material expression of landscape-as-object on the one hand, and a more subjective approach concerned with the way the landscape is perceived and represented. Throughout the following study the landscape in many cases is the primary source of investigation either directly in the field or amplified by a wide range of documentary sources such as surveys and maps, as well as literary and artistic records. The following general discussion introduces themes that are detailed throughout later chapters.

A material world tradition in history and geographical studies is part of an earlier concern with collecting and classifying data and information on landscape and region. Aspects of this older approach have been revived with developing interest in the ordinary, everyday lived and experienced landscape, reflected especially in renewed interest in the local and the vernacular which is probably a reaction to the globalisation of the past half century. The landscape is defined as a tangible, material physical space of fact and artifact. Indeed landscapes are probably more easily conceptualised as material or visual, in the sense that they can be readily recorded, measured or mapped. Historians of landscape have been concerned to understand the evolution, or the 'making' of the landscape through time, to 'describe and account for the ensemble of physical and human forms as they appeared in the field or on the topographical map'.[7] Evans's *Irish heritage: the landscape, the people and their work* (Dundalk, 1942) epitomises this approach in its chapter themes.[8]

Early studies of the English landscape followed a chronological narrative of significant phases in its development commencing with pre-Roman and Roman settlement landscapes and Anglo-Saxon villages and fields. The Domesday landscape of 1086 was systematically reconstructed with subsequent details of the medieval reclamation of woodland, marsh, moor and fen, and the emergence of the built environment in great monasteries, abbeys, cathedrals and parish churches, mills and town houses. From the sixteenth century, focus shifted to enclosure of landscape into fields and hedgerows, construction of country houses and parklands, overlain from the late eighteenth century in places by the mills and factories, roads, canals, railways, and industrial towns of the Industrial Revolution.[9]

(London, 1999). **7** Sauer, quoted in D. Cosgrove, 'Landscape and the European sense of sight — eyeing nature' in K. Anderson et al. (eds), *Handbook of cultural geography* (London, 2003), pp 249–68, p. 251; see W.G. Hoskins, *The making of the English landscape* (9th edition, London, 1970). **8** See also E. Estyn Evans, *Mourne Country: landscape and life in south Down* (Dundalk, 1951; 2nd edition, 1967); idem, *Irish folk ways* (London, 1957); idem, 'The personality of Ulster' in *Transactions of the Institute of British Geographers* (hereinafter *TIBG*), 51 (1970), pp 1–20. For an assessment of Evans see V. Crossman and D. McLoughlin, 'A peculiar eclipse: E. Estyn Evans and Irish Studies' in *Irish Review*, 15 (Spring 1994), pp 79–96 and B.J. Graham, 'The search for the common ground: Estyn Evans's Ireland' in *TIBG*, new ser., 19 (1994), pp 183–201. **9** See H.C. Darby, *The Domesday geography of*

Many of these themes, especially in the modern period, have echoes also in Ireland. In these instances, the focus remained on landscape as object, as container of cultural artifacts, which 'is allowed to speak to its skilled interpreters as hard or factual evidence'.[10] The enduring legacy of this tradition of studying landscape is an emphasis on making sense of it in our terms, measuring, quantifying, classifying and constructing generalisations. So the discussion in Ireland on dispersed or nucleated settlement patterns, clachans and clusters, on origins and classification of types of urban settlement, is part of a nineteenth-century passion for forcing everything into categories.

The main emphasis here is on the landscape as an objective, fixed and finite reality of shape or morphology, which speaks for itself as it were, is not open to multiple interpretations, and has materiality or factuality to do with humanity's occupation and settlement, which can be captured and measured in words or maps or data of some kind. So houses, fields, farms, roads, churches, are all tangible expressions of society imposing its particular cultural order and organisation at different times in the past. These material legacies of landscape order vary from place to place, region to region, country to country, with local vernacular texture resulting in a 'sense of place', in regional landscape variety, in 'scenery'.

In many ways this approach comes closest to the popular understanding of landscape as a material, visual place. There are also hints of a deeper meaning to landscape than its superficial presence, embodied in the changing nature of the relationship between people and their landscape and what it means in different periods. In this context, Irish landscapes may denote more than the eye can see: they are places of memory which can be constructed and re-constructed in different ways at different times.

READING THE LANDSCAPE

A second more subjective approach to landscape study reflects a critique of the older emphasis on material landscapes and a move away from morphology towards representation, meaning and the experience of landscape: 'landscape seems less like a palimpsest whose "real" or "authentic" meanings can somehow be recovered with the correct techniques, theories or ideologies, than a flickering text displayed on the word processor screen whose meaning can be created, extended, altered, elaborated …'[11] This is based on the belief that landscape does not speak for itself, it is 'read' by its viewers, its inhabitants, visitors, tourists, or scholars. There is more

---

eastern England (Cambridge, 1971); *A historical geography of England before 1600* (Cambridge, 1976); Hoskins, *The making of the English landscape.*   **10** R.A. Butlin, *Historical geography: through the gates of space and time* (London, 1993), p. 136; W.G. Hoskins, *English landscapes* (London, 1973), p. 5 talks about 'de-coding' the material expression of landscape.   **11** S. Daniels and D. Cosgrove, 'Introduction: iconography and landscape' in D. Cosgrove and S. Daniels (eds), *The iconography of landscape: essays on the symbolic representation, design and use of*

to landscape than meets the eye. The essential difference between the two approaches is a change in emphasis from describing the nature of the material landscape to deconstructing the nature of the gaze of the observer, be it the peasant squatter on the commons, the landowner in the eighteenth-century demesne, tourists like Arthur Young or Thomas Carlyle, painters and poets, Protestant or Catholic clergymen, or indeed the gaze of historians of landscape today looking back. The first approach emphasises the built environment, evolving infrastructures of settlement, reclamation or enclosure of landscape. The second approach shifts the emphasis to changes in ways of looking at them, through contexts of ideology, power and representation. Landscape 'is not merely the world we see, it is a construction, a composition of that world. Landscape is a way of seeing the world'. This perspective is related to a broader 'cultural turn' in social science which sees histories of landscapes as more than a collection of material artefacts which tell a story.[12]

The most common preoccupation of this more recent perspective is the representation of the landscape in a variety of media such as paintings, photographs, literature, all of which are texts whose conventions universally convey certain meanings. The landscape itself, however, is the ultimate text which can be read through the syntax and grammar of its shape, texture, colour, its streets and fields, hedgerows and trees, its boundaries and buildings, in other words its language of territorial order. We 'know' the language of our local landscape, we instinctively recognise it, though some of us might misread or miss the meaning. We are disoriented in strange foreign places because we don't 'know' their language. Landscapes, in reality or representation, can be edited or modified to change their meaning for society, a pattern characteristic of colonial and postcolonial landscapes, for example. That is why English and Irish immigrants re-inscribed the new colonised landscapes of America or Australia in familiar terms by building in European styles, planting with European species and naming with familiar names in New England or New South Wales. The Irish landscape itself experienced some of these processes following English immigration in the medieval or early-modern period, reflected in English townland names in the Pale or early-modern settlements like Virginia, Kingscourt, Maryborough or Summerhill.

Therefore landscape, whether represented in earth, brick, verse, paint, ink or prose, should be thought of as something 'to be viewed', with the view/gaze organised through certain kinds of aesthetic conventions.[13] There is a politics to landscape representation, which may be ideologically constrained, aesthetically shaped or economically determined, in other words tied to considerations of class,

past environments (Cambridge, 1988), pp 1–10, p. 8. **12** D. Cosgrove, *Social formation and symbolic landscape* (London, 1984), p. 13; D.W. Meinig, 'The beholding eye: ten versions of the same scene' in D.W. Meinig (ed.), *The interpretation of ordinary landscapes*, p. 34; see also R. Muir, 'Landscape: a wasted legacy' in *Area*, 30:3 (1998), pp 263–71. **13** S. Seymour, 'Historical geographies of landscape' in B.J. Graham and C. Nash (eds), *Modern historical geographies* (Harlow, 2000), pp 193–217.

culture, gender and identity. This approach is most commonly rendered in 'élite' landscapes which have the greatest range of representations. So-called high art, for instance, in painting or literature, portrays the landscapes and culture of élites and is still a dominant landscape discourse. Eighteenth-century landed gentry in Ireland were part of a pan-European culture which privileged classical taste in landscape and nature, in paintings, engravings, gardening books, many written in the Latin or French of educated upper classes. Their preferred landscapes were often unpeopled wilder-nesses or the manicured parklands which contemporary eighteenth-century society called 'pleasure grounds'. Indeed, the historiographical significance of this landscape discourse is due in no small measure to its dominance in the historical record: the papers, correspondence, and general documentary survival of élite narratives contrasts with the dearth of records about ordinary places occupied by ordinary people. The stories of the vernacular places of poorer classes (which make up most of the landscape) are mainly to be excavated out of the material landscape itself.

The traditional empirical approach generally assumes innocence in the changes in landscape, ignoring the importance of underlying discourse. The great houses and parklandscapes of the eighteenth century, for instance, were seen as a neutral aesthetic ornamentation of landscape: '… to surround the mansions with wide expanses of smooth, open turf dotted with clumps of noble trees … pastoral arcadian scenes … classical temples and ruins.'[14] However, representations of landscape, in painting, or building or gardening are 'not innocent of a politics … [but] deeply embedded in relations of power and knowledge'. Enclosure, one of the iconic reflections of the age of improvement in the eighteenth century, was driven by agrarian capitalism to produce a transformed and regulated land. Social relations which stood in the way of modernisation were at times ruthlessly obliterated. A study of such a landscape cannot be described in terms of an innocent transformation.[15] Such changes can be read as assertions of power over nature or neighbours; ordering, taming, even torturing a disordered nature or displaying wealth and status. Reading past landscapes produces different perspectives on the consumption of landscape: land was used by farmers to produce commodities but in the eighteenth century, landscape itself became a commodity for consumption by powerful élites – a scene, a pastoral myth, a bucolic idyll, a 'view' to gaze on for pleasure, instead of having to slave in for work. To see and classify it, as if it were a painting (*picturesque*), is only possible for the privileged perspective of the well-off élite: 'Those who work the land very rarely regard it as art. And those who live in sublime landscapes frequently regard them as dreary wilderness from which they long to escape.'[16]

Ordinary landscapes, on the other hand, are ones that people inhabit and work in, landscapes produced essentially through routine practice: most landscapes evolve

14 Terence Reeves-Smyth, 'Demesnes' in F.H.A. Aalen, K. Whelan and M. Stout (eds), *Atlas of the Irish rural landscape* (Cork, 1997), p. 201.   **15** W.J. Darby, *Landscape and identity* (Oxford, 2000), p. 9; see also R. Williams, *The country and the city* (Oxford, 1973).   **16** D. Brett, *The construction of heritage* (Cork, 1996), p. 40. See also D. Bell, 'Framing nature: first steps into the

from the 'simple choices and trivial judgements of everyday life'.[17] People in these landscapes in the past understood their place by local experience, in constructing, arranging, ordering, maintaining, modifying and adapting, naming and re-claiming it – not through abstractions of aerial views or topographical maps, complying with models of geographical order, cultural or economic behaviour. This leads one to think about how different people experienced the landscape in different ways: the gentry élites of pre-famine Ireland with the power to lay-out landscapes for their pleasure, and the leisure to view it from the carriage window or highseat of a car, with the *Post-chaise companion* (1784) or George Taylor and Andrew Skinner's road maps (*c.*1780s) for guidance; the land agent looking for ways to maximise rent through improved husbandry; the tenant farmer walking to the fair, or the peasant / labourer living on the roadside with his dunghill at the door. Their involvement in the landscape was different to ours. We have the advantage of 20:20 vision, being able to see a much bigger context than they ever conceived of: maps of all kinds, aerial photos, satellite perspectives, as well as many generations of commentaries, opinions and representations, theories and concepts, which have moulded the way we think about the landscapes around us.

APPROACHES TO IRISH LANDSCAPES

Both of the main approaches discussed above ask different questions, engaging different sources. Broadly-speaking the approaches combine what might loosely be called 'scientific' and 'artistic' approaches. The first approach utilises empirical sources of information about past landscapes, surveys and maps and archives of data, information on landscape topography, soil quality, land-use patterns, settlement patterns, placenames, field patterns, boundaries, buildings and so on. There are also clues in the landscape itself to be read in field work or excavation. A classic example of an empiricist phase in landscape history is the Ordnance Survey (OS) memoir project of the 1830s, which attempted to assemble an enormous range of geological, historical and economic data to match the topographical detail of the six-inch map survey which was being undertaken. Most of these perspectives on landscape can be quantified and measured to cast light on the characteristics of past landscapes and their evolution and change.

The second approach engages with a different range of sources which explore the idea of the landscape in a different way, involving more artistic insights of

wilderness for a sociology of landscape' in *Irish Journal of Sociology*, 3 (1993), 1–22.
17 C. Harris, 'The historical mind and the practice of geography' in D. Ley and M. Samuels (eds), *Humanistic geography* (London, 1978), p. 133. See also P. Coones, 'Geographical approaches to the study of landscape' in F.H.A. Aalen (ed.), *Landscape study and management* (Dublin, 1996), pp 15–37; T. Cresswell, 'Landscape and the obliteration of practice' in Anderson et al. (eds), *Handbook of cultural geography*, pp 269–81; see also D.W. Meinig, 'Reading the landscape: an appreciation of W.G. Hoskins and J.B. Jackson' in Meinig (ed.),

poetry and painting, writing and folklore. For instance, Seamus Heaney and other Irish writers evoke a landscape of memory in a manner that is quite different from the first approach. His 'Mossbawn' is a place of sounds and smells, light and dark textures, as well as a geographical location on a map. Heaney's is a very particular rendition of the power of place, especially local place, in our lives and expresses a kind of organic link between people and place, where time and space are inextricably interwoven in memory and experience.[18]

Different interpretations of Ireland's past have also influenced approaches to landscape history. Nationalist versions of Ireland's past adopted an insular perspective that has largely downplayed British linkages, avoiding comparative analyses and contexts within the British Isles. In terms of landscape history, for instance, urban settlements were sometimes seen as 'alien' intrusions in an immemorially rural Gaelic/ Celtic world. Though Ireland's landscape experiences diverged in significant ways from England's, the shared political and cultural histories of both islands, and especially the shared identities of the Protestant gentry élites from the seventeenth century onwards, are important to consider: they owned and controlled the land and landscape of Ireland for more than three centuries and participated in a dominant British discourse of landscape. For this reason, comparative contexts within the British Isles are important. Following the Union, many landscape processes in nineteenth-century Ireland must be considered as part of a larger imperial project, though undoubtedly because much of the island of Ireland outside east Ulster did not experience the landscape upheavals of an industrial revolution, its environmental history has been dominated by rural narratives. The post-famine experience of the land in Ireland, with land reform and removal of landowners, also diverged considerably from the British experience. However, Ireland is not unique in this history and fruitful comparisons might be made with the broader history of territorial landownership in Russia and eastern Europe.[19]

STUDYING IRISH LANDSCAPES

Figure 1.1 illustrates the interaction of processes of change that help to understand the mechanisms of landscape order reflected territorially in the shape and patterning of the landscape which are themes in the following chapters. Processes can be grouped into those that are the consequences of locational, environmental, economic, cultural, social or ideological factors. The territorial expression of these processes in varying ways and in different circumstances has resulted in the landscape order which we have inherited today.

The physical landscape of rocks, soils, ecology and plants, for example, is the basic building block which was modified, tamed and transformed by time and the

The interpretation of ordinary landscapes, pp 195–244. **18** S. Heaney, 'Mossbawn' in *Preoccupations* (London, 1980). **19** See D. Cannadine, *The decline and fall of the British aristocracy* (New Haven, 1990).

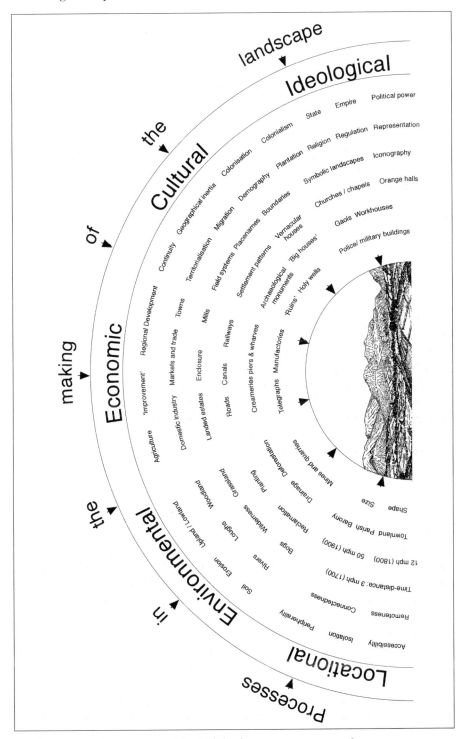

1.1 Processes in the evolution of the Irish landscape

actions of human communities. There was a piecemeal year-by-year, decade-by-decade modification of the physical landscape: drains and ditches were built, enclosures and hedges were laid out, land was reclaimed and abandoned, cabins and villages, roads and lanes spread like necklaces across the physical landscape as the fabric of settlement wove its way across a template of hills and valleys.

The scale, morphology and material qualities of the landscape have evolved slowly over time, building up layers of legacies in landscape in an apparently random fashion. Fundamental characteristics underlying nearly all changes in landscape evolution relate to distance, scale and accessibility. Much of the change can be associated with alterations in energy ratios in humanity's relationship with the landscape: from regimes of muscle-power (animal and human, with limited water and wind power inputs) which constrained much landscape change for centuries, to increasingly high-energy mechanisation which enhanced the potential for engineering and infrastructural change. The speed and range of landscape change escalated through revolutions in transport technology. Changing mobility, for instance, altered the perception and understanding of landscape. Walking (for most), horseback, horse carts, brougham, stagecoach, canal barge, bianconi cars, railway engines all represented increasingly faster and more efficient ways of overcoming the expense of distance, thus expanding accessible parts of landscape and making places closer.

Time-space compression altered perceptions and concepts of landscape as well. Landscapes of foot passengers were slow landscapes, where a day had to be set aside to get in and out of town, where there was time for leisurely observation, chatting, reflecting, looking at the landscape. Railways represented a radical compression of time-space relationships for more and more people in the nineteenth century. Patterns of housing and settlement, networks of roads and lanes, locations and distances of towns, villages and markets all evolved in these earlier technical and economic conditions. From the late twentieth century, a whole new landscape template is being laid down focussed on motorways, with up to two hours being cut off journeys between Dublin and Cork in a couple of years as the old road system inherited from the eighteenth century and earlier is abandoned. Most landscape legacies are characterised by localness: on a day-to-day basis people can more easily identify with routine local landscapes than with regional or remote places. Lasting county allegiances reflect this. So the landscape is the end result of ancestors' efforts at organising their lives, economies, communities and territories locally according to the circumstances and priorities of their times.

Figure 1.2 illustrates the relationship between the unfolding histories of earlier periods and contemporary landscape change. A great many of the social, economic or political events of the past had associated environmental repercussions expressed through agents or processes of change in local or regional landscapes. Thus in the nineteenth century a great many developments directly impacted on Irish land-scapes, such as the Poor Law Act of 1838 which initiated the construction of work-houses throughout the country. It also had more indirect impacts in terms of the effects of its regulations on small holdings and land clearances during the famine.

Diagram: *Historical events and landscape change* — a timeline chart running from 1000 to 2000, with the words **LANDSCAPE** and **IMPACTS** spanning the lower half.

Contexts	1000	1100	1200	1300	1400	1500	1600	1700	1800	1900	2000
Spatial	Predominantly local ->			Increasingly regional ->		Increasingly national ->				Increasingly global	
Political	Tribalism	Clans	Feudalism	War		Colonialism State	Ascendancy	Imperialism	Empire	nationalism	
	Kingship	Warfare	Lordship Overlordship			War State					
Social	Gaelic population	Church/Monastic Reform	Anglo-Norman settlers	Immigrations Borderlands	Pale	British Plantations	Immigrations Settlers	Emigration	Emigration	Immigration	
	Norse settlers										
Economic						Prot Reformation Land confiscation Land surveys	Leases Rents Estate maps	Landed estates	Ordnance Survey	Disestablishment Land reform Farmers Co. Councils	Planning Acts
Settlement	Monastic towns Rath, Bóthar	Abbeys, Cathedrals Tóchar Slite	Mottes Castles	Towns, Boroughs 3-field systems	Tower houses	Plantation towns Enclosure Deforestation	Market towns Manor houses	'Improvements' Tree planting Big house/demesnes	Subdivision	Suburbs	Motorways
						Highway acts		Canals	Railways		

1.2 Historical events and landscape change

In the sixteenth and seventeenth centuries the various plantation schemes were closely associated with radical changes to rural landscapes in terms of local migrations and land reclamation. Immigration and colonisation also has an important local explanatory role in terms of landscape evolution as far back the Anglo-Norman colonisation especially in parts of Leinster and east Munster. Activities as diverse as wars, emigration, land surveys, parliamentary legislation, lease agreements, increasing rental incomes, estate improvements, all induced or facilitated processes of landscape change in one way or another. Some of the earliest examples of topographical description came with Gerald of Wales's account following the Anglo-Norman settlement. Landscape contexts were more incidental in Gaelic sources such as the genealogies and bardic poetry. Gaelic landscape tradition probably grew more out of interest in the storied landscape, the *dinnseanchas*, than the landscape itself. Topographical writing followed British or English settlement, although Roderic O'Flaherty's account of Connacht (1684) reflects an eclipsed native tradition. The exigencies of colonial settlement in the sixteenth and seventeenth century spawned some early explorations in Irish landscape and environment by immigrant British pioneers, whose main objectives were to catalogue opportunities and describe the economic potential of new landscapes being encountered. Accounts of tours in the seventeenth and early eighteenth centuries were characterised by utilitarian interests in investment and improvement. Many of the landowning gentry in the eighteenth century developed antiquarian interests in local landscape, which often nurtured identity with places and landscape that differed from the local community's.

Ireland's landscapes of ruins especially fascinated the new élites, and ruins featured prominently in the popular Romantic renditions of landscape in the eighteenth and early nineteenth centuries: a waterfall at Ballymore Eustace, County Kildare, was described in 1808 as 'very beautiful, resembling much the Salmon Leap [Leixlip, County Kildare], but has a bad background'.[20] But in terms of scholarship, the work of the Ordnance Survey from the 1820s, and individuals associated with it, such as Petrie, O'Curry, O'Donovan, Wilde, Wakeman, and Westropp, and the establishment of archaeological and historical societies, laid the foundations for modern scholarship which eventually flourished in the new universities of Ireland. The Ordnance Survey in the early nineteenth century represented a fundamental stage in the accumulation of information about the Irish landscape: it was committed to providing invaluable information on 'the distinction between bog and cultivated land, the boundaries of counties, baronies, parishes, and townlands, the roads and lanes, the rivers and streams, the seats of gentlemen, the houses of every description, churches, chapels, mills, limekilns, quarries ... every object on which the eye could rest'.[21]

20 George Petrie quoted in P. Murray, *George Petrie (1790–1866): the rediscovery of Ireland's past* (Cork, 2004), p. 44. For discussion on antiquarianism and Romanticism in Ireland, see G.M. Doherty, *The Irish Ordnance Survey: history, culture and memory* (Dublin, 2004), pp 118–29.
21 *Prospectus of the Ordnance Survey of Ireland* (Dublin, 1837) quoted in Doherty, *The Irish*

Local history invariably engages with the local landscape because it is at the level of the local that landscape impinges most. Therefore, local historical journals containing work by highly motivated authors with a lot of local knowledge are important entry points in local landscape history.[22] In recent years there has been a surge in work on landscape history. The *Atlas of the Irish rural landscape* (1997) set a standard not only in analysis, but also in terms of maps and photographs which are important elements in any landscape study. Flowing from this Cork University Press are publishing a new series on Irish rural landscapes, with Geraldine Stout's *Newgrange and the bend of the Boyne* (2002) and Billy Colfer's *The Hook* (2004).

The growing scholarly and popular interest in the Irish landscape which corresponds with some of the most sweeping environmental changes in our history suggests that in future there will be enhanced local and general knowledge about the origins and significance of our landscape heritage. It is hoped that this will lead to a greater awareness of the importance of landscape conservation in the future.

CONCLUSION

This study relies on the work of many researchers and authors in terms of sources and case studies. It does not, however, pretend to be an exhaustive compilation and is intended chiefly as a guide and starting point for students of landscape history by highlighting major themes and elements in the making of landscape, as well as major approaches to studying and understanding its evolution. It is impossible to conduct a comprehensive examination as the nature of each individual local study and the diverse range of local landscapes will uncover wholly unique opportunities for exploration and open endless doors to a myriad of sources. This book is intended, therefore, to be broadly indicative of generic type sources. Only when pondering a problem at local level and subjecting the locality under study to intensive scrutiny will it be possible to ask the questions which send one off on one's investigations. There may be a goldmine of locally relevant records such as an estate survey, a collection of sketches or photos, a series of letters, a diary, or a particularly fruitful travel/tour account. Most of the material referred to in the following chapters is available in the National Library of Ireland, university libraries, or local county libraries which are especially relevant in the case of local studies. While individual chapters contain references to specific sources and their location, Seamus Helferty and Raymond Refaussé's *Directory of Irish archives* (Dublin, 2003) should be consulted for details on 262 major repositories in Ireland and the practicalities of undertaking research in them, such as opening times, facilities, contact details, descriptions of their principal collections and so on. William Nolan's

Ordnance Survey, p. 23. **22** J. Grenham, *Tracing your Irish ancestors* (2nd edition, Dublin, 1999) has a useful county-by-county summary of most major sources pertaining to each county, including details on publications on local history and local journals for each county. For links to other repositories, see http://www.eneclann.ie/MssLink.htm

Tracing the past: sources for local studies in the Republic of Ireland (Dublin, 1982) is useful for sources which focus particularly on landscape history. Peter Collins's *Pathways to Ulster's past: sources and resources for local studies* (Belfast, 1998) also lists sources and repositories of use for local case studies with special reference to the northern parts of the island.

CHAPTER 2

Natural landscapes

Though the traditional model which separates the world into natural and cultural domains has been challenged for not acknowledging that society and environment constitute the same world, and that nature is essentially socially produced and not a given, it helps us to focus on the way the natural has been modified by human agency. The natural landscape is the basic environmental stage which the human population has modified for millennia. In Ireland, it consists of the geological substructure of uplands and lowlands and its drainage systems, its enveloping cover of glacially-deposited sediments, clay and soil, and the consequences of processes of erosion and deposition which have shaped its topography. Altitude, aspect and environmental quality have been controlling factors in the settlement experience. The limestone substrate and its overlying soils have generated lush grasslands; granite uplands are characterised by peat covered moorlands; well-drained, richly-wooded river valleys have wide-ranging soils. As well as providing well-drained rich loams for arable farms, peatland for fuel, sand and gravel deposits for construction, the physical landscape produces rivers and streams for drainage and transport: the variability of environmental qualities has influenced the diversity of settlement processes for generations.[1]

Solid geology has a limited direct relevance for the settlement landscape apart from its influence on drainage, hill and mountain slopes, or its role in the location of extractive industries. In a general sense, some familiarity with geomorphology, soils and surface geology is important in understanding landscape use over the millennia: early societies favoured light, easily accessible and manageable soils. In early medieval times inhabitants of the Midlands showed a keen sense of eskers as routeways from one piece of good land to another. Most of the Irish landscape is owned by farmers and farming has been largely responsible for much of our landscape as we know it, so in many ways it could be argued that the history of landscape is the history of farming in Ireland. Improvements in agricultural

---

1 D. Drew, 'The shape of the land' in D. Gillmor (ed.), *The Irish countryside: landscape, wildlife, history, people* (Dublin, 1989), pp 15–47 provides the best introduction to Ireland's natural landscape for the general reader. For more detailed regional overviews see J.B. Whittow, *Geology and scenery in Ireland* (London, 1974); F. Mitchell and M. Ryan, *Reading the Irish landscape* (Dublin, 1997); P. Coxon, *The quaternary of central western Ireland.* (www.tcd.ie/Geography/IQUA) for evidence of pre-glacial landscapes and the recently published *Natural and cultural landscapes – the geological foundation*, ed. Mathew Parkes (www.ria.ie/committees/geosciences/). See also L.R. Praeger, *Irish landscape* (Cork, 1953) and Praegar's classic *The way that I went* (Dublin, 1969 reprint) which is a commentary on the natural and human

technology in modern times, as well as growth in rural populations and markets meant that virtually every part of the landscape has come within the ambit of farming activity. In the next twenty years as the numbers of full-time farmers in Ireland fall, a great deal of the landscape in the west of Ireland in particular will be abandoned and will probably revert to wilderness for the first time in many generations. Many of the outcomes of farming are popularly perceived to be part of the natural landscape – grassland, hedges, trees and so on, although they are more accurately the result of human management and husbandry over the centuries: in truth little of the countryside is 'natural'.[2] 'Pre-modern' agricultural landscapes may still often be found in remoter areas which were relatively untouched by the intensive agricultural changes that came after the seventeenth-century plantations: remoter islands in lakes, rivers and offshore for instance, or inaccessible glens, where older native plants and ecosystems may have survived. However, the ubiquitous evidence of fossil potato ridges on many mountain sides suggests that few places escaped the pressure of population in the nineteenth century.[3]

The location of extractive activities like quarries and mines clearly reflects the influence of geology. Local quarries throughout the country were used for extracting stone for building and for grave stones. Ballyknockan and its stonemasons in County Wicklow provided granite for local communities as well as for construction in Dublin city from the eighteenth century. In the parish of Boho in County Fermanagh in the early nineteenth century, sandstone for window sills, coping stones, flagstones and headstones was roughly prepared in quarries and carried to the road with ropes suspended on the backs of two or three men.[4] One of the commonest industrial activities was the use of limestone where it lay near the surface. Limestone was burnt for spreading on land or for building mortar: the use of lime for agriculture was a feature of the eighteenth-century Agricultural Revolution and limekilns of all shapes and designs from this period still litter the Irish landscape. The frequent location of limekilns on the edge of lime-rich areas was a measure of the economics of supply of the mineral to lime-deficient areas. Limestone on the Aran islands was transported to parts of Clare and Connemara which had no lime, in return for turf which had been cut away on Aran. South Monaghan, Meath and Louth had limestone which supplied the shale clays farther north in the drumlin belt. Lime kilns were usually built into hillsides in Monaghan or otherwise partly buried for efficiency in generating heat: some limekilns were filled from the top, limestone rocks broken into small pieces mixed with turf and allowed to burn for several days; in others the stone was kept separate from the fuel.

landscapes he encountered on his journeys through the country.   **2** See B. Dunford, *Farming and the Burren* (Dublin, 2002) for a discussion of the symbiotic relationship between farming and the natural environment for centuries; also J. Feehan et al., *The book of the Burren* (Galway, 2001) contains a wide-ranging series of essays on the natural, settlement and cultural landscapes of the Burren.   **3** See The Heritage Council's *Habitats in Ireland* (Kilkenny, 2004) which contains a range of studies of different natural habitats – freshwater and marsh, peatlands, woodlands, coastlands etc. www.heritagecouncil.ie/publications/   **4** Ordnance Survey Memoirs, 1835: see P. J. Duffy, *Landscapes of south Ulster* (Belfast, 1993), p. 38.

Local landed proprietors in the eighteenth and nineteenth centuries were alert to the value of limestone resources and the Shirley and Bath estates in south Monaghan, for instance, leased limekilns that local tenants were expected to use. Shirley also extracted and carted culm (a low-grade coal) on the southern borders of his estate, using it to burn the limestone. Large amounts of limestone were burnt in simple kilns fired with furze, turf and culm in Waterford and Cork in the eighteenth century.[5] Shirley was also actively involved in gypsum mining in the mid-nineteenth century. Many investors in land in the seventeenth century were keenly interested in the mineral or industrial assets of properties whose geology produced landscapes with limited agricultural potential, as at Castlecomer, Coalisland, Avoca and Arigna. Although not a product of local geology, clay deposits near water sources were also exploited for brick-making from the seventeenth century: many of the post-plantation towns in Ulster were constructed from local bricks. In the mid-eighteenth century a Clones land agent was interested in having a brickhouse constructed for the manufacture of bricks. More inferior local bricks were frequently made where clay resources allowed, as in Arney in County Fermanagh in 1835, where the farmers spent the summer season making bricks which were transported to Enniskillen.

Stone walls are an important part of the texture of landscape especially in western and upland regions, comprising in toto up to a quarter of a million miles. They vary from one part of the country to another, reflecting in many cases the parent material from which they are constructed. For this reason stone walls are intimately connected to the natural landscape, blending comfortably into their surroundings and are part of a suite of vernacular elements in local settlement landscapes. Most of the walls in the west of Ireland were constructed following the dispersal of rundale farm clusters either by landowner initiative in the half century before the famine or after the famine by landlords and the Congested Districts Board. These origins are usually reflected in rectilinear networks of walls laid out by survey or plan. Older organic networks of fields representing generations of local communal effort are evident also in places such as Connemara. Walls may be single, one stone width, or double, reflecting custom and perhaps the adaptability of the local stone. Walls in Donegal and Down are narrow, mostly composed of granite boulders which allow the wind to blow through them and deter sheep from jumping over them. Basalt predominates in Antrim, limestone in Connemara and in the Aran islands where the walls are receptacles for the surplus stones in the small gardens. Walls on Aran sometimes have many small stones filling in the bottom to restrict movement of rabbits; others have lintels and small apertures for sheep to pass through. Double walls have two faces to the walls with smaller stones filling the centre, and regular long stones tying both sides together.[6]

5 C. Smith, *The ancient and present state of the county and city of Waterford: containing a natural, civil, ecclesiastical, historical and topographical description thereof* (Dublin, 1746), p. 219; M.J. Conry, *The culm crushers* (Chapelstown, 1999). See C. Rynne, *Industrial Ireland: an archaeology* (Cork, 2006).   6 See P. McAfee, *Irish stone walls: history; building; conservation* (Dublin, 1997).

BOGLANDSCAPES

The boglands covering about one sixth of Ireland are an important component of our natural landscape. They are even more important in local landscape studies where the role of peatlands can be examined in detail as a resource for fuel, for grazing and for squatter settlement in the pre-famine period. In the medieval period, the bogs played a significant role as areas of retreat and security. For this reason colonial settlement policies from the late medieval period usually represented the peatlands (and forests) as hostile environments sheltering Irish enemies.[7] Raised bogs (the 'shaking bogs' of seventeenth-century surveys) are the deep bogs of the Midlands intersected by eskers and glacial deposits which snake their way westwards, along which settlement developed over the millennia. Blanket bogs are shallower features which developed as a result of climate changes *c*.4,000 years ago and are found in the uplands and mountain regions.[8] The presence of tree stumps and ancient timbers in the bogs, as well as the discovery of fieldscapes and house sites in north Mayo, are testament to the comparative speed of the transition to bogland. In general, as a result of their low aerobic levels (that is, with little or no oxygen), peats have a high capacity for conserving organic remains.[9] In this sense peatlands are the ultimate historical source, often preserving organic records from the past including the plant pollen, analysis of which helps us reconstruct local environments in former millennia.[10] Due to the unreliability of this technique for more recent centuries, volcanic ash or tephra from dated Icelandic eruptions, which was deposited as thin layers of microscopic glass within the peat, has been used to date environmental change from the Middle Ages.[11]

Turf as fuel has been an important part of local life for centuries (as well as being an important local source of construction timbers like bog oak) and 'saving' the turf features in folklife and folklore. There were two main methods of harvesting peat: the commonest for centuries was the 'cutting' of turf with a spade-like implement (called the *slán* in most areas) whereby farm families rented or owned turf-banks

7 A. Smyth, *Celtic Leinster: towards an historical geography of early Irish civilization, A.D. 500–1600* (Dublin, 1982); see W. King, 'On the bogs and loughs of Ireland' in *Philosophical Transactions of the Royal Society of London*, xv (1685), pp 948–60 from a discussion by J.H. Andrews, 'Land and people, *c*.1685' in T.W. Moody, F.X. Martin and F.J. Byrne (eds), *A new history Ireland, iii, early modern Ireland, 1534–1691* (Oxford, 1976), p. 455.   8 See J. Feehan and G. O'Donovan, *The bogs of Ireland: an introduction to the natural, cultural and industrial heritage of Irish peatlands* (Dublin, 1996) which is a hugely comprehensive look at all aspects of Irish bogs; J. Feehan, 'Raised bogs' in Aalen et al. (eds), *Atlas of the Irish rural landscape*, pp 108–11; Roy Tomlinson 'Blanket bogs' in ibid., pp 117–21.   9 D. Bellamy, *The wild boglands* (Dublin, 1986) describes bogs as 'living slabs of history.'   10 For critical explanation of pollen analysis, see J. Feehan, *Farming in Ireland: history, heritage, environment* (Dublin, 2003), pp 27–31; on pollen analysis as a research resource, see M. Stout, 'Early Christian Ireland: settlement and environment' in T. Barry (ed.), *A history of settlement in Ireland* (London, 2000), pp 81–109, p. 87.   11 See V.A. Hall and L. Bunting, 'Tephra-dated pollen studies of medieval landscapes in the north of Ireland' in P.J. Duffy, D. Edwards and E. FitzPatrick (eds), *Gaelic Ireland: land, lordship and settlement, c.1250–c.1650* (Dublin, 2001), pp 207–22.

from which the peat was cut. From May it was laid out to dry on the surface in a long-drawn out process before being taken home and stacked for winter. In areas where the peat was cut-away, usually following severe local population pressure as in south Ulster, mud-turf was 'made'. In this case the scrapings of the peat were mixed with water in a bog-hole and the resulting mud was spread on the surface to dry. Both operations usually involved cooperation between neighbouring families.[12]

Viewing boglands as wasteland and wilderness in need of reclamation and taming was a characteristic perspective of the Anglo-American colonial world in the eighteenth and especially the nineteenth centuries. The Bogs Commission which surveyed the larger bogs during the period 1810 to 1814 was a typical government-sponsored improvement initiative aimed at facilitating the drainage of the bogs for agriculture and flax-growing at a time of great population pressure.[13] Indeed, one of the potential benefits of canal developments such as the Grand Canal running through part of the great Bog of Allen, was its role in draining these wet deserts. The maps of the bogs produced by the commissioners are important records of the early extent of these landscapes before the intensive fuel consumption in the crowded nineteenth century and the industrial exploitation of the twentieth century cut away many of the local peatlands.[14] The bogs in twenty-two counties were surveyed by a cohort of exceptionally able engineers and surveyors, products of the new industrial and scientific age, who left a record whose potential has been largely neglected by local historians. In addition to mapping the bogs, they produced recommendations for roads and communications, drainage and rural development.[15] An Foras Talúntais in 1979 produced a map of peatlands which shows the bogs following a century and more of intensive harvesting.

DRAINAGE AND DRAINS

Accompanying fields and field topographies is the drainage network, one of the most pervasive features in the human modification of the Irish landscape. Controlling and managing the flow of water across the landscape was one of the

12 For examples from Ballygawley, Co. Tyrone in 1958, see A. O'Dowd, *Meitheal: a study of co–operative labour in rural Ireland* (Dublin, 1981), pp 140–1.   13 *First report* [*Second* 1811, *Third* 1819] *of the commissioners appointed to enquire into the nature and extent of the several bogs in Ireland and the practicability of draining and cultivating them*, HC 1810 (365).   14 See Aalen et al. (eds), *Atlas of the Irish rural landscape*, p. 109. The one-inch maps of the Geological Survey show bogs in the immediate post-famine period.   15 See *Reports of the commissioners appointed to enquire into the nature and extent of the several bogs in Ireland, and the practicability of draining and cultivating them, 1810–14*. See also reprint series of maps for the Bogs Commissioners published by Glen Maps: *Iveragh Co. Kerry in 1811* (Dublin, 2002) and *Kenmare River in 1812* (Dublin 2003) (both by Alexander Nimmo), and *Wicklow and Dublin mountains in 1812* (Dublin, 2004) (by Richard Griffith) with accompanying essays by A. Horner; see A. Horner, 'Napoleon's Irish legacy: the bogs commissioners, 1809–14' in *History Ireland*, 13, no. 5 (2005), pp 24–8; idem, *Mapping Offaly in the early nineteenth century* (Bray, 2006).

earliest human activities, and was a particularly significant aspect of modern agriculture from the seventeenth century. Drainage schemes began with the natural stream network, making it progressively more efficient in increments over the generations, straightening, deepening, channelling. Artificial drainage networks linked into this, channelling the surface water from fields by means of shores and dutch drains into dykes and ditches (called *siuchs* in Ulster) along newly-emerging field boundaries, down slope to streams, brooks and rivers, along road sides and culverted under roads. Thus it was a network laid down on farms, within townlands, linking up with arterial streams. Culverting and bridging were important human additions to the landscape, enhancing mobility across the landscape and over its natural fluvial obstructions. Walking on any country road in days following heavy rain, one can listen to the landscapes of drains and streams, as the water flows and gurgles along fields and under roads. Examination of these drainages shows the ingenuity of our forefathers in their construction and maintenance. Drainage networks at very local levels can be examined in the first instance in large-scale maps, six-inch and twenty five-inches to the mile, which show the direction of flow by means of arrows.

Much of the network probably dates mainly from the eighteenth and nineteenth centuries. An important part of estate improvement by landowners committed to development of their properties was encouragement of tenants in installing and maintaining drains. In 1741, for example, the agent on the Barrett estate at Clones was writing about drainage and reclamation:

> was lately with Mr Nixon's viewing the great bog about the island and find he has caused several large drains to be made but before he does any good must cut several cross drains which he proposes to have done next summer. I think those already done are cut in very proper places (and will help to dry the bog pretty well against next Spring and in time I believe will turn to a very good account – and so will Stubbing the hills of Lissegerton a good part of that lying on the left of the road towards Knockballymore being rooted up.[16]

The duke of Leinster drained and reclaimed extensive lands around Maynooth in the eighteenth century which continue to exhibit the results of his investment. Other wetlands in west Kildare did not have an outfall to drain off the lands without expensive pumping machinery. William Steuart Trench, who was agent in the mid-nineteenth century on the Lansdowne, Bath, Shirley and Digby estates, was also a substantial improving farmer in his own right, involved in innovative schemes for draining bogland on the Slieve Blooms.[17] During the famine, relief work often comprised drainage schemes and parliamentary legislation in the mid-nineteenth century was aimed at encouraging drainage: in 1847 landlords were given low interest loans under a Landed Property Improvement Act and tenant farmers were

16 Letter from John Todd, agent in Clones to Mr Barrett in London (PRONI, Barrett-Lennard papers, T. 2529/6/c.33).   **17** See J. Feehan, *History of farming* (Dublin, 2004), p. 263.

compensated by the length of field drains installed. Throughout the middle decades of the nineteenth century the Shirley estate ran a 'drainage account' with the purpose of making grants to tenants for land drainage – as well as planting, liming and other improvements to their farms. 'Improvement Books' on the estate recorded examples of drainage and fencing throughout the 1840s: for instance, in a dispute over five perches of fence between two tenants in June 1845, the agent adjudged that a fence should be made on one side, all the material taken out of the drain should be used for 'backing the ditch' and the fence should include proper outlets to drain the inside garden. Another tenant was granted assistance of 10*d.* per perch to drain a 'green bog' by which his 'potatoes and turf are nearly destroyed'.[18]

Wells occupied a significant place in local cultures traditionally, with many holy wells continuing as places of pilgrimage up to the present. Usually associated with a local saint from the early Christian period, miracles were often attributed to these sites. Pattern (patron) days were very common until the early twentieth century. Other wells were notable locally for having curative powers and post-Enlightenment commentators in the eighteenth century attempted scientific assessments of their effects. Charles Smith's histories contain extended accounts of chalybeate and sulphurous wells in Cork and Waterford: Bandon spa water when drunk 'to the quantity of two or three pints … has been found to excite the appetite, ease pains in the stomach, lessen swelling in the legs, and to have cured great numbers of persons overrun with the scurvy'.[19] In the neighbourhood of Clones, County Monaghan, the 'Gallibois' well had the cure for jaundice, where the patient was stripped, soaked and sweated in a neighbouring house.[20] Other curative springs or spas, such as the one at Lucan in County Dublin became fashionable resorts for the wealthy classes in the eighteenth century; expansion of railways in the nineteenth century made them accessible to the growing urban middle class.

ISLANDS OF IRELAND

Because of their relative inaccessibility, Ireland's islands (both coastal and lacustrine) are sometimes the last outposts of landscape and cultural heritage. Habitats, heritage and history, language and material culture, for example, are most immune to change in these situations.[21] The Irish language has lasted longest in such remote places as

18 Shirley papers (PRONI, D. 3531/M/7/1–5).   **19** C. Smith, *The ancient and present state of the county and city of Cork containing a natural, civil, ecclesiastical, historical and topographical description thereof* (2 vols, Cork, 1774), ii, 267.   **20** Rev. P. Skelton, 'The Jaundice Well in 1743', reprinted in the *Northern Standard*, 30 Dec. 1938.   **21** For a colourful introduction, see P. Somerville-Large, *Ireland's islands: landscape, life, and legends* (Dublin, 1999), with superlative photographs by D. Lyons; see also S. Royle, *A geography of islands: small island insularity* (London, 2001); R. Deacon, *Islands of Ireland* (Reading, 1974); K. McNally, *The islands of Ireland* (London, 1978); T.H. Mason, *The islands of Ireland: their scenery, people, life and antiquities* (Cork, 1967).

Clear Island, Inishvickillaune, the Blaskets, the Aran islands, Inishbofin, Inishturk, Achill, Aran Mór and Tory in Donegal and Rathlin off north Antrim. For reasons of inaccessibilty they were frequently sought out by anchorites and other ascetics such as the *Céile Dé* monastic orders in early medieval Ireland. The Skelligs off west Kerry represent one of the most extreme such early Christian centres. And from the nineteenth century, the islands in the west became popularly perceived as quintessentially Irish, the last outposts of authentic Irish life, sought out by participants in the late nineteenth-century cultural revival and the Blasket Island writers added to this perception in the twentieth century.

Because of its remoteness, Clare Island at the entrance to Clew Bay, was selected by the Royal Irish Academy (RIA) for a comprehensive survey of its natural and cultural resources in 1909–11. The survey, published in more than sixty reports in proceedings of the RIA (1911–15), benchmarked the flora and fauna of the island. A follow-up survey was undertaken between 1989 and 2000 to measure the extent of change in the landscape of the island during the twentieth century.[22] The Aran islands have also been studied extensively by naturalists, historians and folkorists. However, their very remoteness has been socially detrimental for Ireland's islands, whose small populations in many instances have had to abandon their homesteads. island communities became very disadvantaged especially following the electrification of the mainland. Brian Dornan provides a comprehensive case study of the past and present of some of Mayo's most remote islands, highlighting their value as laboratories to look at impacts of exogeneous and endogeneous forces on a local society and place.[23]

The Irish coastlands (dunes and *machaire*) are distinctive landscapes which have played an important part in local economies in the past. Today they are experiencing pressure from housing and golf and leisure developments which are exposing the coast to serious erosion.

---

22 J.R. Graham (ed.), *New survey of Clare Island 2: geology* (Dublin, 1999); C. Mac Cárthaigh and K. Whelan (eds), *New survey of Clare Island 1: history and cultural landscape* (Dublin, 1999); C. Manning, P. Gosling and J. Waddell (eds), *New survey of Clare Island 4: the Abbey* (Dublin, 1999); see also T. Collins, 'The Clare Island Survey: an early multidisciplinary success story' in T. Collins (ed.), *Decoding the landscape* (Galway, 1994), pp 114–32.   **23** B. Dornan, *Mayo's lost islands: the Inishkeas* (Dublin, 2000), p. 13; see also S. Royle, 'Settlement, population and economy of the Mayo islands' in *Cathair na Mart*, ix (1989), pp 120–33; D. Keogh, 'Leaving the Blaskets 1953: willing or enforced departures?' in D. Keogh, F. O'Shea and C. Quinlan (eds), *The lost decade: Ireland in the 1950s* (Cork, 2004), pp 48–71 looks at government reports on the removal of the last inhabitants on the Blaskets. On other islands, see also T. Robinson, *Stones of Aran: pilgrimage* (Dublin, 1986) and *Stones of Aran: labyrinth* (Dublin, 1995) which provide detailed personal explorations of the coastal and interior landscapes respectively of the Aran islands; R. Fox, *The Tory islanders: a people on the Celtic fringe* (Cambridge, 1978); F.H.A. Aalen and H. Brody, *Gola: the life and last days of an island community* (Cork, 1969); S. Royle, 'Exploitation and celebration of the heritage of the Irish islands' in *Irish Geography* (hereinafter *Ir. Geography*), 36 (1) (2003), pp 23–31; J. Feehan et al., *The book of Aran: the Aran islands, Co. Galway* (Galway, 1994); E. Lankford, *Cape Clear island: its people and landscape* (Cape Clear, 1999); J. Beaumont, *Achillbeg: the life of an island* (Monmouthshire, 2005).

TREES AND WOODLANDS

Traditions of woodland management (such as coppicing) in Gaelic Ireland for ...e medieval period were disrupted by the wars, upheavals in landownership and asset stripping of the late sixteenth and early seventeenth centuries which particularly affected forest resources. Wood was the plastic/concrete of the pre-modern age, used for barrels and packaging of butter, fish, wine, and for charcoal and iron smelting, building timbers and shipbuilding, and green oak bark was used for tanning. The plentiful supply of oakwoods in seventeenth-century Ireland was as much a driving force for British colonisation as other economic or political considerations.[24]

Kenneth Nicholls has used a range of documentary sources from the late medieval period on fauna, such as the goshawk and capercaillie, to reconstruct circumstantial evidence for the extent of native woodland.[25] The Desmond Survey, the Civil Survey and Books of Survey and Distribution, contemporary sixteenth- and seventeenth-century descriptions, maps such as that of Leix and Offaly *c.*1562 and Robert Lythe's maps describe great oak woods throughout the country. Written surveys often accompanying plantations contain assessments of the economic value and extent of woods. The borderlands and frontier zones which were frequently abandoned by population in the middle ages were often marked by blocks of original forest or regenerated woodland, for example, along the southern shores of Galway Bay, the shorelands of Lough Neagh, on the edges of the midland bogs and the boundaries of autonomous lordships in the late medieval period. The political consolidation of the island in the seventeenth century erased these internal borderlands and ultimately destroyed the most extensive woodlands as well.[26]

24 See E. McCracken, *The Irish woods since Tudor times: their distribution and exploitation* (Newton Abbot, 1971); idem, 'Limerick woods in Tudor times' in *Newcastle West Historical Society*, I (1979), p. 31; N. Carroll, *The forests of Ireland* (Dublin, 1984); W.A. Watts, 'Contemporary accounts of Killarney woods' in *Ir. Geography*, xvii (1984), pp 1–13; V. Hall, 'The vegetational landscape of mid-County Down over the last half millennium: the documentary evidence' in *Ulster Folklife*, 35 (1989), pp 72–85; idem, 'The woodlands of the lower Bann valley in the seventeenth century: the documentary evidence' in *Ulster Folklife*, 38 (1992), pp 1–11; see also *Champion trees: a county by county selection of Ireland's great trees* (Tree Council of Ireland, Dublin, 2005), which is a guide to more than 1,200 ancient trees in Ireland; E. Neeson, 'Woodland in history and culture' in J. Wilson Foster (ed.), *Nature in Ireland: a scientific and cultural history* (Dublin, 1997), 133–56; Mitchell and Ryan (eds), *Reading the Irish landscape.* **25** K. Nicholls, 'Woodland cover in pre-modern Ireland' in Duffy et al. (eds), *Gaelic Ireland*, pp 181–206; see also K. Hickey, 'Wolves – forgotten Irish hunter' in *Wild Ireland*, 4 (3) (2003), pp 10–13. **26** See J.H. Andrews and R. Loeber, 'An Elizabethan map of Leix and Offaly: cartography, topography and architecture' in W. Nolan and T.P. O'Neill (eds), *Offaly: history and society. Interdisciplinary essays on the history of an Irish county* (Dublin, 1998), pp 243–85; R. Tomlinson, 'Forests and woodlands' in Aalen et al. (eds), *Atlas of the Irish rural landscape*, pp 122–32; idem, 'Trees and woodlands of County Down' in L.J. Proudfoot (ed.), *Down: history and society. Interdisciplinary essays on the history of an Irish county* (Dublin, 1997), pp 239–65.

By the seventeenth century the remaining forests of Ireland were important economic resources, lacking the sorts of legal protection prevailing in England, and so accumulating details on extent and quality was an important activity by undertakers and contemporary commentaries. New estates and settlers were quick to cash in these natural assets, as were neighbouring Gaelic landowners: Patrick MacKenna of Truagh in County Monaghan was selling timber to planters in Clogher in the 1610s and 20s; references to fourteen wolves inhabiting Sliabh Beagh in north Monaghan in 1696 suggest the enduring presence of woodland cover for them.[27] William Brereton's report on his trip through Wicklow and Wexford in 1635 paid particular attention to the value of forests: he travelled from Wexford to Clohamon,

> seated upon the bank of river Slane, which doth hence carry down to Ennerscoffe, and so to Wexford, all pipe-staves, boards and other timber which grows in the woods near adjoining. We passed through Sir Morgan Kavanagh's woods, wherein (we were informed in the morning in Carnew) there were lurking about sixteen stout rebels, well appointed, every one of them with his pistols, skene, and darts … Herein there hath been good store of good timber, though now there remains little timber useful, save to burn, and such as cumbreth the ground, but they say he hath better timber in his more remote woods from the river. This is a commodity which will be much wanting in this kingdom, and is now very dear in Dublin. In this wood there runs a little river which divides the counties of Wexford and Catherloe, over when we had passed we went to Clenmoullen, the castle and seat of Sir Morgan Kavanagh, who seems to be a very honest, fair-dealing man, and his lady, a good woman, but both recusants … He showed me a convenient seat for an iron-work, which may be supplied with sufficient water and charcoal … [28]

Sir Thomas Ashe reported in 1703 on the devastation of the woodlands on the south Derry London company estates where there was no timber with bark on it and 'some thousands of Stumps or Bottoms of old trees besides what has been dug up and made charcoal of. All which show there have been vast Quantitys of Timber Carryed off the Farme.'[29]

27 A perfect relation and report of the works, buildings, and fortifications done by the English … begun the 29th of July 1611 (*Cal. S.P. Carew MSS, 1603–24*, p. 223); Letter from John Smith in Clones to Hon. Dacre Barret, Nov. 1696 (PRONI, Barrett-Lennard papers, T. 2529/6/104). **28** 'Travels of Sir William Brereton in Ireland 1635' in C. Litton Falkiner, *Illustrations of Irish history and topography mainly of the seventeenth century* (London, 1904), pp 388–9; see also E. McCracken, 'Charcoal burning ironworks in seventeenth- and eighteenth-century Ireland' in *Ulster Journal of Archaeology*, xx (1957), pp 123–38; R. Loeber, 'Settlers' utilisation of the natural resources' in K. Hannigan and W. Nolan (eds), *Wicklow: history and society: interdisciplinary essays on the history of an Irish county* (Dublin, 1994), pp 267–304.   **29** Sir Thomas Ashe, 'A view or an account of the lands of the Archbishop of Armagh 1703' (PRONI, T. 848) cited in E.A. Curry, 'Landscape development in south Derry in the eighteenth century' in *Studia Hibernia*

By the eighteenth century Irish woodlands were severely reduced and there was increasing parliamentary intervention to encourage planting of new wood and protection of residual remnants. Estates such as that of the earl of Abercorn had penalties to prevent trees and oak bark being stolen. Private tanning using oak bark was illegal because of its nuisance. Waterford and Wexford exporters of timber products in the seventeenth century were reverting to the importation of seeds and saplings in the eighteenth century.[30] Tree planting instead of the destruction of the seventeenth century was a fashionable and notably visible part of eighteenth-century rural landscape improvement: 'Trees stood for order, improvement and superior culture.'[31] An act of 1765 allowed the tenant to claim the trees he had planted provided they were registered with the clerk of the peace for the county.[32]

Although hedgerows and fields are more properly aspects of the cultural landscape, they are included here because they comprise a natural component in seasonal rhythm with the rest of the landscape. Usually they are composed of local native species as well and generally contribute enormously to the quality and sense of place of Irish landscapes. Their variety is well illustrated in the *Atlas of Irish rural landscape* which includes maps showing composition of field boundaries and field patterns in Ireland.[33] Most of the legacy of deciduous trees is to be found in the hedgerows, so that they contribute significantly to the woodland cover in the Irish landscape. Hedges in general reflect the process of modernisation of the landscape which commenced in the seventeenth century – part of the enclosure movement which saw formerly openfield, unenclosed landscapes from the middle ages being enclosed or emparked into rectangular sections.

The enclosure 'revolution' in agriculture was reported in a variety of eighteenth-century commentaries by individuals or agencies on planting, drainage, crop rotations and other improvements, especially in the commercial eastern regions of the country, in the management of landscape for better breeding of stock and cropping. It was usually the landowner who had the greatest incentive and power to stimulate such undertakings by encouraging his tenants to enclose.[34] From the seventeenth century, most estates would have been interested in having at least the outbounds of farms enclosed or fenced. These regularly coincided with the townland boundary which consequently often contains the oldest hedged

(hereinafter *Studia Hib.*), 19 (1979), pp 78–101, p. 84. **30** E. McCracken, 'Irish nurserymen and seedsmen, 1740–1800' in *Quarterly Journal of Forestry*, lix, no. 2, pp 131–9. **31** W.J. Smyth, 'The greening of Ireland – tenant tree-planting in the eighteenth and nineteenth centuries' in *Irish Forestry – Journal of the Society of Irish Foresters*, 54, no. 1 (1997), p. 58. **32** W.H. Crawford, *The management of a major Ulster estate in the late eighteenth century: the eighth earl of Abercorn and his Irish agents* (Dublin, 2001), pp 60–3. **33** John Feehan also comprehensively discusses the origins, biodiversity and composition of hedgerows in *Farming in Ireland*, chap. 14. Roscommon and Westmeath County Councils' Heritage Plans (2005) include tree surveys which show the following common species: hawthorn, blackthorn, gorse, elder, privet, holly, willow, spindle, hazel, guelder rose, snowberry, beech, sycamore, crab apple, elm, damson and yew. **34** See Tomlinson, 'Trees and woodlands of County Down'.

enclosures, with the internal divisions being left to individual farmer initiative, perhaps under supervision.[35] Most of the modern enclosed landscape was probably laid down in the period 1750–1850.

There may have been earlier medieval enclosures in the Pale, as also in other areas in the west of Ireland such as Tulsk in Roscommon and around particular sites where medieval field enclosures can be detected underneath modern fieldscapes.[36] In Céide fields, many are substantial, in one case being a kilometre in length, though John Feehan suggests they may not have been built as walls but simply piles of stones to clear the fields.[37] The extent of the Céide fields is evidence of a substantial degree of social organisation, in contrast to the poorer curvilinear cellular gardens in other parts. Pollen analysis shows they were mainly paddocks for cattle. Walls had the function of enclosing a space as well as providing a repository for clearing stones from the land. Gaelic Ireland's enclosures, either permanent fences or temporary wattle or brushwood, were mainly on the relatively restricted tilled land near the settlements, while the rest of the land beyond this was open grazing land for the herding of cattle. The older field systems are smaller and cellular in structure with the distinguishing feature of modern fields from the eighteenth century being their large and regulated layout. Thomas Raven's maps of planted lands in Ulster in the 1620s and 1630s frequently suggest fences separating bogland from pasture.

Early enclosures generally showed no evidence of hedges, so one could suggest a transition from unenclosed landscape to mearing banks to a hedged (or walled) landscape commencing earliest in the tillage lands of the east, in the planted lands of the north and progressing westwards with the latest enclosure by estates or Congested Districts Board in the marginal rundale landscapes of the west. John Rocque's maps of the Kildare manors of Castledermot and Graney in 1758 show hedgerows along townland boundaries mainly, with almost one third of the area in large fields of more than 100 acres each. By the early nineteenth century these had been subdivided. Elsewhere on the Kildare estate, such as the manor of Maynooth, the landscape was comprehensively enclosed in 1758. Three stages of enclosure have been identified: the gradual engrossing of older openfield strips, the progressive subdivision of larger field enclosures and the creation *ab initio* of carpets of new fieldscapes over extensive areas.[38]

---

35 W.H. Crawford, 'The significance of landed estates in Ulster, 1600–1820' in *Irish Economic & Social History*, 17 (1990), pp 44–61; F.H.A. Aalen, 'The origins of enclosures in eastern Ireland' in N. Stephens and R. Glasscock (eds), *Irish geographical studies* (Belfast, 1970), pp 209–23; F.H.A. Aalen and K. Whelan, 'Fields' in Aalen et al. (eds), *Atlas of the Irish rural landscape*, pp 134–44. The manuscript reports of Ireland in 1682–4, commissioned by William Molyneux, give impressions of piecemeal enclosure in place in various districts – see Andrews, 'Land and people, *c*.1685' in Moody et al. (eds), *A new history of Ireland, iii, early modern Ireland*, pp 465–68.   **36** M. Herity, 'A survey of the royal site of Cruachain in Connaught IV: ancient field systems at Rathcroghan and Carnfree' in *Journal of the Royal Society of Antiquaries of Ireland* (hereinafter *JRSAI*), 118 (1988), pp 67–84.   **37** Feehan, *Farming in Ireland*, p. 39.   **38** Aalen, 'The origins of enclosures', p. 218.

Although there is some possibility of dating hedges by the number of species growing in them (older hedges having a greater diversity of plants), this is not very reliable. Single bank-and-ditch constructions with a hedge on top or on the side of the bank may be an older style of construction than the typical nineteenth-century enclosure of the stone-faced ditch and bank with the hedge planted between the stones.[39] Local studies of hedges might best rely on a good run of documentary records, such as estate maps and surveys, followed by the early editions of the Ordnance Survey. Accounts of the battle of Dungan's hill in south Meath in 1647 refer to the obstruction of the Leinster cavalry by large thorny hedges and banks which can still be detected today. In south Monaghan, Raven's maps of the earl of Essex's estate for 1634 shows a completely unenclosed landscape which is likely to have survived until the late eighteenth and early nineteenth century, when Lord Bath's agent embarked on the re-arrangement of farmholdings and their fields.[40]

Many observers commented on the bare and naked condition of the Irish landscape in pre-famine times. Poor soil and windswept conditions in many western regions accounted for the lack of trees, but so also did the poverty of the people, their desperate need for fuel and timber, and the depredations of livestock (especially goats) which prevented regeneration of plants. Of course the opposite happened following the largescale depopulation in post-famine decades when marginal farmland was abandoned and secondary woodland and scrubland reclaimed fieldscapes again. In the 1820s, 40s and 50s the Bath, Shirley and Templetown estates in Monaghan were distributing free hedge plants to their tenants as encouragement. A survey of the Shirley estate in 1814 had noted that the fences

> on most parts of the estate are remarkably bad, composed of loose stones, serving rather as boundary marks than for protection from cattle and trespass; but in the neighbourhood of Carrick[macross] where quicksets have been planted in many places the goats have destroyed them or prevented their growth … some quicksets have been lately planted by the new roads … no young trees are put in with the quick, which is the cheapest and best mode of raising trees … no time should be lost in encouraging quickset fences.[41]

This was a practice encouraged by most writers on improvements in the late eighteenth century. Ring forts were especially recommended as suitable sites for such planting,[42] and today they make a significant impact in the hill landscapes of south Ulster.

39 Hall, 'The vegetational landscape of mid-County Down', p. 82. **40** P.J. Duffy, 'Farney in 1634: an examination of Thomas Raven's survey of the Essex estate' in *Clogher Record* (hereinafter *Clogher Rec.*), xi (1963), pp 245–56; see also Tomlinson, 'Trees and woodlands of County Down' on Raven's maps of the Clandeboy estates showing woodlands in 1625. **41** 'Remarks on viewing the estate of John Shirley esquire situate at Carrickmacross, in the barony of Farney, in the county of Monaghan, Ireland', ed. P.J. Duffy in *Clogher Rec.,* xii (1987), pp 300–4. Extracts from the Shirley papers are by kind permission of Major Shirley, Carrickmacross. **42** For example, by T. Rawson in the *Statistical survey of the county of*

The first stage in enclosure may have been the erection of an unplanted bank and ditch: Rocque shows some such fences on his map of Maynooth manor in 1757.[43] This was an initial stage in draining and improving the land, which especially followed the construction of new roads. In the larger farm regions of south Leinster and east Munster, government incentives to encourage woodland plantation frequently saw enclosing ditches being planted with tree saplings and quicksets: the standard practice was quickthorns at four to the perch with regular spacing of ash or oak at longer intervals. The Royal Dublin Society offered premiums for planting from 1764 onwards. The Register of Trees (in the National Archives and PRONI) records the planting of tens of thousands of trees by substantial farmers, a great many along field boundaries in the late eighteenth century.[44]

The mapping of trees (2.1) on Alexander Taylor's map of Kildare (1783) reflects the significance of plantations largely linked to estates as centres of improvement and innovation and are still today a pre-eminent feature of the Kildare landscape.[45] Apart from the obvious importance of demesnes, his map also hints at trees being planted on the outbounds of townlands or farms, along some field boundaries, on selected roadsides usually adjacent to a local mansion house or on avenues leading to big houses. The association with the houses of the gentry, and in some cases with slated farmhouses, is clear from his map. In the nineteenth century poorer settlements were notably treeless, with inhabitants too poor to plant or to refrain from cutting down existing trees for fuel or house building. There is a continuous zone of well-planted landscapes in north-east Kildare extending down the Liffey from Ballymore Eustace to Leixlip – Harristown, Brannockstown, Castle Martin, Rosetown, Moorfield, Morristown, Yeomanstown, Landenstown, Firemount, Millicent, Blackhall, Castle Browne, Rathcoffey, Straffan, Lyons, Ardrass, Killadown, Castletown, Westown and others. The period of Taylor's map coincides with what William J. Smyth calls the 'climax phase' in the relationship between landlord culture and trees, when landowners and strong tenants became seriously involved in planting as a result of incentives offered by the RDS and the Irish parliament. Tenant farmers came to play a more significant role in planting after legislation in 1789 and 1791 which gave them extensive rights to fell trees during the lifetime of their leases, provided their trees were registered. The Register of Trees provides a useful indicator of the rate of tenant tree planting in Ireland in the late eighteenth and early nineteenth centuries, and Kildare county ranks highly with its substantial tenants being actively engaged in this enterprise. In the parish of Rathsillagh, for instance, John Bagot, on the marquis of Drogheda's estate, registered 3,500 trees in

Kildare (Dublin, 1807).   **43** See copy of Rocque's map of the manor of Maynooth on display in Rhetoric House, NUIM. See also J.H. Andrews, 'The French school of Dublin land surveyors' in *Ir. Geography*, 5 (1967), pp 275–92.   **44** See W.J. Smyth, 'The greening of Ireland – tenant tree-planting in the eighteenth and nineteenth centuries' in *Irish Forestry*, 54 (1997), pp 55–72; E. McCracken and D. McCracken, *A register of trees for County Londonderry, 1768–1911* (Belfast, 1984).   **45** *A map of the county of Kildare* by Alexander Taylor, 1783; facsimile reprint by the Royal Irish Academy in 1983 with an accompanying essay by J.H. Andrews.

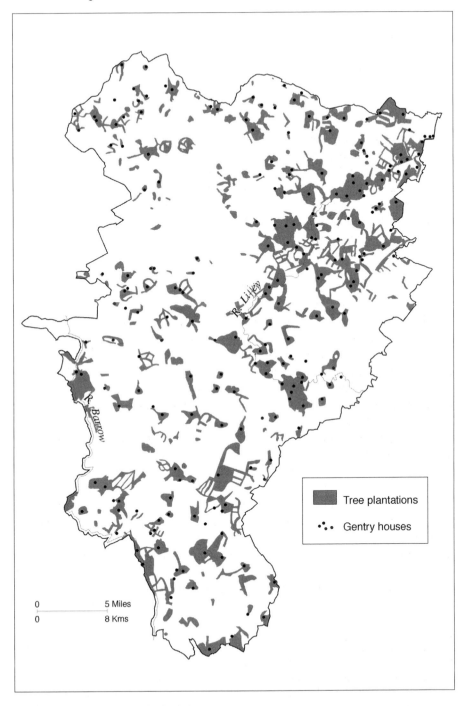

2.1 Tree plantations from *A map of the county of Kildare* by Alexander Taylor, 1783

the period 1817–26. Accompanying affidavits gave precise information on the location of the plantings: for instance, Joshua Huband of Ballygorn planted 184 ash 'on the ditch of the road leading from my dwelling to Maynooth', while at Burtown in Moone parish, Robert Power planted 19 each of ash and alder and ten elm 'in the hedgerows at the back of Castle paddock; 144 ash and 11 alder in the Limekiln field; 121 ash and eight alder in Grove Park, and 28 ash and 36 alder in the paddock at the rear of the dwelling house'.[46]

Hedging and planting on this lavish scale occurred later in south Ulster and the west of Ireland, though east Ulster was to the fore also, notably on estates like Downshire's. In the planted parts of Ulster tenants had considerable freedom in relation to internal enclosures on their farms. In 1820–40 a notable amount of planting of hedges was evident on the Shirley and Bath estates with limited amounts of trees. Of 300 applications for assistance/compensation in 1845, a total of 78 were for thorn quicks. James Marron of Box, for example, applied for 6,000 thorn quicks in August 1845. Applications dried up in 1847 during the height of famine, though by 1848 there were 22 applications for 47,000 quicks.

LAND SURVEY AND LAND CLASSIFICATION

Surveys of land value and potential were associated with the scientific rationalism of agrarian capitalism from the sixteenth and seventeenth centuries. Thus land surveys tabulating or mapping land by its arable qualities, or describing the extents of bog or forest or waste land all date from this period. Surveying and classifying new lands, particularly in terms of their potential usefulness, endured into the nineteenth century as a trope in colonial discourse. In preparing his Down Survey (1655–6), William Petty produced terriers containing information on land quality, suitability for mines and other productive developments, data which were used in his *The political anatomy of Ireland* (London, 1691). The Down and Civil surveys and other plantation surveys repeatedly attempted to classify land as profitable and unprofitable. Raven's 1634 survey of Farney, for instance, referred to 'arable, shrubby wood, pasture, bog, and meadow'. The Civil surveyors were instructed to detail 'profitable' and 'unprofitable' woods, distinguishing bogs and barren mountains, and making clear why it was being classified as unprofitable. Land was to be classified as arable, meadow, rocky pasture, heathy pasture, mountain, 'red bog', 'black bog', 'shaking bog', 'sinking bog', and so on. The barony of Strabane, for instance, is described in the following terms:

46 Quoted in C. Costello, 'Looking back series' in *Leinster Leader*, 4 Apr. 1987; E. McCracken, 'Tree planting by tenants in Meath' in *Ríocht na Midhe*, 8 (2) (1988–9), pp 3–20. Enormous damage was caused to demesne plantations in the hurricane of January 1839 which necessitated increased expenditure of new plantings subsequently (http://www.mayoalive.com/MagApr23/BigWind.htm).

This Barrony is for the most part mountaynouse & woody, cheifly east and southward onely fitt for pasture, Westward, and on the rivers where it is arrable the soyle is butt barren only fitt for oats, and some barly, The woods that weare proffitable heare are all wasted the trees being all barked, & building tymber for the most part cutt downe to reedifie ye buildings burned and destroyed in that late Rebellion.[47]

William Molyneux and Petty in the Dublin Philosophical Society in 1683 assembled comprehensive descriptions of the natural history as well economic and social data from a questionnaire circulated in more than twenty counties which was never published.[48] Roderic O'Flaherty's description of Iar-Connacht from 1684 was part of this projected regional survey.[49] O'Flaherty was one of a number of distinguished Irish scholars who flourished in a time of great difficulty for native society ('I live a banished man within the bounds of my native soil; a spectator of others enriched by my birthright'). According to W. J. Hogan, O'Flaherty's 'knowledge of Geography and natural history is particularly extensive. He knows the source of each river, the families of each townland, their genealogy, patrimony, extent and history of their property, its acquisition and loss. He describes the mountains, lakes, soil and its agricultural productions, and its mineral wealth.'[50]

The following is part of his account of the economic potential of the Aran islands:

47 *The Civil Survey: counties of Donegal, Londonderry and Tyrone*, ed. R.C. Simington (10 vols, IMC, Dublin, 1931–61), iii, 373. **48** Molyneux papers (TCD MS 883); see Andrews, *A paper landscape*, p. 144; idem, 'Land and people, *c.*1685' in Moody et al. (eds), *A new history of Ireland, iii, early modern Ireland*, pp 454–77; J.G. Simms, *William Molyneux of Dublin* (Dublin, 1982). As part of a project to produce a *magnum opus* on Ireland which never materialised, Molyneux and the Dublin Philosophical Society collected surveys of *c.*22 counties and districts of Ireland, including Roderick O'Flaherty's *A chorographical description of West or h-Iar-Chonnaught* (which was published with notes by James Hardiman in 1846) and Sir Henry Piers's 'Chorographical description of the county of West-Meath, written A.D. 1682' which C.Vallancey published in his *Collectanea de Rebus Hibernicis*, vol. 1 (Dublin 1786, reprint Tara, 1981). Nicholas Dowdall's 'Description of the county of Longford 1682' is printed in R. Gillespie and G. Moran (eds), *Longford: essays in county history* (Dublin, 1991), pp 207–11; see also Petty (with Francis Lamb), *Geographical description of ye kingdom of Ireland* (*c.*1689) (IUP reprint, Shannon, 1969 with commentary by J.H. Andrews); J.H. Andrews, 'The making of Irish geography, 1: William Petty' in *Ir. Geography*, 9 (1976), pp 100–3. **49** O'Flaherty, *Chorographical description of West or h-Iar Connacht*, ed. Hardiman. The earliest published report in this series was Piers' choreographical description of West Meath; see also 'A choreographic account of the southern part of the county of Wexford, written *anno* 1684 by Robert Leigh, Esq, of Rosegarland, in that county', ed. H.F. Hore in *JRSAI*, v (1858–9), pp 451–67 and 'Thomas Monk's descriptive account of the county of Kildare in 1682' in *Journal of the County Kildare Archaeological Society* (hereinafter *Kildare Arch. Soc. Jn.*), 6 (1909–11), p. 341. **50** O'Flaherty, *A chorographical description of West or h-Iar Connaught written in 1684 by Roderic O'Flaherty, esq.*, ed. J. Hardiman (Dublin, 1846), facsimile reprint of the first edition (Galway, 1978), with Introduction by W.J. Hogan (unpaginated).

The soile is almost paved over with stones, soe as, in some places, nothing is to be seen but large stones with wide openings between them, where cattle break their legs. Scarce any other stones there but limestones, and marble fit for tomb-stones, chimney mantle trees, and high crosses. Among these stones is very sweet pasture, so that beefe, veal, mutton are better and earlier in season here, then elsewhere; and of late there is plenty of cheese, and tillage mucking, and corn is the same with the sea side tract. In some places the plow goes. On the shore grows samphire in plenty, ring-root or sea-holy, and sea-cabbage. Here are Cornish choughs, with red legs and bills. Here are ayries of hawkes, and birds which never fly but over the sea; and, therefore, are used to be eaten on fasting-days: to catch which, people goe down, with ropes tyed about them, into the caves of cliffts by night, and with a candle light kill abundance of them ... They have no fuell but cow-dung dryed with the sun, unless they bring turf in from the western continent.[51]

His perspective contrasts with the more negative (Cromwellian) assessment of a similar landscape in the Burren as having neither trees on which to hang a man, water to drown him, nor earth to bury him.

In the mid-eighteenth century, the short-lived Physico-Historical Society was involved in endeavours to produce county surveys of Ireland.[52] Charles Smith's *The ancient and present state of the county and city of Waterford: containing a natural, civil, ecclesiastical, historical and topographical description thereof* (1746) was published under the aegis of the society. In 1774 *The ancient and present state of the county and city of Cork* was published by Smith, containing quite detailed topographical descriptions of towns and villages. It lists the stone bridges on the Lee at Inchigeelagh, Drumcurragh, 'a fair bridge, of ten arches, at Ballynaclashen', at Carigadrohid with its 'romantic castle, built on a rock in the river'; Roves-bridge, Inniscarra bridge, and the four bridges in the city of Cork. The ancient monuments such as the 'Danish forts' are described, several of which 'have given names of many places in this county, which begin with the words Rath, Lis, and Dun'.[53] Together with the later writings of commentators such as Mary Delany, Arthur Young, and others, this work was concerned with improving, taming, regulating nature, bringing it into discipline and order. Even wild nature could be rearranged in gardens and parks: Mrs Delany describes the early stages of planning a house and demesne near Clough in County Down in July 1751 which contained all the elements of the pioneering improvement that characterised the age.[54]

In the eighteenth century, as the educated élite throughout Europe became enamoured of science, engineering, geology and statistics, there was a concerted

---

51 O'Flaherty, *West or h-Iar Connaught*, pp 66–8.   52 See G.L. Herries-Davies, 'The making of Irish geography: the Physico-Historical Society of Ireland 1744–1752' in *Ir. Geography*, 12 (1979), pp 92–8.   53 Smith, *The ancient and present state of the county and city of Cork*, ii, pp 261, 407. Smith also published volumes for Down (Dublin, 1744), Kerry (Dublin, 1774) and Youghal (Dublin, 1784).   54 See chap 5, note 113.

attempt to quantify and evaluate landscape, reflected in the establishment of the Dublin Society for the Improvement of Husbandry, Manufacturing and Other Useful Arts in 1731, which became Royal Dublin Society (RDS) in 1820. Much of its energy went into encouraging improvement in agriculture and other aspects of rural life. The county statistical surveys of the early nineteenth century were sponsored by the RDS. William Tighe's *Statistical observations relative to the county of Kilkenny* (1802) is a classic in the series. Section 14 looks at woods and plantations and is a measure of the push for improvement, with a discussion of coppicing oak-wood for millshafts, boat timbers and spokes, an assessment of the demesne woods of Desart, accounts of plantations in County Kilkenny granted premiums by the Dublin Society, trees registered by leaseholders with the Clerk of the Peace 1767–99, descriptions of orchards, nurseries and ozieries. He comments disapprovingly that planting 'is not undertaken extensively; few modern plantations exceeding ten or twelve acres. Many residences are adorned with old and fine trees, that have grown in the most vigorous manner: in the demesne of Castlecomer, are about 200 acres planted by the late Lord Wandesford, now producing large timber ...'[55]

This quest for improvement and economic development reached its apex in the nineteenth century with a vast array of attempts at quantifying, mapping and measuring, cataloguing and enumerating. 'Taming the wilderness' became one of the great projects of nineteenth-century Europe, reflected in an Irish context in the work of the Ordnance Survey, the Geological Survey, the surveys by the bogs commissioners, the Poor Law and Griffith's valuations, the operations of the Board of Works and others. Explorations in Ireland's geology and land value were also stimulated by burgeoning interests in rural and regional economic development and a search for mineral resources, part of a growing imperial interest in social, statistical and political economy surveillance.[56] There were upwards of one hundred commissions of inquiry in the half-century before 1850 in Ireland, which were published in Parliamentary blue books. Boards and inspectorates (for example, the Board of Works in 1831) were set up to make inroads into problems of economic development. London had to interject these extraordinary mechanisms to get things done and to circumvent the local power of the Irish landowning class. The broader context which generated much of this interest was growing population pressure and poverty, requiring an effective taxation and valuation of land and property, and the necessity to develop an infrastructure of roads and piers, dispensaries and hospitals, canals and railways. The problems of agriculture and landholding, as well as the need for railways, required accurate surveys and valuation of land as well as reliable geological maps.

---

55 W. Tighe, *Statistical observations relative to the county of Kilkenny* (Dublin, 1802), pp 567, 573, 575. The county statistical surveys are listed in chap 3, note 115. **56** See R.B. McDowell, *The Irish administration, 1801–1914* (London, 1964); idem, *Public opinion and government policy in Ireland* (London, 1952); idem, *Social life in Ireland, 1800–45* (Dublin, 1957) and idem, 'Administration and the public services, 1800–70' in W.E. Vaughan (ed.), *A new history of Ireland, v, Ireland under the union, 1801–1870* (Oxford, 1989), pp 549 ff; Rena Lohan, *Guide to the archives of the OPW* (Dublin, 1995).

This activity also reflected a nineteenth-century preoccupation with data collection and statistical summaries as part of a developing interest in political economy. In many ways, Ireland was fortunate in the number and quality of key people who were born in the country or came in from Britain, such as Thomas Colby, Thomas Larcom, James Portlock, Thomas Drummond, Richard Griffith, George Petrie, John O'Donovan, Eugene O'Curry, William Wakeman, all part of a wave of young enthusiastic players in a world of imperial opportunity (and prejudice as well): investigators, administrators, bureaucrats, lawyers and civil engineers interested in collecting and assembling ranges of data and information on Ireland which were expected to assist in lifting it out of its poverty, cultural 'backwardness' and underdevelopment. Politicians were also important in this endeavour, like the duke of Wellington who used his powerful influence to progress the Ordnance Survey, or landowning gentry like Spring Rice and others.

The OS Memoir scheme was a classic example of this nineteenth-century endeavour.[57] The survey team assembled by Colby and Larcom, mostly comprising army engineers, was tasked with collecting a wide range of data which would be of use to 'society' and would produce the 'combination of a perfect map with a perfect Memoir'. In Larcom's instructions nothing was to be left out which might be useful to the overall objective of the 'general improvement of the country', with the result that prior to the closure of the project, it was accused of 'the indefinite research of curiosity'.[58] The heads of inquiry sought information on hills, lakes, rivers, bogs, woods, coast and climate; towns, modern and ancient; general appearance and scenery; social economy (improvements and habits of the people); productive economy; divisions of the land. By the time the memoir scheme was closed down, it had only reached south Ulster.[59]

Richard Griffith, from County Kildare, pioneered much of the survey work which helped to provide data on Ireland's physical landscape resources in the nineteenth century.[60] Griffith and a talented team of enterprising officials such as Colonel Colby, Lieutenant Joseph Portlock, George Victor Du Noyer and others were involved in the pioneering work of the Ordnance Survey and the Geological Survey, both products of an age of imperial optimism which saw science as a tool of modernity, civilisation and order. The first important geological map was produced by Griffith in 1838. County geological maps were published at half-inch scale from 1848 and at one-inch from 1856 which became the standard published map. Each one-inch sheet was accompanied by a descriptive memoir including valuable landscape sketches, many by Du Noyer. The Ordnance Survey's now obsolete half-inch and one-inch maps are useful introductions to the physical landscape. Containing contoured colouring they give an immediate and accurate

57 Manuscripts are in Royal Irish Academy. The Institute of Irish Studies has published the memoirs in forty volumes edited by A. Day and P. McWilliams. **58** Quoted in Andrews, *A paper landscape*, p. 164. **59** See Doherty, *The Irish Ordnance Survey*. **60** G.L. Herries-Davies, *Sheets of many colours: the mapping of Ireland's rocks, 1750–1890* (Dublin, 1983); idem, 'A history of Irish geology' in C.H. Holland (ed.), *The geology of Ireland* (Edinburgh, 2001), pp 493–504.

impression of the lie of the land. The current 1:50 000 maps fulfil the same function covering a smaller area but are probably not so effective, and are more useful for studying the human landscape.

Griffith's role as commissioner of the Valuation of Ireland in 1830 saw him take responsibility for the valuation of all the land and property in Ireland. Griffith's Valuation was undertaken by a team of valuators who assessed the land in terms of twelve categories of soil quality. Commencing with the newly constructed six-inch maps of Londonderry, they were instructed to 'observe the slope and altitude of the land, to dig up soil samples, and to divide each townland into "lots" of more or less uniform physical character, each of which would then be assigned a certain value in shillings per acre'.[61] Additional considerations such as accessibility to market towns were taken into account in calculating a final valuation. Farms with associated turf banks had the value of the turbary included in the land value. Griffith's townland valuations have been regularly mapped by geographers as a measure of land quality in an era before scientific assessment of soil. Although provision was made for subsequent re-valuations, the nineteenth-century valuations reflect contemporary conditions: for instance, heavy clay lands which provided suitable soils for flax in south Ulster have comparatively high values, reflecting the former significance of the linen industry.

MODERN LANDSCAPE SURVEY

The Land Utilisation Survey of Great Britain, under the direction of Dudley Stamp, was commenced in 1931 and the Northern Ireland survey started in 1937. Of historical interest now, it is a record of the way land was used before widescale mechanisation, modernisation and the shift in agricultural economies after European integration. It was undertaken with the support of the NI Geographical Association and recruited teachers as voluntary field workers. The land use of each field was mapped in colour on six-inch maps according to a six-fold classification: crop land; grassland; rough grassland and heathland; woodland; gardens, housing estates and orchards; agriculturally unproductive land including lowland bogs. The data were transferred to one-inch maps and published with a memoir.[62] No such survey was undertaken for the Irish Free State.

A National Soil Survey was commenced by An Foras Talúntais in the 1960s and a number of county maps were produced, as well as a national map. The Ordnance Survey of Northern Ireland has also produced a series of seventeen soil maps at 1:50 000 scale.[63] Although these surveys show modern soil conditions that are the

61 J.H. Andrews, *A paper landscape: the Ordnance Survey in nineteenth-century Ireland* (Dublin, 2001), p. 78; see *Instructions to the valuators appointed under the 6th and 7th William IV ...* (1833); see also G. Herries-Davies and R.C. Mollan (eds), *Richard Griffith, 1784–1878* (Dublin, 1980).
62 D.A. Hill, 'The Land utilisation survey in NI' in *Ir. Geography*, 1, no. 4 (1947), pp 101–5.
63 M.J. Gardiner, 'The National Soil Survey' in *Ir. Geography*, 4 (1959–63), pp 442–53. Maps

product of generations of husbandry and improvement, maps such as the 1968 soil map of County Kildare afford a useful interpretive tool in studies of settlement landscapes. The commonest soils in the county are the grey-brown podzols and regosols of the Liffey valley which have the widest landuse potential and were so recognised in the Civil Survey of 1655 (being suitable for 'all manner of corne and cattle'). Clearly these districts were attractive to incoming colonists for centuries as reflected, for example, in correlations with English/Norman placenames. The poorly-drained western boglands remained largely a preserve of Gaelic culture, though there are islands of top-grade land at Kilmeague in the historic 'island of Allen', Timahoe and in the barony of Carbury in the north west.

Selected landscapes in Ireland have been specially designated by a range of environmental agencies and may be important as places where landscape is protected. Most of the coastal landscapes in the west of Ireland have been zoned or are proposed as National Heritage Areas. There are six National Parks which contain unique or historic natural landscapes: Killarney and the Muckross estate with its oak woods and bogland, Wicklow (upland blanket peat, woodland and lakes), Burren (karst limetone pavement and associated flora), Glenveigh (former estate, mountain landscape and estate flora), Connemara (peatlands), and Mayo (extensive blanket bogs). There are also Areas of Outstanding Natural Beauty (NI), Nature Reserves, Environmentally Sensitive Areas and Special Areas of Conservation.[64]

CONCLUSION

Much of the human and cultural landscape which concerns the rest of this book has been constructed, shaped and modified out of the natural landscape. The distinctiveness of local landscapes owes much to the varied character of the natural landscape and the processes of reclamation and change which accompanied human settlement. Depending on the availability of sources it is sometimes possible to

have been published for counties Carlow, Clare, Kildare, Meath, Laois, Limerick, north Tipperary, Offaly, Westmeath, and Wexford, as well as west Donegal and west Cork. Soil classification maps for the remaining areas are in course of production by Teagasc. For Northern Ireland see J.G. Cruickshank and D.N. Wilcock (eds), *Northern Ireland: environment and natural resources* (Belfast, 1982) and C. Jordan, A. Higgins, K. Hamill and J.G. Cruickshank (eds), *The soil geochemical atlas of Northern Ireland* (Belfast, 2000). Much of this work has been overtaken by remote sensing and satellite imagery.   **64** An Foras Forbartha published *Inventory of outstanding landscapes in Ireland* (Dublin, 1977) and *Areas of scientific interest in Ireland* (Dublin, 1981). *Fermanagh. Its special landscapes: a study of the Fermanagh countryside and its heritage* (HMSO, Belfast, 1991) highlights all aspects of its environmental, ecological and built environment. DoENI, *Mourne: area of outstanding natural beauty: policies and proposals* (HMSO, 1989) and *Causeway coast: area of outstanding natural beauty* (HMSO, 1989) are summaries of the major characteristics of the landscape legacy which are worthy of protection by the state. For a regional case study, see E. Wood et al., *The west coast of Ireland: an environmental appraisal* (London, 1996).

reconstruct earlier landscapes of bogs, woodland and wilderness. The late eighteenth century and the nineteenth century which witnessed the most extensive 'humanisation' of the landscape also provides the most comprehensive sources on natural landscape resources as outlined in this chapter. One of the most deep-seated and enduring characteristics of regional and local landscapes in Ireland is the inverse relationship which emerged historically between environmental quality (reflected, for example, in land valuation, soil fertility, marginal land and so on) and economic and social development (reflected by farm structure and output, market economies and urban development).

CHAPTER 3

Cultural landscapes

'The cultural landscape is fashioned out of a natural landscape by a culture group. Culture is the agent, the natural area is the medium, the cultural landscape is the result.'[1] Much of cultural landscape history is to do with 'taming the wilderness', bringing order to wild nature, tidying it up, straightening it out, 'improvement and civilisation', all of which comprise predilections of agrarian capitalism and colonialism universally. The Irish landscape reflects many of these processes, from a pre-modern and early-modern emphasis on taming nature for survival (farming for subsistence) to the more aesthetic post-Enlightenment notion of designing nature for beauty, which continues to dominate our worlds of gardens and scenic landscapes. In this section we look at a number of broad themes in cultural landscape formation mainly relating to systems, structures and processes in the evolution of cultural landscapes. This chapter focusses on processes of territorialisation, naming places, settling landscape, land ownership and management, and administrative landscapes – all having clear impacts on the order and arrangement of the landscape and producing distinctive patterns and textures through which it is possible to read and understand the details of landscape evolution. Chaper four will examine the material legacies of the built environment.

It is possible to construct an inventory of some of the key features in the Irish cultural landscape which can help us appreciate the nature of the cultural accretions which have built up over the generations.[2] Most major elements of our modern cultural landscape developed in the past three or four centuries, though they were influenced by pre-existing structures and boundaries (3.1). Older morphologies were subsumed in modern developments, as for instance, with the shadowy reflections of early medieval monastic settlements in some of our towns and villages or the evidence of early enclosures in street patterns of Kells or Armagh.[3] Political, economic, social and military developments in the past can also be seen as

---

1 C. Sauer, 'The morphology of landscape' in *University of California Publications in Geography*, 2 (1925), p. 46. **2** Feehan, *Farming in Ireland*, p. 298 lists churches and chapels, graveyards and tombstones, cillíns, mass rocks, holy wells, court tombs, passage tombs, wedge tombs, cist tombs, ring barrows, stone circles, moated sites, mottes and baileys, tower houses, linear earthworks, hillforts, ringforts, cashels, souterrains, toghers, *slite*, tracks and pathways, *fulachta fiadh*, middens, booley huts, sweathouses, to which might be added mearings, territorial units, toponyms and placenames. **3** See, for instance, J.H. Andrews, *Kildare*. Irish Historic Towns Atlas, no. 1 (Dublin, 1986); A. Simms, *Kells*. Irish Historic Towns Atlas, no. 4 (Dublin, 1990); R.H. Buchanan and A. Wilson, *Downpatrick*. Irish Historic Towns Atlas, no. 8 (Dublin, 1997).

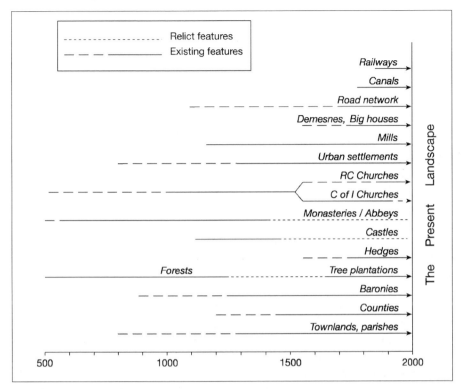

3.1 Evolution of the Irish cultural landscape

contributing to the broad scale cultural evolution of landscape. In this way the narrative of history can be read in the landscape: medieval Gaelic lordship was crucial in the formation of landscape territorial structure; the Reformation and land confiscations of the sixteenth century involved immigrations of planters and settlers; state policies of support for plantation settlement, wars and destruction, investment in housebuilding and so on, were all episodes in the past with decipherable landscape consequences.

TERRITORIAL STRUCTURES

Territorialisation and the evolution of spatial order in the organisation of landscape were a fundamental process in the social and economic morphology of the Irish landscape.[4] This embraced an organic order from a very early period, reflecting

4 See W.J. Smyth, 'Ireland a colony: settlement implications of the revolution in military-administrative, urban and ecclesiastical structures, *c.*1550–*c.*1730' in Barry (ed.), *A history of settlement in Ireland*, pp 158–86; on p. 159 Smyth refers to them as 'enclosures' for living at a variety of levels.

exigencies of local culture, society and landholding, and more rational territorial constructions of the modern state in the nineteenth century. Knowledge of these territories is essential in understanding the history of the Irish landscape. Units such as townlands and parishes represent a vocabulary of landscape without which it would be impossible to understand or to meaningfully describe it. A more prosaic reason for becoming familiar with them is that most knowledge and data about the landscape are relayed through the medium of its territorial template: data on population and economy for the past several centuries are stored in registers of territorial units.

In reading the Irish landscape there is an historic territorial hierarchy of townland, parish, barony and county – units which have evolved from the medieval period or at least have medieval antecedents and were systematically recorded in surveys and maps from the late sixteenth century. In addition to these, there are units that were later created (or adapted) by agencies with specific functions in local or central administration. Counties were adapted from earlier lordships and were set up to administer the laws of the modernising state in the sixteenth century mainly, with some originating in the feudal settlement of the Middle Ages; baronies were based on pre-existing local lordships or 'countries' to adminster local government up until the creation of county councils in 1898. Poor Law Unions and Electoral Divisions were newly constructed to administer a public welfare programme in the nineteenth century, as well as a plethora of other administrative policies. Much earlier, dioceses developed from the 1111 synod of Rathbreasail in response to Roman church reform: these too reflected in their geographies the political realities of pre-Norman Gaelic Ireland. In this way, much of the ancient territorial order in Ireland is 'captured' in the boundaries and units which were formalised in the early-modern period.

Pre-modern territorial structure
In studying pre-modern settlement and geography, the island's fragmentation into kingdoms/lordships in the medieval period is important. There was a modicum of island-wide similarity in territorial structures but with significant local variations on this theme. A late sixteenth-century Elizabethan adventurer reported on this regional diversity:

> But every lord of a seigniorie had one commonly called a brehon, supplyinge
> the place of a judge, yet skilled in noethinge but in the costumes [customs]
> of that parte of the contrie wherein he leived, which were usually as different
> one from the other as could be devised ... They kept commonly they[r]
> consistories and kindes of courts on the toppes of hills.[5]

5 *The chronicle of Ireland by Sir James Perrott, 1584–1608*, ed. H. Wood (Dublin, 1933), p. 20; for Gaelic Ulster, see the preparatory survey for the plantation: 'MS Rawlinson A.237, Bodl. Oxford, Fo. 61. A booke of the king's lands founde upon the last generall survey within the province of Ulster anno le: 1608' in *Anal. Hib.*, iii (1931), pp 151–218. See also Norden's

The territorial units were ultimately spatial expressions of landholding structures which laced the countrysides of late medieval and early-modern Ireland, in some cases reaching back to the tribal septlands of pre-Norman Ireland. They had different nomenclatures in separate lordships, such as tates, ballyboes, polls, gneeves, quarters, sessiaghs and so on.[6] These medieval septlands were subdivided into fractions (halves, quarters, sixths, sixteenths) of primary units such as ballybetaghs whose geographies mirrored local diversity in environmental resources: the size of territorial units ranged from small to large in fertile or marginal landscapes respectively. This parcellation process probably developed within an initial broader framework of larger units which were progressively subdivided by streams and other physical landmarks to accommodate increasing population, settlement and land reclamation.[7] In late medieval Gaelic Monaghan, the ballybetaghs with their intricate tate subsections, were combined into parishes, indicating a link between secular and ecclesiastical territorial order that was universal throughout Christian Europe. The smallest unit in medieval Ireland, which from the later seventeenth century came to be known as townland, is frequently listed in records as far back as the thirteenth century.[8] Although territorial boundaries were sometimes marked in the landscape by boundary crosses, burial sites and earthen banks, they were chiefly preserved in local memory and bolstered by periodic traversing by local tenants.[9]

In preparation for the Ulster plantation, inquisitions of lands systematically described the nature of the landscape territories. The drumlin landscape with intervening wetlands in south Down is described in the following commission outlining boundaries and listing places:

maps of escheated counties of Ulster *c.*1610 (British Library, Cotton collection, MS Augustin I. ii. 44; M. Swift, *Historical maps of Ireland* (London, 1999)).   **6** T. McErlean, 'The Irish townland system of landscape organisation' in T. Reeves-Smyth and F. Hammond (eds), *Landscape archaeology in Ireland* (Oxford, 1983), pp 315–39; see also W. Nolan, 'Some civil and ecclesiastical territorial divisions and their geographical significance' in W. Nolan (ed.), *The shaping of Ireland* (Cork, 1986), pp 66–83; J. Hogan, 'The tricha cét and related land-measures' in *Proceedings of the Royal Irish Academy* (hereinafter *R.I.A. Proc.*), 37 (1928–29), p.189; J.H. Andrews, 'Topography: territorial divisions' in V. Meally (ed.), *Encyclopaedia of Ireland* (Dublin, 1968), pp 142–50; P.J. Duffy, 'Townlands: territorial signatures of landholding and identity' in B. Turner (ed.), *The heart's townland: marking boundaries in Ulster* (Downpatrick, 2004), pp 18–38; W.H. Crawford, 'The study of townlands in Ulster' in R. Gillespie and M. Hill (eds), *Doing Irish local history: pursuit and practice* (Belfast, 1998), pp 97–115.   **7** P.J. Duffy, 'Social and spatial order in the MacMahon lordship of Airghialla in the late sixteenth century' in Duffy et al. (eds), *Gaelic Ireland*, pp 115–37; idem, 'The territorial organisation of Gaelic landownership and its transformation in County Monaghan, 1591–1640' in *Ir. Geography*, 14 (1981), pp 1–26; P. Nugent, 'The dynamics of parish formation in high medieval and late medieval Clare' in E. FitzPatrick and R. Gillespie (eds), *The parish in medieval and early modern Ireland* (Dublin, 2006), pp 186–208.   **8** See for instance *The Red Book of the earls of Kildare*, ed. G. Mac Niocaill (IMC, Dublin, 1964); *Calendar of Ormond deeds, 1172–1603*, ed. E. Curtis (6 vols, IMC, Dublin, 1932–43), i (1172–1350); also *Crichad an Chaoilli, being the topography of ancient Fermoy*, ed. P. Power (Dublin & Cork, 1932).   **9** See, for example, R. Refaussé and M. Clark, *A catalogue of the maps of the estates of the archbishops of Dublin, 1654–1850* (Dublin, 2000), p. 28.

... viewed certain differences betwixt the said Dromsallagh and Lysnegeado belonging to sir Edward Trevor, and Ballymeagh belonging to sir George Sexton, both parties being present at setting forth the meeres, and sondry wytnesses sworne and examyned on both sydes, we fynde the meere and boundes trodden by Neale O'Hyer, begynning at a bottom where a little brooke called Dromsallagh brooke goeth along a ditch called Lemneneigh, in English the Horse Leap, up the hill called Lenneneigh, and thence to the hill called Derilonan, and alonge the said ditch to a forte in the wooddes called Lislonan, leaving the same forte within Dromsallagh, and thence along the like olde ditche to a foarde called Agh Fowke, in English the Dyvell's Foarde, and thence crossing over a bogge to the lower ende of a ditche in the middle of a playne neare Lisnecnow, leaving the said lysse in the Meagh, and alonge the said ditche wyndinge eastwardes toward the bogge, and alonge the bogge a little distance, and then through a playne northwarde, by a stone and an old stumpe of an oke to certen busshes northward where the meere hath been plowed, beyng the meere betwene Lisnegeade and the Meagh, and thence by a hedge in a lowe bottom through woodds called the Glack to the Dingle under the forte of Lisnegeade, leavying the hill Edendaron in the Meagh, and the hills called Dromenyskye within Lysnegeade; which meere so trodden and sett forth as aforesaid is the true meere betwixt the landes of Dromsallagh and Lysnegeade belonging to the said sir Edward Trevor, and the landes of the Meagh belonging to the said sir George Sexton, and so we do order and determyne the same to remayne.[10]

An Inquisition of 1609 described the parish of Magheraculmoney in County Fermanagh as being

bounded on the north uppon the half barony of Coolemckernan, and from thence to a great rocke of stoane called Ardshanckie in bawagh on the north west, and from thence to the river of Termonmcgragh, which river is the auncient meere and bound of the said parishe, unto a mountaine called Urliewe on the north east, and on the east it is bounded by Mononvarrowe, and on the south by Lougherne ... [11]

Out of this medieval world of locally and regionally specific territorial units emerged the modern structures of townlands, parishes and baronies.[12] The early-

---

10 *Inquisitionum in officio rotulorum cancellariæ Hiberniæ asservatarum, repertorium / printed by command of His Majesty King George IV*, vol. 2, p. xliii.   11 *Inq. Cancell. Hib. Repert.*, vol. 2, Appendix VI, Fermanagh, pp 24–34. See also P. Mulligan, 'Notes on the topography of Fermanagh' in *Clogher Rec.*, i (1954), pp 24–34 for comments on various commissions as sources for Fermanagh, which can be supplemented by the topographical references in a Gaelic source, *Me Guidhir Fhearmanach*, ed. an tAth. P. Ó Duinnín (Dublin, 1917).   12 See K. Muhr, 'Territories, people and place-names in Co. Armagh' in A.J. Hughes and W. Nolan

modern period witnessed the emergence of a recognisably modern centralised state to replace the fragmented lordships of the medieval world, though earlier in the Middle Ages the Anglo-Norman colony had adopted pre-existing Gaelic territories as counties and cantreds.[13] One of the initial strategies of the developing English state from the 1500s aimed at decoding the territorial structures, so that policies of state consolidation (through confiscation and plantation) were implemented via a rational, hierarchical structure of territories. The shiring process, for instance, created counties or shires based on pre-existing territorial entities to which sherrifs and local officials were appointed to assist local government. Baronies and parishes were similarly utilised by the state. As part of the modernising process of civil administration, an increasing amount of information was collected and recorded for these spatial entities, especially townlands, parishes and baronies: *The Compossicion Booke of Connought* recorded agreements between the government and landowners of Connacht in 1585, listing all the lands by quarter and townland throughout the province.[14] The lands and landholders in the newly created county of Monaghan were similarly listed in a detailed survey of 1591.[15] Subsequent surveys and maps which featured in the land confiscations and colonisation schemes, from the Ulster Plantation surveys to the Civil and Down surveys of the mid-seventeenth century, are classic examples of this process of surveillance, often replicated in later out-reaches of empire.[16] All were concerned to identify the territorial structures and names to facilitate effective colonisation.[17] There was also a recurring interest in uncovering the territorial codes of contemporary local units in search of an elusive standard acreage for townland, ploughland, seisreach, quarter and so. Many of the mapping surveys were flawed as a result of using false acreage assumptions. Estate surveys in the eighteenth century were often undertaken to correct these sometimes hastily completed surveys of the plantation periods by determining boundaries and areas.

(eds), *Armagh: history and society. Interdisciplinary essays on the history of an Irish county* (Dublin, 2001), pp 295–331. **13** See C.A. Empey, 'The Anglo-Norman County Waterford, 1200–1300' in W. Nolan and T. Power (eds), *Waterford: history and society. Interdisciplinary essays on the history of an Irish county* (Dublin, 1992), pp 131–46 and idem, 'Conquest and settlement patterns of Anglo-Norman settlement in north Munster and south Leinster' in *Irish Economic & Social History*, xii (1986), pp 5–31. **14** *The Compossicion Booke of Connought* transcribed by A.M. Freeman (IMC, Dublin, 1936). **15** The 1591 survey of Monaghan, *Inquisitiones Cancillariae Ultoniae Repertu*, xxi–xxxi: see Duffy, 'Territorial organisation of Gaelic landownership'; idem, 'Patterns of landownership in Gaelic Monaghan in the late sixteenth century' in *Clogher Rec.*, x (1981), pp 304–22. **16** Essential early reading for students of landscape divisions is 'Surveying without maps', chapter 1 of J.H. Andrews, *Plantation acres: on historical study of the Irish land surveyor and his maps* (Belfast, 1985). This wide-ranging essay discusses the composition and meaning of the various territorial units and the history of pre-cartographic measuring. **17** Andrews, 'The mapping of Ireland's cultural landscape, 1550–1630' in Duffy et al. (eds), *Gaelic Ireland*, pp 177–9; Andrews's unpublished catalogue of Irish maps before 1630 is available in NUIM library.

Townlands

There are *c*.63,000 of these units in the country which because of their small size and the amount of data that they record are a fundamentally important source in local studies.[18] Townlands are legacies of a medieval landscape assessment system which emerged as an expression of landholding and a means of imposing cesses and other dues on the population in Gaelic lordships or the manors of Anglo-Norman Ireland. The environmental logic of this assessment system, which usually saw more extensive territories occurring on poorer lands, was also evident at the micro scale, where Monaghan's townlands, for example, invariably encompass a drumlin core, with the boundaries running through intervening wetlands.[19]

Kin groups were associated with this structure of local units which were called a variety of regional names such as tates, ballyboes, polls, quarters, and so on until 'townland' emerged as the standard term. The townland matrix was mapped and used to record information from the seventeenth to the nineteenth centuries. It formed the basic building block of the Ordnance Survey (OS) in 1830s, the territorial and legal framework for subsequent valuations, the administrative structure for Poor Law and revenue collection, and was the ultimate unit of record in the censuses from 1841. Accurately mapping the townland boundaries was an early stage in OS activity, described in boundary register books which recorded the boundaries as pointed out by local meresmen (who had knowledge of the boundaries or 'mearings').[20] Most townland boundaries had been well established in local estate surveys and records by the eighteenth century. In a minority of cases the OS had to delineate new legal boundaries. In some cases, taking account of developments like road and canal construction in the eighteenth century, it re-aligned nearby townland boundaries, subdivided others (into east and west, upper and lower, though *Íochtar* and *Uachtar, Mór* and *Beag* had often emerged as earlier subdivisions in response to local population growth).

One of the most useful tools for the local historian is the townland index map which, though lacking in elegance, is inexpensive and easy to use.[21] Today the

18 For historical background and evolution of the smaller territorial units see, for example, R.C. Simington (ed.), *The Civil Survey, AD 1654–1656*, vol. viii, County of Kildare (Dublin, 1952), pp xiii–xxix; W. Reeves, 'On the townland distribution of Ireland' in *R.I.A. Proc.*, vii (1857–61), pp 473–90; T.A. Larcom, 'On the territorial divisions of Ireland', HC 1847 (764) vol. 1, Accounts and papers, 37 vols (Relief of distress in Ireland: Board of Works), pp 1–5; J. Hogan, 'The tricha cét and related land measures', pp 148–235; T. McErlean, 'The Irish townland system of landscape organisation', pp 315–39.   **19** Duffy, 'Social and spatial order'; idem, 'Perspectives on the making of the Cavan landscape' in R. Gillespie (ed.), *Cavan: Essays on the history of an Irish county* (Dublin, 1995), pp 14–37; idem, 'Geographical perspectives on the Borderlands' in R. Gillespie and H. O'Sullivan (eds), *The Borderlands: Essays on the Ulster-Leinster divide* (Belfast, 1989), pp 5–22.   **20** Andrews, *A paper landscape*, pp 57, 312; see also J.P. Browne, 'Wonderful knowledge: the Ordnance Survey of Ireland' in *Éire–Ireland*, 20 (1985), pp 15–27.   **21** *Indexes to the townland survey* (in one sheet per county) and *Townland indexes* which detail the townlands in several sheets per county; see also the printed gazeteer of townlands: *General alphabetical index to the townlands and towns, parishes and baronies of Ireland* (Dublin, 1861; reprint Baltimore, 1992).

Ordnance Survey of Ireland and Ordnance Survey of Northern Ireland provide digital townland maps through which it is possible to map data much faster and more conveniently with the assistance of Geographical Information Systems or GIS. The latter is a system for storing and managing spatial data, essentially a database system which links maps to data and which will be increasingly useful in future for local historians wishing to analyse large amounts of data by local spatial units. Researchers looking at a local parish or townland, of course, should not expect to find their study areas written up, though there are growing numbers of local histories on townlands being produced by an expanding body of local historical studies.[22]

Parishes

The parish is potentially one of the most interesting geographical units in studies of the Irish landscape. It is the earliest local community territory with a rudimentary administrative system, where baptism and burial were generally the markers of parochial status. There were variations in parish organisation between Gaelic and English Ireland, between the roles of erenaghs and coarbs, churchwardens and vestries. Parishes emerged following the twelfth-century reform of the church in Ireland and the institution of dioceses at the synod of Rathbreasail in 1111. It has been generally assumed that parishes with their accompanying tithe payments for pastoral services came with this reform and were introduced earliest in the Anglo-Norman colonised areas. Recent scholarship suggests that the parish geographies of the twelfth or thirteenth century were not conjured out of thin air and that they had much earlier roots in Gaelic tuatha which were reorganised formally as post-reform parishes.[23]

During the upheavals of the Tudor period – and periodic disturbances in earlier centuries – parish life and pastoral services were severely disrupted and churches in many places were ruined and abandoned.[24] But the territorial structure of the

---

22 See P. Connell, D.A. Cronin and B. Ó Dalaigh (eds), *Irish townlands: studies in local history* (Dublin, 1998); W.H. Crawford and R.H. Foy (eds), *Townlands in Ulster* (Belfast, 1998); Crawford, 'The study of townlands in Ulster'; T. Canavan (ed.), *Every stoney acre has a name: a celebration of the townland in Ulster* (Belfast, 1991); Turner (ed.), *The heart's townland*. Other townland databases can be accessed such as at http://www.seanruad.com/. A useful summary website is at http://scripts.ireland.com/ ancestor/browse/records **23** See J. Blair and R. Sharpe, *Pastoral care before the parish* (Leicester, 1992) and FitzPatrick & Gillespie (eds), *The medieval and early modern parish in Ireland*. The best sources for parishes is to be found in Roman papal correspondence on taxation especially, as well as calendars of state documents for the Middle Ages: *Calendar of documents relating to Ireland*, ed. H.S. Sweetman (5 vols, HMC, London, 1875–86), v, nos 693–729; S. Ní Ghabhláinn, 'The origin of medieval parishes in Gaelic Ireland: the evidence from Kilfenora' in *JRSAI*, 126 (1996), pp 37–61; K. Nicholls, 'Rectory, vicarage and parish in the western Irish dioceses' in *JRSAI*, 101 (1971), p. 62; M. Hennessy, 'Parochial organisation in medieval Tipperary' in W. Nolan and T. McGrath (eds), *Tipperary: history and society: Interdisciplinary essays on the history of an Irish county* (Dublin, 1985), p. 63; Nugent, 'The dynamics of parish formation'. **24** See Andrews, 'Mapping Ireland's cultural landscape' on roofless ruins, though Andrews also considers that this may have been a stylistic convention by surveyors.

3.2 Civil parishes in Ireland (courtesy of the Department of Geography, UCC)

parish was virtually indestructible in a way that the church building was not: its sites and boundaries were indelible in the landscape and embedded in local memory. Reports of inquisitions sitting in different places in the late sixteenth and early seventeenth centuries were preoccupied with the tenurial characteristics of Irish parishes taken over by the reformed Established Church. The inquisitions of Ulster prior to the Ulster Plantation, for instance, give detailed outlines of parishes with complex and sometimes ambiguous accounts of their tenurial and rental arrangements.[25]

The 1609 inquisition to enquire into the churchlands of Cavan refers to polls ('every poll containing two gallons, every gallon containing two pottles, and every sixteene pols makinge a ballibet'), with a range of annual assessements payable to the bishop of Kilmore, from cash to 'breads with butter proportionablie' or 'mathers of butter', day labourers, 'cesse, coyny and other charges', from two to twelve 'reape hookes.' Another enquiry of 1609 reported the sworn testimony of 24 jurors (mostly O'Neales, O'Quinns, McIvers, O'Develyns, O'Hagans) on the lands of the arch-bishop of Armagh in the barony of Dungannon giving details, some of which are unclear today, on the names, tenure and territorial structure of some of the lands of the erenaghs who were the traditional caretakers of churchlands in Gaelic Ireland:

> out of the erenagh land of Donoghmore, contayninge thirtene tullaghes, everie tullagh contayninge one balliboe and one sessiagh, every sessiagh contayninge a third parte of a balliboe, the yearly rent of forty shillings per ann. and sixe shillings and eight pence Irish for everie bloodshed; and alsoe, a yerely cosherie in the said lord archbusshopp his visitation, yf he come himself in person, and not otherwise; and alsoe, out of the erenagh land of Kyllishell, contayninge twoe small balliboes; the yearly rent of three shillings and foure pence per ann. and one mutton, thirtie cabdell meadors of oates, and a cosherie yerely ... ; and out of the erenagh land of Ardboo als Ballileigh, conteyninge thirtene tullaghes, (whereof one tullagh was free to the erenagh), the yerely rent of fower markes per ann. and one cosherie yerely in his visitation, as before, and not otherwise, and that the herenagh of this land was to beare twoe third parte of the chardge in repairing and mainteyninge the parish church ... ' (Appendix II Tyrone).

The parish as a convenient spatial scale emerged as an important summary unit in the Civil Survey (1654–6), the Down Survey (1654–59) and the Book of Survey

---

25 See also C.F. McGleenon, 'The medieval parishes of Ballymore and Mullabrack' in *Seanchas Ard Mhacha*, 12 (2) (1987), pp 46–7, and M.A. Costello, *De Annatis Hiberniae*, vol. 1 Ulster (Maynooth, 1912) which includes details on Inishmacsaint parish from Inquisition of Ulster, Sept. 1603. Erenagh families customarily provided the parochial clergy also, with duties of hospitality to travellers, wayfarers, and the poor, often involving the maintenance of a house or hostel for such purposes *Inq. Cancell. Hib. Repert.*, vol. 2, Appendix II, Tyrone.

and Distribution (*c*.1660–80), and for the registration of hearth monies and poll taxes in the seventeenth century. Grand Jury records regularly used the parish. With the nineteenth-century censuses, it continued as the preferred local unit for most data and townland data were summarised by parish. The OS recognised the importance of the parish by producing individual parish maps of counties as indexes of their first edition six-inch survey. The OS Memoir project was the most ambitious data-gathering exercise in the nineteenth century and was essentially a parish survey which never progressed beyond south Ulster.[26] Mitchell's *Guide to Irish parish registers* is a useful index to the civil parishes of Ireland listed by county, with corresponding Church of Ireland and Catholic parishes. In *The new genealogical atlas of Ireland* (Baltimore, 1986), Mitchell maps the baronies, Poor Law Unions and civil parishes by county and provides a useful basis for studying the actual geographies of the parishes, for instance.[27]

In looking at parishes it is important to distinguish between civil, Church of Ireland and Catholic parishes, and not to assume that today's Catholic parish, for example, is necessarily the historic parish. The civil parish is the closest we can get to the historic medieval parish. The Church of Ireland inherited most of this parish network at the Reformation and was careful to maintain the boundaries, rights and tithes to which each parish was entitled historically. Small Church of Ireland congregations, however, necessitated some change and parish centres were abandoned and parish unions instituted which generally respected the boundaries of the older parishes.[28] The result was that the disEstablished Church in 1869 held 1,518 parishes in comparison to 2,428 civil parishes mapped by the Ordnance Survey. Because of its official status as the Established Church, it has more abundant sources than, for instance, the Catholic church. Among the most important sources which are a by-product of its official status are the Tithe Applotment Books (for the period 1823 to 1837 in The National Archives) listing tithe payers by townland within the parish. Tithes were taxes on agricultural holdings payable to Church of Ireland parishes. Changes to parish boundaries or alterations to its legal status by way of unions or divisions could only be made by order of the Privy Council in Dublin and are thus well recorded. Parish vestries were the main unit of local government up to the Poor Law Unions, and had responsibility for the construction of local roads not funded by the county, as well as care of poor. Annual vestry meetings were in principle open to all denominations. Churchwardens and sidesmen were elected annually to assist with the administration of the vestries. The

---

26 Doherty, *The Irish Ordnance Survey*. Templemore parish was the only memoir published as *Ordnance Survey of the county of Londonderry, volume the first: memoir of the city and north-western liberties of Londonderry, parish of Templemore* (Dublin, 1837); see *Ordnance Survey memoirs of Ireland*, ed. Day & McWilliams.   **27** B. Mitchell (ed.), *The guide to Irish parish registers* (Baltimore, 1988); idem, *Guide to Irish churches and graveyards* (Baltimore, 1990) shows the location of churches and cemeteries.   **28** P.J. Duffy, 'The shape of the parish' in FitzPatrick & Gillespie (eds), *The medieval and early modern parish in Ireland*; T.C. Barnard, *Cromwellian Ireland: English government and reform in Ireland, 1649–1660* (Oxford, 1975), pp 160–6; P.J. Duffy, *Landscapes of south Ulster: a parish atlas of the diocese of Clogher* (Belfast, 1993), pp 5–6.

Presbyterian church was not organised on a parochial basis after *c.*1800, falling back instead on the more local organic identity of the townland.[29]

Although the Roman Catholic church lost its parochial properties in the sixteenth century, popular allegiance to the parish territories endured through generations of oppression and disturbance. With a largely underground clergy for many periods in the seventeenth and eighteenth centuries, parishes were often left to their own devices. Stations, which were a response to penal conditions in the eighteenth century when masses took place in private houses, were adopted officially to help consolidate the geography and coherence of parish identities.[30] When the church began to reorganise its parochial structure in the late eighteenth and early nineteenth centuries, it largely adhered to the geographies of the older historic (civil) parishes which in many cases outside Ulster's large parishes might encompass unions of several civil parishes. In the archdiocese of Cashel, for example, there are 46 Catholic parishes and 130 civil parishes, but the boundaries of most of the Catholic unions incorporate the older parish boundaries.[31] The diocesan archives of the Catholic church are useful as indicators of the reorganisation of many dioceses after the disorder of the eighteenth-century penal legislation. Many dioceses like Clogher and Meath, for instance, have records relating to the bishops re-imposing their authority on parishes and priests. There may also be material on the re-organisation and territorial management of parishes.[32]

Placenames
Naming places is a primary act of geographical appropriation, a demonstration of control over nature, the landscape and everything in it. Names create landscapes: an

29 On parish administration see T.C. Barnard, *A new anatomy of Ireland: the Irish Protestants, 1649–1770* (New Haven, 2003); FitzPatrick & Gillespie (eds), *The medieval and early modern parish in Ireland*; see also S. Hood, 'Church of Ireland sources for the historical geographer: a case study of the Meath diocesan archive' in H.B. Clarke, J. Prunty and M. Hennessy (eds), *Surveying Ireland's past: multidisciplinary essays in honour of Anngret Simms* (Dublin, 2004), pp 385–414; J. Johnston, 'Clogher parish – some early sidesmen, 1662–1734' in *Clogher Rec.,* xiv, no.1 (1991), pp 89–91. **30** See P. Mulligan, 'The life and times of Bishop Edward Kernan' in *Clogher Rec.,* x, no. 3 (1981), pp 323–48; T. O'Connor, 'Thomas Messingham (*c.*1575–1638?) and the seventeenth-century church' in *Ríocht na Midhe,* xi (2000), pp 88,95, 99. Official diocesan archive material on decisions relating to changes in Catholic parochial territories are difficult to come by and may be better sought in Roman archives. **31** Based on T. Ó Muirí, *Pobal Áilbe – Cashel and Emly atlas* (S.I., the archdiocese of Cashel and Emly, 1970); Duffy, *Landscapes of south Ulster,* pp 6–8, 25; see also K. Whelan, 'The Catholic parish, the Catholic chapel and village development in Ireland' in *Ir. Geography,* xvi (1983), p. 4; idem, 'The Catholic church in County Tipperary, 1700–1900' in Nolan & McGrath (eds), *Tipperary: history and society,* pp 215–55; Dean A. Cogan, *The diocese of Meath, ancient and modern* (3 vols, Dublin, 1867); P. Fagan, *The diocese of Meath in the eighteenth century* (Dublin, 2001); F. O Fearghail, 'The Catholic church in County Kilkenny, 1600–1800' in W. Nolan and K. Whelan (eds), *Kilkenny: history and society. Interdisciplinary essays on the history of an Irish county* (Dublin, 1990), pp 197–250. **32** J. Grenham, *Tracing your Irish ancestors* includes a county reference guide to Roman Catholic parish registers, with outline maps of Roman Catholic parishes for each county.

unnamed place on a map is quite literally a blank space.[33] Place-naming is a fundamental cultural act, with language being a crucial marker of cultural identity. Continuing controversies about town names, re-naming places, signage, street names, new housing estate names are all indications of persisting underlying tensions about identities in a post-colonial Irish landscape.[34] In Ireland, markers of identity of the dominant (anglophone) culture were clearly inscribed in landscape by the colonial élite: King's/Queen's counties, Kingstown/Queenstown, Londonderry, Virginia, Newtownhamilton, Newtownstewart, Hillsborough, Brookborough, Smithborough, Jonesborough, Summerhill (and its accompanying Springvalley), Prosperous, Newbliss, as well as the overt imperialism of Wellington Quay, Victoria Terrace, and many of the streets in Dublin. Garrison towns like Fermoy had their Messhouse Lane, Barrack Street, Artillery Quay, Prince Albert Street. In many instances a nationalist erasure of these names attempted to inscribe new identities: after independence 'the usual swift rechristening has blotted [the colonial names] out. A local Gaelic League fanatic ... did the baptizing. He sat up night after night with a plan of the town and found a name for every alleyway ...'[35]

Gaelic culture supported a rich oral tradition of place lore – *dinnseanchas*. Nollaig Ó Muraíle refers to the dozens of placenames which pepper many of the medieval Gaelic poetry and genealogical collections, as for instance in Mac Fhirbhisigh's Book of Lecan compiled in the late fourteenth century.[36] The more formal *dinnseanchas* in Ireland consists of epic tales of heroes and the Fianna, recounting stories associated with particular sometimes 'sacred' places which give symbolic meaning to the forms of hills, rivers and other features.[37] Local folklore fulfills a similar role in understanding aspects of the relationship between people and landscape in the past. 'Placenames ... transform the sheerly physical and geographical into something that is historically and socially experienced.'[38]

The 'historical, cultivated world' of Henry Glassie's Fermanagh provides the concepts to explain life in place. Much of what modern society characterises as superstition governed relations with land: traditions of 'fairy paths', the 'lone bush'

---

33 See C. Tilley, *A phenomenology of landscape: places, paths and monuments* (Oxford, 1994), p. 19; Glassie, *Passing the time*, p. 609 writes about turning earth into landscape by claiming it with names.   **34** See C. Nash, 'Irish placenames: post-colonial locations' in *TIBG*, new series, 24 (1999), pp 457–80.   **35** S. Ó Faolain, *An Irish journey* (London, 1940), p. 60. **36** N. Ó Muraíle, 'Settlement and place-names' in Duffy et al. (eds), *Gaelic Ireland*, pp 223–45. For a regional case study of Irish settlement names, see D. Mac Giolla Easpaig, 'Placenames and early settlement in County Donegal' in W. Nolan, L. Ronayne and M. Dunlevy (eds), *Donegal: history and society. Interdisciplinary essays on the history of an Irish county* (Dublin, 1995), pp 149–82; see also P. Power, *The place-names of Decies* (Cork, 1952).   **37** See *The metrical dindshenchas*, ed. E. Gwynn. Todd Lecture series (RIA, Dublin, 1913) which dates from the eleventh century and contains the legends of naming significant mountains and other notable places in Ireland that formed part of the landscape lore of élite groups in ancient Irish society. See also D.C. Harvey, 'Landscape organization, identity and change: territoriality and hagiography in medieval west Cornwall' in *Landscape Research*, 25 (2) (2000), pp 201–12. **38** Tilley, *A phenomenology of landscape*, p. 18.

or 'fairy thorn', have often in the past prevented the destruction or modification of features in local landscapes, such as ring forts or hawthorn bushes, or influenced the location of buildings or roadways. Traditions of holy wells and wells with special curative powers (*tobar*) abounded throughout Ireland until fairly recently – some holy wells, adorned with the grateful tokens of supplicants, still exist as secret legacies of a lost age. Glassie reported in one instance:

> When we have crossed the level fields and come upon the Arney, it is flowing southward. We pause by a lone tree on the riverbank. 'In the Penal Days, under Cromwell,' she says, 'the Irish people used to come across the River there and say their prayers under that tree. They would have their services under it. And on the side of it there's a place where the grass never grows. That's where the priest stood.' ... A patch of bare dirt, strangely free of grass, lies beneath and to one side of the Penal Tree: sacred earth.[39]

Irish speakers especially maintained an intimate relationship with the natural features in their landscape on which they lavished names: fields, hills and hollows had labels comemmorating some ancient owner or legend. Many parts of the West of Ireland where Irish has lasted longest as a living language are rich in local names. Sean Lysaght has referred to the way in which the loss of Irish as vernacular may be an obstacle to understanding this 'old Gaelic relationship with the natural world'.[40] The result is a sort of depleted landscape, preserved in folk museums like Turlough, in County Mayo, with the earlier names for much of its elements lost to everday life. R. Lloyd Praeger pointed to the deceptiveness of pronunciation of Irish placenames by English-speaking outsiders: P.W. Joyce would never try to translate an Irish placename until he heard the local pronunciation. However, after almost two centuries of speaking English in most parts of the country, even local pronunciations are suspect at this stage.[41] Most of John O'Donovan's efforts for the Ordnance Survey in the 1830s were devoted to searching out old people who spoke Irish, to hear their pronunciation of the local names. Following the policy of the Survey, he then produced standardised renditions of the names in English phonetics – an exercise prefigured by William Petty nearly two centuries earlier – which, while execrated by many purists, probably ultimately served to preserve the original pronunciation for posterity.[42] The more than 3,000 Field Name Books of

39 Glassie, *Passing the time*, pp 188–9.   **40** S. Lysaght, 'Contrasting natures: the issue of names' in Wilson Foster (ed.), *Nature in Ireland*, pp 440–60, p. 440, though he warns against giving a special privilege to the Gaelic terms of a primitive rural community, which is principally a legacy of the nationalist cultural revival of the late nineteenth century.   **41** For instance, the townland of Gibberwell in Co. Wexford, evolved from Tybirculle ('Tobar' or well) in a 1356 record to Luberivill in the 1659 'census' to the OS Gibberwell. See R. Lambert, *Rathangan: a County Wexford parish* (Rathangan, 1995), p. 37.   **42** On Petty, see Y.M. Goblet (ed.), *A topographical index of the parishes and townlands of Ireland* (Dublin, 1932), p. xiii; on the OS and John O'Donovan's role in placenaming, see Andrews, *A paper landscape*, pp 120–6; Doherty, *The Irish Ordnance Survey*.

the Ordnance Survey, containing the result of researches by O'Donovan, O'Curry and other Irish scholars employed by the Survey, laid the foundations for placename and toponymic scholarship, as well as Irish cultural history into the twentieth century.[43]

In spite of frequently poor local comprehension of literal meaning, Irish placenames have resounding social and cultural meaning. Even if the Irish language is no longer a familiar everyday language of the people, undoubtedly the euphony of the placename as a shadow of the older disconnected language is embedded in local consciousness. The sounds of names are frequently invoked by local song-writers and poets as signifiers of locality or local identity.[44] Although they are usually seen as emblematic of rurality, these names have endured in the city as well: Ballymun, Finglas, Drumcondra, Cabra, Glasnevin, Drimnagh, and Crumlin in Dublin; Shankill, Falls, Ardoyne, Finaghy, Glengormley, Knockbreda, Ligoniel in Belfast, are all names of former townlands which have been absorbed by expanding urban landscapes.[45]

Although the British state tried to legislate (in 1665) for the replacement of the 'barbarous and uncouth names by which most places were called' with 'new and proper names more suitable to the English tongue', such developments had limited impact. Later, in the eighteenth century, new names occasionally came into common usage, reflecting new developments in the landscapes, as was the case with three new townlands which emerged in the vicinity of Newport in County Mayo in the eighteenth century called Bleachyard, Barrackhill and Weaversquarter,[46] or Bleachgreen (in Kilkenny and Sligo), and Bleachlawn (in Westmeath). Curiously the extensive linen industry of Ulster failed to displace older Gaelic townland names. In parts of the country where settler communities were relatively strong, or in what might be called 'élite landscapes' where landowning gentry were socially dominant, name displacement also occurred, with older names being supplanted by fashionable designations that reflected an anglicised milieu. The Dartrey-Cootehill area on the Monaghan-Cavan borderlands, for instance, was transformed by the houses and parklands of the landowning class in the eighteenth century which erased many of the Gaelic names recorded in seventeenth-century surveys: Dawson Grove replaced parts of Dromore, Kilcrow and Carsan. Dyanmore was replaced by Freame Mount and Fairfield displaced Lisnespeenan and Feddan. Newbliss replaced Mullaghnashanner in the early eighteenth century. Elsewhere, names such as Annsborough, Willsborough, Bailieborough, Lanesborough, Cootehill, Cootehall, Castle Blayney, Castle Caulfield, Castle Coole, Castle Dawson, Castle Archdale all reflect the successful imposition of new settlement by landowning élites.[47]

43 The Name Books are in the National Archives.   **44** See P.J. Duffy, 'Unwritten landscapes: reflections on minor place-names and sense of place in the Irish countryside' in Clarke et al. (eds), *Surveying Ireland's past*, pp 689–712.   **45** See É. de hÓir, 'Sracfhéachaint ar logainmneacha Bhaile Átha Cliath' in *Studia Hib.*, 15 (1975), pp 128–42; A.J. Hughes, 'Deirdre Flanagan's "Belfast and the place-names therein" in translation' in *Ulster Folklife*, 38 (1992), pp 79–97.   **46** See R. Gillespie, 'An historian and the locality' in Gillespie & Hill (eds), *Doing Irish local history*, pp 7–23, esp. pp 10–11.   **47** See also P. O'Flanagan, 'Placenames

Though settlement names are numerous in Gaelic landscapes, in general Gaelic naming was a more passive, descriptive representation of landscape than Anglo-Norman or English naming which more commonly commemorated a process of active settlement and reclamation. A great many of the Gaelic root words in placenames (as well as Welsh toponyms) distinguish between a variety of natural environmental characteristics, as in *drum, cor, cnoc, gleann, inis, cluain, tullach, mullach, coill, ros, carraig, magh, srath, cabhán, leacht, poll.* Townland as well as minor names may be important indicators of processes of settlement, colonisation and reclamation. English townland names, concentrated in the Pale region, often tell a story of active colonisation and environmental change for hundreds of years.[48] Burntfurze (two each in Kildare and Kilkenny), Blackditch (ten instances, mostly in Kildare and Meath), Blacktrench in Kildare, Redbog (six in Louth, Meath, Kildare and Kilkenny) reflect the process of reclamation of the land in the Middle Ages. The County Kildare Civil Survey recorded the townlands of Thornberry, Thornhill and Furryhill. The numbers of Moortowns throughout east Leinster represent in most cases reclaimed marsh or bogland. Blackwood, Shortwood, Allenwood, Broadleas, Whiteleas, Wheatfields, Newland, Loughtown, Kingsfurze, Kingsbog, and Ironhills all contain landuse references. Newhaggard (four in Meath and Dublin) and Pollardstown (in Kildare in 1331) are also significant.

In the *Bulletin of the Ulster Place-name Society*, approximately 2,500 minor names (that is, below the level of townland) are listed for counties Antrim and Tyrone, each followed by the townland in which it occurs.[49] John O'Donovan was sceptical about the usefulness of recording many of the minor placenames in Ireland which he considered to be ephemeral and of local significance only – like 'Peter Bryan's Bullock Hole' on sheet 37 of the County Fermanagh six-inch map.[50] Such ordinary minor names, however, are a manifestation of vernacular landscapes which have changed and evolved and probably fallen out of usage over the past half-century. As far back as 1328 names of minor units were recorded in the vicinity of Maynooth: Athecosteran (5 acres), Atheryn (7 acres), Lympitisfelde (20 acres), Ballybrody (20 acres); Moneyscaddan (50 acres); Athenek alias Aghpeike (14 acres); Mellaghesfeld (14 acres); Crenegele alias Cravile (36 acres); Scotingis (42 acres); Atheclare (16 acres); Johannisfelde (17 acres); Moriceisfeld (13 acres); Hoxclonyn

---

and change in the Irish landscape' in W. Nolan (ed.), *The shaping of Ireland* (Cork, 1986), pp 111–22. **48** Until the systematic recording of most of the names in the large surveys of the seventeenth century, it is impossible to guage the extent to which many names, especially in Gaelic regions, were in a constant state of flux. See T. Jones Hughes, 'Town and Baile in Irish place-names' in Stephens & Glasscock (eds), *Irish geographical studies*, pp 244–58 and P.J. O'Connor, *Atlas of Irish place-names* (Newcastle West, 2001). **49** *Bulletin of the Ulster Place-name Society*, series 2, vols 1–3 contains an index of minor placenames from the 6" OS (third edition) maps of the six counties of Northern Ireland. See also the parish index in Duffy, *Landscapes of south Ulster* which contains *c.*6000 townland and minor names in the parishes of Clogher diocese. **50** Referred to in Andrews, *A paper landscape*, pp 121, 124. O'Donovan was convinced that many of the minor names on the coast and shores of the west would change in the following generation.

(2 acres); Holwemede (8 acres); Inchepolyn (4 acres); Rothmede (7 acres); Coliesmede (1 acre).[51] Emerson's survey of the earl of Kildare's lands in the area of Kildare town for 1674 contains 'a feast of field and other place-names.'[52] Rocque's 1757 map of Barrogstown on the earl of Kildare's estate had 26 fields all individually named: Barnfield, Commonhall, Three-corner field, Barn close, Low park, High park, Quarry field, Lodge field, Clump field, Hare cover field, Obelisk field, Obelisk croft, Obelisk lawn, Broad croft, Coltsfoot field, Old Pasture, Narrow croft, Well park, Quarry meadows, Moulding field, Anne's acre, Spring field, Paddock, and Crodaune.

Field names, many of them in Irish, were abundant features of the landscape into the twentieth century, whose meaning is often now forgotten by local people, though the sounds and rhythms persist in English.[53] The Irish Folklore Collection contains many summaries of such minor names assembled in 1938, in most cases as lists without reference to maps or the landscape: Clontibret parish in County Monaghan, for example, contained the footstick field, the smoothing iron, the black garden, the cowan, the gussett, the parawhack, glenmore, purgatory field, mass-stone field.[54] Ó Muraíle has referrred to the 'astonishingly rich substratum of microto-ponymy still surviving … [in forms that are] utterly undisguised and undistorted'.[55] A total of 7,500 such minor names have been recorded for County Kerry; 1,600 from the three western parishes in Cork county along with 1,400 from the Gaeltacht parish of Ring in County Waterford, 1,100 from two parishes in west Donegal, 800 from one townland in north Mayo and so on. Ó Muraíle has collected more than 600 micro names in nine townlands on Clare Island in Clew Bay, over 600 from a dozen townlands in Tourmakeady Gaeltacht and 500 from Achill Island.[56]

The 1975 study of the 850-acre townland of Kilgalligan in the remote corner of north-west Mayo is a classic in the genre.[57] There were 802 mostly Irish names in

51 *Red Bk Kildare*, ed. Mac Niocaill, pp 97–8. The Ath- names may refer to the Irish *Achadh* (for field).   **52** A. Horner, 'Thomas Emerson's Kildare estates surveys, 1674–1697' in *Kildare Arch. Soc. Jn.*, xviii, 3 (1996–7), pp 399–429, p. 403. See C. Thomas, 'Place-name studies and agrarian colonization in north Wales' in *Welsh History Review*, 10 (2) (1980), pp 155–71 which traces ranges of field and minor names from the middle ages. See P.J. Duffy, 'The territorial identity of Kildare's landscapes' in W. Nolan & T. McGrath (eds), *Kildare: history and society* (Dublin, 2006), pp 1–34.   **53** S. Ó Catháin and P. O'Flanagan, *The living landscape. Kilgalligan, Erris, Co. Mayo* (Dublin, 1975); Duffy, 'Unwritten landscapes'; E. Lankford, *Suirbhé Logainmneacha Chorcaí* (11 vols, Cork, 2005): this survey has about 105,000 minornames collected in Cork with about 240,000 references to Cork names altogether and around 60,000 for Kerry with other references adding *c.*10,000 more (personal communication). **54** National Folklore Collection (hereinafter NFC), University College Dublin, Schools collection, NFC S936.   **55** Ó Muraíle, 'Settlement and place-names', p. 225.   **56** N. Ó Muraíle, communication. See also C. Mac Cárthaigh and K. Whelan (eds), *New Survey of Clare Island 1: history and cultural landscape* (Dublin, 1999). Some of these names were first recorded on William Bald's map of Co. Mayo, surveyed in 1809–16; many were recorded for the first time in 1996. See also the Cork and Kerry Placenames project directed by E. Lankford, author of *Cape Clear island: its people and landscape* (Cape Clear, 1999) and *Suirbhé Logainmneacha Chorcaí.*   **57** Ó Cathain & O'Flanagan, *The living landscape.*

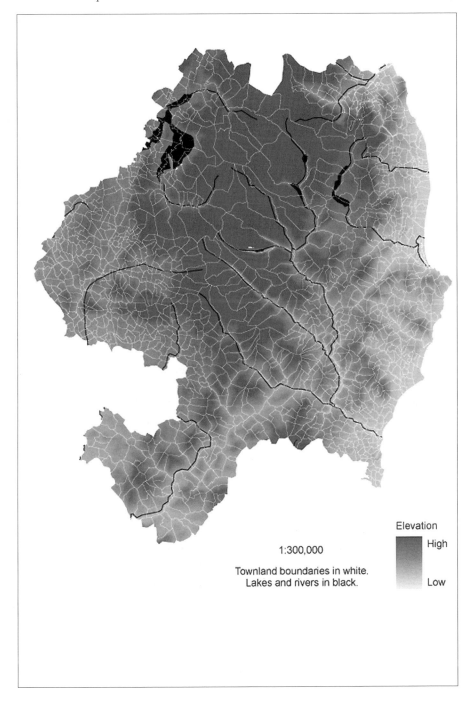

Elevation

1:300,000

Townland boundaries in white.
Lakes and rivers in black.

High

Low

3.3 The townlands of County Wicklow (courtesy of the Ordnance survey of Ireland)

this Irish-speaking district, emblematic of the relationship between community, settlement and place in the past. The local community in north-west Mayo has recently surveyed a fifteen townland area known as Dún Chaochán, mapping hundreds of minor placenames.[58] The coast and shore lands of Ireland are especially rich in placenames, where every rock and inlet has its own distinctive name, reflecting their importance as a resource for fishing offshore and for beachcombing. The Hook peninsula in Wexford has a similar richness, with up to a third of the names in Irish.[59] *Suirbhé Logainmneacha Chorcaí*, published in 2005 under the direction of Eamon Lankford, is the most ambitious placename project, consisting of eleven volumes which include comprehensive details and maps of field names and other minor names.

The survival of these thousands of minor names in Gaeltacht areas or areas which were recently Irish-speaking testifies to the extraordinary richness of this topoynmical tradition in Irish. Tim Robinson's work in Galway is a latter-day *dinnseanchas* of innumerable place-names in Connemara and the Aran Islands:

> Róidín Seoirse … is a narrow, grassy, walled track that angles its way between the fields and up the hillside for half a mile, then pauses by a wet hollow before scrambling around it and up the scarp behind it. The hollow is Turlach na mBráthar, the turlough of the friars; nobody knows why but it might have belonged to the Franciscans of Cill Éinne. It is fed by the run-off from a long narrow ravine crossing the plateau south of it called Gleann Ruairí Óg, the glen of young Ruairí (and again nobody knows who he was), the significance of which is that it divides Ceathrú an Chnoic, on the east, from Ceathrú na gCat, the quarter of the cats, on the west. The former was the land of the Hill Farm, the latter the quarter in which the villagers had their land; the cats were probably pine martens, which are no longer seen in the islands … [60]

Robinson's experience of the cultural landscape, folklore and local history of Connemara was first published in articles in the *Connacht Tribune*. Publishing in local newspapers (and other media) is an important means of arousing local interest in history and heritage and, as with Robinson's project, can result in readers (or listeners) contributing additional valuable material for local projects: it facilitates access to a much larger population than would be possible with orthodox fieldwork.

---

58 *Dún Chaochán, landscapes, seascapes, placenames, stories, songs.* CD-rom (Belmullet, 2000) and Uinsíonn MacGraith agus Treasa Ní Ghearraigh, *Logainmneacha agus oidhreacht Dhún Chaocháin* (Béal an Átha, 2004). See the locally-produced map, *An Blascaod Mór*, published in Dún Chaoin (n.d.) which maps and lists over one hundred names, field names and shore names in Irish. Most of the 'field'/ garden names are in fact patronymics as in Gort fhada Eoghain Uí Shúileabháin, Trasnán Mharas Mhuiris Uí Chatháin, Garraí Thomáis Uí Chriomhthain and so on. **59** B. Colfer, *The Hook peninsula* (Cork, 2004), p. 190. **60** T. Robinson, *Stones of Aran. Labyrinth* (Dublin, 1995), pp 87–8; idem, *Stones of Aran: pilgrimage* (London, 1990) and *Mapping South Connemara* (Roundstone, 1985).

Some of the earliest recorded place names are included in the Irish genealogies and often written down some centuries after they originated.[61] The legal documents of the Norman colony and state papers of the late medieval and increasingly the early-modern periods (fiants, chancery inquisitions, calendar of patent rolls and seventeenth-century surveys and inventories)[62] all represent important archives of name records. Yann Goblet highlights the importance of seventeenth-century maps for their toponomastic details and the variety in spelling of placenames which were often written down on the spot by surveyors: '… the D.S. [Down Survey], the barony maps and the *Hiberniae Delineatio* are all together the most perfect collection of Irish place-names in the unforfeited as in the forfeited area towards the middle of the xvii th century'.[63] In combination with the Civil Survey and the Book of Survey and Distribution this is an enormously significant repertory of Irish toponyms. The first section of Goblet indexes the parishes by barony and county and the second section indexes *c.*24,000 townland names by parish and county – more than a third of all the townlands recorded by the Ordnance Survey (OS) in the 1830s, encompassing almost half of the land area of Ireland.

The OS Name Books and Letters (mostly written by John O'Donovan reporting to the Survey headquarters in Dublin) are important sources for placename researches. The hundreds of Name Books are held in the National Archives and contain summaries of spelling variants, listing recorded occurrences of the names, location and other details of the townland.[64] Typescripts and carbon copies of the Letters for twenty counties were made in 1926 and can be found in the National Library of Ireland, NUIM and other repositories.[65] For students of local history, the OS Letters should be perused in conjunction with the OS six-inch maps in order to get a picture of conditions at local level in pre-famine Ireland. On-line versions of various editions of the six-inch maps, 25-inch and large-scale manuscript town maps, are being made available by the OS, with a facility for searching for a range of recorded features, such as raths, churches, burial

61 See P. Power (ed.), *Crichad an Chaoilli, being the topography of ancient Fermoy* (Cork, 1932). On the MacFhirbhisigh's Book of Genealogies, see Ó Muraíle, 'Settlement and place-names', p. 241; *Leabhar mór na nGenealach: The great book of Irish genealogies compiled (1645–66) by Dubhaltach Mac Fhirbhisigh*, ed. N. Ó Muraíle (Dublin, 2003–4). **62** *Red Bk Kildare*, ed. Mac Niocaill records grants, agreements and extents of lands dating from early thirteenth and fourteenth centuries in Kildare, Limerick and Connacht. It contains a wealth of placenames, mostly rendered in Latin, with introductory abstracts and table of contents in English from *c.*1514, and an index of persons and places provided by the editor. See also S. Pender (ed.), *A census of Ireland c.1659* (IMC Dublin, 1939; 2002). **63** Goblet (ed.), *A topographical index of the parishes and townlands of Ireland*, pp xiii–xiv. **64** See J. Prunty, *Maps and map-making in local history*. Maynooth Research guides for Irish local history series (Dublin, 2004), pp 138–42. **65** The original manuscripts are held in the RIA. Some have been published: *OS Letters Meath: letters containing information relative to the antiquities of the county of Meath collected during the progress of the OS in 1836*, ed. with intro. by M. Herity (Dublin, 2001); also, *Kildare, Donegal*, ed. with intro. by M. Herity (Dublin, 2001); *John O'Donovan's letters from County Londonderry (1834)*, ed. G. Mawhinney (Ballinascreen Historical Society, 1992); *The OS letters: Wicklow*, ed. C. Corlett and J. Medlycott (Roundwood, n.d., [2000]).

grounds.[66] A flavour of O'Donovan's fieldwork methods is provided in the following Letter from Meath:

> This morning (Thursday) I got the names of the Townlands in the Parish of Dunboyne from Andrew Dowd, a native and resident of the Parish, as were his father and grand-father … Dunboyne Ph. in which is the village of that name is called in Irish *paráiste dhun bóinne*, for which I could get no meaning. In Jarratstown TL are two fields, 'Church Meadow' & 'Relic Field', both of which together the people call the *reilicín*. This was formerly a burying place, & they say that as yet unbaptised children are buried there. I asked were there any old walls of a church, and was told there is a stump of a wall about 20 perches from the *reilicín*, about which no one knows anything.[67]

P.W. Joyce's *Irish names of places* represents the first attempt at a comprehensive index and explanation of Irish placenames, mainly townland names, which was made possible by the earlier publications of the Ordnance Survey. It was published in three volumes, the first two in 1869 and 1871 which examine the contextual meanings of Irish placenames ranging from the *dinnseanchas* through land divisions and environmental toponyms, and the third in 1913 which contains an extensive index of townlands with suggested derivations and examples of occurrences. In excess of 10,000 names are discussed.

The Northern Ireland Place-Name Project in Queen's University has published a number of volumes in a projected series of thirty-five volumes on the counties of Northern Ireland. Townland and some other names (towns, villages, hills and water bodies appearing in the 1:50 000 OS maps) in each parish are comprehensively examined. In keeping with orthodox placename scholarship, the historical evolution of the spelling of each name is noted, showing pre-1700 spellings with sources and dates, followed by a selection of post-1700 forms. For example, the parish of Ramoan in County Antrim consists of thirty-seven townlands.[68] The earliest occurrence of the parish name is in the Book of Armagh's reference to the church of R[á]th Muadáin being founded by St Patrick. The name is later traced through a range of sources such as the ecclesiastical taxation of *c.*1306, fiants of Elizabeth (1570) and numerous references through the seventeenth century. The townlands in the parish are then discussed in alphabetical order. The Placenames Branch of the Ordnance Survey of Ireland has published official versions of the placenames of the main centres of population (mainly Post Office locations) and physical features in the country.[69] *Liostaí Logainmneacha. Contae Mhuineacháin* (Dublin, 1996) contains the official versions of all the townland, parish and barony names in the county.

66 www.irishhistoricmaps.ie/historic/. See J. Prunty, *Maps and map making*, pp 252–67.
67 *OS Letters Meath*, ed. Herity, p. 114.   **68** F. Mac Gabhann (ed.), *Place-names of Northern Ireland* (8 vols, Belfast, 1993, 1995, 1996, 1997, 2004), vol. vii, County Antrim, p. 227.
69 *Gazetteer of Ireland: the names of centres of population and physical features* (Dublin, 1989); see

The Liam Price notebooks contain the field notes of Liam Price who was passionately interested in the local history, archaeology and folklore of Wicklow in particular. His notebooks, which also cover parts of Carlow, Kildare, Laois and Offaly, as well as west Mayo, are deposited with the Placenames Branch of the Ordnance Survey and demonstrate his wide-ranging interest in most aspects of the historical antiquities, placenames and landscapes he visited from the 1920s to the 1960s. The following extract (1944) provides a flavour of his work which is very much in the spirit of John O'Donovan:

> The grove in the S part of the townland [Stranahely] … was called 'Bala-clava', because it was planted in the year of the Battle of Balaclava, 1855. … A small piece of the river, where the 'Knickeen River' is written on the map, was called 'the Raheen River': there was a raheen, just behind the house which is shown on the map just near this river, in Knickeen. These three fields in Knickeen were called (S to N) 'the Long Stone Field', 'the Clash Field', and 'Knickeen Bank'. The old house which is shown on the map a little to the NW was Hanlon's; it is down now. Where the track crosses a drain a little to the N of this, Fenton said 'You crossed a "cassock" over a wide drain'. I said 'Isn't that called a "kish"'? and he said 'We call it a "cassock"'. (Evidently 'ceasach', 'a road over boggy ground': much the same as 'ciseach': cf. 'ceas', 'a basket', and 'cis', 'a wicker basket'.)[70]

Deirdre Flanagan and Laurence Flanagan, *Irish place names* (Dublin, 1994) is a very useful handbook explaining in brief the derivation and meaning of more than 3,000 of the names of villages, towns, cities and physical features in Ireland. The first part consists of an alphabetical list of the root words which most commonly form Irish placenames (such as *baile*, *cathair*, *lios*) with accompanying maps of the distribution of the commonest, and the second part is a gazeteer of all the placenames discussed. A similar approach was taken by Patrick O'Connor in his *Atlas of Irish place-names* which maps the distribution of more than seventy of the commonest name elements and discusses the meaning and locations of the names in time and space.[71]

PROCESSES OF SETTLEMENT

Smooth meadows, trim hedges, trees in line, crisp white houses arrayed on green fields: this landscape of farmwork is a work of art. No part of it has gone untouched. Will has intervened everywhere. Rocks have been broken and

---

also the Ordnance Survey's *The placenames of Ireland in the third millennium* (Dublin, 1992) containing a collection of papers on Irish placenames.   **70** *The Liam Price notebooks*, ed. C. Corlett and M. Weaver (2 vols, Dublin, 2002), ii, 409–10; Liam Price's *Placenames of Wicklow* were published in seven volumes between 1945 and 1967.   **71** P. O'Connor, *Atlas of Irish place-names* (Newcastle West, 2001), p. 51.

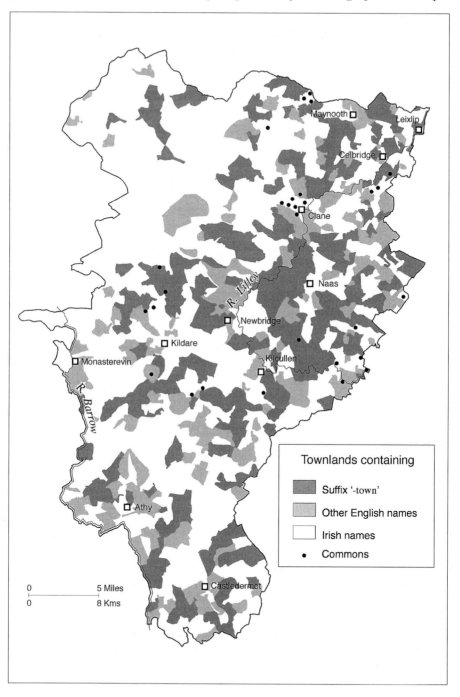

3.4 Placenames in County Kildare

assembled. Earth has been moved and molded. Shaped with spades, shaved with scythes and billhooks and cattle, the land is an enormous piece of sculpture, continually presenting a collective idea of beauty.[72]

The idea of the landscape as the most recent stage in an ongoing narrative of modification and change, undertaken by each generation in turn according to economic and social exigencies of the time, is captured in terms such as palimpsest, syncretism (adaptation of site for subsequent purposes), and more common expressions of evolution, incremental development, dereliction, maintenance or obliteration. The nature of ownership of the land is important. For the past century the farmers of Ireland have been the owner occupiers whose activities directly impact on the landscape. But in terms of landscape history, the earlier structure of ownership, and within it levels of landholding, needs to be understood.[73] This involves considering control of land and what happened on it, or in modern planning parlance 'development control'. 'Planning', whether by a landowning élite in the eighteenth and nineteenth centuries or by the state or local authorities in the twentieth, was affected in some manner by the nature of landownership and landholding. The predominantly colonial nature of Irish landownership for many centuries and, within its parameters, the progress of settlement, has been of critical importance in the shaping and development of regional and local landscapes. At its most basic level an ecological paradox is evident in which the smallest farms, the poorest infrastructure and highest levels of underdevelopment have been associated with the poorest most marginal land resources in the west and north-west of the country.

In general over the past three or four centuries as population has grown, settlement within a framework of big and small estates moved uphill and expanded into more marginal landscapes. Scarce soil resources were reclaimed and incorporated in small patches of potato ridges, which later reverted to wilderness in the face of demographic decline. Settlement studies have also been traditionally concerned with the evolution of ordinary, working landscapes, which of course accounts for the dominant proportion of today's landscape legacies.

One of the most ubiquitous themes in settlement history hinges around open-field and enclosed landscapes – the fundamental manner in which the land resources of the community were organised, with hedged enclosures especially reflecting a rational, ordered modernity in the landscape. Field and settlement systems were responses to variations in tenure, local economies, technologies, and the nature of agriculture. In many places these structures overlay earlier historic field sytems which centuries of arable cultivation have obliterated, except where they have been preserved in blanket peatlands, as in the Céide fields of north Mayo.

---

72 Glassie, *Passing the time*, p. 442.   **73** K. Cahill, *Who owns Britain* (London, 2001), presents comprehensive data, county by county, on landownership in Great Britain (where approximately 5,000 landowners still own up to one-third of the land area of the island) and Ireland and its historical experience over the past 150 years.

In some parts of Leinster, in aerial photographs or the low light of winter, traces of the ridge-and-furrow landscapes of earlier medieval open fields are visible underneath the patchwork of modern fields.[74] On mountain sides in the west, for example in Killary harbour, the fossilised remains of the arable ridges of overgrown and abandoned nineteenth-century rundale landscapes are also visible.[75] Detailed fieldwork, more comprehensive analysis of the large-scale OS maps of the nineteenth century, better aerial photography and geomagnetic surveying techniques have enormously increased the numbers of indicative landscape sites in Ireland.

Sources for medieval settlement landscapes are patchy, with Anglo-Norman Ireland being better recorded than Gaelic Ireland. The Leinster Pale by the late medieval period exhibited a semblance of English control and more intensive settlement. The late fifteenth century saw the commencement of construction of a Pale ditch and boundary to prevent cattle being stolen, with evidence of timber pallisades in places being maintained by local landholders. Medieval documents from English Ireland, such as charters and extents, do not provide much useable information on landscape conditions. Ostensibly detailed extents such as early fourteenth-century examples in a number of Tipperary manors, record castles, buildings such as chapels, mills, dovecotes, with tenants names, their status and the amount of land held and rents paid. Only buildings belonging to the demesne and capable of valuation were included and there is nothing on the location of farmsteads. The use of the term *villatum* (or *vill*) is ambiguous like most settlement terms in Ireland – referring to a village settlement at times and to a territorial unit such as townland or ballyboe at others. Many of the places mentioned in sources such as *The red book of the earls of Kildare or The calendar of Ormond deeds* are fieldnames or other names which have long disappeared.[76]

Limited information is available on the organisation of agriculture in the manors, referring to categories of land such as woodland, open country, roads and pathways, scrubland, bogs and pasture. Knowledge of land measures, land units and land assessment is often lost. For instance the church land with Oughterard in

74 D.N. Hall, M. Hennessy and T. O'Keeffe, 'Medieval agriculture and settlement in Oughterard and Castlewarden, Co. Kildare' in *Ir. Geography*, 18 (1985), pp 16–25; D. Kelly, 'The Porchfield of Trim – a medieval "open-field"?' in *Ir. Geography*, 38 (1) (2005), pp 23–43. **75** Mis-named 'lazy beds' because it involved turning the sod, with the grassy surface allowed decompose and fertilise the growing tubers.   **76** *Cal. Ormond deeds*, ed. Curtis, i; *The red book of Ormond*, ed. N.B. White (IMC, Dublin, 1932); *Red Bk Kildare*, ed. Mac Niocaill; J. Bradley, *Treasures of Kilkenny: charters and civic records of Kilkenny city* (Kilkenny, 2003); see B.J. Graham, 'Anglo-Norman manorial settlement in Ireland: an assessment' in *Ir. Geography*, 18 (1985), pp 4–15 and idem, 'Urban genesis in early medieval Ireland' in *Journal of Historical Geography*, 13 (1) (1987), pp 3–16; Mark Hennessy, 'Manorial organisation in early thirteenth-century Tipperary' in *Ir. Geography*, 29 (1996), pp 116–25; idem, 'Manorial agriculture and settlement in early fourteenth-century Co. Tipperary' in Clarke et al. (eds), *Surveying Ireland's past*, pp 99–117. On Anglo-Norman settlement and landscape, see Empey, 'Conquest and settlement: patterns of Anglo-Norman settlement in north Munster and south Leinster'.

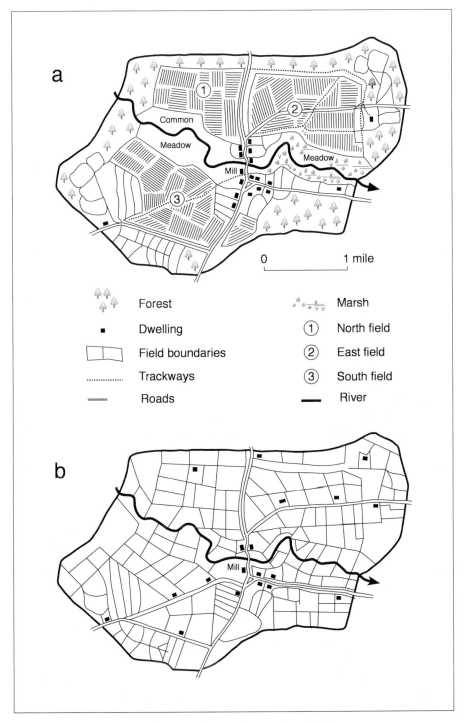

a

Common

Meadow

Meadow

Mill

0   1 mile

Forest   Marsh

Dwelling   ①   North field

Field boundaries   ②   East field

Trackways   ③   South field

Roads   River

b

Mill

3.5 From (a) medieval open fields to (b) a modern enclosed landscape

Kildare had fifty 'day-works' of arable land and in 1543 there was a reference to a grant of a 'half-indell of pasture'.[77] Much of the documentary evidence 'is ambivalent, forever contaminated by the uncertainties that attend the translation from legal theory to the realities of the medieval landscape and the perceptions which feudal seigneurs had of that landscape and their tasks.'[78] The same is also true of Gaelic medieval sources such as annals, genealogies, bardic poetry in which topographical detail is often formulaic and legalistic, symbolic or idealist.[79]

Seventeenth-century surveys like the Civil Survey and the Down Survey have been used by historical geographers especially to provide insights into the medieval landscape. Seventeenth-century maps, however, are often too generalised to discern in detail the nature of rural settlement or the existence of 'villages' or house clusters or the morphology of surrounding agricultural landscapes. The 'national' surveys by William Petty were purposefully interested in territorial denominations and boundaries, with some internal detail on more significant infrastructural features such as castles, bridges, fords and roads. Thomas Raven's maps of Farney in Monaghan in 1634, however, suggest the existence of several embryonic clusters of thatched cabins in an unenclosed countryside and contemporary descriptions seem to support such a scenario; his maps of the Clandeboye estate in 1625 depict plantation settlements in a largely unenclosed countryside.[80]

Broadly speaking, two principal types of open-field systems were based ultimately on the complexity of their land-use management. Stronger agricultural areas were characterised by open unenclosed fields, incorporating rotation systems of two, three or more large 'fields' cultivated by agreement usually, with associated commons in woodland, marsh and meadows (3.5). Individual landholding portions in strips or furlongs were separated by low-level boundary markers or mearings, which following continual ploughing resulted in characteristic ridge and furrow landscapes. Stock were herded off the cultivated fields, or folded on them in winter. These landscapes were often referred to as 'champion' (from *champagne*) lands by English observers in the sixteenth and seventeenth centuries. This was a field 'system' by which the population usually living in a village-type settlement communally arranged and managed their cultivated lands. The open fields were cultivated in rotation in that a half or a third or a quarter of land lay fallow at any one time (two, three or four field systems): the better lands, such as found in the north European lowlands, could tolerate more intensive use. Increasingly intensive use was usually a response to population pressure. A changeover from two-course to three-course rotation allowed greater livestock carrying capacity because of increased fodder, which in turn provided more manure to fertilise and tolerate

---

77 Hall et al., 'Medieval agriculture and settlement' examines agriculture in medieval Kildare.   **78** Graham, 'Anglo-Norman manorial settlement', p. 12.   **79** See K. Simms, 'References to landscape and economy in Irish bardic poetry' in Clarke et al. (eds), *Surveying Ireland's past*, pp 145–68.   **80** Duffy, 'Farney in 1634'; 'A booke of survey of ffarney and Clancarvile in the kingdom of Ireland [by] Wm Smith 1612' (Longleat Library, Irish papers, Box 1, bundle 1); Hall, 'The vegetational landscape of mid-County Down', p. 81.

more intensive cultivation. It also generated more horsepower for ploughing, and more meat and food to support a growing population.

Ultimately, however, there was an economic and geographical limit, where much of the woodland and meadow had to be retained for livestock or fuel and was protected by customary law. So when limits were reached, often at what became the boundaries with adjoining parishes, alternative landuses were sought, or outmigration took place.[81] Examples of such landscapes were found in former Anglo-Norman manorial regions particularly within the Pale, for example at Ballymore-Eustace, Newcastle Lyons, Rathcoole, and Dalkey.[82] In some of these places the older strips or furlongs were fossilised in later hedged enclosures and in relict farm villages in south Kilkenny where fragmented farmholdings in the nineteenth century reflect a late eighteenth-century enclosure of the open fields.[83] Similarly residual elements of common lands in Kildare survived as separate townland units through the eighteenth and into the nineteenth century. Anngret Simms suggests that many Anglo-Norman manors in eastern Ireland differed from English settlements in having to adjust to pre-existing Irish land divisions. Townland units in the seventeenth century resulted in a more dispersed settlement pattern in the Irish manors.[84]

A simpler field system has been identified in Ireland and other parts of Atlantic Britain as 'Celtic' because of its geography and some evidence of earlier tribal associations.[85] In the nineteenth century it was usually characterised as a rundale system. Many rundale settlements were extremely large villages which appear to have grown up by a process of organic expansion from an initial couple of houses, where holdings were subdivided and new houses erected beside the original, with little or no intervention by the landowner. This form of settlement was the most

81 For general discussion on field systems and settlements see C.T. Smith, *An historical geography of western Europe before 1800* (London, 1978), pp 190–259; R.A. Dodgshon and R.A. Butlin (eds), *An historical geography of England and Wales* (London, 1978), pp 151–69; D.B. Grigg, *The dynamics of agricultural change: the historical experience* (London, 1982); B.K. Roberts, *Landscapes of settlement: prehistory to the present* (London, 1996); see also Reeves-Smyth & Hammond (eds), *Landscape archaeology in Ireland* and Aalen, *Man and landscape in Ireland*. **82** Aalen, 'The origin of enclosures in eastern Ireland' in Stephens & Glasscock (eds), *Irish geographical studies*, p. 213. **83** See J. Burtchaell, 'The south Kilkenny farm villages' in W.J. Smyth and K. Whelan (eds), *Common ground: essays on the historical geography of Ireland* (Cork, 1988), pp 110–23. **84** A. Simms, 'Rural settlement in medieval Ireland: the example of the royal manors of Newcastle Lyons and Esker in south County Dublin' in B.K. Roberts and R.E. Glasscock (eds), *Villages, fields and frontiers: studies in European rural settlement in the medieval and early modern periods* (Oxford, 1983), pp 133–52; idem, 'The geography of Irish manors: the example of the Llanthony cells of Duleek and Colp, County Meath' in J. Bradley (ed.), *Settlement and society in medieval Ireland: studies presented to FX Martin* (Kilkenny, 1988), pp 291–315; idem, 'The origins of towns in medieval Ireland: the European context' in J.–M. Duvosquel and E. Thoen (eds), *Peasants and townsmen in medieval Europe: studia in honorem Adriaan Verhulst* (Ghent, 1995), pp 99–116; idem, 'Change and continuity in an Irish country town: Kells, 1600–1820' in *Proceedings of the British Academy*, cviii (2002), pp 121–50. **85** See R.A. Dodgshon, *From chiefs to landlords: social and economic change in the western highlands and islands, c.1493–1820* (Edinburgh, 1998).

ecologically, economically and socially effective way to combine the limited resources of poorer communities in the early-modern period for survival in difficult environmental conditions.[86] This was a one-field rotation system which evolved particularly in more marginal western landscapes such as the Burren in Clare, Connemara, Achill and west Mayo, and Donegal as a device to make the most efficient use of local environments. The arable soils of what was called in some places the 'infield' were cultivated continuously with potatoes, oats, rye and manured fairly intensively by the livestock – or by seaweed and sand in coastal communities. Rougher heathlands in the 'outfield' were used for communal grazing, and periodically cultivated when need arose. More distant uplands in some places were used for summer grazing and booleying (or transhumance). In many cases such summer grazing resolved an important vitamin deficiency for stock in the lower grazing lands. Dry cattle were also out-wintered on mountains in parts of the west for this reason. Many of the larger grazing farms of south Meath rented winter grazing in the Burren. Rundale was also in evidence in the uplands of the east such as the Wicklow and Cooley mountains, as well as in more marginal midland bogs, for instance.

Arable cultivation occurred in small blocks of ridges with traditions of periodic redistribution of lots in some places. By the nineteenth century population pressure in many places meant that the outfield was permanently cultivated with the emergence of a highly complex and disorderly farmscape where shares got progressively smaller. Many families in Achill, for instance, held their few acres fragmented into small portions which were mixed in with neighbours: one farmer had two ridges near his house, then several hundred yards further another three or four ridges. Some of the pieces were no larger than a table, with farms sometimes in thirty or forty plots, none of them separated by fences. Rathlackan in north Mayo, for instance, had fifty-six farms in 1,500 fragments in 1918.[87] Families cultivated their small portions with whatever crops they wanted – potatoes, hay, rye, oats being separately cultivated on each small section. As the hay was harvested first, the cow had to be herded on the aftergrass to prevent it trespassing or injuring

86 K. Whelan, 'The modern landscape: from plantation to present' in Aalen et al. (eds), *Atlas of the Irish rural landscape*, pp 79–84; also F.H.A. Aalen 'Imprint of the past' in Gillmor (ed.), *The Irish countryside*, pp 83–120; D. McCourt, 'The dynamic quality of Irish rural settlement' in R.H. Buchanan, E. Jones and D. McCourt (eds), *Man and his habitat: essays presented to E. Estyn Evans* (London, 1971), pp 126–64; E.A. Curry, 'Landscape development in north-west and south-east Derry, 1700–1840' in G. O'Brien (ed.), *Derry and Londonderry: history and society. Interdisciplinary essays on the history of an Irish county* (Dublin, 1999), pp 321–58; B.S. MacAodha, 'Clachan settlement in Iar-Connacht' in *Ir. Geography*, 5 (1965), pp 20–28; K. Whelan, 'Famine and post-famine adjustment' in Nolan (ed.), *The shaping of Ireland*, pp 151–64; K. Whelan 'Landscape and society on Clare Island, 1700–1900' in Mac Cárthaigh & Whelan (eds), *New survey of Clare Island 1*, pp 73–98; Mary Cawley, 'Aspects of continuity and change in rural settlement patterns' in *Studia Hib.*, 22–23 (1982–3), pp 106–27. 87 J. Kilbane, 'The heritage of mountain grazing in Achill: the booley, land use and commonage' (unpublished BA thesis, Galway-Mayo Institute of Technology, 2002); see Evans, *Irish folk ways*, p. 24.

neighbours' crops. The children or wives of the farmers might spend all day standing with their cows on their grassy patch.[88] Rows and disputes were frequent in these conditions where land was such a precious commodity, with older members falling out for decades. Indeed, locals in west Mayo believed 'Lord Rundale' introduced this system to keep the Irish fighting with each other! Before the establishment of permanent fences, landowners were frequently called in to adjudicate between disputing tenants who often employed local surveyors to advance their cases.

These general thematic models of open-field systems gradually gave way to enclosed landscapes from the seventeenth century. Enclosure was the most central feature of improvement which marked the progress of the agricultural revolution from the seventeenth century and the application of rationalism and science to farming. In England, and to an extent in Ireland, such new approaches to farming meant the dispossession of many of the smaller tenantry and cottier classes and appropriation of older common lands. Enclosure in 'parks' or fields through processes of 'assarting' (clearing land for cultivation) of woodland, forest and reclaimed marshland, facilitated many other improvements such as reclamation and drainage, crop and livestock development. It occurred from the seventeenth century on the well-endowed 'champion' lands of the east and the planted lands in Ulster and Leinster. 'The relatively short period during which the main enclosure movements occurred, the autocratic nature of estate organisation combined with the scientific approach implicit in the "new husbandry", and the relatively level terrain, explain the essentially uniform character of the enclosure pattern now existing over the bulk of eastern Ireland.'[89]

Head tenants especially were expected in many early Ulster leases to fence in all the outbounds of their premises. Leases on the Bellaghy estate in Derry for instance did not require enclosure of individual farms or fields; the fencing and ditching of the 'outmears and bounds' of the premises was required initially. New leases in 1764 forbade rundale and ordered each tenure to be enclosed by a mearing or ditch or stone wall with tenants to make '30 perches of Ditch 5 ft wide and 4 ft deep set with Whitethorn or Crab Quicks ... and to ... plant Ash or Oak trees in the said ditches ... until the farm be divided into Parks not exceeding 7 acres in any one Park'.[90] In this Ulster region woodland clearances were initially divided into parks enclosed by ditches planted with quicksets as islands in a sea of scrub timber, water and bogland. As the land was gradually reclaimed it was subdivided into smaller field units.

In general, from the seventeenth century the enclosure movement was implemented more systematically through the landed estates system than by individual tenant farmers, leading to a uniform rectilinear modern fieldscape, with

88 Children were very much exploited in traditional agricultural landscapes – minding younger children, herding the cattle, or (in Monaghan) 'holding the rod' to keep the corn erect for scythesmen, gathering stones, gleaning the stubble, fetching water. **89** Aalen, 'Origin of enclosures in eastern Ireland', pp 219–20. **90** Curry, 'Landscape development in south Derry in the eighteenth century', p. 93.

only residual common lands in east Leinster being enclosed by acts of parliament in the late eighteenth century. Leases from the Kingston estate in south Tipperary in 1727, for example, required tenants to fence in all outbounds – the inner enclosures could follow.[91] With obscure ownership or title, some commons escaped systematic enclosure and attracted squatter settlements of landless and labouring families up to the famine decade, as for instance in Tirmoghan, Loughanure, or Baltinglass in Kildare, which reflect a process of disorderly piecemeal enclosure into small acreages (see 7.1). At the height of interest in improvement during the late eighteenth century, commentators such as Arthur Young and the authors of the county statistical surveys regularly adverted to the necessity to enclose.[92] Many estates gave quick-sets and saplings to their tenants as encouragement, employed agriculturists and established model farms to demonstrate the advantages of enclosure. Such improvements came later in the west: Lord Palmerston's emigration scheme in the mid-nineteenth century was followed by surveys of residual farms which were formed into squares, strips or parallelograms, with ditches and hedges along new straight roads. He would not tolerate any resistance to his squaring and improvements – resisters 'must quit my estate for I will not allow the obstinacy & perverseness of one or two men to stand in the way of the advantages of the rest of the tenants'.[93] In Cork many estate owners intervened directly in such improvement in the 1820s following the eradication of the middleman system, such as Sir John Benn-Walsh who commenced with a division into fields of five acres and then divisions of farms by 'large bounds ditches and dikes.'[94]

In parts of Monaghan and Fermanagh there is evidence of farm clusters and open-field landscapes in the eighteenth century which probably developed like the rundale settlement in western regions: Blackstaff in south Monaghan contained up to forty houses. Re-letting of the Bath estate in 1777 was followed by the break-up of many clusters and the enclosure of much of the landscape with hedges.[95] In other parts of Monaghan county, enclosures by the early nineteenth century seem to have been mainly banks and ditches. Many of the fences in the north of Muckno parish, for instance, consisted of loose stone walls and sod banks in the 1820s. Lord Templetown established a nursery to provide quicks to his tenants and the parish priest was the first to start fencing and planting his farm. Overall in Ireland, there

---

91 W.J. Smyth, 'Estate records and the making of the Irish landscape' in *Ir. Geography*, 9 (1976), pp 29–49; see L. Clare, *Enclosing the commons: Dalkey, the Sugar Loaves and Bray, 1820–1870* (Dublin, 2004).　　**92** See J. Dubourdieu, *Statistical survey of County Down* (Dublin, 1802), p. 57, where he notes that enclosures were very poor, only a ditch and bank with no hedges in many parts and suggests that landowners should provide quicks so that 'the nakedness of our land will not much longer be a reproach to us.' In contrast, Coote details the well-managed, trimmed quickset hedges in Stradbally, Queen's County in 1801 (C. Coote, *Statistical survey of County Laois* (Dublin, 1801), p. 116).　　**93** Quoted in T. Power, 'The Palmerston estate in County Sligo: improvement and assisted emigration before 1850' in P.J. Duffy (ed.), *To and from Ireland: planned migration schemes, c.1600–2000* (Dublin, 2004), pp 111–12.　　**94** J.S. Donnelly, jn., *The land and people of nineteenth-century Cork* (London, 1975), pp 66–7.　　**95** Duffy, *Landscapes of south Ulster*, p. 21.

was a frontier of settlement change moving from east to west from the eighteenth century, which gradually saw clustered settlements being replaced by dispersed farmsteads.

This process of landscape reorganisation accelerated in the west through the second half of the nineteenth century, exemplified most notoriously on Lord George Hill's estate in Gweedore in Donegal.[96] The Encumbered Estates acts of 1848 and 1849 spurred on many landowners to enhance the social and economic efficiency of their estates. In some cases the fragmented rundale landscape was fossilised in new enclosed fieldscapes with ownership being scattered among a range of landholders. The Congested Districts Board (CDB) and the Land Commission in the late nineteenth and early twentieth centuries were deeply involved in rearranging farmholdings for more effective agriculture.[97] 'Striping' the land was the commonest mechanism adopted, where long narrow sections (subdivided into fields) roughly proportionate to each farmer's rundale plots and including a share in the mountain commonage, were allotted to each farmer, with in many cases a new house being built on the roadside adjacent to the newly allocated holding. In many situations such rearrangement was facilitated by local migration, migration to the Midlands or emigration of selected households.[98]

96 Lord George Hill, *Facts from Gweedore* (London, 1887; reprint with intro. by E. Estyn Evans, Belfast, 1971); E. Estyn Evans, 'Some survivals of the Irish open-field system' in *Geography*, 24 (1939), pp 24–36; on rural settlement and field systems see Aalen & Brody, *Gola*; D. McCourt, 'The decline of rundale, 1750–1850' in P. Roebuck (ed.), *From plantation to partition: essays in honour of J.L. McCracken* (Belfast, 1981), pp 119–39 for evidence on the contraction of rundale; D. McCourt, 'The dynamic quality of Irish rural settlement' in Buchanan & McCourt (eds), *Man and his habitat*, pp 126–64; J. Burtchaell, 'A typology of settlement and society in County Waterford *c.*1850' in W. Nolan and T. Power (eds), *Waterford: history and society. Interdisciplinary essays on the history of an Irish county* (Dublin, 1992), pp 541–78; see case studies by W.J. Smyth, 'Social, economic and landscape transformations in County Cork from the mid-eighteen to the mid-nineteenth century' in P. O'Flanagan and C.G. Buttimer (eds), *Cork: history and society. Interdisciplinary essays on the history of an Irish county* (Dublin, 1993), pp 655–98; W. Nolan, 'Society and settlement in the valley of Glenasmole, *c.*1750–*c.*1900' in F.H.A. Aalen and K. Whelan (eds), *Dublin city and county: from prehistory to present* (Dublin, 1992), pp 181–228; K. Whelan, 'Pre- and post-famine landscape change' in C. Portéir (ed.), *The great Irish famine* (Cork, 1995), pp 19–33.   **97** At its peak, the CDB (established in 1891) operated over a third of the land surface of Ireland. One of its most comprehensive reorganisations was undertaken on Clare Island in 1895. See W.L. Micks, *An account of the constitution, administration and dissolution of the Congested Districts Board for Ireland, from 1891 to 1923* (Dublin, 1925); Whelan, 'Landscape and society on Clare Island'; W. Nolan, 'New farms and fields: migration policies of state land agencies, 1891–1980' in Smyth & Whelan (eds), *Common ground*, pp 296–319.   **98** Nolan, 'New farms and fields', pp 296–319; M. Whelan et al., 'State-sponsored migrations to the east midlands in the twentieth century' in Duffy (ed.), *To and from Ireland*, pp 175–96; P.J. Sammon, *In the Land Commission: a memoir, 1933–1978* (Dublin, 1997) contains some appendices on the 1923 Land acts; the Gaeltacht colonies in Co. Meath; the use of migration in re-arrangements of congested holdings; Land settlement in Co. Meath; comparison of land settlement achievements by the Estates Commissioners and the CDB under British administration, with the achievements of the Land Commission under Irish government; how an estate was acquired and how a resale scheme was prepared, approved and operated.

LANDED ESTATES

Up until the mid-nineteenth century, the most pervasive expression of private initiative in landscape change was the estate system, through whose structures from the eighteenth century most of the lineaments of landscape were laid down by tenants and townspeople. These landed estates emerged from a medieval world dominated by territorial lordship, a legacy of Gaelic lineages, Anglo-Norman manors or monastic granges, in which economic and political control was territorially dispersed. Landownership was transformed by the expanding colonial ventures of the new centralised British state, through military subjugation, confiscation and plantation, and the operation of a 'national' market in rents and property. Economic integration of the British Isles extended the commodity value of land and its agricultural products, as well as woodland, charcoal, mining and so on, all of which introduced important changes in local environments.[99] The Civil Survey and accompanying Down Survey and the Books of Survey and Distribution record the embryonic stage of this landownership in the seventeenth century.[1]

In much of the east of the country the landed estates had a largely positive influence in terms of landscape change, facilitating 'improvements on nature' which are still evident in mansions and parklands, estates and industrial villages, enclosures and hedgerows, woodland plantation, farmhouses, cottages and other buildings. The estate system had more negative repercussions in marginal lands of the country especially in parts of the west (and in pockets throughout the Midlands), where what might be characterised as a landscape crisis existed in pre-famine decades. Land was largely beyond the control of the management of many non-resident or speculator landowners as was reflected in mushrooming, straggling and impoverished clusters of cabins in grossly fragmented fieldscapes and reclaimed wasteland.[2] After

99 See H. O'Sullivan, 'The Magennis lordship of Iveagh in the early modern period, 1534–1691' in Proudfoot (ed.), *Down: history and society*, pp 159–202; R. Gillespie, *Colonial Ulster: the settlement of East Ulster, 1600–1641* (Cork, 1985) and idem, *Transformation of the Irish economy, 1550–1700* (Dundalk, 1991); P.J. Duffy, 'The evolution of estate properties in south Ulster, 1600–1900' in Smyth & Whelan (eds), *Common ground*, pp 84–109; P.J. Duffy, 'Colonial spaces and sites of resistance: landed estates in 19th-century Ireland' in L.J. Proudfoot and M. Roche (eds), *(Dis)Placing empire: renegotiating British colonial geographies* (Aldershot, 2005), pp 15–40 **1** For coverage by these sources see W. Nolan, *Tracing the past: sources for local studies in the Republic of Ireland* (Dublin, 1982), pp 50–6. Earlier Ulster Plantation surveys also record the establishment of the early-modern estate system: see, for instance, Sir T. Phillips, *Londonderry and the London Companies, 1609–1629 – being a survey and other documents submitted to King Charles 1* (HMSO, Belfast, 1928); Philip Robinson, *The plantation of Ulster. British settlement in an Irish landscape, 1600–1670* (Belfast, 2000).   **2** See, for example, P. Connell, *The land and people of County Meath, 1750–1850* (Dublin, 2004). For regional case studies of the history and development of landed estates, see the county series published by Geography Publications, Dublin: counties published to date are Tipperary, Wexford, Kilkenny, Dublin, Waterford, Cork, Wicklow, Donegal, Galway, Down, Offaly, Derry and Londonderry, Laois, Tyrone, Armagh, Fermanagh and Kildare. See also L.J. Proudfoot, 'The estate system in mid-nineteenth-century County Waterford' in Nolan & Power (eds), *Waterford: history and society,*

the famine, in these chaotic localities, more and more state intervention was necessary through Encumbered Estates acts, for instance, and also late nineteenth-century land acts dispossessing landlords, and policies of the Congested Districts Board and the Irish Land Commission.

In the seventeenth and eighteenth centuries, when central government had relatively limited local impact, landownership was a keystone in the rural economy. It was at the forefront of the impetus towards rural development (characterised as 'improvement') in the eighteenth and nineteenth centuries, until the post-famine decades when the state took on more and more local government functions in the face of the private estate system's failure. Up to then, land 'was a source of income, a source of political power, and the great source of food, fuel, space, and sport. Neither chapel nor meeting-house, presbytery nor manse, could be built without some landlord's co-operation. Taxes on land supported county government, workhouses, dispensaries, and (in the form of a rent-charge) the Irish church,'[3] articulated principally through county, barony, and parish units.

Within the estate system, a range of other agencies were involved in the re-fashioning and modification of rural and urban landscapes. Middlemen such as large leaseholders, merchants and shopkeepers were responsible for much development, with landowners encouraging and facilitating their investments. Tenant farmers also had roles to play in terms of constructing working landscapes of houses, hedges, drains and lanes.[4] Different levels of ownership, reflected in leases and subleases, had different opportunities and inputs in modifying or maintaining local landscape. A pyramid of power existed, from great estates of some tens of thousands of acres, ranging down through resident and non-resident fee simple owners to tenants-in-chief with freehold leases conferring virtual ownership on the holder, through layers of leased landholdings to the most menial tenant on an annual contract.[5] Apart from large landowners, there were institutional forms of landownership such

pp 519–40; W.A. Maguire, *Downshire estates in Ireland, 1801–1845* (Oxford, 1972); K. Trant, *The Blessington estate, 1667–1908* (Dublin, 2004); G. Lyne, *The Lansdowne estate in Kerry under the agency of William Steuart Trench, 1849–72* (Dublin, 2001); J. Sheehan, *South Westmeath: farm and folk* (Dublin, 1978); J. Bell, 'The spread of cultivation into the marginal land in Ireland during the eighteenth and early nineteenth centuries' in C.M. Mills and C. Geraint (eds), *Life on the edge: human settlement and marginality* (Oxford, 1998), pp 39–44. **3** W.E. Vaughan, *Landlords and tenants in mid-Victorian Ireland* (Oxford, 1994), p. 13. **4** See T. Jones Hughes, 'The large farm in nineteenth-century Ireland' in A. Gailey and D. Ó hÓgáin (eds), *Gold under the furze: studies in folk tradition presented to Caoimhín Ó Danachair* (Dublin, 1982), pp 93–100, on the role of larger farms of more than £100 valuation in the making of the landscape; Crawford, 'The significance of the landed estates in Ulster' and idem, 'Economy and society in south Ulster in the eighteenth century' in *Clogher Rec.*, viii (1975), pp 241–58. **5** See *Return of owners of land of one acre and upwards, in the several counties, counties of cities and counties of towns in Ireland* (Dublin, 1876); J. Bateman, *The great landowners of Great Britain and Ireland* (Leicester, 1971). U.H. Hussey de Burgh, *Landowners of Ireland 1878* excludes owners of less than 500 acres or £500 valuation. See T. Jones Hughes, 'The estate system of landholding in nineteenth-century Ireland' in Nolan (ed.), *The shaping of Ireland*, pp 137–50 and idem, 'Landholding and settlement in the counties of Meath and Cavan in the nineteenth century'

as the twelve London Companies in Ulster, the Irish Society, the Established Church and its bishoprics, educational institutions like Trinity College, the Armagh, Dungannon and Enniskillen schools, and Crown estates, all with considerable variety in wealth of properties and policies and landscape consequences. But ultimately the landed estate was the legal territorial unit within which environmental change occurred, whether or not under the direct impetus of the owner. In a general sense it was the gentry élite who up until end of the nineteenth century had the most power, influence, authority and motivation to bring about change. Many of them believed they had an unquestionable right and duty to manage their landscapes and the people in them: 'the rich man in his castle, the poor man at his gate, God made them high and lowly, each to his own estate': Cecil Frances Alexander's hymn expressed the authority of a privileged élite. Intermarriage between gentry families often reflected strategies to conserve power locally, as well as consolidating it with marriages from further afield.[6]

Ownership was used to facilitate improvement in towns using leases to control landuse or to implement a coherent urban plan, or encourage a better quality of housing.[7] The pattern of landownership within towns often affected their morphological development: for example, Carrickmacross was divided between two large

in P. O'Flanagan, P. Ferguson and K. Whelan (eds), *Rural Ireland, 1600–1900: modernisation and change* (Cork, 1987), pp 104–46; L.J. Proudfoot, 'Spatial transformation and social agency: property, society and improvement, *c*.1700–1900' in B.J. Graham and L.J. Proudfoot (eds), *A historical geography of Ireland* (London, 1993), pp 219–57, and L.J. Proudfoot, 'The management of a great estate: patronage, income and expenditure on the duke of Devonshire's Irish property, *c*.1816–1891' in *Irish Economic & Social History*, xiii (1986), pp 32–55; W.H. Crawford, 'The influence of the landlord in eighteenth-century Ulster' in L.M. Cullen and T.C. Smout (eds), *Comparative aspects of Scottish and Irish economic and social history, 1600–1900* (Edinburgh, 1977), pp 193–203.   **6** E. Somerville and M. Ross, *Irish memories* (London & New York, 1925), p. 71 noted that 'matches were a matter of mileage, and marriages might have been said to have been made by the map.'   **7** L.J. Proudfoot, 'Landlord motivation and urban improvement on the duke of Devonshire's Irish estates, *c*.1792–1832' in *Irish Economic & Social History*, xviii (1991), pp 5–23; J.H. Andrews, 'Changes in the rural landscape of late eighteenth-and early nineteenth-century Ireland: an example from County Waterford', unpublished paper, Freeman Library, TCD. B.J. Graham and L.J. Proudfoot, 'Landlords, planning and urban growth in eighteenth- and nineteenth-century Ireland' in *Journal of Urban History*, 18 (1992), pp 308–29; B.J. Graham and L.J. Proudfoot, *Urban improvement in provincial Ireland, 1700–1840* (Dublin, 1994); L.J. Proudfoot and B.J. Graham, 'The nature and extent of urban and village foundation and improvement in eighteenth- and early nineteenth-century Ireland' in *Planning Perspectives*, 8 (1993), pp 259–81; L.J. Proudfoot, *Urban patronage and social authority: the management of the duke of Devonshire's towns in Ireland, 1764–1891* (Washington, 1995); T.C. Barnard, 'Landlords and urban life: Youghal and the Boyles, 1641–1740' in *Group for the Study of Irish Historic Settlement Newsletter* (Autumn 1995), pp 1–4; A. Horner, 'The scope and limitations of the landlord contribution to changing the Irish landscape, 1700–1850' in V. Hansen (ed.), *Collected papers presented at the permanent European conference for the study of the rural landscape* (Copenhagen, 1981), pp 71–7; P. Connell, *Changing forces shaping the nineteenth-century Irish town: a case study of Navan* (Maynooth, 1978); also various case studies in Andrews and Simms (eds), Irish country towns series.

estates with sometimes contrasting policies; Navan was fragmented among several owners which led to squatting in poorly supervised portions. Landscape management to develop sustainable settlements and environments (such as conservation of arable lands, woodland and bogland resources) was the clear objective of many landowners into the nineteenth century. This is evident in the correspondence and regulations of estates such as Downshire, Devonshire, Shirley and Bath.[8]

Leases afforded mechanisms for forms of development control by landowners and though many leases were more honoured in the breach than the observance, a great deal of the order and shape of the landscape today owes its origin to the terms of leases. In general, the format of leases was fairly standard – reserving rights of the landowner (or lessor) to such things as minerals, quarries and turf bogs; stating the term and length of lease (for example, three named lives or other durations); specifying the rent to be paid on the first of May and first of November each year; outlining the obligations of the tenant (or lessee) to provide duty work days for landlord, or to make roads; listing penalties for non-payment of rent (for example, by distraining for arrears), penalties for alienation (or selling without permission of landlord); covenants to build a house (of specified dimensions sometimes) and keep it in repair, to make enclosures (for example, ditches planted with whitethorn quicks and trees), perhaps to plant an orchard, maintain drains and watercourses and so on.

Dacre Barrett's agent in Clones described a lease agreement in 1718 which had clear intentions for the town's development:

> If your honour pleases to consent … I have made a bargain with Mr John Rogers for Shankhill. He is to pay your Honour £18 a year for 21 years from May instant, and give up his old lease which has six years of it unexpired. He is to build a good new house of lime and stone or brick 50 foot long in the clear and 18 foot wide and 10 foot high on the side walls with upright gable ends with a good oak or ash roof and a double chimney, in three years from the commencement of his lease on the penalty of £30 Sterling, plant an orchard and ditch and plant as the rest of the new leases are obliged to do.[9]

An early seventeenth-century Essex lease in Farney had Sir John Dillon agreeing to build a substantial house of twenty rooms, and establish twenty-four British households in eight years. He was to 'forke and root up' the underwoods and the 'stragling shrubs', coppice the woodlands, enclose the land with quick sets and plant orchards.[10] Most of this was never achieved. In the late eighteenth century the Bath

8 See, for instance, *Letters of a great Irish landlord: a selection from the estate correspondence of the third marquess of Downshire, 1809–45*, ed. W.A. Maguire (Belfast, 1974) and W.A. Maguire, *The Downshire estates in Ireland, 1801–1845* (Oxford, 1972); *General report on the Gosford estates in County Armagh, 1821, by William Greig*, ed. W.H. Crawford (Belfast, 1976). **9** Letter from Edmond Kaine to the honourable Dacres Barrett, May 1718 (PRONI, Barrett-Lennard papers, T. 2529/6/c.38 386); see also R. Gillespie, *Settlement and survival on an Ulster estate: the Brownlow leasebook, 1667–1711* (Belfast, 1988). **10** P.J. Duffy, 'A lease from the estate of the earl of Essex, 1624' in *Clogher Rec.*, xiii (1990), pp 100–14.

estate agent wrote to the landlord in England on the advisability of having all leases within each parish falling in at the same time so as to maintain effective control over extensive areas.

In rural areas eighteenth-century leases often laid down broad prescriptions for enclosure: on the Bellaghy estates in Derry, 'whole townlands, and later large lease-holdings into which the townlands were divided, formed the basic units of enclosure right from the start. Open-field systems where they developed, operated within this primary open-textured reticle of enclosures. As landlords encouraged more tenants to take leases and hold their farms in severalty, the enclosure net tightened, as leasehold boundaries proliferated.'[11] The Kingston estate and O'Callaghan estates in Tipperary required tenants to build houses complete with stone chimneys and to enclose three English acres around the house with a double ditch set with whitethorn which was to be planted with an orchard. Land surveyors were employed by the estates from the 1780s into the mid-nineteenth century in re-shaping the landscape, with leases requiring quick sets, slated houses and outbuildings to be built, fir and elm trees to be planted on roadsides, orchards and vacated or consolidated holdings to be re-designed. As on the Devonshire estate, small holders were pushed out to reclaim moorland, with the largest farms dominating the best lowland soils.[12]

Estate owners were also actively involved in tree planting or encouraging their tenants to do so. According to the Register of Trees, Headfort demesne planted *c.*31,000 trees in 1830. Tenants in ninety parishes in County Meath registered trees in 1841, with the parish of Kells planting a total of 124,000 trees between 1808 and 1844, 53,000 by the marquis of Headfort alone.[13] From 1844 until the 1860s the Improvement Books for the Shirley estate contain records of gates, drainage allowances, trees and thorn quicks by the thousand, which were approved and granted to the tenants by the estate. In many ways the books represent a day-by-day catalogue of the nuts and bolts of landscape management influenced to a significant degree by the improving principles of estate administration.

The Dublin Society (Royal Dublin Society from 1820) which was dominated by gentry and ascendancy interests, was established in 1731 to promote the development of agriculture, industrial science and art. In the eighteenth century, parliamentary support for economic development generally in Ireland was often channelled through the aegis of the Dublin Society. It offered premiums for agriculture and planting from the mid-eighteenth century. County statistical surveys were published for twenty-four counties, taking up where an earlier endeavour had failed in the mid-eighteenth century.[14] Providing overviews of the

11 E.A. Currie, 'Land tenures, enclosures and field-patterns in Co. Derry in the eighteenth and nineteenth centuries' in *Ir. Geography*, 9 (1976), pp 50-62, p. 60.   12 Smyth, 'Estate records', pp 29-49; see also Smyth, 'Social, economic and landscape transformations in County Cork'; Crawford, *The management of a major Ulster estate*.   13 McCracken, 'Tree planting by tenants in Meath 1800 to 1850'; McCracken & McCracken, *A register of trees for County Londonderry*; Smyth, 'The greening of Ireland', p. 58.   14 See Herries-Davies, 'The

state of economy and landscape in each county, according to headings provided by the Society, they reflected contemporary interest in all aspects of economic development.[15] Apart from improvements encouraged throughout the tenanted lands of estates, most landlord investment was directed at the development of their private demesnes and parks.[16] Demesnes became the most extensive man-made features in the Irish landscape: Carton, for example, is clearly discernible in satellite imagery of Ireland.

Much of this work was driven by requirements of leisure, as well as display – indeed installation of 'pleasure grounds' was *de riguer* in the later eighteenth century. Hunting, for instance, called for deerparks and hareparks, coverts, gorses, decoys, or grouse moors in the West of Ireland. Playing at being cottars or sailors, or country picnics, called for ornamental lakes, canals, water features or *cottages ornées*. Summer called for iced drinks and ice houses. In addition more general concerns with improvement by many estates spurred interest in the most up-to-date demesne farm and farm buildings. Walled gardens, with high brick walls to retain solar heat (some containing flues to carry heat internally from peat furnaces) provided exotic soft fruits and vegetables for the table. Demesnes went through fashionable design phases from classical layouts to Romantic pastoral creations. The severe lines of earlier classical gardens were replaced by Brownian landscapes that were charac-terised by such features as 'sinuous shelter belts of trees around the park boundary, copse planting, and man-made lakes, "rivers" and hills … considerable use was made of the natural variety' of local topographies to achieve desired effects with

making of Irish geography: the Physico-Historical Society of Ireland' which had precedents a half century earlier in the activities of the short-lived Dublin Philosophical Society. Surveys of counties Cork, Waterford, Kerry, Down and Dublin were published between 1746 and 1774 under the aegis of the Physico-Historical Society. See also D. Clarke, *Dublin Society's statistical surveys* (Athlone, 1957). **15** Arthur Young, *A tour in Ireland*, originally published in 1780, re-published by Blackstaff Press Dublin, 1983, provides an all-Ireland commentary. With the exception of Tipperary, county statistical surveys were published for the following counties: Antrim by Dubourdieu (1812); Armagh by Coote (1804); Cavan by Coote (1802); Clare by Dutton (1808); Cork by Townsend (1810); Donegal by McParlan (1802); Down by Dubourdieu (1802); Dublin by Archer (1801); Galway by Dutton (1824); Kerry by Radcliff (1814); Kildare by Rawson (1807); Kilkenny by Tighe (1802); King's Co. by Coote (1801); Leitrim by McParlan (1802); Londonderry by Sampson (1802); Mayo by McParlan (1802); Meath by Thompson (1802); Monaghan by Coote (1801); Queen's Co. by Coote (1801); Roscommon by Weld (1832); Sligo by McParlan (1802); Tipperary (in MS in NLI); Tyrone by McEvoy (1802); Wexford by Fraser (1807); Wicklow by Fraser (1801). **16** On demesnes, see Reeves-Smyth, 'Demesnes'; idem, 'The natural history of demesnes' in Wilson Foster (ed.), *Nature in Ireland*, pp 549–72; L.J. Proudfoot, 'Landscaped demesnes in pre-famine Ireland: a regional case study' in A. Verhoeve and A.J. Vervloet (eds), *The transformation of the European rural landscape: methodological issues and agrarian change, 1770–1914* (Brussels, 1992), pp 230–37; A. Horner, 'Carton, Co. Kildare: a case study of the making of an Irish demesne' in *Quarterly Bulletin of the Irish Georgian Society*, xviii, nos 2 & 3 (Apr.–Sept. 1975), pp 45–103; P. Friel, *Frederick Trench and Heywood, Queen's county: the creation of a Romantic demesne* (Dublin, 2000); F. O'Kane, *Landscape design in eighteenth-century Ireland* (Cork, 2004).

minimal effort.[17] By the mid-nineteenth century, there were *c*.7,000 demesnes in Ireland, accounting for nearly one million acres or over 6 per cent of the land area.

Accompanying often lavish mansions, much rental of the estates in the eighteenth and nineteenth centuries was invested in the most fashionable landscape designs, classically exemplified in Carton, Castletown, Westport, Curraghmore, Belvedere and many others. Detailed maps of these were often produced to match the picturesque views frequently commissioned from fashionable painters: John Rocque's maps probably represent the most artistic achievement of a cartographer in eighteenth-century Ireland. As far as possible these elaborately contrived landscapes were insulated with trees and enclosing walls from the utilitarian workaday landscapes on the estate symbolising a social chasm in Irish society which endured into the late nineteeth century. By the early twentieth century, the landed gentry 'lived within their demesnes making a world of their own, with Ireland outside the gates'.[18]

In many parts of Ireland variations in the rigour of estate management by landlords and agents resulted in variations in patterns of settlement landscapes. During the demographic explosion in the half century before the famine especially, poorer tenant or landless families searched the countrysides, squatting in interstices in the landscape of estates where control was lax or non-existent: on non-resident properties, marginal land on roadsides, bog edges, mountain sides or commons. The famine period saw the weaknesses of the estate system exposed following a couple of generations of mismanagement and population escalation which were well documented in such contemporary commissions of enquiry as the Poor Enquiry and the Devon Commission.[19] A witness to the Poor Enquiry (1835) reported on conditions in the Trim district in County Meath where evicted tenantry 'sought shelter in the cabins of the peasantry on the adjoining estates, but only for a time, for they would not be allowed by the proprietors to remain there.'[20] In 1835 the small Rothwell estate in Monaghan cleared fifty-two cottier families who ended up drifting through neighbouring properties in search of a space. A failed emigration scheme from Kerry to Canada in 1826 resulted in the tenants coming back and 'pitching like a flock of plover, upon a bog in the same place they left'.[21] Destruction of the houses of emigrants was aimed at preventing such returns.

17 L.J. Proudfoot, 'Landownership and improvement, *c*.1700–1845' in Proudfoot (ed.), *Down: history and society*, pp 203–37, p. 214.   **18** D. Fingall, *Seventy years young: memories of Elizabeth, countess of Fingall* (London, 1937) quoted in P. Somerville-Large, *The Irish country house: a social history* (London, 1995), p. 355.   **19** *First, second and third reports of his majesty's commissioners for inquiring into the condition of the poorer classes in Ireland*, 1835, 36, 37 and the Devon Commission (*Commission of inquiry into the state of the law and practice in respect to the occupation of the land in Ireland, 1845*). For sources on famine records, see A. Eiríksson and C. Ó Gráda, *Estate records of the Irish famine* (Dublin, 1995) which provides a comprehensive list of estate collections and their location, arranged by county. See also W.E.Vaughan, *Landlords and tenants in Ireland, 1848–1904* (Dundalk, 1984) and J.S. Donnelly, jnr., *Landlord and tenant in nineteenth-century Ireland* (Dublin, 1973).   **20** Quoted in Connell, *Land and people of County Meath*, p. 146.   **21** *Devon Commission*, appendix (part iv), pp 491–93, quoted in P.J.

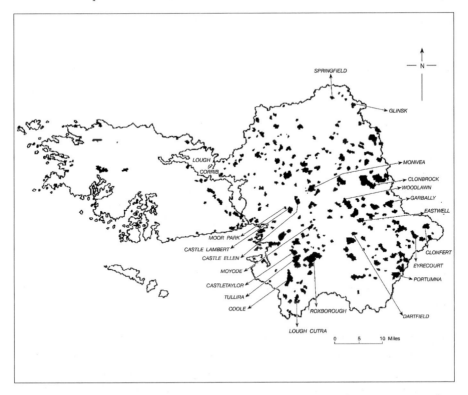

3.6 Demesnes in nineteenth-century County Galway (adapted from B.S. MacAodha, 'Demesnes in the western part of Ireland' in *Hommes et terres du Nord*, Institut de Géographie de Lille, 1988)

SOURCES ON ESTATE LANDSCAPE

A range of general surveys of Ireland were undertaken in the early nineteenth century which accompanied the county surveys of the Dublin Society. Most of them gave prominence to the role of members of the landowning gentry in their localities. Edward Wakefield, William Shaw Mason and Samuel Lewis published accounts which ultimately undermined the viability of the Ordnance Survey's ambitious memoir scheme of the 1830s. More systematic databases such as the first Townland Valuation and Griffith's Tenement Valuation catalogued the complex landholding and farming landscapes of the mid-nineteenth century.[22] Following

Duffy, 'Irish landholding structures and population in the mid-nineteenth century' in *Maynooth Review*, 3 (2) (1977), pp 1–27. See *First report of the select committee of the house of lords on colonisation from Ireland* quoted in D. Fitzpatrick, 'Emigration, 1801–70' in Vaughan (ed.), *A new history of Ireland, v: Ireland under the Union, 1, 1801–1870*, p. 589.   **22** E. Wakefield, *An account of Ireland, statistical and political* (2 vols, London, 1812); W. Shaw Mason, *A statistical*

the Encumbered Estates acts, the reports of the landed estates courts contain details on the condition of each of the encumbered estates being sold, including maps and plans of houses. The Irish Land Commission records relating to land purchases under the Land acts prior to 1923 contain an enormous range of data on the economic and social condition of farms on each estate, including inspectors' reports and surveyors' reports which describe the condition of landholding on each estate. Like the Baseline reports of the Congested Districts Board these are important records of local settlement landscapes.[23]

Private estate papers are important records of landscape history. Estate records provide only partial samples of past landscape experience, representing in many cases survivals from better run estates: indifferently managed properties probably left fewer records.[24] There is a wide range of record types which document local landscape change. Account books, improvement books, manor court books and other notebooks often contain details of expenditure on building, drainage, decisions on disputes over land and farm boundaries, often relating to the demesne farm and estate farms. Shirley's visitation books recorded farm inspections in the 1850s and 1860s. Drainage and Improvement acts after the famine resulted in the collection of a lot of data on local reclamation schemes. Correspondence, often two-way, between land agents and non-resident proprietors in England, Dublin or elsewhere, served to leave important records about the role of the estate in landscape development, plus other correspondence with some of the tenants, other estate officials or merchants. Shirley corresponded from Warwickshire with his adult sons in Carrickmacross in the 1840s and 50s on a wide range of matters, especially relating to the house, gardens and deerpark, as well as the tenants. In the mid-nineteenth century Lord Palmerston (in England) was regularly informed by his agent on the progress of attempts at removing rundale, squaring fields, planting hedges and trees. But many resident landowners kept good records also, as evidenced in the correspondence of the marquis of Downshire.[25]

---

account and parochial survey (3 vols, Dublin, 1814–); S. Lewis, *Topographical dictionary of Ireland* (2 vols & atlas, London, 1837). Valuation records are available in the National Archives and the Valuation Office in Dublin and PRONI in Belfast. The first townland valuation is in manuscript form. Griffith's Valuation has been published by Eneclann in Dublin: http://www.irishorigins.com/   **23** *On the verge of want: a unique insight into living conditions along Ireland's western seaboard in the late 19th century*, reports of the Congested Districts Board, ed. J. Morrissey (Dublin, 2001), for a selection of CDB inspectors reports from the 1890s; see also Nolan, *Tracing the past*, pp 110–14.   **24** Collections are available in the National Library, National Archives and PRONI; see T. Dooley, *The decline of the big house in Ireland* (Dublin, 2001) and idem, *The big houses and landed estates of Ireland* (Dublin, 2007). See also local repositories, such as the archives in Strokestown House, and private collections. As many landowners also held property in Britain, British archives are important, such as the Bath papers in Longleat, Shirley in Warwickshire County Record Office, Palmerston papers in Southampton. See http://scripts.ireland.com/ancestor/browse/records/land/estate.htm and also B. Donovan & D. Edwards, *British sources for Irish history, 1485–1641: a guide to manuscripts in local, regional and specialised repositories in England, Scotland and Wales* (Dublin, 1997).   **25** On land agents in general, see Barnard, *A new anatomy of Ireland*, pp 208–38.

Surveys and valuations provide important insights into the landscapes of estates, and the layout, value, extent and appearance of farms. Annual reports and valuations by agents on the Bath and Shirley estates, sent to the home estates in Wiltshire and Warwickshire, provide important recurring reviews. William Greig's report on the Gosford estates was exceptional in its detail.[26] One early nineteenth-century prescription recommended that agents should have an accurate survey and valuation undertaken of the estate *in fields*, reporting on the circumstances of each tenant, the condition of their farms, the state of their houses and offices, the quality of their stock, the numbers and ages of their children. Repeating this exercise at regular intervals would enable the proprietor to 'distinguish and encourage the deserving, as well as trace out the improvement that might progressively take place on the estate'.[27] Some agents actually followed this approach or modifications of it.

Valuations and surveys were frequently accompanied by maps of the estate. Estate maps are perhaps the most useful in providing visual evidence of estate landscapes, mainly during the eighteenth century, which was characterised by John Andrews as the 'golden age of the Irish land surveyor', though some have survived from the seventeenth century. However, the quality of their detail and accuracy varies.[28] 'Country surveyors' worked at local level, producing surveys for tenant farmers, assisting with bog divisions, laying out the lines for new roads. Cartographers and surveyors like John Rocque and Bernard Scalé produced superlative maps for great landowners like the earl of Kildare and the marquesses of Downshire, Devonshire or Bath in the 1750s and 1770s, undertaken often when a re-letting of estates was taking place to evaluate settlement changes and the condition of the property.[29] Much earlier, in 1634 Thomas Raven was engaged by the earl of Essex to produce a survey of his lands in Farney in south Monaghan which provide a unique glimpse of this lightly colonised landscape. His maps show the tates (townlands) together with more than 400 hundred cabins and houses, wells, mills, churches along with indications of land quality within the townland units. Unfortunately this amount of detailing of local landscapes did not continue as standard practice with Irish surveyors until the later eighteenth century. The 'French school of Rocque' contained wide-ranging detail within each townland: hachured relief, buildings in block plan (a Rocque innovation, contrasting with earlier pictorial depictions of buildings), gardens and farmyards, containing hay or corn stacks in some cases. Arable land was shown with brown stippling to represent ridges or furrows, meadow and pasture in light green. Tree symbols showed

26 *General report on the Gosford estates*, ed. Crawford. **27** W. Blacker, *The management of landed property in Ireland*, Prize Essay, RDS (Dublin, 1834). **28** See Andrews, *Plantation acres*; P.J. Duffy, 'Eighteenth-century estate maps' in *History Ireland*, 5 (1) (1997), pp 20–4. Local historical journals frequently publish articles on local maps: for example, J.H. Andrews, 'An Elizabethan map of Kilmallock' in *North Munster Antiquarian Journal*, xi (1968), pp 27–35 and idem, 'Henry Pratt, surveyor of Kerry estates' in *Journal of the Kerry Archaeological and Historical Society*, 13 (1980), pp 5–38. **29** Rocque's maps of the Kildare estates are currently held in the University Library, Cambridge. Recently discovered wall maps of Maynooth and Rathangan manors are held in NUIM, Rhetoric House.

orchards and woodlands; hedges were depicted by lines of bushes. There are also springs, mills, quarries, forges, pigeon houses, prehistoric forts and field names. Individual fields were numbered in sequence within each townland, accompanied by details of the area, and sometimes the content and the tenant of the field.[30]

The best summary of holdings of estate papers in public collections such as the National Library or the National Archives is in R.J. Hayes (ed.), *Manuscript sources for the history of Irish civilisation* (11 vols, Boston, 1965) and a supplement of three volumes edited by D. Ó Luanaigh in 1979. Hayes' *Guide to the periodical sources for the history of Irish civilisation* (9 vols, Boston, 1970) classifies sources by place, name and subject. Eventually this will probably be superseded by on-line resources such as Irish history Online, a bibliography of Irish historical writing which is in progress.[31] The National Library of Ireland and the National Archives of Ireland have large collections of estate papers, as well as the Public Record Office of Northern Ireland (PRONI) which has an extensive and well-calendared collection of estate papers for Northern Ireland and selected estates in the Republic.[32]

Landownership conferred on gentry privilege and authority which led them as a class to become involved with improvement, not only in the material landscape but also in the moral order of its inhabitants.[33] Ideas on ordered landscapes and tidy houses assumed accompanying order in lifestyles and behaviour. E.J. Shirley's annual address to his tenants before returning to England in the autumn frequently invoked such paternalistic principles. In 1839, among recurring admonishments about excessive drinking and carousing at fairs in Carrickmacross and the need to read the bible, he hoped to see 'an encreased degree of *improvement comfort and respectability*. To promote this and to encrease a love of *order, tidiness and cleanliness* is the anxious desire of my heart ... ' [his emphases]. He went on to deal with related matters of improved husbandry, being pleased to see

> the effects of lime on the estate – it has been brought into general use but remember the ground must be drained, before the good effects of Lime can be shewn. ... I propose that my steward should provide a pair of horses, man and plough for the use of such of the neighbouring tenants as require them (for the usual price) ... and thus I conclude the tenant will benefit by having his land *better ploughed* ... I must again repeat my last years advice about *early cutting the turf*; if this business had been done during the dry weeks in the

30 J.H. Andrews, 'The French school of Dublin land surveyors' in *Ir. Geography*, 5 (1967), pp 275–92; A. Horner, 'Thomas Emerson's Kildare estates surveys, 1674–1697' in *Kildare Arch. Soc. Jn.*, xviii (3) (1996–7), pp 399–429. **31** It currently contains in excess of 30,000 items published between 1989 and 1998: www.irishhistoryonline.ie/. **32** See P. Collins, *Pathways to Ulster's past: sources and resources for local studies* (Belfast, 1998); idem, *County Monaghan sources in the PRONI* (Belfast, 1998) examines the records of eight large and a number of smaller collections of estate records from the county. **33** See M. Busteed, 'The practice of improvement in the Irish context – The Castle Caldwell estate in County Fermanagh in the second half of the eighteenth century' in *Ir. Geography*, 33 (1) (2000), pp 15–36.

Spring, and commencement of summer when *my own turf* was cut, and most of it brought home, great distress would have been prevented … The cutting of Timber trees I have witnessed with much pain as an injury to the appearance of the country not to be soon repaired. The only addition wanted to the naturally beautiful features of this neighbourhood is *Wood*.[34]

These ideas on what might be characterised as a morality of landscape are abiding themes in nineteenth-century private and public correspondence: tidiness was next to godliness. The reports and letters of the well-educated army officers on the OS Memoir scheme are imbued with assumed 'racial' correlations between improvement, 'civilisation' and the cultural backwardness of the inhabitants.[35] William Steuart Trench, agent on the Shirley, Lansdowne and Bath estates was convinced of the practical lessons to be learnt from careful husbandry, pointing out that 'cleanliness and decency within … will induce it to be extended further, and you will seldom see a man who has his house and homestead decent who will leave his land in weeds and neglect'.[36] It is a theme which runs through the correspondence of the marquis of Downshire also.[37]

This discourse of social and landscape improvement was well represented in published work by active landlords, land agents and surveyors. Effective land management within the estate system was seen to be the panacea for all Ireland's ills in the nineteenth century. One of the classics in this mode was Trench's *Realities of Irish life* published in 1868 which promoted his own dogmatic views on estate management, already well publicised in newspaper columns.[38] Armagh landowner Colonel William Blacker was also a prolific promoter of his ideas which had clear implications for landscape development and aesthetics.

I look forward to the prospect of seeing their estates peopled with a thriving tenantry, and covered with neat and respectable cottages, and the farm divided by hedge-rows of useful and ornamental timber, with underwood for fuel. The cattle being kept from injuring these plantations, they would soon come to a luxuriant growth; and, I am confident, would not only yield a quantity of valuable timber, but also sufficient faggots to afford a cheerful fire in the winter's evenings; and if the farmer has a lease, and registers the trees

---

34 Address to his tenantry (PRONI, Shirley papers, D. 3531/C/3/1/7). On this theme of moral improvement and model estates, see T. Dunne, ' "A gentleman's estate should be a moral school": Edgeworthstown in fact and fiction, 1760–1840' in Gillespie & Moran (eds), *Longford: essays in county history*, pp 95–121. **35** Discussed in Doherty, *The Irish Ordnance Survey*, pp 44–54. **36** See P.J. Duffy, 'Management problems on a large estate in mid-nineteenth century Ireland: William Steuart Trench's report on the Shirley estate in 1843' in *Clogher Rec.*, xvi (1997), pp 101–23. **37** *Letters of a great Irish landlord*, ed. Maguire. **38** See G.J. Lyne, 'William Steuart Trench and post-famine emigration from Kenmare to America, 1850–55' in *Journal of the Kerry Archaeological and Historical Society*, 25 (1992), pp 105–16; W. Steuart Trench, *Realities of Irish life* (London, 1868).

planted as here recommended, he may have, at the expiration of his tenure, even if the farm be a very small one, one hundred or two hundred trees, from twenty to forty years old, according to the duration of his lease, … if the cattle are home fed, and thus prevented from injuring them; and these trees he cannot be prevented from selling at their full value; and if his landlord even should turn him out (which in such a case is not likely) he would not go away empty handed, and thus the bank of his ditch would be to him a *savings bank*.[39]

ADMINISTRATIVE GEOGRAPHIES

Regional administration of economy and society depended on the utilisation of existing territorial structures or, as the administrative machinery of the modernising state in the nineteenth century generated a need, for tailor-made territorial divisions. The eighteenth-century Irish parliament had a relatively constricted role in local affairs which was mainly regulatory with some revenue functions. It was dominated by a landed gentry who ensured that government intervention in their lives and localities, as well as revenue impositions, were kept to a minimum.[40] But following the union with Great Britain, the nineteenth century witnessed much greater intervention by the state in local affairs, aimed at addressing regional inequalities and more efficient allocation of resources.[41] This was evidenced in commissions of enquiry sitting in provincial centres, census enumerations, sweeping topographical and mapping projects, national property valuations and taxation assessments reaching into every barony, parish and townland. All of this increased surveillance by the modern imperial state has left an enormous legacy of information on landscape, society and settlement for local historians today. The Post Office and its administration was also an exercise in territorial management and an expression of the modernisation of state bureaucracy, and the evolution of its local structures would repay research.[42] Postal districts or 'walks' along which post boys carried the letters gradually evolved from the eighteenth century, accompanying the establishment of

---

39 W. Blacker, *Essay on improvement to be made in the cultivation of small farms* (Dublin, 1837), p. 63; see also T. De Moleyns, *The landowner's and agent's practical guide* (London, 1860). **40** For detailed examples of gentry dominance in eighteenth-century politics, see Barnard, *A new anatomy of Ireland*; for background to seventeenth- and eighteenth-century administrative structures, see E.M. Johnston-Liik, *History of the Irish parliament, 1692–1800* (6 vols, Belfast, 2002), where there is a summary introduction to the operation of county Grand Juries and the statutory powers granted by parliament.   **41** See V. Crossman, *Local government in nineteenth-century Ireland* (Belfast, 1994); McDowell, 'Administration and public services, 1800–1870'. See also J.J. Lee, *The modernisation of Irish society, 1848–1918* (Dublin, 1973) for a critical assessment of state intervention.   **42** Post Office surveyors established the postal network from the eighteenth century and the author Anthony Trollope worked as a post office surveyor in Ireland from 1841 until 1859. See R.H. Super, *Trollope in the Post Office* (Ann Arbor, 1981). Many of the records of the Irish postal service were destroyed in the GPO in 1916.

sub-offices throughout the countryside. By the late eighteenth century mail coach services were established and continued to expand up to the 1840s.[43]

Both the home parliament and the UK parliament operated through local government structures which were embedded in the legacy of territorial structures that had been fixed in surveys and maps of the seventeenth century. From the 1620s counties formed the basic unit of administration of the common law through the county Grand Jury, though much of the county geography of Leinster and Munster dated from the earlier medieval English settlement. Until the institution of county councils in 1898, local administration was part of the jurisdiction of the Grand Jury which met at the quarterly assizes. It consisted of twenty-three, usually of the principal landowners in the county or their agents, who were selected by the sheriff of the county at each session. The Grand Jury was responsible for the administration of justice, implementing the county cess which paid for the upkeep of roads and bridges (through compulsory local labour), the construction of gaols, and for the maintenance of a county infirmary (under an act of 1765).[44] The Grand Juries managed the counties through their baronies. Like the counties, which were essentially territorial entities that pre-dated colonial settlement, the baronies were pre-colonial subsections of earlier lordships (usually minor lordships or septlands) which were convenient units for taxation and allocation of resources within counties. County and baronial presentments, which are printed summaries of tenders for infrastructural works submitted to the Grand Juries, form important sources of information for the eighteenth and nineteenth centuries.[45]

The main problem surrounding the fiscal management of Grand Juries, which left the system open to local manipulation and corruption, was the lack of a reliable method of revenue assessment. The county cess was struck each year in a largely arbitrary manner which owed its origin to the lack of a comprehensive survey of land and property in the country. This deficiency was grounded in many of the original plantation surveys of the sixteenth and seventeenth centuries which attempted to establish a standard extent for many of the local territorial units encountered throughout the country (discussed above). Up to the early nineteenth century, some county administrations continued to calculate baronial cess liability on the basis of obsolete (and areally ambiguous) ploughlands, cartrons and other units, many still relying on the area estimates of Petty's Down Survey. The government continued trying to translate ancient territorial assessments into statute acres for more equitable distribution of taxation. Ultimately, it was the elusiveness of this ratio and the need to raise a viable local taxation which led to the initiation of the OS townland survey and the townland valuations which followed it in the 1830s and 40s.

43 M. Reynolds, *A history of the Irish Post Office* (Dublin, 1983).   **44** The *Journals of the house of commons of the kingdom of Ireland … , 1613–1791* (28 vols, Dublin, 1753–91; reprinted and continued, 1613–1800, 19 vols, Dublin, 1796–1800) have an extensive amount of local and regional detail and data.   **45** Available for irregular sequences in the NAI and PRONI; see J.C. Lyons, *The Grand Juries of Westmeath, 1727–1853* (2 vols, Ledestown, 1853), which can be consulted in Westmeath County Library.

One deficiency which was clear to Grand Juries from early on was the absence of reliable maps of county areas. From the 1740s the Physico-Historical Society in Dublin commissioned a number of county maps to accompany a series of county reports which, with the exception of John Rocque's Dublin map, were of small-scale and limited value. From the 1770s parliamentary grants were made to Grand Juries to undertake county surveys which would assist in assessments of land for taxation purposes and the allocation of resources for road construction and associated works. A series of much improved county maps were produced, listed by Andrews as follows: Down (1739, 1755), Dublin (1750, 1760, 1821), Kildare (1752), Armagh (1760), Wicklow (1760 and 1798), Queen's County [1763], (1805), Louth (1766, 1777), Antrim (1782), Carlow (1789), Monaghan (1793), Donegal (1801), Wexford (1811), Cork (1811), Tyrone (1815), Kildare (1783), Clare (1787), Westmeath (1808), Londonderry (1814), Longford (1814), Meath (1817), Waterford (1818), Galway (1819), Leitrim (1819), Sligo (1819), Roscommon (1825), and Mayo (1830).[46]

At a more local level than counties and baronies, parish vestries which depended on tithes assessed on cultivated land (grassland being exempt) and payable to the Church of Ireland, relied on inadequate estimates of area and content of parishes. Most tithe calculations were based on the out-of-date maps of the Down Survey which were inadequate in terms of measuring parishes and internal townland units. The expansion of tillage in the late eighteenth century and the rising agitation against tithes by the non-Church of Ireland tenantry brought pressure to bear for a more transparent and equitable evaluation. In 1823 the first government survey was instituted to compile a parish-by-parish survey of titheable land. Landowners, tenants, land areas and tithe payable by townland are listed. The Tithe Applotment Books represent the first reasonably comprehensive list of landholders (landless labourers and cottiers being exempt) in the country by townland and parish since the mid-seventeenth century. The tithes survey was quite rapidly superseded from the late 1830s by the detailed local territorial and landholding profiles of the Ordnance Survey six-inch maps and Griffith's Valuation which provided the ultimate accurate basis for local taxation for the rest of the nineteenth century. These surveys facilitated central government's efforts at constructing functional spatial entities for the first time in Ireland designed to administer the new Poor Law at local level.

Escalating problems of poverty in the early nineteenth century, resulting from rapidly expanding rural populations and growing landlessness, often exacerbated at local level by estate clearances, were manifested in rising levels of 'pauperism.' The Poor Law act (1838) introduced a workhouse system designed to provide relief for the destitute poor. The workhouses were supported by a tax (a rate per £ valuation) on property assessed under a Poor Law valuation of land which was more systematic and transparent than the tithe survey. Workhouses were erected in central urban locations within districts called Poor Law Unions (PLUs) from which the rates were collected. In order to facilitate the fair allocation of the rates burden

---

46 Andrews, *Plantation acres*, pp 333–85; idem, *Shapes of Ireland: maps and their makers, 1564–1839* (Dublin, 1997), p. 281.

among landowners and tenants, and to administer the election of local members to the Board of Guardians of the workhouses, Unions comprised Electoral Divisions (EDs, DEDs after 1898). These spatial units were carved out of the surrounding parishes and townlands in areas of roughly equal size, reasonably accessible on foot to workhouses for destitute families. Consequently PLUs regularly consisted of fragments of parishes and groups of townlands, often crossing county and barony boundaries. In this manner the older, even ancient, territorial realities were overridden for the first time in the interests of efficient delivery of what today would be termed social welfare services. Through the latter half of the nineteenth century Union electioneering, which saw the gentry landowning class from 1850s displaced from their positions of power on Boards of Guardians, provided a curtain-raiser to the eventual establishment of county councils in 1898. Because of local variations in pauperism, often correlating with poorly managed estates, landowing gentry especially on large and well-managed properties, lobbied to have ED boundaries coincide with estate boundaries, so that they would not be liable for the rates burden on neighbouring mismanaged properties. At the height of the famine which ultimately undermined and bankrupted the workhouse system, with rates of up to and over 5 shillings in the £ in many EDs, poorer tenants were forced to emigrate and indeed some Unions assisted the emigration of many inmates.[47]

As the local administrative role of the state expanded from the mid-nineteenth century, more and more functions were added to the PLUs: rural dispensary and rural sanitary districts, for instance. From 1863 the dispensary districts were designated as Superintendant Registrars Districts for the compulsory registration of births, deaths and marriages. These newly constructed units were also used in the census of population. While the census commissioners from 1821 used the parish and barony as the basic units for data collection, and by 1841 the townland was the smallest unit of record, some data was summarised by PLUs and EDs from 1851.[48]

CONCLUSION

From the evolution of its territorial structure and associated placenames to the arrangement of working landscapes of fields, settlements and estates, what has

---

47 Many Poor Law records are in the care of county councils: see Seamus Helferty and Raymond Refaussé, *Directory of Irish Archives* (Dublin, 2003). Clare County Archives service (www.clarelibrary.ie/local-studies/ clarearchives.htm) holds the Board of Guardian minute books for Corofin, Ennis, Ennistymon, Kilrush and Tulla Poor Law Unions. Limerick County Library holds the Board of Guardian records, Rural District Council records among others. Fingall County Archives contain some Grand Jury minute and presentment books (1818–98), as well as Board of Guardian and Rural District Council records. See John O'Connor, *The workhouses of Ireland: the fate of Ireland's poor* (Dublin, 1995).   **48** For details on boundary changes between 1841 and 1901, see E.M. Crawford, *Counting the people: a survey of the Irish censuses, 1813–1911*. Maynooth Research Guides for Irish Local History series (Dublin, 2003), pp 87–107.

sometimes been called by historical geographers the 'humanisation' of the landscape encompasses the gamut of changes made by society on the face of landscape. Local communities for centuries have left the marks of their culture and economy, social order and organisation on the Irish landscape. For local historians, therefore, the Irish landscape is a repository of narratives of settlement in town and country for a thousand years, but principally for the past few centuries of the modern era.

CHAPTER 4

Built environment

The most ubiquitous examples of human modification of the environment are found in the buildings and constructions which accompanied the course of settlement in the landscape. The role of the local historian is to explore the context and evolution of these structures over time. In the vicinity of Maynooth in north Kildare, for example, the following range of buildings is found: some traditional thatched houses and larger two-storey farmhouses from the later eighteenth and the nineteenth centuries mainly, as well as the great house at Carton, two-storey Quaker houses, herds' houses, rectories, ruins of castles at Maynooth and Donadea (with an accompanying terrace of estate houses, as well as gate lodges, hunting lodges, lime kiln and ice house), schoolhouses, churches and chapels, lock-keepers' houses, railway stations, and mills. As with most aspects of landscape history, there is a greater amount of information on buildings erected from the eighteenth century approximately. Inevitably also, in quantitative and spatial terms, the most significant built environments are urban: cities, towns and villages represent concentrated sites of building and construction. In rural areas, society's impact is more diffuse and dispersed through what is usually perceived as a natural landscape, although in reality much of the countryside is man-made.

The most extensive modifications to the built environment in Ireland histori-cally probably took place in the last half of the eighteenth century and the first half of the nineteenth century – building, development and improvement in landscape and townscape which were probably comparable to the impact of the tiger economy of the 1990s. For a century after the famine, on the other hand, apart from the city of Dublin and the eastern counties of Ulster, the morphology of town and country experienced limited development. In most rural areas and in many smaller towns and villages, settlement contraction and abandonment left the main parameters of landscape relatively unchanged; the edges of towns were fossilised at mid-nineteenth century boundaries and waited until the 1960s to see significant suburban expansion. Up to then, settlement landscapes in Ireland reflected the impacts of dereliction as result of chronic population decline: in the 1950s, 'many of the villages suggest the phrase in which they have been despairingly described as consisting of a dozen inhabited houses, a dozen ruined houses, and half a dozen public houses'.[1] In spite of the rash of new housing over the past thirty years, many parts of the rural landscape are still marked by derelict housing from the late nineteenth and first half of the twentieth century.

---

1 Praeger, *Irish landscape*, p. 12.

One of the consequences of the current phase of extensive building and construction in Ireland is the enormous change to landscape. Apart from the controversial destruction of archaeological sites in the paths of motorways, the face of the landscape in many places is being radically re-engineered by roads, extensive shopping facilities, industrial/business parks, suburban expansion and rural housing that is usually discordant with the inherited form and scale of the landscape. Tower cranes and earth-moving machinery can rapidly transform familiar landscapes, generating a form of landscape amnesia, where the connection with the previous remembered landscape is broken. In this context, there is a pressing need for photographic records to be made of most towns, villages and parts of countrysides undergoing extensive change. This could be a voluntary undertaking before commencement of major developments or it could be mandatory for developers or Local Authorities. Indeed some older construction companies have valuable photographic collections which help in examining the development of many housing schemes around Dublin in the first half of the twentieth century.[2]

Emerging housing and settlement patterns in rural and urban areas reflect the continuing impact of earlier templates in the landscape, for example, farm and field, road and lane networks. Rural houses are slotted into farm and fieldscapes, and along by-roads, so that the legacy of modern rural settlement continues to be greatly influenced by geometries and geographies laid down in the pre-modern, horse-cart era. In the same way, most of the urban development which has occurred in the past century has also been shaped by these earlier structures. Suburban expansion, before the enormous earth-moving machinery today, often sensitively fitted into older patterns of by-roads and enclosures. Many of the streetscapes in older suburbs of Dublin, such as Rathmines and Rathgar, echo an older road system which linked the villages of two and three centuries ago. Drumcondra Road and Grace Park Road, for instance, with their college grounds and older buildings originally located on the north edge of city, were embedded in carpets of suburban housing from the 1930s and 40s. Today, suburban expansion in towns like Maynooth and Celbridge similarly fossilise earlier fieldscapes: housing developments, for instance, reflect purchase by field, as it were, with developers attempting to fit an appropriate road and housing layout into the older fieldscape. Planners are also interested in many cases in retaining features of the older landscape such as hedges, tree plantations or perhaps earlier features of estate landscapes which have acquired 'heritage' value, like the Wonderful Barn, or the Obelisk (or Conolly's Folly) in Leixlip and Celbridge.

2 R. McManus, *Dublin, 1910–1940: shaping the city and suburbs* (Dublin, 2002); S. Ó Maitiú, *Dublin's suburban towns, 1847–1930: governing Clontarf, Drumcondra, Dalkey, Killiney, Kilmainham, Pembroke, Kingstown, Blackrock, Rathmines and Rathgar* (Dublin, 2003). Local photographic clubs have sometimes undertaken surveys.

RURAL SETTLEMENT

Rural housing patterns in Ireland are notably dispersed, with houses in general scattered across the countryside, individually located on their farms. The small and complexly intermeshed structure of holdings makes for a dense network of rural farmhouses. This pattern of rural housing is generally relatively recent – a product of plantation settlement in the seventeenth century and of reform and rationalisation by estates from the later eighteenth century in eastern counties and in the later nineteenth and early twentieth centuries in western regions.

Two main forms of rural housing dominated in the sixteenth and seventeenth centuries – individual farmsteads and farm clusters and villages.[3] A variety of maps from the sixteenth and seventeenth centuries, usually accompanying colonial settlement schemes, suggest the significance of house clustering. Robert Lythe's map of much of the southern half of Ireland in 1569 shows a fairly dense distribution of small settlements, concentrated in the Pale, but also noteworthy throughout the rest of the country. Raven's map of Gaelic south Monaghan in 1634 suggests the existence of small cabin clusters located within the network of townlands.[4]

Grouped or nucleated housing often located around tower houses of the medieval period. Clustered rundale settlements were found in extensive parts of western regions by the time of the Ordnance Survey six-inch survey in 1830s, as well as in more marginal landscapes in the east, such as the Wicklow glens, or midland bogs. It is possible that such clusters were characteristic of much more extensive parts of the country as far back as the sixteenth and seventeenth centuries. Squatter settlements on older commons dating from the medieval period were also characteristic of many former manorial lands in Leinster. Eighteenth-century surveys both in map and inventory form suggest such clustering.[5] In a map survey by Bernard Scalé of the marquis of Bath's estate in south Monaghan in 1777, a number of farm clusters are clearly evident, some with more than twenty houses. In the OS six-inch survey in 1834 they had all disappeared in consequence of estate reorganisation.

In much of the north and west, the 'street' was an element in micro landscapes – the street was the yard space outside the house, suggesting perhaps an earlier existence of space between houses. In many situations these farm clusters were also

---

3 Terminology for rural settlement histories often lacks precision. Clachan is a Gaelic term for settlement clusters in parts of Scotland which found its way to Ulster in the seventeenth century and was popularised in settlement studies by E. Estyn Evans in the 1940s: see P. Robinson, 'The use of the term "clachan" in Ulster' in *Ulster Folklife*, 37 (1991), pp 30–7. '*Baile*' is an ambiguous term which is very extensive in Irish placenames and has been adopted for a settlement cluster, though in many places it has historically referred to territorial rather than settlement units. '*Sráid bhaile*' means roughly a 'street village', though this is also ambiguous. This confusion has led to misinformed or misleading claims about traditional or indigenous forms of rural settlement. **4** See Aalen et al. (eds), *Atlas of the Irish rural landscape*, p. 183; J.H. Andrews, 'The Irish surveys of Robert Lythe' in *Imago Mundi*, xix (1965), pp 22–31. **5** See, for instance, Sir Henry Piers account of parts of Westmeath in 1682 discussed by Andrews in 'Land and people, *c*.1685', pp 464–5.

associated with temporary booley settlements on the mountain upland pastures – reflecting an older transhumance tradition. In County Kildare, the evidence of Emerson's late seventeenth-century survey and Rocque's maps of the 1750s, and other evidence such as leases, indicates that considerable adjustments were made in settlement patterns and landscape on the Kildare estates.[6] Settlement appears to have become more road-oriented. The distribution of houses had changed considerably, with many townlands having a lot fewer, reflecting proactive alterations to the pattern of settlement. Agricultural reform and dispersal of settlement clusters accompanied the elimination of much of the commons and the reorganisation and successive subdivision of fields in many areas up to the Ordnance Survey in the 1830s. By then the greatest concentrations of farm clusters were to be found in western seaboard counties, along the north, in the upland mountains of the east and in other marginal landscapes in the Midlands (4.1). This formed a very distinctive pattern of local housing which contrasts radically with today's pattern.

Most of the dispersed single farmsteads developed in the modern period. Some scholars have suggested a continuity with early medieval dispersed farmsteads represented by the thousands of ring forts in the countrysides but there is no direct lineage. In a general sense, change in settlement landscapes may be thought of as being generated by private agencies (landowners or farmers) and/or public intervention by the state or local authority, which were especially prominent in local life and landscape in the nineteenth century.[7] A great many of the rundale clusters were broken up in nineteenth-century programmes of land reform undertaken by individual landowners or in the west of Ireland by the Congested Districts Board (CDB). Landlords in post-famine decades in many of the poorer regions were interested in schemes of improvement which involved re-designing the landscape, breaking up rundale clusters, rearranging fields and roads, building bridges, drains, and improving fences – practices which had taken place in other more favoured regions through the eighteenth century. The CDB was responsible for breaking up and re-ordering thousands of rundale house clusters and intricately meshed fields and gardens in the late nineteenth and early twentieth century. A number of models of improved houses which often echoed traditional building styles were developed and located on newly built roads and newly striped fields.

The Irish Land Commission in its programmes of land reform in the twentieth century continued to re-arrange these settlement clusters. Its policy of migrating selected farmers from such clusters and relocating them locally or in eastern counties allowed the re-distribution of residual farms. Clusters endured into the 1960s in parts of Connemara when newer houses were built in ribbon developments along the roads.[8] Residual examples of these clusters continue along parts of the Atlantic seaboard in Connemara, Achill and west Donegal. Examination of the

6 Horner, 'Thomas Emerson's Kildare estates surveys, 1674–1697'; Duffy, 'Territorial identity of Kildare's landscapes', pp 20–2. **7** P.J. Duffy, 'Trends in nineteenth- and twentieth-century settlement' in Barry (ed.), *A history of settlement in Ireland*, pp 213–15. **8** B.S. MacAodha, 'Clachan settlement in Iar-Connacht' in *Ir. Geography*, 5 (1965), pp 20–8.

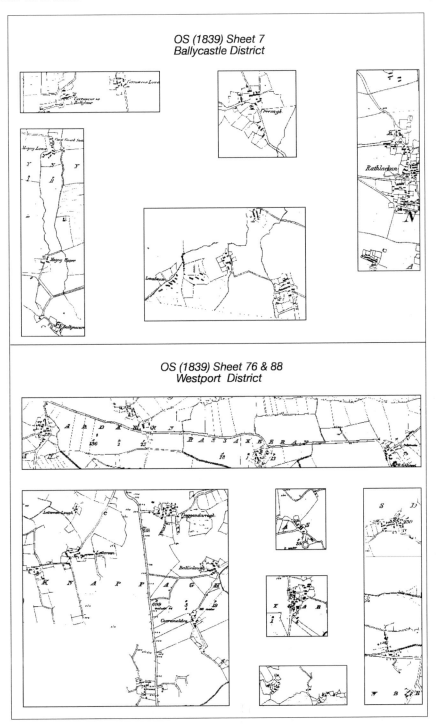

4.1 Farm clusters, County Mayo, 1839

pattern of rural housing today in parts of the east midlands indicates a link with the earlier matrix of farms: the Land Commission's creation of small holdings out of large grazing farms in Meath and Kildare in the 1940s, 50s and 60s subsequently facilitated the emergence of an extensive belt of rural commuter settlement across the countryside in the past thirty years.[9]

In addition other settlement forms appeared in the post-famine period, often the result of organic growth and new services developing in strategic locations in the countryside, such as cross-roads settlements near public houses, rural dispensaries and national schoolhouses. More often than not these were combined in 'chapel villages', agglomerations of houses around newly erected Catholic chapels which continue as local centres in many districts of scattered settlement today.[10] All of these settlement types can be discerned in the six-inch maps first published by the Ordnance Survey in the 1830s and 40s and subsequent editions.[11]

In general for rural areas, settlement is mainly farm-related and road-oriented, with the latter being very much a feature of the evolving pattern today. In the first instance, rural patterns were determined largely by their relationship with farms and farm structure – reflected for instance in locations of farm-houses and labourer cottages. Farming was the dominant economic activity in the rural landscape for the past hundreds of years and so the social and spatial organisation of landscape by this primary economic activity has influenced the arrangements of housing throughout the country. The most characteristic pattern was farmhouses located in their individually worked farms, linked to the road network by avenues or lanes. In the larger farm regions of the east and south-east of Ireland, associated labourer cottages were located on the fringes of the farms along roadsides, or on edges of villages, bogs or commons – but all essentially determined by the labour require-ments of nearby farms.

Road-oriented housing patterns reflect the evolution of settlement mainly by poorer, usually landless rural classes in the past couple of centuries – communities of labourers in tillage regions of the east and south-east, or (landless) cottiers in small farm regions of south Ulster and elsewhere, for instance. These settlements often followed the improvement of roads from the late eighteenth century and the opening up of marginal regions in the nineteenth century, reflecting settlement on largely unsupervised land sites. Such squatter settlement took the form of either single closely dispersed houses or small linear clusters. The road network was later

9 P.J. Duffy, 'Recent housing change in Kilclone, Co. Meath' in Aalen et al. (eds), *Atlas of the Irish rural landscape*, pp 244–9; idem, 'Rural settlement change in the Republic of Ireland – a preliminary discussion' in *Geoforum*, 14 (2) (1983), pp 185–91. 10 K. Whelan, 'The Catholic parish, the Catholic chapel and village development in Ireland' in *Ir. Geography*, 16 (1983), pp 1–15; idem, 'Town and village in Ireland, 1600–1960' in Verhoeve & Vervloet (eds), *The transformation of the European rural landscape*, pp 298–305. 11 Andrews, *A paper landscape* discusses the early decisions of the OS to map all houses and other features 'attached to the ground' (pp 57, 79, 129, 196); see also J.H. Andrews, *History in the Ordnance map* (Dublin, 1974). Six-inch, twenty-five inch and large-scale manuscript town plans are available in scanned format from the Ordnance Survey: *website*: www.irishhistoricmaps.ie/historic

used by estate owners involved in re-organising their tenant farms, by Poor Law
Union housing, by the Congested Districts Board later in the nineteenth century,
Local Government Board and County Council labourer cottage schemes and Land
Commission farmhouses in the twentieth century, all using roadside locations for
houses.

URBAN SETTLEMENT

General 'ethnic' classifications of Irish towns have been popular starting points in
historical studies of urban settlement: towns which originated as early Christian
sites, as Viking seaport settlements, as Gaelic market centres, or Anglo-Norman
settlements, Tudor or Stuart plantation towns, as well as estate towns, garrison
towns, Victorian seaside resorts or industrial settlements.[12] Apart from plantation
towns like Derry, most Irish urban settlements originated as pre-industrial market
centres, or port settlements, with Belfast being the only true industrial city
accompanied by a number of small industrial towns in east Ulster. Origins are
frequently manifested in the morphology of towns, the study of which has been
part of a broad European scholarship in geography, where the plan of the town
broadly reflects organic growth in the medieval period and more planned
morphologies in the post-plantation period.[13] Some question the obsession with
settlement classification schemes and emphasise the importance of trying to
appreciate landscapes of practice. Contemporary local inhabitants at any time did
not necessarily live in a 'clachan', a cluster, a 'town' or a 'proto-town': 'medieval
people did not need to work out which category their home-place belonged to'.[14]

Plantation towns of the sixteenth and seventeenth centuries offered the
opportunity to put into practice models of settlements in a market economy. The
Ulster plantation has been regarded as an example of regional town planning in
practice, well represented in contemporary maps illustrating embryonic towns
showing house layout, market squares, market crosses and so on.[15] Andrews has

---

12 Irish Historic Towns Atlas series; R.A. Butlin, *The development of the Irish town* (London,
1977); J.H. Andrews and A. Simms (eds), *Irish country towns* (Cork, 1994) and idem (eds), *More
Irish country towns* (Cork, 1995); B.J. Graham, 'The definition and classification of medieval
Irish towns' in *Ir. Geography*, 21 (1988), pp 20–32; J. Bradley, *Walled towns in Ireland* (Dublin,
1995). **13** See L. Swan, 'Monastic proto-towns in early medieval Ireland: the evidence of
aerial photography, plan analysis and survey' in H.B. Clarke and A. Simms (eds), *The
comparative history of urban origins in non-Roman Europe* (2 vols, Oxford, 1985), i, 77–102.
14 T. O'Keeffe, 'Reflections on the "dispersed-nucleated" paradigm in medieval settlement
archaeology' in *Ruralia III* (2000), pp 103–5. **15** See Robinson, *The plantation of Ulster*;
W.H. Crawford, 'The creation and evolution of small towns in Ulster in the seventeenth and
eighteenth centuries' in P. Borsay and L.J. Proudfoot (eds), *Provincial towns in early modern
England and Ireland: change, convergence and divergence* (Oxford, 2002), pp 97–120; R. Gillespie,
'The small towns of Ulster, 1600–1700' in *Ulster Folklife*, 36 (1990), pp 23–31; W.H.
Crawford, 'Evolution of towns in County Armagh' in Hughes & Nolan (eds), *Armagh: history
and society*, pp 851–80; R.H. Buchanan, 'Towns and plantations, 1500–1700' in Nolan (ed.),

Leabharlanna Fhine Gall

reviewed the intention and reality of plantation settlements in Ireland and the anchor role in plantations played by urban centres in Munster and Ulster for instance. Many of the towns were very small, but they did aspire to some kind of planned intervention in a predominantly pastoral landscape and they symbolised in their (sometimes theoretical) streets and squares 'abstract concepts of order, authority and un-Irishness … by drawing out a new landscape with that simple but appropriately named appliance, the ruler'.[16] Patents for markets and fairs were often used by landowners as drivers of settlement and economic development.

In general settlement terms, plantation policy envisaged settlers coming together in some sort of nucleated, defensible site: planters were enjoined in their agreements to build a stated number of stone houses 'after the English manner'. Dillon's lease in Farney from the earl of Essex in 1624 stipulated that he build a house of twenty rooms within four years as well as two mansion houses and also settle twelve households of British men and women within four years and twelve in the following four years.[17] In the Ulster Plantation, a number of follow-up surveys provided feedback on compliance by planters. As Philip Robinson has shown in Ulster, settlers soon adopted local custom and seem to have dispersed through the landscape. Peterstown on the Essex estate in 1634 had vanished from the scene twenty years later.[18]

From the British plantations onwards there was a greater degree of intervention in Irish settlement structure, whether by agents of the state, or more commonly individual landowners who endeavoured to have their towns settled and developed along pre-determined lines, as for example in Blessington, Castlecomer, Collon, Cootehill, Slane, Castlebellingham and many others. There were many examples of urban renewal too in the later eighteenth century, where older disorderly structures inherited from the Middle Ages were swept aside and replaced by fashionable high streets, malls and squares. The town of Westport in County Mayo is one of the best examples of the latter development, where Lord Altamont commissioned James Wyatt to design his town on classical lines. The older settlement of Nedeen in south Kerry, established by William Petty, was re-developed as Kenmare by his descendent the first Lord Lansdowne in the late eighteenth century. Other examples of renewal are Maynooth, Monasterevin, Tullamore, Birr, and Tyrellspass.[19] The Georgian

The shaping of Ireland, pp 84–98; G. Camblin, *The town in Ulster* (Belfast, 1951); R.J. Hunter, 'Towns in the Ulster Plantation' in *Studia Hib.*, 11 (1971), pp 40–79. **16** J.H. Andrews, 'Plantation Ireland: a review of settlement history' in Barry (ed.), *A history of settlement in Ireland*, pp 140–57, p. 147. Andrews has also critically examined the nature of early town maps in Ireland and their representation as plans or bird's eye pictorial views: see 'Classifying early Irish town plans' in Clarke et al. (eds), *Surveying Ireland's past*, pp 217–42; also R. Loeber, *The geography and practice of English colonisation in Ireland from 1534 to 1609* (Athlone, 1991). **17** Duffy, 'A lease from the estate of the earl of Essex 1624'. Monaghan was not an official plantation county. **18** Robinson, *Plantation of Ulster*. **19** See Graham & Proudfoot, 'Landlords, planning and urban growth in eighteenth- and nineteenth-century Ireland'; Susan Hood, 'The significance of the villages and small towns in rural Ireland during the eighteenth and nineteenth centuries' in Borsay & Proudfoot (eds), *Provincial*

period witnessed a great deal of redevelopment in Irish towns and cities, reflected in the work of the Wide Streets Commissioners in Dublin (established by parliament in 1757), as well as fashionable blocks and squares in Limerick, Cork and Galway.[20] *The Journal of the Irish House of Commons* catalogues the Irish parliament's financial incentives towards erection of market houses, bridges, harbours and other improvements in Irish towns during this important formative building period. In the nineteenth century a great many towns experienced what Patrick O'Connor calls the 'architecture of authority' imposed by the colonial state – constabulary barracks, court houses, gaols, dispensaries, post-offices, workhouses, fever hospitals, dispensaries and national schools.[21]

Reading a town's past in its morphology, street plans, housebuilding projects and suburban expansion is the most common historical research strategy, making use of maps, plans, surveys and street directories from the seventeenth century onwards. John Rocque's eighteenth-century map of Dublin county has generated many historical studies.[22] There was a range of interests and agents involved in the making and shaping of most Irish towns. The landowner clearly had the greatest incentive to see his town being developed and the patronage of powerful families was important in terms of parliamentary support and injection of capital locally, as in the Aungier estate in the late seventeenth century. But in many cases the landowner had insufficient resources, and management of leases was an important stimulus to development. From the middle of the eighteenth century, long leaseholders gradually acquired much of the power to develop the infrastructure and buildings of towns. Landlords simply became receivers of rent with limited input into the development of the town, relying largely on middlemen and substantial tenants with capital to carry projects through. In the nineteenth century also there was an increasing amount of regulation by the state of urban and municipal governance, in health, housing and sanitary legislation for instance.[23] Construction of open spaces and parks became an important municipal activity from the late seventeenth

towns, pp 241–61; see also L.M. Cullen, *Irish towns and villages* (Dublin, 1979) which contains an admirably illustrated summary of a wide range of Irish settlements and T. Jones Hughes, 'Village and town in mid-nineteenth-century Ireland' in *Ir. Geography*, 14 (1981), pp 99–106. **20** See E. Sheridan, 'Living in the capital city: Dublin in the eighteenth century' in J. Brady and A. Simms (eds), *Dublin through space and time* (Dublin, 2001), pp 66–135. **21** See Prunty, *Maps and mapmaking*, p. 264 for House of Lords, Westminster, records relating to Irish infrastructural developments. P. O'Connor, *Exploring Limerick's past* (Newcastle West, 1987), p. 104; see also P. Dargan, 'The morphology of Irish towns: Renaissance town planning in Ireland: Georgian Dublin' in *Geographical Viewpoint*, 27 (1999), pp 17–24. **22** For example, J.H. Andrews, *Two maps of 18th century Dublin and its surroundings by John Rocque* (Ashford Kent, 1977); R. McManus, 'Windows on a hidden world: urban and social evolution as seen from the mews' in *Ir. Geography*, 37 (1) (2004), pp 37–59; N. Burke, 'An early-modern Dublin suburb: the estate of Francis Aungier, earl of Longford' in *Ir. Geography*, 6 (4) (1972), pp 365–85; L.M. Cullen, 'The growth of Dublin, 1600–1900: character and heritage' in Aalen & Whelan (eds), *Dublin city and county: from prehistory to present*, pp 79–120. **23** See, for instance, F.H.A. Aalen, 'Health and housing in Dublin, c.1850–1921' in Aalen & Whelan (eds), *Dublin city and county: from prehistory to present*, pp 279–304.

century.[24] Brian Graham and Lindsay Proudfoot have examined themes of morphology, social and landowning contexts in the development of the fabric of Irish
towns.[25]

Estate papers most usefully throw light on the process of urban development in
the eighteenth century. The correspondence between agent and landlord in the
Barrett-Lennard estate, for example, makes reference to leases to encourage building
in Clones in the early years of the eighteenth century, as well as the re-building of
local mills. In 1741 the agent was reporting proudly on the progress of the town's
development which mirrored activity prevailing in many Irish towns at the time
when the main components of the urban structures were emerging:

> The houses in this town go on very well Mr Guthrys and Mr Ramadge are
> both ready for roofing and Mr Bennett is building a pretty little house in a
> direct line with his present dwelling house. Maxwell Cross is preparing
> material of brick stone and lime to go on with his building next Spring. The
> widow Graham … has finished her malt kiln almost, so that when John
> Stone? the builder's house is new built (which lies in the middle of the
> Diamond facing the Cross) equal to Mr Watts brick house this Town will cut
> a very handsome figure … besides the market house when built as I intended
> it provided you approve of the enclosed plan will be no small addition to its
> beauty … I have at last got Mr Ramadge to fix the place for building his
> Brickhouse which is near Ringsend on the right hand side of the road and
> the bleach yard is to be on the left hand of the Road … I hope to have them
> both finished in six or seven weeks if not sooner and shall write next post to
> Alderman Dawson to provide the furnace and other utensils and also fir deal
> boards for Ramadge's dwelling house and staircase five score deals, for those
> and window shutters, and for framing the doors and window shutters 20
> whole deals … [26]

24 See I. Strati, 'Reflections on the origins of public green spaces in Dublin City' in *Chimera*,
18 (2003), pp 56–61; idem, 'Historical Geographies of Dublin's public green spaces – from
their origins to 1756' (PhD thesis, Trinity College Dublin (2003)).   **25** L.J. Proudfoot,
'Patrician urban landlords: research on patronal relations in nineteenth-century 'estate towns'
in the British Isles' in D. Denecke and G. Shaw (eds), *Urban historical geography: recent progress
in Britain and Germany* (Cambridge, 1988), pp 175–88; B.J. Graham & L.J. Proudfoot, *Urban
improvement in provincial Ireland, 1700–1840*; L.J. Proudfoot, *Property ownership and urban and
village improvement in provincial Ireland, c.1700–1845* (London, 1997); idem, *Urban patronage and
social authority*; Graham & Proudfoot, 'Landlords, planning and urban growth in eighteenth-
and early nineteenth-century Ireland'; see also Graham & Proudfoot, 'A re-definition of
Irish landscape: revisionist attitudes to landlords and their transformation of place' in *L'avenir
des paysages ruraux européens. Entre gestion des héritages et dynamique du changement* (Lyon, 1992),
pp 95–8; T. Jones Hughes, 'Village and town in mid-nineteenth century Ireland' in *Ir.
Geography*, 14 (1981), pp 99–106.   **26** Letter from John Todd, Clones, to Mr Barrett
(PRONI, Barrett-Lennard papers, T. 2529/6/c.33 181). In 1718 agent Kaine referred to
'200,000 bricks making an hour to build in your honour's town of Clonnis' (T. 2529/6 c.37
310). See J. Prunty, 'Estate records' in W. Nolan and A. Simms (eds), *Irish towns: a guide to*

Similarly Carrickmacross in County Monaghan was largely the product of collaborating strategies of Shirley and Bath, on the boundary of whose properties the town lay, both of them employing the same agent for much of the eighteenth century which ensured common policies being implemented into the pre-famine period.

These various interests were involved in the construction of landmark buildings in Ireland's developing townscapes from the eighteenth and into the nineteenth centuries: market houses, court houses, town halls and club/fraternities buildings – linen halls, assembly rooms, Masonic halls, Orange halls, and so on. In bigger centres, clubs such as the Kildare Street Club in Dublin, or the Limerick County Club,[27] hotels and public houses (some ostentatiously called 'emporiums') developed in the later eighteenth and nineteenth century as mobility increased, for example, with bianconi traffic. Banks were one of the most well-endowed institutions in all towns, usually among the best built structures in the town, following the removal of the Bank of Ireland's monopoly in 1821, and the Northern Bank, Provincial Bank, Hibernian and Royal banks were established within a decade. The twentieth century was marked by a proliferation of cinemas or picturehouses, many of them examples of art deco in the 1930s and 40s.[28]

The most comprehensive recent coverage of source material on Irish towns can be found in William Nolan and Anngret Simms (eds), *Irish towns: a guide to sources* (Dublin, 1998) which is essential introductory reading for students interested in studying Irish towns. Its wide-ranging themes include: early history of Irish towns; maps, prints, drawings and photographs; buildings and archaeology of Irish towns; medieval and plantation records; records of central and local government from 1700; estate records; church records; newspaper, directories and gazetteers; literary sources. It also reprints Desmond McCabe's select bibliography of materials on Irish towns in the modern period which were originally printed during the period 1969 to 1993.[29]

Classification of origins and morphology is the basis on which the *Irish Historic Towns Atlas* (*IHTA*) project has been undertaken by the Royal Irish Academy. To date the following towns, covering most of the generic types of urban centres, have been completed: Carrickfergus, Belfast (Parts 1 and 2), Downpatrick, Kells, Trim, Mullingar, Athlone, Maynooth, Dublin (Part 1), Bray, Kildare, Kilkenny, Fethard (Tipperary), Bandon, and Derry-Londonderry. The standard model for the *IHTA* is an essay on the origin and development of each town, a topographical section with details on placenames, legal and proprietorial status, streets, boundaries, and

sources (Dublin, 1998), pp 121–36.   **27** See Dooley, *The decline of the Big House in Ireland*, pp 61–4.   **28** See J. Keenan, *Dublin cinemas* (Dublin, 2005).   **29** See also A. Simms and P. Fagan, 'Villages in County Dublin: their origins and inheritance' in Aalen & Whelan (eds), *Dublin city and county: from prehistory to present*, pp 79–120; Cullen, 'The growth of Dublin', pp 251–78; W.H. Crawford, 'The creation and evolution of small towns in Ulster in the seventeenth and eighteenth centuries' in Borsay & Proudfoot (eds), *Provincial towns*, pp 97–120; idem, Crawford, 'Sources for studying Ulster towns in the nineteenth and twentieth centuries' in *Ulster Local Studies*, 18 (1996), pp 95–100.

population through time, with a selection of large-scale maps of the town at various stages in its history. The focal map is normally a reconstruction for *c.*1840 based on the large-scale manuscript town plans of the Ordnance Survey and the Valuation Office. As part of a Europe-wide project, the atlas offers the opportunity to compare aspects of urban settlement history across a wide canvas. John Bradley has initiated such a study by examining the impact of religion on Irish urban landscapes.[30]

Simms and Andrews's *Irish country towns* (Dublin, 1994) and *More Irish country towns* (Dublin, 1995) incorporate short case studies of Kells, Downpatrick, Carrickfergus, Maynooth, Enniscorthy, Bandon, Lurgan, Ennistymon, Castlecomer, Bray, Sligo, Athlone, Dungarvan, Mullingar, Kildare, Carlingford, Bangor, Coleraine, Carrickmacross, Tullamore, Monasterevan, Athenry, Tuam, Westport, Roscrea, Cashel, Tralee, Youghal and Wexford. Patrick O'Connor's *Exploring Limerick's past: an historical geography of urban development in county and city* (Newcastle West, 1987) surveys the evolution of medieval settlement, the development of seventeenth-century villages, the early-modern city, the rise and fall of Kilmallock, the growth of the estate town of Newcastle West, and urban developments in the eighteenth and nineteenth centuries.[31] In *Dublin, 1910–1940: shaping the suburbs* (Dublin, 2002) Ruth McManus examines the social, economic and planning context of new housing projects at Marino, Drumcondra and Crumlin in the first half of the twentieth century and the role of public and private housing initiatives. Seamas Ó Maitiú, *Dublin's suburban towns, 1834–1930* (Dublin, 2003) explores the role of local government in Dublin townships, in particular Rathmines, focussing on property development, housebuilding and the provision of services such as water, street lighting and drainage.[32]

The historical development of the fabric of a small county town like Monaghan from the eighteenth century involved street-widening projects, replacement of unsightly thatched houses with more fashionable slated buildings and encourage-ment of landmark architectural statements. By the middle of the nineteenth century Monaghan exhibited all the hallmarks of a self-conscious county town: market house, town hall, courthouse, gaol, barracks, infirmaries, churches, hotels and inns and up to fourteen different kinds of school. In addition to its visible landscape

---

30 J. Bradley, 'The Irish historic towns atlas as a source for urban history' in Clarke et al. (eds), *Surveying Ireland's past*, pp 727–46; Patrick O'Connor has produced a unique variant on the IHTA theme in his *Hometown: a portrait of Newcastle West, Co. Limerick* (Newcastle West, 1998), presenting large-scale maps of parts of the town with accompanying historical accounts. See also J. Crowley et al., *Atlas of Cork City* (Cork, 2005) which is a lavishly illustrated profile of the city.   31 Also P.J. O'Connor, 'The maturation of town and village life in County Limerick, 1700–1900' in Smyth & Whelan (eds), *Common ground*, pp 149–72. There are innumerable wide-ranging case studies of individual towns: see, for example, A.R. Orme, 'Youghal, County Cork – growth, decay, resurgence' in *Ir. Geography*, 5 (3) (1966), pp 121–49 and T.C. Barnard, 'Landlords and urban life: Youghal and the Boyles, 1641–1740' in *Group for the Study of Irish Historic Settlement Newsletter*, 5 (Autumn 1995), pp 1–4 where the rise and decline of the town followed the seventeenth-century involvement and then the eventual withdrawal of the Boyle family from the locality. See also W.G. Neely, *Kilkenny: an urban history, 1391–1843* (Belfast, 1989).   32 Ó Maitiú, *Dublin's suburban towns, 1834–1930*.

expression, like all towns it had a developing subterranean network supporting its surface buildings – an infrastructure of drains, pipes and cables which helped it work as a town, linking up its buildings and functions like the arteries in the body. Up to the late nineteenth century, as in most country towns, water was supplied by local wells and handpumps and refuse was dumped in surrounding ditches and the streets. Indeed townspeople also had to cope with the downside of being a market-place for the surrounding countryside, as in Clonmel for example: 'Pig fairs were held on the Mall and the pigs were noted for their habit of rooting up the street surface, much to the annoyance of some inhabitants.'[33] Animals were slaughtered on the public streets in many town shambles until the mid-nineteenth century. Ideas on municipal improvement and concerns about health and sanitary conditions, not to mention sensitivities about public taste and morality, led to drainage and culverting, paving and cobbling of streets, drainage of waste water from roof gutters and streets, and from the households and water closets of the well-to-do. As wells became polluted, water was piped from nearby lakes or streams. Later gas lighting and electricity linked up streets and some buildings.[34]

An essay on the population of Dublin, published by William Whitelaw in 1805, refers to the slum housing conditions in parts of the city which endured for the next century and more. Indeed many of the older elegant streets and squares of Dublin deteriorated in consequence of post-famine immigration of poverty-stricken people. Except for the overcrowding, many of the descriptions also matched contemporary accounts of the poorest rural cabin-dwellers, as well as conditions in the back lanes of smaller country towns.[35]

As well as the politics of municipal and social improvement, the engineering history of the infrastructure in towns and country (such as piped water supplies, sanitation, gas lighting and electrification, and also public transport) is a valid local historical enterprise. The Wide Streets Commission set the pace for planning and environmental improvements in Dublin from 1757 until the middle of the nineteenth century. Reflecting a growth in municipal consciousness and identity as the capital city of the kingdom of Ireland, it was given powers to control and design the layout of the city's main streets. Dame Street, Parliament Street, Westmoreland

---

33 Sean O'Donnell, *Clonmel, 1840–1900: anatomy of an Irish town* (Dublin, 1998), p. 78. The problem of animal manure which was a public nuisance in all country towns was exacerbated in Clonmel by Bianconi's horses in the 1820s and 30s. **34** P.J. Duffy, 'The town of Monaghan: a place inscribed in street and square' in E. Conlon (ed.), *Later on: the Monaghan bombing memorial anthology* (Dingle, 2004), pp 14–32; O'Donnell, *Clonmel*, pp 82–92. **35** See T. Graham, 'Whitelaw's 1798 census of Dublin' in *History Ireland*, 2 (3) (Autumn 1994), pp 13–14; see also McManus, 'Windows on a hidden world', pp 37–59; J. Prunty, *Dublin slums, 1800–1925: a study in urban geography* (Dublin, 1998) examines the post-famine development of slums in the Liberties and on the Gardiner estate; Sheridan, 'Living in the capital city: Dublin in the eighteenth century'; B. Murnane, 'The recreation of the urban historical landscape: Mountjoy Ward, Dublin *c.*1901' in Smyth & Whelan (eds), *Common ground*, pp 189–207; Aalen, 'Health and housing in Dublin *c.*1850 to 1921' and idem, *The Iveagh Trust: the first hundred years, 1890–1990* (Dublin, 1990); Crossman, *Local government*, pp 69–70.

Street, D'Olier Street and Sackville Street all reflect their endeavours. Gas lighting was first introduced in Dublin in the 1820s and from the mid-nineteenth century in many smaller towns. Up until perhaps the 1960s, there was a notable divergence in material living standards between town and country in Ireland. The rural townlands had no electricity until the mid-twentieth century, making do with oil lamps, candles, open hearths and pot ovens. Water was carried from the well, fuel from the bog. There was a much greater degree of work, energy and muscle power involved in rural living than in the more comfortable landscapes of town. Town and country were 'light' and 'dark' landscapes respectively: people in some towns spoke of life 'beyond the lights'.[36] Towns with their strong sense of community endeavour or municipal pride, or local landowner or merchant influence, contrived local responses to infrastructural needs: one of the earliest hydro-electric schemes was established in Clifden.[37]

BUILDINGS IN TOWN AND COUNTRY

The following section will briefly survey a selection of structures which form part of the fabric of the built environment, highlighting a wide range of studies which examine the social and architectural significance of buildings situated in town and country. For the local historian these are landscape signatures of society's relation-ship with its environment over generations – from the domestic residential impacts of powerful local élites for a millennium, through the infrastructural investments of local and central government especially from the early-modern period, to the innumerable local vernacular contributions of ordinary inhabitants of town and country.

'Ruins'

In many senses Ireland is a land of ruins, reflecting destruction and warfare of the past, as well as depopulation of settlements in more modern times. The town of Trim is a classic example, comprehensively examined by Michael Potterton.[38] The passage of time had an especially marked impact on the Irish landscape. Inter-lordship feuding in the Middle Ages was responsible for much destruction, with borderlands being particularly vulnerable to damage. Gaelic 'resurgence' from the fourteenth century overran the medieval English colony and economic contraction within the colony led to many of its outlying manorial settlements being deserted.[39] Towns like Ardee and Dundalk were regularly razed, as were fortified defences on the perimeter of Dublin. However, the wars and disturbances accompanying the

---

36 S. Ó Maitiú, communication.   **37** This impetus for improvement is evident in many town corporation and council records and local newspapers of the nineteenth century. **38** M. Potterton, *Medieval Trim: history and archaeology* (Dublin, 2005).   **39** See R. Loeber, 'An architectural history of Gaelic castles and settlements, 1370–1600' in Duffy et al. (eds), *Gaelic Ireland*, pp 271–314.

subjugation of Gaelic Ireland in the sixteenth and seventeenth centuries were responsible for most of the ruins littering the landscape today. The Protestant Reformation, which confiscated most monastic property and transferred all church buildings and lands to the Established Church, had different landscape consequences in Ireland to England. Because most of the population in Ireland maintained its allegiance to Rome, the material legacy of the ecclesiastical buildings was largely abandoned by the new church. Contemporary maps frequently show destruction and burning of buildings in progress in this period.[40] Extensive tracts of Munster, Ulster and Leinster were subjected to scorched earth military tactics in the late sixteenth century. The Civil Survey records the consequences of years of war and upheaval in its recurring catalogue of settlements and castles in ruins.

Our extensive medieval ruins inspired the antiquarianism of the later seventeenth and eighteenth centuries and shaped the emergence of a romanticism about a Celtic past, generating many misguided theories on Irish history, relating to Phoenicians, Danish forts, phallocentric round towers and so on.[41] This was due in no small measure to the disjuncture between the newly emerged colonial élites of the seventeenth and eighteenth centuries and the cultural and material landscape. Kevin Whelan invokes a geological metaphor, with lower/ older strata of ruins being upthrust into later periods as permanent reminders of a disrupted past to haunt the new landowning order.[42] The eighteenth- and early nineteenth-century interest in antiquarianism was often a colonial obsession with the conquered, vanished, 'failed' world of previous hegemonies. Eventually antiquarianism laid the foundations for a more systematic and scientific approach to ancient structures initiated by the Ordnance Survey in the early nineteenth century. Ruined buildings represented the collapse of a former ordering of landscape space, with the lines between order and disorder (civilisation and barbarism) becoming decayed and abandoned. This is dramatically reflected in lonely stranded burial grounds, often with associated medieval church ruins, located in the middle of an eighteenth-century field network. There are also remains of eclipsed industries of the eighteenth and nineteenth centuries, in crumbling mills and warehouses along rivers like the Barrow, Nore or Boyne which were the highways of pre-famine Ireland. More recent house ruins in derelict and abandoned uplands and marginal lands of the west highlight where fields and farms, lanes and boreens have long surrendered to fern and briar in the face of emigration.

Pre-modern landscapes especially have been the area of interest of Irish archaeology for generations, which until recently has largely ignored early modern and modern landscapes. Many of the most important survivals are monuments to

40 G.A. Hayes-McCoy, *Ulster and other Irish maps, c.1600* (Dublin, 1964); Andrews, 'The mapping of Ireland's cultural landscape'; Swift, *Historical maps of Ireland.* **41** See Sir James Ware, *De Hibernia et antiquitatibus* (London, 1654). **42** K. Whelan, 'Reading the ruins: the presence of absence in the Irish landscape' in Clarke et al. (eds), *Surveying Ireland's past*, pp 297–328: see also V. Kreilkamp, 'Fiction and empire: the Irish novel' in K. Kenny (ed), *Ireland and the British empire* (Oxford, 2004), pp 154–81.

the dead – tombs and burial structures, such as passage graves (which often have astronomical characteristics for agricultural societies), as well as structures for storage, defence and security (like souterrains), more domestic fieldscapes (like Céide), and early historic house structures (such as Lough Gur). Earthen structures or stone built structures like henges, promontory forts, cashels, cahers, duns, ring forts (or stone built cahers), medieval house structures, mottes and baileys and so on have been extensively examined by archaeologists.

Medieval buildings

Castles, tower houses and fortified buildings reflect a transition in architecture from the medieval to the early-modern landscape, with emphasis on defensive protective structures. Anglo-Normans reputedly introduced stone castles into Ireland, as well as earthen mottes. Later in the fifteenth century the tower house became the dominant structure. As one of the most notable buildings in the later medieval rural and urban landscape, tower houses were erected by both Anglo-Normans and Gaelic Irish as refuges of security in unstable landscapes of the late medieval period, reflecting the fragmented political lordships of the period, with concentrations especially along borderlands. They were important centres of nucleation built by lords to consolidate their hold on surrounding territory, from frequently imposing situations which dominated surrounding countrysides, protected moveable property like livestock and reflected power in a status-conscious society.[43] They were often associated with churches, mills and weirs, as well as possibly a village at parish centres. Defence continued to be an important consideration in the war-torn seventeenth century, and into the eighteenth century with the construction of barracks and coastal structures.[44] A great proportion of these medieval built landscapes were abandoned, while many more continued or acted as anchors of continuity in subsequent modern developments, frequently reflected, for example, in parts of Meath and Kildare in the juxtaposition of farmhouses and older tower houses, or estate mansions and medieval parish centres.[45] The early-modern

43 T. Barry, 'Tower houses and terror' in Clarke et al. (eds), *Surveying Ireland's past*, pp 119–28; K. Simms, 'Native sources for Gaelic settlement: the house poems' in Duffy et al. (eds), *Gaelic Ireland*, pp 246–67 for literary evidence on medieval buildings in Gaelic Ireland; C.J. Donnelly, 'Tower houses and late medieval secular settlement in County Limerick' in ibid., pp 315–28; Aalen, *Man and the landscape in Ireland*.   **44** R. Loeber, 'An architectural history of Gaelic castles and settlements, 1370–1600' in Duffy et al. (eds), *Gaelic Ireland*, pp 271–314; idem, *The geography and practice of English colonisation in Ireland from 1534 to 1609* (Athlone, 1991); P.M. Kerrigan, *Castles and fortifications in Ireland, 1485–1945* (Dublin, 1995); J. Prunty, 'Military barracks and mapping in the nineteenth century: sources and issues for Irish urban history' in Clarke et al. (eds), *Surveying Ireland's past*, pp 477–534.   **45** Kilyon House in Co. Meath has a medieval church site, holy well and pattern day. See Donnelly, 'Tower houses and late medieval secular settlement in County Limerick'; T.E. McNeill, 'The archaeology of Gaelic lordship east and west of the Foyle' in ibid., pp 346–56; H.G. Leask, *Irish churches and monastic buildings* (3 vols, Dundalk, 1955–60), idem, *Irish castles* and castellated houses (reprinted Dundalk, 1995); R. Stalley, *The Cistercian monasteries of Ireland: an account of the history, art and architecture of the white monks in Ireland from 1142–1540* (New Haven, 1987); A.

elimination of local lordships, imposition of more state control and instigation of plantation settlement witnessed the beginnings of house-building as statements of power and status in the landscape. The high gabled, tall houses built in Ulster and elsewhere from the early seventeenth century were built to view the landscape and gardens rather than as look-outs for defence.[46]

Ecclesiastical buildings and burial grounds

Churches, whether of wood or stone, were among the first significant central places in the Irish landscape – more so than the castles or the houses of lords. In pre-Norman Ireland or later medieval Gaelic Ireland where towns were largely absent, parish churches enjoyed what might be characterised as rural centrality, either in larger ecclesiastical settlements, or local churches with burial grounds. Burial grounds gave churches lasting significance for local communities. Parish centres were also occasional meeting places for hundreds of years, often revered sites or places of sanctuary, frequently marking earlier pre-Christian locations.

Early medieval churches and monastic foundations were extremely numerous throughout the country, reflecting kinship lineages. Many were small, often containing a number of buildings in a circular enclosure, some accompanied by tenth and eleventh-century round towers, others with simple but sophisticated drystone corbelled structures like Gallarus. Round towers have a certain iconic significance following eighteenth-century antiquarianism and later nineteenth-century cultural revival. The most significant impact in terms of buildings was a product of monastic foundations from the Continent which followed twelfth-century church reform and Anglo-Norman settlement. Invited into Ireland by either Gaelic or Norman lords, these monastic orders usually brought with them elements of continental ecclesiastical architecture (such as distinctive twelfth- or thirteenth-century Romanesque styles) as well as incorporating elements of the earlier Christian phase, and reflected building booms in parts of the country throughout the Middle Ages. The principal foundations of abbeys were initially Cistercian, Augustinian and Benedictine, most of them adopting a cloister form of building plan. Upwards of forty Cistercian abbeys were built in the hundred years following the erection of their first centre at Mellifont (1142). Franciscan and Dominican friaries were

Gwynn and R.N. Hadcock, *Medieval religious houses: Ireland* (Harlow, 1970); P. Harbison, *Guide to the national monuments in the Republic of Ireland: including a selection of other monuments not in state care* (Dublin, 1975); D. Sweetman, *Irish castles and fortified houses* (Dublin, 1995); Kerrigan, *Castles and fortifications*; T. McNeill, *The castle in Ireland. Feudal power in a Gaelic world* (London, 1997); C.T. Cairns, *Irish tower houses: a Co. Tipperary case study* (Athlone, 1987); J. Lyttleton and T. O'Keeffe (eds), *The manor in medieval and early modern Ireland* (Dublin, 2005); R.E. Glasscock, 'Moated sites, and deserted boroughs and villages: two neglected aspects of Anglo-Norman settlement in Ireland' in Stephens & Glasscock (eds), *Irish geographical studies*, pp 162–77. **46** T. Reeves-Smyth, 'Ireland's 'great rebuilding' and the revolution in domestic architecture, 1610–1640' and T. O'Keeffe, 'Plantation culture and the birth of the Georgian order: the seventeenth-century castles of Munster', Plantation Ireland: settlement and material culture, 6th Annual conference, IPMAG with GSIHS, UCC 24–26 Feb. 2006.

introduced in the thirteenth and fourteenth centuries. Friaries were characterised by towers separating the choir for the friars from the nave for the laity. More than one hundred Franciscan houses were built in the late medieval period.[47] Cathedrals, abbeys and church buildings in general have significance beyond their material reflections of wealth and authority. They have always had important symbolic and ritual significance, built for the glory of God and to instil respect and awe in the laity and this aspect of religious buildings has often endured through to present-day ruins.

'Historically parish centres were powerful settlement foci and community anchors' highlighting the endurance of the centralising and symbolic functions of parishes after the Reformation in Dublin, Kilkenny and Tipperary counties.[48] While most of the churches of the eighteenth and nineteenth centuries exhibit distinctive styles of architecture (neo-Romanesque and so on), many also show local vernacular influences, as exemplified in many places in the 'barn chapels' and T-plan designs of Catholic chapels, built by local craftsmen using local skills and materials. Thatched masshouses were relatively common features in the eighteenth century, usually off-the-beaten track in town and country which contrasted with the more central locations of the Church of Ireland. Following Catholic Emancipation in 1829, modestly-designed Catholic churches were erected, with more flamboyant Gothic revival styles emerging in the later nineteenth century when buildings moved to dominant locations in towns especially: the ceremonies accompanying the laying of the foundation stone of Monaghan cathedral in 1861, for instance, spoke volumes about the new position of the Catholic church.[49] The Church of Ireland's Board of First Fruits erected hundreds of churches throughout Ireland in the late eighteenth and early nineteenth centuries which, while abandoned or in ruins, continue to add much distinction to the Irish landscape in the uniformity of their tower and hall design.[50] Being the Established Church it has an extensive archive of records. There is much material on churches, glebe houses and parochial organisation, including photographs from the late nineteenth century. In Meath diocese, for instance, censuses were undertaken for 1749 and 1766: that

47 B. de Breffny, R. Ffolliott, and G. Mott, *The churches and abbeys of Ireland* (London, 1976); Leask, *Irish churches and monastic buildings*; P. Harbison, *Pilgrimage in Ireland: the monuments and the people* (London, 1991); L. Bitel, *Isle of saints: monastic settlement and Christian community in early Ireland* (Cornell, 1990); E. FitzPatrick and C. O'Brien, *The medieval churches of County Offaly* (Dublin, 1998); Bradley, *Settlement and society in medieval Ireland*; T.B. Barry, *The archaeology of medieval Ireland* (London, 1987); J. Bradley, *Walled towns in Ireland* (Dublin, 1995). **48** W.J. Smyth, 'Property, patronage and population' in Nolan & McGrath (eds), *Tipperary: history and society*, p.126; idem, 'Exploring the social and cultural topographies of sixteenth- and seventeenth-century County Dublin' in Aalen & Whelan (eds), *Dublin city and county: from prehistory to present*, pp 153–8. **49** P.J. Duffy, 'The town of Monaghan: a place inscribed in street and square' in note 34 pp 14–32; see also T. C. Barnard, *A guide to sources for the history of material culture in Ireland, 1500–2000* (Dublin, 2005), pp 56–9, 105–7. **50** C. Casey and A.Rowan, *The buildings of Ireland: north Leinster* (London, 1993), pp 61–72.

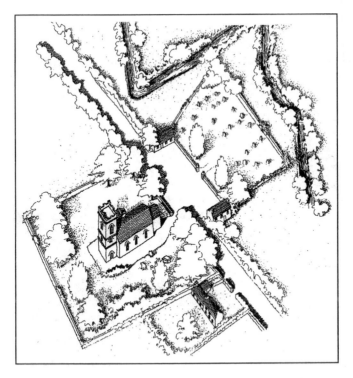

4.2 A distinctive local landscape: Ballintemple Church, County Cavan; from P. & M. Shaffrey, *Irish countryside buildings* (Dublin, 1985), p. 73

for Navan in 1766 provides valuable insights into the geography of the town and its residents.[51]

Burial grounds are one of the earliest features in the landscape, often today accompanying a ruined church building, surrounded by yew trees, containing ranges of headstones and monuments. Early Christian burial grounds occur throughout Ireland in great numbers, servicing local small communities and possibly in many cases early settlement clusters. They are frequently raised above the level of the surrounding landscape, reflecting generations of interments, surrounded often by circular wall enclosures mirroring the secular rath enclosures of the period. Gravestone slabs are important sources of information on local society. The Anglo-Norman settlement introduced European style burial and monuments. From the medieval into the early-modern period, wealthy élites

---

51 See P. Shaffrey and M. Shaffrey, *Irish countryside buildings: everyday architecture in the rural landscape* (Dublin, 1985), pp 71–86; S. Hood, 'Church of Ireland sources for the historical geographer: a case-study of the Meath diocesan archive'; A. Rowan 'Irish Victorian churches: denominational distinctions' in Kennedy & Gillespie (eds), *Ireland: art into history*, pp 207–30; Mitchell (ed.), *A guide to Irish churches and graveyards* shows the location of churches and cemeteries.

erected slab monuments with mortality symbols (usually depicting hell and damnation) which originated in Europe after the Black Death. By the late seventeenth century a fashion for smaller vertical headstones with short inscriptions of name and date of death spread into other classes. By the later eighteenth century symbols of resurrection and salvation became popular. Burial stones, monuments, slabs and headstones all convey messages to the skilled interpreter – names and ages, relationships, sometimes cause of death, mortality symbols, and moralistic inscriptions. The more modern stones tell of families, with implications for demographic structure and kinship, though earlier stones often convey more details because the stone monument was seen as the last record of the deceased.[52]

Schools

School buildings are also one of the commonest structures found throughout the country, often in conjunction with churches. These range from nineteenth-century buildings erected by agencies involved in education, many of them proselytising agencies, such as the Kildare Place Society, or landlord endowments, or the model schools erected under the National Education commission from 1848 in most county towns. Many of these private school buildings are distinctive local architectural statements reflecting educational and philosophical principles. The state national school system commencing in early 1840s was the most important innovation in the mid-nineteenth century and represented the beginnings of a standardised building plan being imposed on local landscapes. Prior to this, in the absence of landlord assistance, local communities established their own so-called 'hedge' schools in barns, stables and local houses. The national schools of the 1840s and 50s, some of which continue in use, have a simple distinctive style. There followed in the twentieth century a series of school designs which can still be recognised in most parts of the country marking the period when they were erected. The distinctive plan with central classroom block and arcaded shelters with water tower commenced in mid-twentieth century and remains the most ubiquitous.[53]

52 See H. Mytum, 'A long and complex plot: patterns of family burial in Irish graveyards from the 18th century' in *Church Archaeology*, 5/6 (2004), pp 31–41; idem, 'Graveyard survey in west Ulster' in ibid., pp 112–14; R. Gillespie, 'Irish funeral monuments and social change, 1500–1700: perceptions of death' in Kennedy & Gillespie (eds), *Ireland: art into history*, pp 155–68; R.J. Hunter, 'Style and form in gravestone and monumental sculpture in Co. Tyrone in the seventeenth and eighteenth centuries' in Dillon & Jefferies (eds), *Tyrone: history and society*, pp 291–326; R. Loeber, 'Sculptured memorials to the dead in early 17th–century Ireland: a survey from *Monumenta Eblanae* and other sources' in *PRIA*, 81, sect. C, 11 (1981), pp 267–93. See also local studies of burial monuments in most local historical society journals.   **53** Shaffrey & Shaffrey, *Irish countryside buildings*, pp 78–83.

Mansion Houses and Estate Buildings

The term 'Big House' has entered the vernacular lexicon with reference to the mansion/manor houses of the landowning classes erected between the seventeenth and the late nineteenth centuries. The several thousand mansion houses were – and continue to be – important additions to the landscape, dramatic statements of power and examples of showy display in an era of gentry privilege.[54] In the mid-nineteenth century Evelyn Shirley, the landlord near Carrickmacross in County Monaghan, captures the self-conscious aura of such a house in a letter to his son describing the arrangements for a ball held in Lough Fea House in November 1848 (which, in retrospect, was unfortunate timing with famine stalking much of the countryside). He provides elaborate details on the lighting arrangements ('200 candles and six lamps in the Hall ... In the Conservatory we had 500 coloured lamps'), on the supper, on the dancing till after six in the morning, on the feeding of servants and footboys in the coach house ('cold meat and bread and beer but no whiskey').[55]

The Big Houses represented conspicuous consumption by gentry élites, with exotic designs like mock Gothick, Tudor/Elizabethan, Jacobean, 'Jacobethan,' 'College' (as in Lough Fea) and so on. The product of a comparatively small coterie of fashionable architects and designers, mansion houses were accompanied by suites of other buildings, whether functional, ornamental or folly: out-offices in elaborate designs, dove cotes, meat houses, ice houses, shell cottages, boat houses, gate lodges, mausoleums, including in some cases underground passages for use by domestic staff: housing for estate workers and officials in Carton had steps up or down at entrances reflecting the status of the occupier. There were also dower houses, as well as follies (some of which were artificial 'ruins' like the Jealous Wall at Belvedere in County Westmeath), temples, obelisks, gazebos and *cottages orneés* such as Swiss cottages and so on. Some of the most dramatic examples are Conolly's Obelisk or Folly between Carton and Castletown, The Wonderful Barn near Leixlip, and those at Killua, Kilruddery, and Dangan castle. The Marino Casino (or Casino Marino) built by Lord Charlemont is the ultimate elaborate folly.[56]

Many estate owners built elaborate houses in provincial Ireland, in Dublin and in England. Lord Charlemont had his houses in Dublin and Armagh; the duke of Leinster at Carton built a town house in Dublin; Thomas Dawson built an exten-

---

54 See Dooley, *The big houses and landed estates of Ireland* (Dublin, 2007). N.C. Johnson, 'Where geography and history meet: heritage tourism and the Big House in Ireland' in *Annals of the American Association of Geographers*, 86 (3) (1996), pp 551–66 which looks at the historical background and more recent development of Strokestown House in Co. Roscommon as a museum.	**55** Letter from E.J. Shirley to E.P. Shirley, 20 Nov. 1848 (PRONI, Shirley papers, D. 3531/C/2/1).	**56** For commentaries on the ideology of housebuilding, see L.J. Proudfoot, 'Placing the imaginary: Gosford Castle and the Gosford estate, ca.1820–1900' in Hughes & Nolan (eds), *Armagh: history and society*, pp 881–916; idem, 'Place and *mentalité*: the "big house" and its locality in County Tyrone' in Dillon & Jefferies (eds), *Tyrone: history and society*, pp 511–42.

4.3 The Shell Cottage, Carton, County Kildare by Paul Ferguson

sive mansion at Dawson Grove in Monaghan in the 1770s, as well as Cremorne House in Chelsea. Richard Castle was one of the most popular architects for the landowning class in mid- eighteenth-century Ireland who had a hand in Carton, Summerhill, Powerscourt, Russborough, Hazlewood, Westport and many other houses. James Wyatt (responsible for the layout of Westport town in County Mayo), James Gandon, Robert Adam and William Chambers were popular British architects who designed many of Ireland's mansion houses of the later eighteenth century.[57] Together with stuccodores (like the Lafranchini brothers), gardeners and painters, they were responsible for creating a whole new phase in Irish buildings and landscape design mainly from the mid-eighteenth century to the mid-nineteenth century. One of the many medium-sized country houses designed by Castle was John Preston's Bellinter House in the Boyne valley in County Meath. As with all these houses, the main floor and first floor represented the domestic and formal family spaces, the basement offices being servants' workplaces, with the

57 See J. O'Brien and D. Guinness, *Great Irish houses and castles* (London, 1992), pp 258–60 for a list of eighty-six architects and craftsmen who were popular with the landed gentry in Ireland in the eighteenth and nineteenth centuries mainly. James Malton and many other artists in the eighteenth and nineteenth centuries have left a rich legacy of house portraits from town and country. See Chapter 5.

servant quarters and kitchens in one of the wings and the stables in the other. In the 1901 census it consisted of twenty-two rooms and forty-six outbuildings – drawing rooms, large and small dining rooms, billiard room, bedrooms with dressing rooms attached.[58]

Irish landowners did not invest as much as their English counterparts in tenant housing. Land agent William Steuart Trench pointed out that on the Shirley estate in 1842, only £16 14s.11d. (out of a rental income of £22,954) had been spent on three tenants' houses.[59] Many of the better managed properties and mansions were accompanied by labourer houses in villages, or ranges of terraces as in Donadea in County Kildare, as well as gate lodges and model farmyards for the demesne farm as in Carton, Westport, and Glaslough. Some estates in the nineteenth century were involved in attempts to improve the housing of their tenants, especially their labourer's houses, as in the duke of Leinster's estates in Kildare or the de Vesci estate near Abbeyleix, or on Bath estate in Monaghan. Many landowners in the post-famine period invested more in tenant housing: the Lansdowne estate subsidised the construction of houses for 123 tenants in the 1850s and 60s. The owner of a 29,000 acre estate in Kerry boasted in 1880 that over the previous thirty years he had 'built over eighty houses and offices, slated or tiled … made nearly twenty-three miles of road, built nine bridges, made twenty three miles of fences [presumably roadside], thorough drained about 500 acres, and planted about 150 acres of waste land'.[60] The Shirley estate was keen on improving housing conditions, paying particular attention to unsightly and untidy structures on the roadside. The estate possessed house plans in 1844 for a farmer holding 10–20 acres ('stairs to be of stone, two storey, 2 up 2 down, 13 foot 6 inches x 10 foot 6 inches and kitchen

---

58 There are extensive sources on Irish houses, for example: T. Reeves-Smyth, *Irish country houses* (Belfast, 1994) which is a pocket guide containing short historical profiles of thirty Irish 'Big Houses.' The Knight of Glin, D.J. Griffin and N.K. Robinson, *Vanishing country houses of Ireland* (Dublin, 1988) looks at a sample of derelict houses; see also M. Heron, *The hidden houses of Ireland* (Dublin, 1999); Maurice Craig, *Classic Irish houses of the middle size* (London, 1976); T.C. Barnard, *Making the grand figure: lives and possessions in Ireland, 1641–1770* (Yale, 2004) examines early house building in Sligo, Roscommon, Tipperary, Cavan and Clare and looks at garden layouts, as well as interior furnishings and decorations in houses; M. Bence-Jones, *Burke's guide to country houses, vol. one – Ireland* (London, 1978); idem, *A guide to Irish country houses* (London, 1988); idem, *Life in an Irish country house* (London, 1996) profiles twenty–three Big Houses; B. de Breffny and R. Ffolliott, *Houses of Ireland* (London, 1975); M. Craig, *History of Irish architecture* (London, 1982); E. McParland, 'A bibliography of Irish architectural history' in *Irish Historical Studies* (hereinafter *IHS*), xxvi, no. 102 (1988), pp 161–212; R. Loeber, 'Irish houses and castles of the late Carolingian period' in *Bulletin of the Irish Georgian Society*, 16 (1973), pp 1–69; D. Guinness and W. Ryan, *Irish houses and castles* (London, 1971); B. Jones, *Follies and grottoes* (London, 1974); J. Howley, *The follies and garden buildings of Ireland* (New Haven, 1993); E. Malins and the Knight of Glin, *Lost demesnes: Irish landscape gardening, 1660–1845* (London, 1976); D. Cannadine, *Lords and landlords: the aristocracy and the towns, 1774–1967* (Leicester, 1980); P. Somerville-Large, *The Irish country house* mentions up to 140 houses; T. Dooley, *A future for Irish historic houses* (Dublin, 2003).
59 Trench's report on the Shirley estate, Aug. 1843 (PRONI, Shirley papers, D. 3531/S/55).
60 Quoted in Donnelly, *The land and people of nineteenth-century Cork*, pp 165–69.

13 foot 6 inches x 12 foot six inches'); for a tenant of 30–60 acres (kitchen, parlour, dairy, scullery, four bedrooms, with plans for outoffices for cow house, cart house, stable, barn over cow/carthouse, corn store over stable and so on). There was also a plan for a farmyard layout and a house for a labourer or small farmer.[61] Most of these were more aspirational than real, however, as few of them were actually built.

Like many other landlords, by the mid-nineteenth century Shirley and Bath also began making financial contributions towards the erection of schools and chapels on their properties. In Leinster and Munster and more commercial agricultural regions especially, the townland farm, usually a large well-appointed farmhouse, often appropriating the townland name, incorporated some of the vanities of the Big House, with touches of classical elegance, built in box style, frequently over a basement, with avenue to a front door distinguished by fanlights and reached by steps. Other substantial houses which also mimicked the Big House were merchants houses in the hinterlands of cities like Cork, Waterford and Galway, or linen merchant, bleacher or mill-owners houses in Ulster.[62]

Vernacular buildings

Vernacular buildings, including fences, gate piers and other furniture of the local environment are especially important signatures of the local in landscape. In the absence of documentary evidence, vernacular buildings are often the only source of information on life and landscapes of households of more modest or poorer circumstances and are an important subject matter for local historians. They are ordinary, everyday, workaday constructions by craftsmen, tapping into their local culture and heritage, and intimately connected with the environmental resources of their locality. Most elements of the vernacular blend into the landscape to a greater extent than élite architectures (which often transported construction materials from further afield, such as the popular Portland stone from Wales, or wood product from Europe or the Empire). The reasons for particular styles of building are often lost to us today: the unnecessarily large gate piers probably simply reflect tradition. For historians, geographers, cultural anthropologists and archaeologists, vernacular architecture is important because in a globalising world this unique and characteristic flavour of our landscape is being eroded or obliterated. Estyn Evans was the first to examine systematically a wide range of vernacular features in the Irish landscape – houses, outbuildings, gate posts and piers, thatched roof styles, hearth and interior furnishings, all coming to the end of their lives when

---

61 Improvement books 1844–78 (PRONI, Shirley papers, D. 3531/M/7/1); P.J. Duffy, 'Management problems on a large estate in mid-nineteenth century Ireland: William Steuart Trench's report on the Shirley estate in 1843' in *Clogher Rec.*, xvi (1) (1997), 101–22. **62** K. Rankin, *The linen houses of the Lagan valley* (Belfast, 2002) illustrates accounts of some dozens of houses in Waringstown, Donacloney, Dromore, Hillsborough, Lisburn, Lambeg, Edenderry; see also J.H. Murnane and P. Murnane, *At the ford of the birches: the history of Ballybay, its people and vicinity* (Monaghan, 1999), pp 254–93; idem, 'The linen industry in the parish of Aughnamullen and its impact on the town of Ballybay, 1740–1835' in *Clogher Rec.*, xii, no. 3 (1987), 334–68.

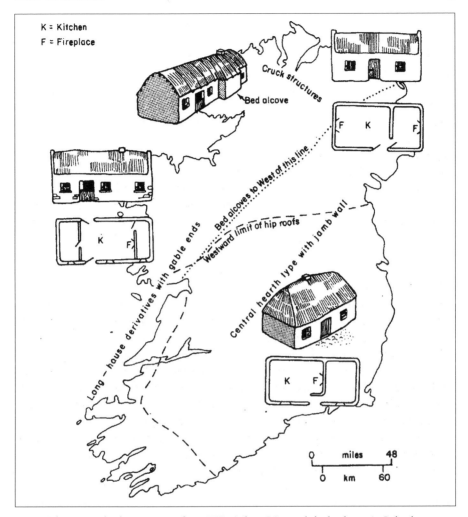

K = Kitchen
F = Fireplace

Cruck structures

Bed alcove

Bed alcoves to West of this line

Westward limit of hip roofs

Long - house derivatives with gable ends

Central hearth type with jamb wall

F K F

K F

K F

miles   48

km   60

4.4   Irish vernacular house types; from F.H. Aalen, *Man and the landscape in Ireland* (London, 1978), p. 251

he was writing in the 1940s.[63] Piers or gate pillars, for example, mortared with cone-shaped tops, were especially common in east Ulster and down the east coast as far as Wexford and reflected regional styles of construction. House types, roof types, materials used, location of hearth and doors, construction of chimneys, outshots, lobby entrances and so on had distinctive geographies.[64]

63 E. Estyn Evans, *Irish heritage: the landscape, the people and their work* (Dundalk, 1942), *Irish folk ways* (London, 1957) and *Mourne Country* (Dundalk, 1951).   **64** Today most of these elements of the vernacular landscape are only to be found in folk museums, such as the Evans-inspired Ulster Folk and Transport Museum, the Ulster-American Folk Park, Turlough Park, Bunratty Folk Park and many local museums and heritage centres.

Few Irish farmhouses pre-date *c.*1700, with seventeenth-century warfare leading to widespread destruction of property.[65] The typical farmhouse from the late seventeenth century was a modest thatched structure, one-storey high with an elongated, rectangular plan, rarely more than one room deep, with one room opening onto another. Local materials were used – stone or mud for the walls, straw or rushes for thatch. There were contrasts in vernacular building styles between the poorer, more mountainous and wetter west and north-west regions, and the richer lowlands of the east and south, which also mirrored differences in farm structures and agricultural economies. In the former, stone dwellings with gable ends and hearths on the gables were characteristic, part of a long-house tradition which incorporated both byre and dwelling until the nineteenth century. These have been called 'direct-entry' houses with opposite doors opening directly into the living area. There was a tradition of single-room houses built over a cowbyre, or half-houses to be extended later when resources allowed, in Gweedore and the Rosses in Donegal, as well as parts of Derry and Tyrone. In the east and south, hip-roofed houses of mud walls with central hearths and lobby entrances predominated. In the late eighteenth and early nineteenth centuries, substantial two-storeyed thatched houses, with a more formal ordering of plan and façade, began to appear, reflecting wealth accumulation, and are found more in the north of Ireland and the lowlands of the south and east associated with planter families and larger farms. Many of these substantial farmhouses incorporated some formal architectural elements such as central chimney stacks. Often such houses were named after the townland, as in Jenkinstown House or Culmullin House, in County Meath, for example.[66]

The tens of thousands of landless labourers in pre-famine Ireland typically occupied one-roomed cabins made of mud or sod, which were classically biodegradable and have literally melted from the Irish landscape, in many cases with the class that built them.[67] In 1823 Bishop Doyle described passing 'through a large part of the Bog of Allen, where a colony chiefly of Connaught people, have dug out habitations from the immense cliffs of turf, where fire and water seem to be the only elements given them for subsistence; yet they are healthful, and seem to be blessed with a numerous progeny.'[68] Those which remained in the post-famine decades were

65 Thomas Dineley, *Observations in a voyage through the kingdom of Ireland … in the year 1681*, ed. J. Graves (Dublin, 1870) has descriptions of local houses, chimneys etc.   **66** See F.H.A. Aalen, 'Buildings' in Aalen et al. (eds), *Atlas of the Irish rural landscape*, pp 145–79; idem, 'Vernacular rural dwellings of the Wicklow mountains' in Hannigan & Nolan (eds), *Wicklow: history and society*, pp 581–624; B. Walker, 'A Donegal building type: farmhouse or farm building?' in *Ulster Folklife*, 35 (1989), pp 1–7; A. Gailey, 'Vernacular dwellings of Clogher diocese' in *Clogher Rec.*, ix (1977), pp 187–231 and idem, 'Vernacular housing' in A.J. Rowan (ed.), *North west Ulster: the counties of Londonderry, Donegal, Fermanagh and Tyrone* (London, 1979), pp 87–103; K. Danaher, *Ireland's vernacular architecture* (Dublin, 1975); J. Feehan, *Laois: an environmental history* (Stradbally, 1983), chapter xiii on 'buildings in the landscape'.   **67** See L. Shields and D. Fitzgerald, 'The "Night of the Big Wind" in Ireland, 6–7 January 1839' in *Ir. Geography*, 22 (1989), pp 31–43 which destroyed an enormous number of houses poorly sited and constructed in the West of Ireland.   **68** Quoted in Rev. M. Comerford, *Collections*

gradually replaced in public housing programmes under the Labourers' acts from 1883. County councils erected *c.*50,000 cottages by 1921 mainly in Munster and Leinster where labourers were most numerous.[69] The government in the 1930s continued to fund cottages for labourers and small farmers (who in some cases were worse off) in the hope of arresting emigration and stabilising rural populations. The Congested Districts Board and its successor the Irish Land Commission also replaced large numbers of small-farm houses in the west of Ireland in the late nineteenth and first half of the twentieth century. The Land Commission settlements in the Midlands from the 1940s introduced many hundreds of new farm buildings. Several models of house designs were used, many of them incorporating elements of local building traditions.

A significant number of vernacular houses remains in Fingal in north Dublin, many still thatched, some with open hearths and canopies of clay, wattle or stone. Farmyards in these landscapes are mainly of the small courtyard type. Examples occur in Kitchenstown, Balrickard, Bog of the Ring, Rush and Lusk.[70] An example of a small farmer's house in Stalleen in the Boyne Valley consists of a modest single-storey associated with a holding of seven acres. Its central hearth and lobby-entrance, hipped roof of oaten straw (now under corrugated iron) are very characteristic of eastern Ireland. Stalleen also contains the remains of one-roomed labourer houses.[71]

In north Kildare a smattering of interesting vernacular buildings survives, though they are being rapidly inundated by modern housing. In Rathcoffey, for instance, a small chapel, according to local tradition dating from *c.*1710, contains features of a traditional barn structure and a number of houses nearby show traces of vernacular origins (central hearths and hipped roofs). Painestown contains a newly renovated house (and former shop) which is mud-walled and thatched. At Ballynagappagh is a long, thatched house with mud walls, which was associated with a farm of *c.*80 acres in Griffith's Valuation. It may pre-date the long, straight, late eighteenth-century road on which it now stands. There are examples of a farmhouse and a bog-edge squatter's house in Downings and Drehid townlands. South County Wexford continues to hold an important collection of traditional thatched houses,

relating to the diocese of Kildare and Leighlin (3 vols, Dublin, 1883–6), iii, 85; see also J. Bell, '"Miserable hovels and substantial habitations": the housing of rural labourers in Ireland since the eighteenth century' in *Folk Life*, 34 (6) (1996), pp 43–56. **69** F.H.A. Aalen, 'Ireland' in C.G. Pooley (ed.), *Housing strategies in Europe, 1880–1930* (Leicester, 1992), pp 132–64; A-M. Walsh, 'Root them in the land: cottage schemes for agricultural labourers' in J. Augusteijn (ed.), *Ireland in the 1930s* (Dublin, 1999), pp 47–66. **70** See B. O'Reilly, *Living under thatch: vernacular architecture in Co. Offaly* (Cork, 2004); idem (ed.), *Vernacular buildings of east Fingal* (Dublin, 1993); Dept of Environment and Local Government, *Report on the present and future protection of thatched structures in Ireland* (2 vols, Dublin, 2005). DoELG, *An introduction to the architectural heritage of Fingal* (Dublin, 2002). See also The Heritage Council's *Policy paper on Irish thatched roofs and the national heritage* (Kilkenny, 2002); M. Higginbotham, *Reports on thatched dwellings in Ireland: Dublin, Kildare, Wexford, Wicklow and the Aran Islands* (Dublin, 1987–90). **71** G. Stout, *Newgrange and the bend of the Boyne* (Cork, 2002), pp 152–6.

supported by a locally revived thatching tradition. Poulwitch farm in Mayglass is a thatched one and a half-storey lobby entrance mud-walled house which was probably built in the late seventeenth or early eighteenth century. Kilmore Quay contains approximately seventeen thatched houses built in the vernacular style.

The manuscript enumeration schedules of the 1911 census, in conjunction with field interviews with older residents, provided the following information on Loughloon village, near Westport in County Mayo: it contained twenty-five stone-built houses in 1911, all of which were thatched and the same size, mainly three rooms and a couple of small outbuildings: each also had a duck house, henhouse and pig house. Sedge or rush thatch was used mainly on the outhouses, which did not last as long as the oat, wheaten or rye thatch on the dwelling house. Wheaten or rye thatch also lasted longer on the sunny side of the roof. Reeds were used for the 'buntacht', or starting off the thatching. Most of these houses had a 'cailleach' (or outshot) near the fire which belonged to the old people.

William Carleton has described the material living conditions of many such houses in his stories from the early nineteenth century. In 'Dandy Kehoe's wedding', Ballycomaisy, though clearly ironic in tenor, had many of the elements of a pre-famine landscape of poverty:

> Most of the houses were of mud, a few being of stone, one or two of which had the honour of being slated on the front side of the roof, and rustically thatched on the back, where ostentation was not necessary. There were two or three shops, a liberal sprinkling of public houses, a chapel, a little out of the town, and an old dilapidated market house near the centre.[72]

Such housing conditions, which appalled some of the officer reporters in the Ordnance Survey Memoirs in the 1830s, continued in some places into the twentieth century. In 1905 J.M. Synge described a house in Connemara, where the smoke exited through a hole in the roof and a boy of ten, minding three babies, shared the room with a cow, two calves and a few sickly-looking hens.[73]

Other local buildings in the vernacular tradition were the blacksmith forges which in the era of horsepower lay at the heart of local rural communities, as well as byres, pigsties, hen houses, booley huts and other outbuildings.[74] Sweat houses (with holy wells), the Irish equivalent of the Scandinavian sauna, also reflected the role of traditional folk medicine in rural society. The twentieth-century countryside was marked by parish halls and later dance halls, of determinedly functional rather

---

72 W. Carleton, 'Dandy Kehoe's christening' in *Traits and stories of the Irish peasantry* (2 vols, 6th (William Tegg) edition, London, 1865), i, 182–3. **73** J.M. Synge, quoted by A.M. Dalsimer, '"The Irish peasant had all his heart": J.M. Synge in The Country Shop' in A.M. Dalsimer (ed.), *Visualizing Ireland: national identity and the pictorial tradition* (Boston, 1993), p. 210. **74** Many of these were small corbelled buildings in places where timber was scarce: see, for example, R.H. Buchanan, 'Corbelled structures in Lecale, County Down' in *UJA*, 19 (1956), pp 92–112.

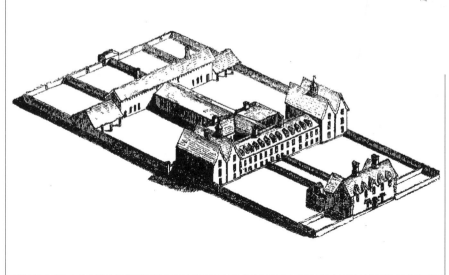

4.5 Workhouse design, 1840s

than aesthetic significance, handball alleys (now derelict structures rapidly falling out of folk memory), and local branch creameries which are similarly abandoned. Older GAA halls have been largely succeeded by modern community centres.

Workhouses

Workhouses were important additions to townscapes in the nineteenth century. Under the 1838 Poor Law Act, 130 workhouses were built throughout the country by 1846, one of the first interventions by the state to address rising numbers of poor landless people – 'paupers' in the contemporary idiom. With their rather forbidding standard architectural design by English architect George Wilkinson, and internal regimes intended to discourage applicants, many are still extant today.[75] They were usually sited in urban places centrally located in the Union. For those who entered Irish workhouses in the 1840s conditions were miserable. Dormitories were cramped with poor ventilation. Beds usually consisted of a platform of planks and a straw mattress covered in rough rags. There was a lack of water and the only toilet facilities were large urination tubs in each ward which often overflowed. All meals had to be eaten in total silence and even plates might not be provided for food. Visitors could only be met in the presence of one of the workhouse officials. The onset of famine in the 1840s overwhelmed the workhouse system which in many regions proved totally incapable of coping with the numbers of paupers.[76]

75 See M.H. Gould, *The workhouses of Ulster* (Belfast, 1983).   **76** See J. O'Connor, *The workhouses of Ireland* (Dublin, 1995) which looks at the construction of the workhouses, their management during the mid-nineteenth century and includes in appendixes contracts for their construction in the 1840s; also Lyne, 'William Steuart Trench and post-famine

studies of individual workhouses can be found generally in local historical journals.[77]

Military structures

Ireland with its strong colonial experience was intensively garrisoned from the eighteenth century with barracks in a great many towns and villages. During Britain's wars with her continental rivals, especially France, Ireland was always perceived as a vulnerable back door to the British Isles. In the mid-nineteenth century there were more troops (a large proportion of them Irish) in Ireland than there were in Britain.[78] Barracks in many of Ireland's garrison towns had an important social and economic as well as architectural influence on the town. Extensive and imposing architectural statements, they often provided a unifying theme which had long-term implications for the evolving morphology of the urban space of the town, as for example, in Mitchelstown, Fermoy, Athlone, Longford, Newbridge, Roscrea and Templemore. Throughout the country the armed Irish Constabulary (RIC after 1867) occupied hundreds of barracks, many of which continued as Garda Síochána stations in the twentieth century.

Industrial landscapes

With the exception of north-east Ulster, Ireland experienced more limited environmental impacts of the age of industry which transformed extensive parts of the British and north European landscapes. Ireland remained a predominantly rural and agricultural economy with consequently mostly benign effects on its landscapes. Industrial activity had a mainly local impact as well, as evidenced by comparatively small amount of charcoal and iron ore activity in the seventeenth century, later some coal mining in Castlecomer, Coalisland and Arigna coalfields, and localised examples of mining works which lasted into the nineteenth century at Glendalough, Glenmalure, Avoca in Wicklow and Allihies in west Cork.[79] Ironworks from the seventeenth centuries required very basic infrastructure of accommodation and trackways and have only shadowy remnants in the landscape.[80]

emigration from Kenmare to America, 1850–55'; http://users.ox.ac.uk/~peter/workhouse/ contains a comprehensive range of data and details (including many photographs and illustrations) on Irish workhouses.   **77** R. Barrett, 'Dunshaughlin workhouse, 1838–1849' in *Ríocht na Midhe*, xvi (2005), pp 105–19, for example, examines the background of the Poor Law and its local application in Meath.   **78** See Prunty, 'Military barracks and mapping' in Clarke et al. (eds), *Surveying Ireland's past*, pp 477–534. Forts, pillboxes and blockhouses built by the defence forces at the outset of the second world war are discussed at length by Stout in her *Newgrange and the bend of the Boyne* (Cork, 2002).   **79** A.R. Orme, *Ireland* (London, 1970) p. 223 suggests that Castlecomer and Arigna coalfields recapture the atmosphere of pre-Industrial Revolution British coalfields. In many of these cases, the relict remains in the landscape of pumps and old machinery, shafts and spoil heaps, as well as local records (seen in Arigna Visitor Centre) might repay investigation. See W. Nolan, *Fassadinan: land, settlement and society in southeast Ireland, 1600–1850* (Dublin, 1979), pp 142–8.   **80** See C. Rynne, 'Mining and quarrying' in Aalen et al. (eds), *Atlas of the Irish rural landscape*, pp 221–4; idem, *A life of usefulness: Abraham Beale and the Monard ironworks* (Cork, 2001).

Mills

Mills are the most common industrial structure in the landscape and were a crucial by-product of the rural economy. From the early medieval period horizontal water mills had smaller wheels, providing less power than the vertical mill wheel which marks the modern period. Water mills were most common in Ulster with its intricate lakelandscapes. Many preliminary plantation surveys in the sixteenth and seventeenth centuries, which were interested in the potential assets of an area, drew particular attention to opportunities for water-powered mills.[81] In 1695 John Leslie of Castle Leslie in Monaghan leased the corn mills of the estate for four years at £25 annual rent together with the yearly duties of providing '24 fat hens, 2 fat sows, 3 sacks of malt, feeding for 2 sows and their followers 4 of which to be fattened for pork or bacon, feeding for poultry and half of what fish is taken at the said mills; to allow a house and garden at each mill for wives and to keep the mills and lands in good repair.'[82] On Ulster estates tenants were tied to local corn mills, paying tolls of one-sixteenth of the grain. The corn was frequently winnowed on a nearby elevated site. Wind power was especially important during the tillage expansion of the second half of the eighteenth century when many windmills were built, especially in the commercial cereal lands of Leinster. There are quite a number surviving today as characteristic masonry stumps, particularly concentrated in the Ards peninsula and south-east Wexford.

In the late eighteenth century milling and warehousing, springing directly from a booming agricultural economy, which succeeded the woodland-based charcoal smelting and tanning of the seventeenth century, made the greatest impacts in south Leinster and east Munster, along river valleys like the Barrow.[83] Many of these mills are imposing structures of stone, such as New Haggard mills near Trim or Slane mill in Meath. John Feehan refers to corn mills in the 1840s in County Laois at Mountmellick, Coolrain, Portlaoise, Castletown, Rathdowney, Donaghmore, Abbeyleix and Stradbally, bolting mills at Durrow, Rathdowney, Coolrain, woollen and cotton factories in Mountmellick (as well as an iron foundry, breweries, distilleries, tan yards and a flour mill), spinning and weaving mills at Mountrath (and a brewery and malting establishment) and a mill for rape oil at Donaghmore, woollen factories and bolting mills at Abbeyleix, woollen factory and brewery in Ballinakill and tobacco, candle and soap factories in Portarlington.[84]

The complex processes involved in linen manufacture resulted in substantial engineering and building activity throughout the countrysides of Ulster especially, until the industry concentrated in the towns of east Ulster in the latter half of the nineteenth century. Most of the early mills were established in the hilly countryside

81 For example, 'A booke of survey of ffarney and Clancarvile' by William Smith, 1612 (Longleat Library, Bath Papers, Irish box 1); see also R. Loeber, 'Biographical dictionary of engineers in Ireland, 1600–1730' in *Irish Sword*, 13 (50) (1977), pp 30–44; 13 (51) (1977), pp 106–22; 13 (52) (1978–9), pp 230–55; 13 (53) (1979), pp 283–314.   **82** Deeds of agreement, 6 Apr. 1695, Leslie papers, Appendix B, no. 186, PRONI.   **83** See the Kings River valley in Kilkenny mapped by Jack Burtchaell in Aalen et al. (eds), *Atlas of the Irish rural landscape*, p. 228.   **84** Feehan, *Laois: an environmental history*, p. 343.

to avail of water supplies and space for bleachgreens. Landowners interested in encouraging the industry offered favourable leases for the erection of mills and ancillary works such as bleachgreens. Local small-scale impacts were significant in pre-industrial Irish landscapes, with corn mills, scutching mills and beetling mills closely integrated in local economies, located on quite small streams – which were engineered with millraces, dams, ponds, and sluice gates. The cluster of linen mills on the River Callan in mid-Armagh, and in the Lough Egish district in mid-Monaghan were vibrant rural industrial landscapes which reflected the ready availability of water power.[85] The lakes and streams in Aghnamullen parish in south Monaghan were controlled by an intricate system of sluice gates and dams which powered up to two dozen mills in the early nineteenth century. Creeve bleach green and district contained fourteen water mills in 1846, with ponds which provided water during periods of heaviest use. The first mills were erected on leases granted by Lord Massereene in 1749. Lord Cremorne leased lands to Alexander Jackson of Ballybay in 1785 for the erection of 'bleaching works, races and greens' which had a noteworthy local landscape impact in the mid-nineteenth century. Most of the mills were three stories high and one of the bleaching greens was 57 acres in extent.[86] In Griffith's Valuation House Books (1839), the local extent of the linen industry in the townlands of Aghnamullen parish is well represented, in spite of the decline of the industry as it retreated to east Ulster[87]:

> Creeve: six beetling mills, bleach mill, lapping sheds, offices etc., turf houses, yard wash house, vitriol house, workshops, smithy, three engine houses, boiler house
> Drumfaldra: two corn mills (former bleaching mills)
> Corwillin: scutching mill (formerly beetling mill), old beetling mill, boiling house, stores, sheds and offices
> Bowelk: beetling mill
> Lisnagalliagh: corn mill (former beetling mill)

85 W.J. Smyth, 'Locational patterns and trends within the pre-famine linen industry' in *Ir. Geography*, 8 (1975), pp 97–110; W.H. Crawford, 'The origins of the linen industry in north Armagh and the Lagan valley' in *Ulster Folklife*, 17 (1971), 42–51; idem, *Domestic industry in Ireland* (Dublin, 1971); idem, *The impact of the domestic linen industry in Ulster* (Belfast, 2005); see also B. Collins, P. Ollerenshaw and T. Parkhill (eds), *Industry, trade and people in Ireland, 1650–1950* (Belfast, 2005). For an index of mid-nineteenth century mills, see W.E. Hogg, *The millers and the mills of Ireland about 1850* (Dublin, 1997) which lists mills and millers by townland, type of mill, dimensions of water wheels and valuation; see also Valuation Office Ireland, mills books associated with the Townland Valuation; C. Rynne, *Industrial Ireland*, pp 194–234.   **86** OS *Memoirs of Ireland: counties of south Ulster*, ed. Day & McWilliams, pp 71–2. **87** From Murnane and Murnane, *At the ford of the birches*, pp 254–92; see also idem, 'The linen industry in the parish of Aughnamullen, Co. Monaghan' in *Clogher Rec.*, xii (1987), pp 334–68. To encourage the industry, the Linen Board granted spinning wheels according to the amount of flax grown: over one acre-four spinning wheels, 3 roods – 3 wheels, 2 roods – 2 wheels, 1 rood – 1 wheel.

Derrygooney: two corn mills (formerly a beetling mill), tuck mill, mill races, mill dam

Shantonagh: two mills

Reduff: beetling mill

Cornacarrow: spinning mill

Laragh: carding mill, two beetling mills, hackling house, spinnning mill, bleaching mills, flax mill, corn mill

Even the most modest scutching mill sometimes had a mill row to accommodate its workers in Ulster. Industrial villages or towns were also established by some landowners or investors in improvement in the eighteenth and nineteenth centuries, as in Portlaw, Prosperous, Collon, Monivea, Stratford-on-Slaney, for example, often reflecting contemporary utopian interests among gentry to improve the lives, welfare and behaviour of tenants.[88] Prosperous was a small industrial town erected around a cotton mill in the early 1780s, close to the Grand Canal. It was a response to government incentives encouraging the dispersal of industry (with its potential for agitation and unrest) from Dublin and six long, straight roads converge on the village of the kind widely sponsored at the time by the Grand Juries. Despite its optimistic name, the cotton enterprise collapsed in the 1790s and the settlement was burnt down in the 1798 uprising and never survived competition with Lancashire after the Union. At its peak, *c.*5,000 were employed: most of the handloom weavers lived in local cabins, though remnants of some of the original weavers' houses survive. Stratford-on-Slaney was established by Lord Aldborough in County Wicklow in the late eighteenth century with textile mills employing over a thousand in the 1830s, exploiting links with industrial developments in Lancashire, but it too failed. In the nineteenth century more successful industrial settlements were established in Bessbrook in County Armagh, based on industrialisation of the linen industry and Portlaw, County Waterford, based on the cotton industry.[89] Both succeeded in constructing extensive mill works and laid out formal urban streetscapes with superior housing for their workers.

In addition most towns in Ireland had small local manufactories in the eighteenth and early nineteenth centuries such as distilleries, breweries, tobacco manufactories, chandlers and craft industries like nail makers and spade makers, all of them usually catalogued in Lewis's *Topographical dictionary* (1837). New economic realities after the Union witnessed the demise of many of these industries or the consolidation and concentration of activity in fewer but bigger enterprises. There

88 See D. Macneice, 'Industrial villages of Ulster, 1800–1900' in P. Roebuck (ed.), *Plantation to partition: essays in Ulster history in honour of J.L. McCracken* (Belfast, 1981), pp 172–90; Graham & Proudfoot, *Urban improvement in provincial Ireland, 1700–1840*; E.R.R. Green, *The industrial archaeology of County Down* (Belfast, 1963); F. Hamond and M. McMahon, *Recording and conserving Ireland's industrial heritage* (Heritage Council, Kilkenny, 2002). **89** See T. Hunt, *Portlaw, County Waterford: portrait of an industrial village and its cotton industry* (Dublin, 2000).

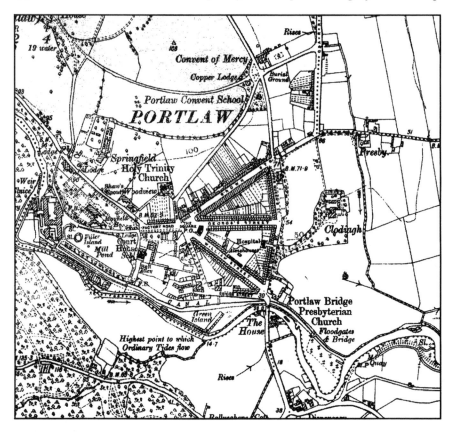

4.6 Portlaw, County Waterford, cotton town of the Malcomsons, 1860s

were approximately 2,200 malt houses associated with a widespread brewing and distilling industry scattered throughout the island in the late eighteenth century, though these had declined to 388 producing twice the output in 1835.[90]

The mechanisation of the linen industry concentrated capital and development in the Belfast region and along the Lagan valley, with large industrial towns dominated by textile mills, factories and rows of rebrick back-to-back houses resembling the emerging industrial landscapes of the north of England. Shipbuilding and its downstream industries in Belfast drew thousands of in-migrants to the rapidly growing city from throughout Ulster.[91] By mid-nineteenth century there were up to twenty iron foundries in Belfast and other towns manufacturing machinery and boilers for the mills and workshops of the city, as well as fittings and

90 L.M. Cullen, *An economic history of Ireland since 1660* (London, 1972), p. 123.   91 PRONI, *Problems of a growing city: Belfast, 1780–1870* (Belfast, 1973); C.E.B. Brett, *Georgian Belfast, 1750–1850: maps, buildings and trades* (Dublin, 2004); R. Gillespie and S. Royle, *Belfast, part 1 to 1840*. Irish Historic Towns Atlas, no. 12 (Dublin, 2003).

transport infrastructure for new towns in the province. The linen industry had mechanised early on, with scutching mills from mid-eighteenth century, carding and hackling mills in the early decades of the nineteenth century, and spinning mills gradually taking over from hand-spinning in the early nineteenth century. Wet-spinning mills expanded rapidly from 1825 and by 1850, sixty-three of the sixty-nine flax spinning mills in Ireland were located in Ulster. The penultimate stage of linen weaving was slower to mechanise owing to the persistence of low-cost handloom weaving in rural areas. From 1850, however, power looms were rapidly introduced into the north. The final production stage in the linen industry was bleaching, which in fact was the first to experience 'industrial' processes. Mills which used large quantities of water for washing and 'beetling' the webs of cloth were established early in the eighteenth century, with large bleachgreens in accompanying fields where the brown webs were spread to bleach in the sun. During the early nineteenth century, the bleaching process concentrated in larger establishments in the east of the province, and smaller bleachgreens like those in Creeve in Monaghan fell into decline.

Coastal works

During the Middle Ages, the English settlements centred on the east coast supported a range of small port towns trading across the Irish Sea – from Carrickfergus south through Carlingford, Dundalk and Drogheda to Youghal on the south coast. Dublin, Cork, Galway, Limerick and Waterford had substantial facilities of wooden wharfs, as at Wood Quay in Dublin, with cranes and repair and coppering yards, as well as the administrative buildings which supported customs, excise and money transactions. The smaller fragmented Gaelic lordships had less regional trade, with less need for elaborate port facilities. Gaelic harbours required only sheltered anchorages and safe landing places where lesser quantities of goods could be offloaded from smaller boats.[92]

By the early nineteenth century, the maritime economy of much of the west remained comparatively underdeveloped and following the Union, the Board of Works was involved in investment in piers and quays to assist local development of the fishing industry, for example. Many of these were important works of engineering, such as Clifden and Cleggan, designed by engineers like Alexander Nimmo in the 1820s.[93] Others were the result of Congested District Board initiatives in the late nineteenth century, in many cases extending the older piers to take advantage of the boom in herring and mackerel fishing.

Marking the dangerous meeting zones between landscape and seascape, light-houses are aesthetically attractive features of the built environment, which in the north Atlantic world feature regularly in postcard collections. They are usually

---

92 See C. Breen, 'The maritime cultural landscape in medieval Gaelic Ireland' in Duffy et al. (eds), *Gaelic Ireland*, pp 418–35. A map of Castlemaine castle *c*.1570, reproduced in Swift, *Historical maps of Ireland*, p. 29, shows a landing place.   **93** K. Villiers-Tuthill, *Alexander Nimmo & the western district: emerging infrastructure in pre-famine Ireland* (Clifden, 2006).

4.7 'Bleach green', wood engraving from a drawing by J.H. Burgess in Mr and Mrs S.C. Hall, *Ireland: its scenery, character, &c* [3 vols, London, 1841–3], vol. III, p. 94. Reproduced by permission of the Librarian, NUI Maynooth, from the collections of St Patrick's College, Maynooth

socially as well as physically solitary buildings of great grace and beauty, representing extraordinary feats of engineering and architecture in some of the most hazardous and hostile environments in the country, as for example, the Fastnet Rock Lighthouse in Cork or Eagle Island, County Mayo. The Hook lighthouse is one of the earliest, reputed to have been first constructed in the twelfth and thirteenth centuries to guide shipping into Waterford.[94] The records and logs (in the care of the Commissioners of Irish Lights, Dublin) kept by lighthouse keepers represent an important source of information on the social history of these buildings.

Coastguard stations are frequently imposing structures whose histories have largely been forgotten. Like the RIC barracks, they were part of the fabric of authority of the British state in the nineteenth century, the eyes and ears of Empire

94 D.B. Hague and R. Christie, *Lighthouses: their architecture, history and archaeology* (Llandysul, 1975); K. McCarthy, *Lighthouses of Ireland* (Sarasota [Fla.], 1997) discusses thirty lighthouses round the coast, with further reading on each one; B. Long, *Bright lights, white water: the lighthouses of Ireland* (Dublin, 1997); R.M. Taylor, *Lighthouses of Ireland* (Cork, 2004); B. Colfer, *The Hook peninsula, County Wexford* (Cork, 2004).

4.8 Rosmoney Coastguard Station, County Mayo

or Castle designed to stamp out smuggling, poitín making, plunder of wrecks and to maintain surveillance and security along the coast. Many of the coastguards were Englishmen from the west country, some of whose surnames can still be found in coastal communities in the west of Ireland. Seven to a boat, they rowed on patrol up and down their beat up to 20–30 miles per day. During the Great Famine the coastguard in remote western districts was given responsibility for relief distribution. The buildings were substantial barrack-like structures which in many cases continue to withstand Atlantic gales. Coastguard files in the Admiralty records at Kew in London record details on the names of officers, living conditions and local circumstances of each station.[95] Martello towers were erected (1804–10) around the coast at strategically important points such as Cork harbour, Dublin Bay, the Shannon estuary, Galway Bay and Lough Foyle, as a signalling defensive network during the Napoleonic war.

Infrastructural developments
In a general sense, infrastructural investment in the pre-modern period was mostly privately generated by local lords in areas under their control. Occasionally, in the fifteenth century, there were crown subsidies awarded for the erection of fortified houses of fixed dimensions on the borders of the Pale. The emergence of a more powerful modern state apparatus in the seventeenth and eighteenth centuries saw

95 W. Webb, *Coastguard! an official history of HM coastguard* (HMSO: London, 1976); B. Scarlett, *Shipminder* (London, 1971); E.P. Symes, 'The coastguard in Ireland' in *Irish Sword*, xxiii (2002), pp 201–10.

an increased degree of public investment by the parliament in Dublin, though as in England most of the infrastructural developments in the eighteenth century were privately funded. Private landowning interests in Ireland remained dominant and were keen to restrict government intervention although availing of opportunities for appointments to sinecures in the administration. Taxation policies were limited and government legislation aimed at enabling or subsidising local private initiatives, such as inland navigation schemes, turnpike trusts, military barracks and the promotion of linen manufacture, were controlled by the propertied classes who managed to corner most of the public investment.[96] Most local investment in roads or market houses, for instance, came through Grand Juries at county and barony levels. Gaols, however, like barracks, were the result of government initiative.

Records of the eighteenth-century Irish parliament contain wide-ranging information on local initiatives supported by the Dublin government in the so-called 'age of improvement', recording the genesis of much that is valued in modern heritage landscapes. For instance, in the early 1780s amounts ranging from £500 to £10,000 were granted to the trustees of Cork Harbour for its improvement; to the Dublin Society (£10,000) for improvement of husbandry and other useful arts – 'one half ... to be applied to the encouragement of agriculture and planting'; to the company of undertakers of the Grand Canal to complete the new Circular Road around the City of Dublin; to Protestant Charter schools; to St Patrick's hospital; to the Board of First Fruits for building new churches; for the erection of Dungarvan quay; for improvement of the Boyne navigation; for the erection of the Dublin Baths; to rebuild Kilkenny College; to construct a bridge over the Liffey at Island Bridge, to improve the turnpike road at Chapelizod; to the Commissioners for making wide and convenient passages from Dublin Castle to the Parliament House, for various county infirmaries, and to the Commissioners of Barracks (£12,000) to complete the barracks at Longford and Palatine Square in Dublin.[97]

Following the Union, the British administration took a more proactive role in addressing regional inequalities, and local communities were to become more aware of increasing intrusion in their lives by agents of the state, such as the Bogs Commissioners, the Geological Survey, the Ordnance Survey, Griffith's Valuation and government commissions of enquiry like the Devon Commission, and census enumerators. The Board of Works was established in 1831 to centralise and supervise state investment in roads, canals and other public works, especially in more remote districts. Although it was the age of laissez-faire economics, there was growing pressure on the state to assist with the modernisation of infrastructure to encourage regional development. Improving accessibility through connecting places was an important part of the story of landscape evolution and so investment in infrastructure such as roads, canals, railways, as well as telegraph, telephone and

---

96 See Barnard, *A new anatomy of Ireland*, pp 164–72.   **97** *Journal of the House of Commons of the kingdom of Ireland*, vol. x, 12 Oct. 1779–2 Sept. 1780, appendixed table of payments 1777–79; see also Johnston-Liik, *History of the Irish parliament*.

electricity have helped to reduce the problems of distance and remoteness. They also of course helped to open up areas to emigration in the nineteenth century.

Roads

Roads represent the most universal way to experience the landscape. Vidal de la Blache suggested that the road 'sows seeds of life – houses, hamlets, villages and towns.'[98] Roads are primary aspects of settlement landscapes, linking houses and towns, though the history of roads will show that apart from the organic evolution of trackways, the development of public roads was a long-drawn out process with significant economic and landscape implications.[99] Roads have a direct physical impact on the landscape: the average width of a modern four-lane motorway today excluding the land on either side is 27 metres compared with a minimum width of 12 feet in 1727, 30 feet for new roads in 1759 (including a minimum of 14 feet of gravelled surface) and of 42–52 feet which was set as the width for the new mailcoach roads authorised by parliament in 1792.

In the medieval period, although roads were bad and life was local, élites like lords and clergy, for instance, travelled incessantly through their territories. This was the only way to keep them in order and to maintain their coherence. The medieval world was a local world with no integration of the economy on a national basis. Towns were limited to their hinterlands, with interregional links being poorly developed. Drover tracks for the movement of animals often forged main route-ways. Alfred Smyth has mapped routeways across the midland eskers which appear to have linked up monastic settlements in early medieval Ireland.[1] Walking was the main mode of transport for most people in the Middle Ages, with horseback travel being expensive and available only to élites such as the Italian bankers of the thirteenth century and the grey merchants (so-called from the dust on their long-distance packhorses) who travelled throughout the island in the later Middle Ages: creels and panniers and slide cars are legacies of these primitive road conditions. Towns on navigable rivers did best because river transport was the easiest and fastest way to move material and goods.[2] With the gradual transition from seventeenth-century horseback travel to increasing eighteenth-century wheeled traffic, roads necessarily improved. And the multiplication of wagons and coaches, carriages, gigs and other horse-drawn cars into the nineteenth century led to further road improvements.

---

98 E. de Martonne (ed.), *Principles of human geography by P. Vidal de la Blache* (London, 1926), p. 370. **99** J. Killen, 'Communications' in Aalen et al. (eds), *Atlas of the Irish rural landscape*, pp 206–19; K.B. Nowlan (ed.), *Travel and transport in Ireland* (Dublin & New York, 1973); J.H. Andrews, 'Road planning in Ireland before the railway age' in *Ir. Geography*, 5 (1964), pp 17–41; L.M. Cullen, 'Man, landscape and roads: the changing eighteenth century' in Nolan (ed.), *The shaping of Ireland*, pp 123–36. **1** Smyth, *Celtic Leinster*. **2** Gillespie, *Colonial Ulster*, pp 21–4 discusses transport by road in Co. Down in the difficult conditions of the early seventeenth century. See also W.H. Crawford, 'The construction of the Ulster road network 1700–1850' in *The history of technology, science and society, 1750–1914: symposium, September 1989*

By the early seventeenth century Ireland was being incorporated into the new British state with the beginnings of consolidation of an integrated island-wide economy. According to the 1615 Highway Act, road maintenance was the responsibility of the parishes through which they passed, with a parish vestry levy of six days labour per annum (between Easter and summer), horses and tools being provided by the local inhabitants. Beginning in 1710, a series of acts of parliament conferred responsibility for maintaining roads and bridges in their jurisdiction on county Grand Juries. Monetary investment in roads switched to a presentment system (tenders made by contractors) under the Grand Jury Act of 1765 to be maintained on a county or barony basis.[3] This was part of a rising interest in improvement of trade and transport in the eighteenth century. For instance, the expansion of the linen industry and cereal agriculture in the second half of the eighteenth century necessitated a significant upgrading of roads to bear more wheeled traffic, especially the heavier scotch carts which came in from the mid-eighteenth century. 'Presentment' roads were distinguished by a classicism in their design, running straight as in the Lanesborough to Roscommon or Urlingford to Cashel roads; reflecting the dominance of local landowner interests on the Juries, often the only diversions were around the new landlord demesnes and houses, with many also being designed to pass close to new landlord houses or towns. Carleton lampooned the operations of Grand Juries in the early years of the nineteenth century:

> 'Our party voted about thirty miles of roads to repair *thoroughly* and you know that although you only *veneered* them, we said nothing.' 'But', replied Val, 'who ever heard of a bridge without water; and I know there's not a stream within three miles of it'.
>   'Never mind that,' replied M'Small, 'let me have the bridge first, and we'll see what can be done about the water afterwards. If God in his mercy would send a wet winter next season, who knows but we might present for a new river at January assizes'.[4]

Grand Jury cess and labour duty on the local population was used to maintain roads, drains and fences along the roads; maintenance of roadside drains was especially important to keep the road in good order. There was only intermittent interest in long distance road maintenance beyond county boundaries. Taylor's map of Kildare (1783) demonstrates the role of new roads in opening up development of the midland bogs, since the publication of Noble and Keenan's map in 1752. The intended line of a new turnpike road from Clane through Allenwood to the Offaly border is shown striking through the Bog of Allen. In some of John Rocque's maps

(University of Ulster, Coleraine) and R. Muir, *The new reading the landscape* (Exeter, 2000), p.106. **3** Andrews, 'Road planning in Ireland', pp 17–41. **4** W. Carleton, *Valentine McClutchy: the Irish agent; or, chronicles of the Castle Cumber property* (Dublin, 1845), pp 57–8 quoted in Crossman, *Local government*.

of the Kildare estates in the mid-eighteenth century, roads can be seen clearly cutting across the grain of older field boundaries on the one hand, while in other instances the road network obviously forms the frame for later enclosures.

Parliamentary legislation for turnpike roads was introduced in 1729 to encourage private investment in a national system of tolled roads. However, investment only took place in wealthier regions where more traffic was generated. Turnpikes often resulted in local landscape changes by bypassing older medieval towns. Heavier traffic, especially mail coaches from 1790s, called for improved road engineering with lower gradients. The late eighteenth- and early nineteenth-century period was the golden age of horse-drawn transport. Mail coach links gradually expanded through the eighteenth century with regular mail services from 1789. Irish roads were better than English ones by 1800, principally because of lighter traffic in Ireland. The increase in road traffic generated by the Industrial Revolution resulted in more pressure on the English network. In Ireland too, the limited number of roadside trees and hedges allowed the wind and sun to dry out many of the roads more quickly.

Mail coach roads greatly improved in the early nineteenth century when responsibility passed from the Post Office to the Board of Works. Stage coaches got bigger so that by the 1830s they could carry over twenty people, more than half of them on cheaper fares on the outside. When the Napoleonic wars ended, Carlos Bianconi introduced a national public transport system by purchasing ex-army horses cheaply. His 'bians' (as his cars became known) linked the provincial and country towns, establishing interregional connections, with Anna and Samuel Hall's influential *Tour* of 1840 claiming that Bianconi did more to improve the condition of the country than any other person. He was mainly responsible for initiating a mobilty revolution among the middle classes who were his prinicipal customers. When rail transport developed he established feeder lines connecting railway stations. The main roads from Dublin to the cities and towns of the country were little more than 20 feet wide with a coating of gravel stones, which were poorly drained in winter. Athough the process of road improvement gradually diffused westwards, large parts of western counties were still poorly served by the mid-nineteenth century. The inveterate traveller on Irish roads at the time, John O'Donovan, wrote from western counties about wretched and non-existent roads in the 1830s. Boreens and bridle ways were the commonest forms of roadway in much of the west, largely unsuited to any wheeled vehicles. Patrick Lynch, an Irish language scholar and song and music collector, described his travails in the barony of Tirawley as he journeyed towards Erris in Mayo in 1802:

> a dreary, bleak mountainous country. I came to place called Duliag, where there was but one house; I stayed there all night, and gave the people some tobacco for their hospitality. I got up early and made a journey of upwards of four miles that day. I had to cross a great moor, such as I had never seen before, which fatigued me very much, until I crossed a great river, called Avonmore,

> where abundance of salmon are caught. When I found myself growing feeble, on the side of the mountain, I espied a sorry looking cabin ... [5]

Internal movement was frequently easier along the coasts and lakes of the west: drowning tragedies in Annaghdown and Westport arose from boating traffic to Galway via Lough Corrib and from Achill to Westport Quay. From 1822 the government was becoming increasingly involved in road building in the west through parliamentary grants to the Board of Works which assisted the development of small service settlements like Belmullet, Louisburgh, Newport, Clifden, Roundstone and Cahersiveen in the early nineteenth century. The road from Louisburgh in west Mayo through Doolough to Leenane is a late example of these works. Indeed the famine catastrophe was exacerbated by the absence of roads which inhibited outside relief efforts in many of the worst affected western districts. There was better access by sea, but only to a narrow hinterland. The Congested Districts Board in the late nineteenth century was also investing in a local infrastructure of roads and piers.

Road building frequently had an immediate impact on settlement expansion in pre-famine Ireland and there are recurring references to cabins following the building of new roads into unreclaimed land. The O'Callaghan, Devonshire and many other estates all encouraged land reclamation and new farm settlements in marginal lands on their properties.[6] Roadsides often afforded the cheapest unsupervised spaces in the countryside for squatter settlement by impoverished cottiers and 'the long acre' represented free grazing. The development of the railways in the post-famine decades had the effect of taking long distance traffic off roads which were consequently poorly maintained in the later nineteenth century.

Estate owners were interested in the development of proper roads and the following letter from 1741 illustrates the jostling which occurred between landowners for the completion of roads.

> ... Geo Hamersley had got a good deal of the new road leading from Clones to Cumber bridge gravelled and very well made as far as the Teahill and he and I have since pushed it on through the bog of Clamorian and Clinkeen pretty near the Crossroad leading from the old one to Hanwisty house so that passengers and carriages with them can already avoid going over the Teatirll[?] which is a great comfort to them ... Some roads in another part of this Parish are so well pleased with what we have already done in order to forward us have promised to give of 12 or 14 of their Tates ... We should have some of it done this summer but was obliged to give your Tenants smaller

---

5 From *Annals of the Irish harpers*, reprinted in *A walk in Ireland: an anthology of walking literature*, compiled by M. Fewer (Cork, 2001), pp 21–5, 24. See Alexander Nimmo's reports on the roads of Connemara in Villiers-Tuthill, *Alexander Nimmo & the western district*. **6** Proudfoot, 'The management of a great Irish estate'; Smyth, 'Estate records and the making of the Irish landscape'.

tasks on account of the great sickness that has been in the Parish and still is, scarce a cabin in the country or house in this Town that has not or is not visited with a spotted fever or the flux ... As to the Monaghan Road I think I formerly mentioned we can't attempt doing anything at it until that to Comber be finished and that cant be done till the latter end of next summer it will be then time enough to move at the Assizes for a presentment if I find it necessary ... I find Willoughby and Ward were both testy on account I putting a stop to the new road leading from hence to Knockballymore and the little piece of new road leading through a small meadow at the foot of the Teahill into this Town, for when I told Mr Willoughby you were angry at his opposing you in the Monaghan Road he desired I would acquaint you that they had more reason to be angry at your opposing the going on of those two roads ... I told Mr Ward it was unreasonable to go on with the Road towards his house as laid out because it would spoil a very good bleach yard, but he swore it would not do it the least prejudice.[7]

Lord Blayney in Monaghan was praised for putting up road signposts at cross roads in the vicinity of Castleblayney which were 'not so high as to be visible to hawks and eagles only'.[8] In many regions there were no signposts because the impoverished local people cut them down for firewood. Other road 'furniture' such as milestones, gravel boxes and letter boxes reflected occasional interest by Grand Juries, local estates or government agencies. Milestones were erected from the eighteenth into the nineteenth century to assist the Post Office in establishing postal delivery charges. Letter or pillar boxes were erected from the 1850s.

Canals
Navigable waterways marked an important early stage in the transport revolution, as the movement of goods was speeded up and extended geographically, though they were superseded fairly suddenly by the growth of railways in the middle years of the nineteenth century.[9] Commissioners of Inland Navigation were appointed by parliament in 1729 to provide public funding. From the middle of the eighteenth century there was growing interest by parliament in 'navigation schemes' – part of a range of projects which fed into a surge of interest in economic development and improvement. Canals were seen as a measure which would help drain the midland bogs (seen as a constraint on development), as well

---

7 Letter from John Todd agent to Mr Barrett, Sept. 1741 (PRONI, Barrett-Lennard papers, T. 2529/6/c.33).   8 Quoted in Nowlan, *Travel and transport in Ireland*, p. 55.   9 See R. Delany, *A celebration of 250 years of Ireland's inland waterways* (Belfast, 1986); idem, *The Grand Canal of Ireland* (Newton Abbot, 1973); W.A. McCutcheon, 'The Lagan Navigation' in *Ir. Geography*, 4 (1962), pp 244–55; idem, *The canals of the north of Ireland* (Dawlish, 1965); idem, *The industrial archaeology of Northern Ireland* (Belfast, 1981); V.T.H. Delany and D.R. Delany, *The canals of the south of Ireland* (Newton Abbot, 1966); Canon Elison, *The Boyne navigation* (Dublin, 1983). Records of Grand Canal Company, as well as the Barrow Navigation and the Royal Canal are in the possession of CIE.

as improve trade. New canals were mooted along with canalised riverways such as the Boyne, Barrow or Lagan Navigations. Newry Canal commenced in 1731 to access Tyrone coal for transportation to Dublin, passing into Lough Neagh and thence via canal through Coalisland. The Grand Canal opened to Sallins in 1779 (a nine-hour journey for passengers from Dublin); it had reached Monasterevin in 1785, employing almost four thousand labourers (later called navvies/navigators) and the Shannon was finally reached in 1803. The Royal commenced in 1790 but was slow in getting out of Dublin and it was 1817 before it reached the Shannon. Other plans to link rivers and lakes – especially Lough Neagh and Lough Erne via the Ulster Canal – were mooted in 1814. Commencing in 1833, in order to reduce costs it had the narrowest locks in Ireland which meant that boats from other canals could not pass through it. When completed in 1841, it connected Coalisland with Wattlebridge on the Upper Erne but was never a success and its fate was sealed by the expanding railway network. The Ballinamore and Ballyconnell Canal was initially planned as a drainage improvement scheme designed to provide relief for hundreds of labourers in 1846 and 1847: there were more than 3,000 employed daily in 1849. Completed in 1860 it was an economic failure (allegedly one load of Arigna coal was transported to Enniskillen) and fell into ruin by the 1870s, until its restoration in the late 1990s.[10] The Cong Canal, linking loughs Corrib and Mask, commenced at the height of the famine in 1848 and was abandoned largely due to the expansion of the railways and the expense involved in holding water supply in the porous limestone substrate.

Canals have made an important landscape contribution which endures: the stone work of these waterways is still in a high state of preservation and is being enhanced by a growing number of restoration works. Apart from the actual canal channel and towpaths, there were locks and accompanying buildings, stabling for tow horses, aqueducts as over the Lagan at Moira or Rye Water at Leixlip, lockhouses and cottages, hotels and inns, quays and harbours, warehouses and distinctive hump-backed canal bridges which continue as attractive features of the landscape. Canal workers were often involved in assisting with building of local Catholic chapels in the districts they were passing through. In many parts of the Midlands, from the 1790s onwards, local disturbances, resistance to company wages or agitation against local landlords, frequently resulted in breaches in canals; in some cases they were simply attempts to 'create' employment locally. Although faster passenger barges (fly-boats) were introduced in 1834, canal traffic was eventually superseded by railways and many ceased operations in the 1850s. Coach traffic also competed and set up connecting services with canal boats. Bianconi was to the fore in establishing feeder lines to the canals and later the railways.

---

10 See P.J. Flanagan, *The Ballinamore & Ballyconnell Canal* (Newton Abbot, 1972); D.B. McNeill, 'Public transport in Fermanagh' in *Clogher Rec.*, xi, no. 3 (1983), pp 257–72.

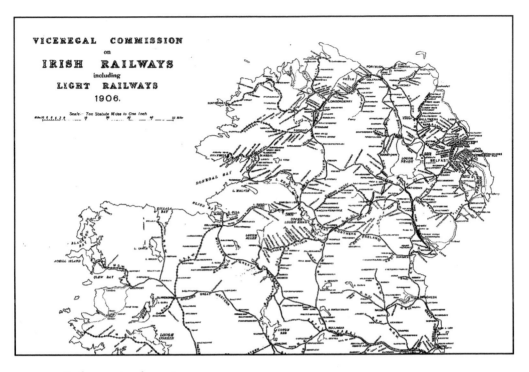

4.9 Railway network, 1906

Railways

Nationally the railways, like the major roads, consolidated the influence of Dublin as capital of the country, but also facilitated the penetration of the island in the nineteenth century by the growing industrial colossus of Britain. Prior to the railways, there was more scope for the development of regional economies in the country. Cork and other cities had their own network of communications focussing their hinterlands. Lewis's *Topographical dictionary* (1837) records towns with a myriad of local industries such as breweries, distilleries and tobacco manufacturing centres, many of which declined in the more open market brought in by the train.

The Drummond (Railway) Commission was set up in 1836, two years after the opening of the Dublin and Kingstown line. It was an important overview of the Irish economy, examining the potential for railways and looking for best routes as a matter of policy. The most vibrant market economy was located in east Ulster, Leinster and Munster. It recommended state investment in Irish railways and two main trunk routes from Dublin to Belfast and Dublin to Cork with connections to Limerick (the Limerick Junction is a relict of this plan) and Galway.[11] However,

11 *Reports of Commissioners appointed to consider and recommend a general system of railways for Ireland*, xxxiii (1837), xxxv (1837–8).

contemporary economic circumstances and British capital favoured private rail companies which went ahead with their own projects, leaving the state a regulatory role, adjudicating disputes and making some funding available.

The lines radiating out of Dublin in a few years consolidated and speeded up Dublin's role and influence, absorbing the capital and labour of the regions and intervening in local regional hegemonies, wiping out local industry by flooding markets with cheaper railed-in commodities from England – and ultimately also draining the population of extensive rural localites to the ports and emigration.

The railway network expanded from *c.*360 miles in 1848 to a peak of 3,750 miles by 1920. A broad guage of 5'3" was adopted on the early mainlines, which became the standard Irish gauge. The Midland Great Western Railway (MGWR) built the line from Dublin to Galway via Athlone in 1851. The Great Southern and Western Railway (GS&WR) was extended from Portarlington to Tullamore, Athlone and Sligo in 1859. A line to Westport was completed in 1866.[12] Following construction of main lines radiating from the capital, competition between companies gradually resulted in the construction of link lines and spurs filling in local regions with a mesh of lines, or the absorption of lines built by smaller companies, as for example, the Sligo and Ballaghaderreen Junction Railway. Disputes between companies resulted in arbitration and allocation of territories to each company, such as the GS&WR and the MGWR which competed for western traffic.[13]

The local and regional impact of the railways was significant, for instance, in moving cattle to fairs and to railheads and consolidating the cattle trade between the west and east. East Ulster was the most industrialised region of Ireland in the nineteenth century, with Belfast resembling an outlier of Lancashire in terms of industrialised landscapes. The railways of the Ulster Railway, later the Great Northern (GNR), laid a mesh of lines across this landscape, consolidating Belfast's dominance as the industrial capital of the north. The lines established labour linkages between Belfast and the manufacturing and mill towns of the Lagan valley and south and west Ulster.

Railways also assisted local mobility, and holiday excursion trains developed very soon after construction. The 'Bundoran Express' ran from Dublin into the mid-twentieth century. The MGWR ran a Tourist Express to Galway and Clifden from 1903 until the Clifden line closed in 1935. Indeed passenger and holiday traffic by a growing middle class to seaside towns like Bray, Tramore, Portrush, Kilkee, Ballybunion and Bundoran was one of the more enduring features of railway traffic

12 S. Maxwell Hajducki, *A railway atlas of Ireland* (Newton Abbot, 1974) contains maps of all the lines in Ireland; S. Johnson, *Johnson's atlas and gazeteer of the railways of Ireland* (Leicester, 1997) has hugely detailed maps showing crossings, junctions with details on the years of opening and closing of all lines. There are numerous local histories of individual lines, for example, P.J. Flanagan, *The Cavan and Leitrim Railway* (Newton Abbot, 1966); E.M. Patterson, *The Clogher Valley Railway* (Newton Abbot, 1972); R.M. Arnold, *The golden years of the Great Northern Railway* (Belfast, 1976).   **13** The Irish Railway Records Society located in Heuston Station holds transport archives from the eighteenth century including waterways, roads and railways.

in an Ireland which failed to industrialise significantly. Investment in hotels by railway companies was a feature of this period. The slow stagnation of most Irish towns in the hundred years from the mid-nineteenth century ultimately reduced the economic viability of most lines with their limited freight traffic, and many closed down following Independence.

The most significant landscape impact of railways throughout Europe arose from the need to maintain a level and straight line, necessitating cuttings and embankments, or in mountainous terrain, tunnels. Bridges, culverts, cuttings, embankments, viaducts and other engineering feats represented unprecedented changes in local landscapes and townscapes. The Boyne viaduct at Drogheda, and others such as Mallow (blown up in 1922) or Monard, the Shannon viaduct at Athlone, dramatic sweeps on the narrow gauge lines in Donegal and Newport in County Mayo, the 12 arches at Ballydehob in west Cork were all impressive additions to the Irish landscape. Huge quantities of earth to construct embankments were moved by horse cart and trucks hauled by horse on rails. The Mallow viaduct was constructed in 1848, often at night by the light of paraffin lamps and tar barrels:

> With the arch-sheeting being cut and dressed by 150 stonemasons on site, it required the combination of quantity surveying, classical engineering and traditional block building to deliver the bridge. Nothing like Mallow Viaduct had ever been seen in Munster. It excited the admiration of the building fraternity and the general public alike. It measured 515 feet across from buttress to buttress, the span of each arch being 45 feet. Apart from its visual impact, it showed how the railway builders could set their stamp upon a remote rural area when possessed of the money, ingenuity and labour to shape the landscape to the needs of the iron road.[14]

William Dargan was one of the pioneering contractors who had gained experience building canals in England and employed thousands of navvies who moved along the line quickly, living in huts and sheds and temporary shelters. During the famine, railway construction was an important source of employment in the south on the Great Southern and Western and the Midland Great Western. Alexander Somerville, a radical Scottish commentator on social and political affairs for a range of newspapers in the mid-nineteenth century, reported on a railway contractor he had met, presumably Dargan, whom he estimated was employing 30,000 men on his railway projects.[15]

Stations and ancillary buildings were a new and impressive addition to the built environment, ranging from the palatial establishments erected as headquarters for railway companies in Dublin to some of the picturesque local stations along the lines. Architectural styles ranged widely, reflecting ostentatious or even imperial

14 K. O'Connor, *Ironing the land: the coming of the railways to Ireland* (Dublin, 1999), p. 64.
15 Alexander Somerville, *Letters from Ireland during the famine of 1847*, ed. K.D.M. Snell (Dublin, 1994), p. 32.

pretensions of companies or their shareholders (or sometimes the local gentry), with Gothic, baroque, Egytian, Victorian, Scottish-baronial, Classical or bizarre castellated flights-of-fancy, all executed in cut stone, brick or brick-and-granite-dressing.[16] Private railway companies, seen by some as a demonstration of the benefits of the Act of Union, invited subscription from interested investors. Developing in an era when landlords were still socially and politically pre-eminent, the local geographies of railway were often influenced by them: as shareholders they frequently tried to attract lines to run through their estates or towns. Evelyn Philip Shirley's correspondence in 1856 and 1868 shows that he was keen on the construction of a line from Dundalk to Carrickmacross, to match lines to other towns in Monaghan county. In other cases, local landowners were significant obstacles to the location of railway works: Mrs Leslie at Ballybay and Captain Coote at Cootehill objected to any station buildings which would interfere with views from their houses or would impact on the amenities of their demesnes.[17]

Railways transformed Ireland in terms of accessibility which was especially significant for the generations of emigrants in the decades after the famine. Assisted emigration from the Shirley and Bath estates in south Monaghan was facilitated by the railway connections from Iniskeen to Drogheda and Dublin. The land agent in 1849 negotiated with the railway company for third class carriages to transport his emigrants on the first leg of a journey to Australia.[18] Railways therefore quite suddenly transformed relationships of local landscapes with the outside world. In the 1940s the railways were still a major channel for emigration from rural Ireland, as evidenced by recurring images of train stations with weeping mothers bidding farewell to sons and daughters. In Fermanagh, 'when the trains came out, anyone who had an idea of emigration, they were known to go to Clones and take the train down to Enniskillen to see how they'd like travelling: to get used to it ... It was imagined that you get sick very quick on either rail or ship.'[19]

There was increasing government intervention from the 1870s to subsidise light railways in the remoter poorer regions, mainly in Antrim, Clare, Donegal, Mayo, Galway and Kerry, where private enterprise showed no interest. These lines fed into mainlines and were sometimes owned or worked by mainline companies. The Tramways Act of 1883 resulted in *c.*600 miles of narrow gauge (3 foot) railway in western counties: for example, the MGWR was extended from Galway to Clifden in 1890s as a government relief measure for the local population. The West Clare Railway and the Connemara Railway promoted tourism as well as facilitating out migration.[20] The Achill line which was used especially by the local community to

16 See J. Sheehy, 'Railway architecture: its heyday' in *Irish Railway Record Society Journal*, xii, 68 (1975), pp 125–38.   **17** Correspondence on Ballybay railway and railway station (Leslie papers, PRONI, D. 3406/D/6/1); Murnane and Murnane, *At the ford of the birches*, pp 448–58: Shirley papers PRONI, D3531/C/3/10.   **18** See P.J. Duffy, 'Embarking for the new world – a group migration to south Australia in 1849' in J.M. Wooding and D. Day (eds), *Celtic-Australian identities* (Sydney, 2001), pp 43–56.   **19** National Folklore Collection 1743: memories of the railway collected in Lisnakea, 1965.   **20** See K. Villiers-Tuthill, 'The Connemara Railway 1895–1935' in *History Ireland*, 3, no. 4 (Winter 1995), 35–40.

consolidate seasonal migration links with England and Scotland, was marked by tragedy at its opening in 1894 and its closing in 1937, on both occasions transporting the bodies of emigrants killed en route to Great Britain or in Scotland.[21]

Wiring the landscape

The mid-nineteenth century was important in terms of transport developments in the landscape: the speeding up of transportation, 'shortening' of distances and decreasing cost, meant more mobility and traffic, more buildings and greater material changes to landscape. Also important in terms of connecting landscapes and dissolving distance was the transformation of the perception of space by linking up landscapes and areas with information and communications. While information diffusion became increasingly reliable with the amalgamation of the British and Irish Post Office in the 1830s, before the electric telegraph, signalling systems depended on sight lines, such as the martello towers built in Ireland during the Napoleonic war – or the mechanical telegraph in revolutionary France.

Telegraph cables marked an important phase in the consolidation of far-flung spaces in the emerging United States in the latter half of the nineteenth century, when lines were installed along the fast-expanding railroads. Telegraph in both Europe and the US became an important aspect of train operations, with messages first about train movements, then about business, being sent up and down the lines. Poles and wire for construction and repair, as well as security and surveillance, were easily and quickly installed by railroads. In the US the railroad companies bought up telegraph companies. In the UK, however, the state was more involved with the infrastructure of telegraphy, which was recognised as an important strategic asset, and took over the network in the 1890s.[22] Telephone networks were initially developed by private companies in cities, connected by trunk lines which later linked up outlying towns and villages along the railway network. The United Telephone company opened the first exchange in Dublin's Dame Street in 1880 and the first telephone cable to Britain was laid at Donaghadee in 1893 and from Howth in 1913. The Post Office took over the developing telephone network in 1912.

The modern automatic telephone districts are territorial legacies of the early geographies of telegraph and telephone networks. The network commenced in cities with trunk lines extending along railways. Urban landscapes were the first to be wired up both by telecommunications and electricity: they were in practical terms the most convenient and viable market spaces. Rural landscapes were 'empty' distances between cities that were connected by telegraph. Poles and trunk lines were erected through the countryside, along mainline railways and roads, gradually incorporating additional links. Dublin city, for instance, had the earliest comprehensive phone network in Ireland. By the time of the war of independence, the

---

21 See J. Beaumont, *Rail to Achill* (Usk, Oakwood, c.2002). **22** See C.R. Perry, *The Victorian Post Office: the growth of a bureaucracy* (Woodbridge, 1992).

telephone in south Dublin was an important means of communication for those 'rebels' involved. The networks extended to link up outlying towns and villages, with tentacles of wires extending gradually to incorporate smaller points within rural hinterlands. Trunk calls to Monaghan town from Dublin, for instance, passed through Clones exchange, a reflection of the earlier geography of railway linkages.

Manual telephone exchanges in rural areas, such as that in Smithboro in Monaghan, for instance, usually closed down at night. Party lines often included several houses sharing the same line in rural districts. Extension of telephone connections from early days reflected needs of government administration and social status in the community: usually the first telephone number was the Post Office, followed perhaps by the police barracks, the doctor, possibly the priest, veterinary surgeon, the Big House, and larger farmers.[23]

The wiring of the landscape by telegraph and telephone was a highly significant process of territorial integration. The manual exchange districts which slowly evolved from the early twentieth century, generally matching postal districts, were consolidated in the mid-twentieth century and formed the basis for the subsequent automatic exchange zones. The network of manual telephone exchanges through-out the country had a notable social impact (similar to banks and local government offices): apart from obviously linking up places by communications, employment of female telephonists especially facilitated internal migration by women into new communities.

Wireless technology was also a significant chapter in connectivities of landscape. Wireless and radio linked up extensive geographical areas, which transformed the timing and accessibility of remoter places to simultaneous information. Indeed wireless communication was seized on as a powerful propagandist tool for con-solidating regional attitudes by fascist governments in the 1930s and 40s. Wireless radio, operated by wet batteries in the absence of electricity before 1950 for most rural communities in Ireland, meant instantaneous linkage with Belfast following the establishment of 2BE in 1924, and Athlone/Dublin stations after the foundation of 2RN in 1926 (Radio Éireann from 1932). Micheál Ó Hehir from 1938 linked local, national and county identities in his GAA football and hurling commentaries on Irish radio.

Electrification of the landscape came later in the twentieth century, with rural electrification being the most comprehensive wiring of the land after the second world war, a process taking place in much of the U.S. and Europe at the same time.[24] As with telephone, urban areas were the earliest to be cabled for electricity

---

23 Eircom archives are available in the National Archives of Ireland, Bishop Street, Dublin. BT Group Archives including material on Ireland before 1921 are located in Holborn in London: archives@bt.com   24 On Ireland, see M. Manning and M. McDowell, *Electricity supply in Ireland: the history of the ESB* (Dublin, 1984) and M.J. Shiel, *The quiet revolution: the electrification of rural Ireland, 1946–1976* (Dublin, 1984); see also *REO News* (1947–61) which was the newsletter of the rural electrification organisation. Detailed files on the establishment and progress of rural electrification are available in the ESB Archives in Harold's Cross, Dublin.

by private supply companies, or some local authorities with private generators in the late nineteenth century. Ultimately (as was the case with other infrastructural services such as railways and telephones) success in comprehensive coverage and transmission was dependent on public regulation by the state. The Electricity Supply Board (ESB) was established in 1927 and took over existing urban operations. The Shannon scheme (operational in 1929) was the new state's significant initial investment and for the first decade it concentrated on servicing cities and town of *c*.500+ population, with high tension main lines running through the countryside to service cities. The Rural Electrification Scheme, based on experience in Scandinavia, commenced after the second world war in 1947. In order to respond to the rapid rise in demand for electricity, additional hydro-electric power stations were commissioned at Erne, Pollaphuca and Golden Falls, as well as peat-fired power stations at Ferbane, Portarlington and Allenwood. A coal-fired plant was opened at Arigna in 1958. Further peat-fired stations were opened at Lanesboro and Rhode.

Electricity differed significantly from the telephone which was seen as responding to private demand, incurring an economic cost which made its installation expensive for rural consumers up to the 1970s. Rural electrification was heavily state-subsidised; charging the economic costs of the infrastructure would have excluded most rural customers and for efficiency it was essential that a maximum take-up was achieved. Thus the Rural Electrification Scheme was accompanied by an intensive recruitment campaign. In expediting the electrification programme, a strategic decision was taken to use the Roman Catholic parish as the basis for the development, as it represented a strong territorial community, with parish priests and other leaders in the community acting as informal agents for the scheme.[25] As well as the engineering significance of the development, it also had important social consequences, in terms of outsiders coming in, many with engineering skills from de-mobbed post-war military. During 1947–8, 760 miles of line were constructed: 'Assuming that a digging gang of say eight or ten men turned out 100 pole holes a week or roughly ten kilometres, the design and pegging, wayleaves, re-canvass, mapping, distributing, fitting, hoisting, coppering, servicing … and metering would all have to go at the same pace'. In December 1948, 37,159 poles and 2,795 km of line had been erected and 7,131 rural consumers connected. By December 1956 a total of 544,361 poles and 47,781 km of line had been erected supplying 195,645 consumers.[26]

To a greater extent and more rapidly than the telephone, electrification integrated all rural and urban landscapes, lighting up the rural darkness, transforming standards of living, assisting with the mechanisation of farms and rural households at a time of considerable rural despondency, and facilitating a significant convergence of rural and urban living standards. It revolutionised rural and farm life. In terms of the built environment, for instance, it was followed by a rash of

25 The MSS parish maps of the ESB are on deposit in Russell Library, Maynooth College. See the *REO News* which commenced in 1948. **26** *REO News*, Dec. 1948 and Dec. 1956.

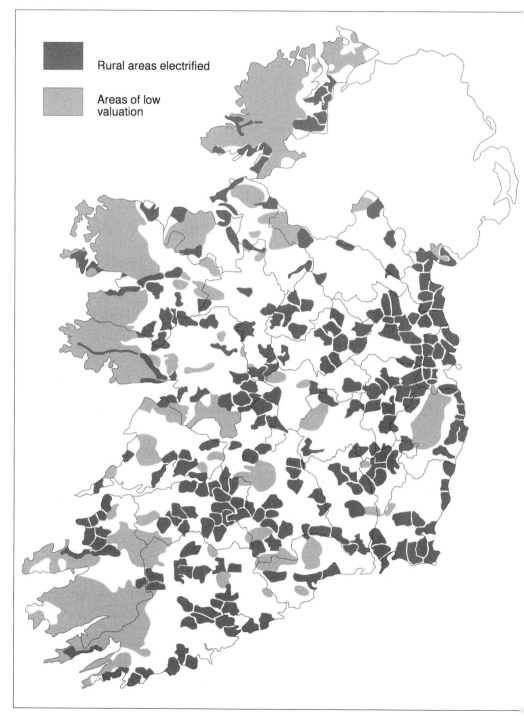

Rural areas electrified

Areas of low
valuation

4.10 Progress of rural electrification, 1952; based on ESB archives, Harold's Cross, Dublin

bathroom extensions to rural houses, as well as new and remodelled farm buildings, such as dairies, milking sheds, chicken and mushroom houses. Indeed the beginnings of the new house-building boom of the 1960s was not unconnected with this new energy source provided to rural communities.

Timing the landscape

Associated with the development of transport and communications was a fundamental transformation in the way time and distance were perceived in local communities. Up until the later nineteenth and early twentieth century, time was measured locally – usually still as 'time immemorial,' sunrise and sunset, which varied between east and west in summer and winter. Local clock time was synchronised with the ringing of church bells.[27] Slow travelling times in spatially constrained locales made this acceptable. For the man sitting on a cart plodding to the forge or the fields or the fair, or walking to the town, or along a canal towpath, time and the tempo of life was delimited by local horizons: how long it took to get to the chapel or the village. Pre-industrial timing of the landscape over wider distances was mainly of interest to wealthy élites – landowners, merchants or government officials who travelled to Dublin or London or the Continent. In the eighteenth century it may have taken a couple of days to get from Carlow to Dublin, and even in the mid-nineteenth century, it took many hours.

Trains speeded life in an unprecedented manner and local time became untenable, as journey times quite suddenly rose from *c.*8–10 mph to as high as 50 mph and more.[28] As well as bringing goods in and people out, trains also brought 'railway time' to countrysides – a central characteristic of modernisation of landscapes and societies. Thus there may have been a twenty or thirty minute differential between the time in rural west Limerick and the city, which may have kept 'railway' time. More standard timing, timetabling and scheduling the day in measurable chunks of time were all characteristics of modernity which came with the railway and machine age. Older people and rural places held onto 'old time' into twentieth century. By the early 1930s a long day's work on farms in Glaslough or Iniskeen in County Monaghan was completed by the sound of the late train and its steam whistle as it approached the station.

Bianconi was first to change popular attitudes to time, contracting to take the mails from Clonmel to Cahir in 1815; by the mid-nineteenth century he had more than one thousand horses drawing his 'bians' throughout the country to strict timetables.[29] The notion of the capital (whether it was London, Paris or Dublin) consolidating the space of the nation by imposing standard time is reflected in the

27 Ireland was approx. 25 minutes behind GMT until 'summer time' (or daylight saving) was introduced in 1916 as an energy-saving policy during the war.   **28** See W. Schivelbusch, *The railway journey: the industrialization of time and space in the nineteenth century* (New York, 1986), although the train journey to Clifden or Achill took up to ten hours in the early twentieth century.   **29** M. O'C. Bianconi and S.J. Watson, *Bianconi: king of the Irish roads* (Dublin, 1962); O'Donnell, *Clonmel*, p. 78.

shortening of time-distances to the cities, from days to hours. Railway time was the first significant time-space standardisation: trains had chronometers set by Dublin time. By the last third of the nineteenth century, telegraph lines along the railway helped the rapid adoption of standard times which were essential for the smooth running of trains. Each station and town en route could then adjust its clocks so that more and more of the landscape was incorporated into 'Dublin' time as it diffused down the track, down the urban hierarchy and into surrounding villages and countrysides. Until the early twentieth century, however, many places operated on both local time and railway/Dublin time. For local communities Dublin time was normally irrelevant, except insofar as they had occasionally to catch a train. Only with the first world war did the state impose 'summer' time or daylight saving which introduced Greenwich Mean Time (GMT) as standard.

The mobility revolution transformed time-distances as well as landscape accessibility. Pedestrian worlds were characterised by a slow, leisurely, local gaze; speeded up trains and later cars brought an inevitably different perception of places as people whizzed faster through the landscape (reflected in later 'road movies' in America, the ultimate motorised landscape). The M50's 'Westlink', 'Western Parkway' and 'Southern Cross' are examples of Ireland's new rapid-transit landscapes, where people move from one point to another with fleeting or no connection with intervening places and landscapes. These new routeways are rupturing pre-existing landscape associations and networks.[30]

SOME PRIMARY SOURCES

One of the most important primary sources in exploring the building fabric of Irish towns and villages (and to lesser extent settlement change in rural areas) is the Valuation of the 1830s and 40s which details the buildings in each street.[31] The first Townland Valuation is useful for general aspects of settlement in rural areas before the famine, containing details on mansion houses and industrial buildings and its Field Books have been used successfully in studies of linen mills, for instance.[32] Griffith's Valuation is potentially the most useful source for settlement studies and for profiling change at local level into the twentieth century. The initial valuation was published as *The General valuation of tenements in Ireland* (1848–64), arranged by townlands or streets in parishes and produced in Poor Law Union volumes. All tenements (properties) are detailed for each townland/street with the names of

30 Though Schivelbusch, *The railway journey*, p. 23 suggests that the mid-nineteenth-century railway, cutting straight through the landscape at unprecedented speed, represented the first major sensory disconnection between the traveller and the landscape.   **31** The scope and purpose of the Townland (including Poor Law) Valuation and the Primary (or Griffith's) Valuation are comprehensively described in Prunty, *Maps and map-making*, pp 145–53. **32** See Smyth, 'Locational patterns and trends within the pre-famine linen industry'. Manuscript copies are available in the Valuation Office, Irish Life Centre, Dublin.

occupiers (usually the tenant), immediate lessors (often but not invariably the main landlord), short description of the tenement, acreage and rateable valuation of land and buildings. The data on tenements are linked to accompanying OS maps where index numbers and boundaries are shown in red ink. This information was regularly updated in manuscript revisions (or Cancellation Books) into the twentieth century and are available in the Valuation Office in Dublin or PRONI in Belfast.

For rural areas, changes in rural settlements can be examined for decades in the mid-nineteenth and early twentieth century.[33] For local studies, the Field Books and House Books on which the published valuations were based are useful sources whose quality varies according to individual valuers. Griffith's grading system for houses in the House Books was based on an A, B, C quality letter system according to the age, state of repair, deterioration and dilapidation of buildings.

The Ordnance Survey Letters, written mainly by John O'Donovan, contain descriptions of the condition of local structures, of mostly antiquarian interest, in the 1830s. For students of local history, the OS letters should be perused in conjunction with the contemporaneous OS six-inch mapping survey. Letters for a number of counties have been published. For the province of Ulster, the OS Memoirs also represent an important record of aspects of the built environment described by parish and town, including accounts of public buildings, 'gentlemen's seats', and references to schools, churches, chapels and meeting houses, glebe houses, dispensaries, mills, roads and bridges.[34]

The 1901 and 1911 census manuscript returns are also important sources for studies of the built environment.[35] The 1901 'House and Building returns' (Form B1) contain summaries of farmhouses and other buildings in each townland. Columns record data on the type of building (residential, school, manufactory, public-house etc.), number of outoffices, whether the building was inhabited or uninhabited, construction details (stone, brick, concrete, mud, wood), roofing (slate, iron, tiles, thatch), number of rooms, windows in front, and house class (1–4) which was used since the 1841 census. 'Returns of Out-Offices and Farm-Steadings' (Form B2) detail all the outbuildings, whether stable, coach house, harness room,

33 See W.J. Smyth, 'Nephews, dowries, sons and mothers: the geography of farm and marital transactions in eastern Ireland, *c.*1820–*c.*1970' in D.J. Siddle (ed.), *Migration, mobility and modernization* (Liverpool, 2000), pp 9–46 for changing settlement landscapes 1841, 1851 and 1970. **34** Manuscripts of the OS Letters and OS Memoirs are in the care of the RIA. Typescript copies made in the 1920s are available in a number of libraries. Some county letters have been published: *John O'Donovan's letters from County Londonderry (1834)*, ed. G. Mawhinney (Ballinascreen, 1992); *The antiquities of County Clare, compiled from the OS letters of John O'Donovan and Eugene O'Curry* (Ennis, 2003); *The OS letters: Wicklow*, ed. C. Corlett and J. Medlycott (Roundwood, n.d. [2000]); *OS Letters Meath: letters containing information relative to the antiquities of the county of Meath collected during the progress of the OS in 1836*, ed. M. Herity (Dublin, 2001); also volumes published for *Kildare, Dublin, Donegal, Kilkenny*. See Day & McWilliams (eds), *Ordnance Survey memoirs of Ireland*. **35** The 1901 returns only are available for NI on microfilm in PRONI; both 1901 and 1911 are available for the whole of

cow house, calf house, dairy, piggery, fowl house, boiling house, barn, turf house, potato house, workshop, shed, store, forge, or laundry. These details show interesting regional contrasts, reflecting variations in rural wealth, farm size and local agricultural economies. For towns the data on numbers of rooms can be used in conjunction with the House Books of the valuation for longitudinal studies of urban housing change.

Street directories became popular as the nineteenth century progressed and can sometimes be helpful in reconstructing the land-use and occupational profile of houses in each of a town's streets. They are available in the National Library of Ireland and for specific counties in the county library. Pigot's and its successor Slater's directories gradually extended their coverage of Irish towns throughout the nineteenth century. For a small town like Ballybay in County Monaghan, Pigot's for 1824 contains a summary description of the town, followed by details on gentry and clergy, shopkeepers and traders, publicans, doctors, surgeons and apothecaries, merchants and tradesmen – profiling the occupational structure of the town community which in turn reflects on the built fabric. *Slater's Directory* (1846), for instance, details gentry and clergy, bakers, surgeons and apothecaries, blacksmiths, boot and shoe merchants, hotels, leather sellers, tailors, ironmongers, linen and woollen drapers, milliners and dressmakers, spirit dealers and publicans, along with persons with miscellaneous skills (schoolmaster, harness maker, umbrella maker, reed maker, miller). Timetable details are provided for coaches and cars: this detail on regional communications is also provided in most of the OS memoirs.[36] Later versions of Slater's in the 1860s and 70s have further information on schools, banks, booksellers and binders, earthenware dealers, flax merchants, carpenters, grocers, nail makers, oil and colour merchants, timber merchants, dispensaries, auctioneers, butchers, blacksmiths, car owners and car makers, wallpaper dealers, undertakers, saddlers and harness makers.[37] For those interested in streetscape and building profiles, Henry Shaw's *New city pictorial directory* provides valuable drawings for Dublin in 1850.

Maps must rank as the most important source for studying the morphology of Irish settlement landscapes – ranging from plantation maps and plans, through estate maps and Grand Jury maps to the Ordnance Survey commencing with the first edition six-inch maps, and later editions and larger scales. Many large-scale manuscript maps of towns were produced and have recently been included in a national digital record by the OS.[38] Up until John Rocque's innovative mapping projects of the 1750s, most buildings were represented pictographically in maps,

Ireland in the NAI. **36** A number of nineteenth-century directories and almanacs have been published in CD-ROM as part of The Archive CD Books project, see www.archivecdbooks.ie **37** *Slater's National Commercial Directory* (from 1846) *Slater's Royal National Directory*; see Murnane and Murnane, *At the ford of the birches*, pp 551ff; R. Ffolliott and D.F. Begley, 'Guide to Irish directories' in D.F. Begley (ed.), *Irish genealogy: a record finder* (Dublin, 1981), pp 75–106. **38** See Historical Mapping Archive, www.irishhistoricmaps.ie/historic/index

often providing a bird's-eye view of settlements. The purpose of most sixteenth- and seventeenth-century maps was to portray the resources and economic potential of the landscape: thus outlines of boundaries were important, as well as other material or environmental assets such as woodland, arable land, stone buildings and castles, bridges and so on, many of which also may have had military value as landmarks.[39] The houses of the ordinary Gaelic inhabitants were usually only haphazardly recorded as being too inconsequential or insubstantial to be system- atically surveyed. The Ulster plantation surveyor, Thomas Raven, depicted houses in his maps of Farney in south Monaghan in 1634 as being circular or ovoid, with thatched roofs and no chimneys. Such huts or cabins were depicted elsewhere and may have been the precursors of the two- or three-roomed traditional house. The pictographs may be useful to the discerning reader in illustrating some of the architectural features of buildings in the pre-modern or early-modern landscape. The Farney maps show a range of buildings from thatched cabins to stone slated houses. Although there are no towers as in some other parts of Ireland at this time, the principal Gaelic lord, Ever McColla's house is shown as a fairly substantial building with simple extensions and what look like dormer-type windows. Prior to these sketches the only evidence on buildings is provided in Gaelic poems such as those described by Katherine Simms.[40] John Rocque and his successor Bernard Scalé, who specialised in detailed estate maps in the second half of the eighteenth century, introduced the modern practice of representing buildings in plan form, contenting themselves with providing inset vignettes of views of scenes of mills and other local buildings.

There is also a wide range of surveys, guides and inventories containing descrip- tions and illustrations of particular buildings in selected areas of coverage. The Irish Architectural Archive in Merrion Square, Dublin, for instance, is the primary repository of a wide range of records on Irish architecture, including photographs, drawings, engravings and manuscripts. 'National monuments' and archaeological remains comprise a distinctive group of structures which have been given significance since the antiquarianism of the eighteenth century and are maintained by Dúchas – the Heritage Service and the Office of Public Works (OPW) located in St Stephen's Green, Dublin. The Records of Monuments and Place section (formerly Sites and Monuments Record) in the OPW in St Stephen's Green, Dublin, is responsible for maintaining an inventory of the built environment up to 1700. County archaeological surveys and inventories have been published by Dúchas so far for Louth, Monaghan, Carlow, Galway, Donegal, Meath, Cork (vols 1–3), Wexford, Cavan, Laois, north Kerry, North Tipperary, Leitrim, Waterford, Galway (vols 1–2), Laois, Cavan, Wexford, Offaly, and Wicklow. Dúchas is responsible for the National Inventory of Architectural Heritage which publishes

39 See Andrews, *Plantation acres*; Hayes-McCoy, *Ulster and other Irish maps, c.1600*; Swift, *Historical maps of Ireland*; J. Feehan and A. Rosse, *An atlas of Birr* (Dublin, 2005) contains a rich array of historical maps of Birr and its hinterland.   **40** Simms, 'Native sources for Gaelic settlement: the House Poems'.

county surveys of architectural heritage.[41] Lavishly illustrated surveys have been published in hard copy with CD-Roms for counties Carlow, Laois, Meath, Kerry, Kildare, Waterford, Roscommon, Leitrim and Wicklow, Kilkenny, Offaly, Westmeath, Sligo, and South Dublin County and Fingal. Themes in the Carlow volume are town settlements, the courthouse, barracks, schoolhouses, commercial buildings, urban residences, country houses, vernacular buildings, ecclesiastical heritage, buildings of transport and industry, and street furniture. Local authorities also hold records of listed structures which are protected from inappropriate development. The Northern Ireland Monuments and Buildings Record includes the Sites and Monuments Record (SMR) from prehistoric to plantation periods, the Industrial Archaeology Record, the Buildings Record which includes non-industrial architecture on more than 8000 post-plantation buildings, and data on 650 historic gardens.[42]

An Foras Forbartha (Environmental Research Institute), established in 1969, undertook a series of architectural surveys in most counties of the Republic. These unpublished surveys are part of the National Heritage Inventory, and are sometimes available in local libraries. Inventories of several towns were published, for instance, *Ennis: architectural heritage* (1981) and *Galway: architectural heritage* (1985), as well as for Cobh, Kinsale, Tullamore, Bray and Carlow. A separate survey for Monaghan town was published by the Ulster Architectural Heritage Society (UAHS) and An Taisce in 1970. This listed significant streets, squares and buildings, as well as exterior and interior monuments and decoration.[43] The UAHS has also published similar surveys for a range of other centres and districts in Ulster including Lisburn, Banbridge, Portaferry and Strangford, Antrim and Ballymena, City of Derry, west Antrim, Dungannon and Cookstown, Glens of Antrim, North Antrim, Coleraine and Portstewart, Enniskillen, towns and villages of east and mid-Down, Rathlin island, North Derry, Donaghadee and Portpatrick, Carrickfergus, the town of Cavan and areas within the city of Belfast.[44] An Taisce has published short studies of selected towns including Adare and Slane, as well as a survey of listed buildings in Dublin at a critical time of change.[45]

Penguin commenced a series entitled *Buildings of Ireland* in 1974. Three volumes have been published to date, covering north-west Ulster (counties Derry, Donegal, Fermanagh and Tyrone), north Leinster (Longford, Louth, Meath and Westmeath) and Dublin.[46] These are excellent guides to buildings in the landscape, with com-

41 See www.buildingsofireland.ie/niah/   42 SMRs for the Republic are in DoE, 6 Ely Place, Dublin 2; for NI in the Environment Service, 5–33 Hill Street, Belfast. For details on SMR see Prunty, *Maps and map-making*, pp 174–9; N. Brannon, 'The built heritage and the local historian' in Gillespie & Hill (eds), *Doing Irish local history*, pp 116–127.   43 C.E. Brett, *Historic buildings, groups of buildings and areas of architectural importance in the town of Monaghan* (Ulster Architectural Heritage Society and An Taisce, Belfast, 1970).   44 See also J.S. Curl, *Moneymore and Draperstown: the architecture and planning of the estates of the Drapers' Company in Ulster* (Belfast, 1979).   45 '*Urbana*': *Dublin's List 1 buildings: a conservation report for An Taisce, The National Trust for Ireland* (Dublin, 1982). Dublin County Council has published some surveys also, for example, *Swords: heritage buildings* (Dublin, 1987).   46 Rowan, *North west*

prehensive overviews of architecture in Ireland from the early Christian era
Elizabethan, Stuart, Georgian, Victorian and twentieth century periods, inclu
detailed gazeteer of settlements and places and their significant buildings.
example, Charlestown, north of Ardee, has descriptions of Charlestown parɪ
church (CoI), its sexton's house and cemetery gateway; mid-nineteenth century
Rahanna House, late Georgian Harristown House, Cardistown House (1865 two
storey Italianate house); the early medieval remains of Clonkeen Old church and
St Malachy's church, an early nineteenth-century T-plan Roman Catholic church.
They also contain maps and indexes of places mentioned in the text.

Jeremy Williams, *A companion guide to architecture in Ireland, 1837–1921* (Dublin,
1994) is arranged as a gazeteer by county and by town or nearest town within each
county. Entries are briefly informative: in County Mayo, Mulranny is listed with its
Roman Catholic church of 1904, Great Southern Hotel built by T. M. Deane in
the late 1890s and Rossturk Castle built in 1860s; Newport has short notes on its
Roman Catholic church and its railway viaduct.[47] Sean Rothery, *A field guide to the
buildings of Ireland: illustrating the smaller buildings of town and countryside* (Dublin, 1997)
includes more than two hundred line drawings and descriptions of a sample of
typical buildings ranging from early Christian, through friaries and abbeys, castles
and fortifications, vernacular and architectural houses, estate buildings, transport and
industrial buildings and lighthouses. It includes a ten-page glossary of architectural
terms.[48]

Patrick and Maura Shaffrey's *Irish countryside buildings: everyday architecture in the
rural landscape* (Dublin, 1985) and its companion volume *Buildings of Irish towns:
treasures of everyday architecture* (Dublin, 1983) provide overviews of ordinary buildings in the Irish landscape, with chapters focussing on country estates, settlement
patterns, farm buildings, dwelling houses, ecclesiastical buildings and schools,
commercial and military buildings, transportation, streetscapes and shopfronts. They
are beautifully illustrated by Maura Shaffrey, with an appendixed essay on building
and roofing materials: stone, brick, mud, concrete, timber, iron, glass, plaster, paint,
thatch, slates, tiles, and corrugated iron.[49] Alan Gailey's *Rural houses of the North of
Ireland* (Edinburgh, 1984) comprehensively examines an array of rural buildings in
Ulster and north Leinster, from the point of view of building materials and styles
in walls and roofs, hearth and chimney, as well as house types and relationships
between Irish and British vernacular types, including a five page glossary of terms.[50]
C.E. Brett has been responsible for a wide range of guides to the built environment
in Ulster and Northern Ireland.[51] Hugh Weir of Ballinakella Press in Whitegate,

Ulster; C. Casey and A. Rowan, *North Leinster* (London, 1993); C. Casey, *Dublin* (New Haven,
2005). **47** See K.C. Kearns, *Georgian Dublin: Ireland's imperiled architectural heritage* (Newton
Abbot, 1983). **48** See S. Rothery, *Everyday buildings of Ireland* (Dublin, 1975). **49** See P.
Shaffrey, 'Settlement patterns: rural housing, villages and small towns' in F.H.A. Aalen (ed.),
The future of the Irish rural landscape (Dublin, 1985), pp 56–79. **50** Also A. Gailey, 'Traditional
buildings in the landscape: conservation and preservation' in Aalen (ed.), *The future of the Irish
rural landscape*, pp 26–45. **51** C.E. Brett, *Courthouses and market houses of the province of Ulster*

County Clare, has published an historical architectural profile of selections of notable houses in a number of counties in Ireland, for example, *Houses of Clare* (1986, reprinted 1999), *Houses of Kerry* (1994), *Houses of Cork: north* (2002) and *Houses of Wexford* (2004). Containing line drawings of many of the houses, entries follow a standard pattern covering location (by townland and grid reference), families associated with the houses historically, description of the houses' current condition, their main architectural characteristics and history. There is an introductory county map showing the numbered location of each house. The Wexford volume contains details on more than a thousand houses. Kevin V. Mulligan's *Buildings of Meath: a selection of protected structures* (Kells, 2001) examines castles, houses, churches, mottes, bridges, villages, shopfronts, monuments, thatched houses and cottages. Richard Pierce and Alistair Coey's *Taken for granted: a celebration of 10 years of historic buildings conservation* (NI Historic Buildings Council, 1984) includes more than one thousand listed buildings in town and country – public, commercial and educational buildings, cottages and small houses, mansions and castles, bridges and estate buildings. The compilation of an inventory of rural architectural heritage at risk in counties Cavan, Fermanagh and Leitrim commenced in the 1990s.[52] The Department of the Environment and Local Government in the Republic of Ireland has produced a series of important booklets containing advice on conservation of buildings and landscape which include background historical notes on the features being discussed.[53] Local authorities in the Republic of Ireland are now in the process of publishing county heritage plans highlighting significant aspects of local enviromental hertiage which will be important for raising popular awareness of future conservation needs.

CONCLUSION

The built environment is one of the most interesting and fruitful areas of research in local historical studies. The legacy of buildings of all shapes and sizes represents one of the most distinctive elements in local landscapes, a part of our environment with which we continue to interact closely on a daily basis. Infrastructural developments of the past three centuries are also important: much of the modern morphology of transport and communications infrastructure has only been laid down in the past couple of centuries. More attention should be paid to it and its contribution to local landscape difference. With the raised awareness of local heritage there is increasing attention being paid to historical data on this most

(Belfast, 1973); idem, *Buildings of County Armagh* (Belfast, 1999); idem, *Buildings of County Antrim* (Belfast, 1996); idem, *Georgian Belfast, 1750–1850: maps, buildings and trades* (Belfast, 2004). **52** Funded by Peace and Reconciliation through Co-operation North and undertaken with the support of local historical and heritage groups. **53** Booklets on the following have been published: windows, mortars and renders, stone walling, brickwork and stonework, paving and street furniture, roofs, ironwork, shopfronts, settings and landscape.

material aspect of our surrounding landscapes.[54] There is a plethora of information available on most aspects of the built environment in many of the repositories detailed in Helferty and Refaussé's *Directory of Irish archives*. Just as consumer spending in the post-second world war period reflected changing lifestyles which impacted on the built environment in town and country, delving into eighteenth- and nineteenth-century business records might also be rewarding: building cycles may be reflected in house constructions and extensions, improvement in domestic interiors or investment in farms at local level. Such changes helped the construction or modification of some of the buildings discussed in this chapter and may well be reflected in the records of small town merchant houses throughout the country.[55]

---

54 K. Villiers-Tuthill, *Alexander Nimmo & the western district* (Clifden, 2006) provides excellent insights into sources for the modernisation of infrastructure in Connacht in the nineteenth century. **55** Business Records Survey, National Archives. See also Barnard, *A guide to sources for the history of material culture in Ireland*; M. Dunlevy, 'Dublin in the early nineteenth century: domestic evidence' in Kennedy & Gillespie (eds), *Ireland: art into history*, pp 185–206.

CHAPTER 5

Visualising landscapes

One of the crucial ways of understanding landscape as a production of cultural and economic discourse is the way in which it was represented in visual and written media. This is the theme of the following two chapters. Most people would put the visual before the verbal in that paintings, drawings or photographs seem to best capture a place at a moment in the past: 'No other kind of relic or text from the past can offer such a direct testimony about the world which surrounded people at other times.'[1]

Our concepts of landscape are still powerfully influenced by a landscape aesthetic which emerged in Europe in the later seventeenth century and is reflected in the legacy of fine art to be found in national and municipal galleries and museums. The most common objects of vision were the sites/sights favoured by the upper classes. What happened to landscape in the eighteenth and nineteenth centuries, therefore, was improvement (on nature) for viewing (by educated élites), display (by privileged ownership) and representation (in the exclusive medium of 'high' art – painting). Local historians have difficulty finding representations of ordinary, everyday landscapes. There is a recurring dichotomy between élite and vernacular landscapes – parklands or sublime landscapes for gazing, repose, leisure and pleasure versus ordinary workaday landscapes of labour, production and industry. In terms of historical research, the élites are the main sources of record, and were interested in both types of landscape as manifestations of improvement and progress. Raymond Williams has noted, however, that a 'working country is hardly ever a landscape':[2] it was unworthy of recording in paint or prose, being detailed instead in more prosaic accounts, extents and surveys.

Artists as painters were selective in what they saw as being important in a scene, responding to their patron's commission and the nature of contemporary landscape aesthetics. Eighteenth- and nineteenth-century representations of landscape reflect cultural and ideological subtexts in what Williams called the enamelled pastoral of the privileged gaze, where romantic and pastoral landscapes were drained of much reality and meaning, but were infected instead with a (pre-industrial) nostalgia, peace, serenity and leisurely freedom which belied the real historical experience.[3]

1 J. Berger, *Ways of seeing* (London, 1972), p. 10; see also H. Prince, 'Landscape through painting' in *Geography*, 69, pt 1, no. 302 (Jan. 1984), pp 3–18, p. 15. 2 Quoted in W.J. Mitchell (ed.), *Landscape and power* (Chicago, 1994), p. 15; A. Bermingham, *Landscape and ideology: the English rustic tradition, 1740–1860* (Los Angeles, 1986) is concerned with illuminating the relationship between the aesthetics of the painted landscape and the economics of the enclosed one. 3 See Kennedy & Gillespie (eds), *Ireland: art into history.*

And they also reflect the inequality in past landscapes, where wealth controlled space and place as spectacles and reflections of power.

The picturesque and romantic in poetry and painting in England were essentially constructions of a rural pastoral idyll where nature and humanity lived in harmony, where inhabitants of the wilder mountain landscapes were binaries of primitive but authentic, natural but healthy, frugal as opposed to the corruptness of industrial cities now exploding onto the landscape. These grew out of anti-urban/ industrial sentiments and filtered down to the emerging middle class through writings, cheaper lithographic prints and engravings, postcards, dioramas and panoramas of the nineteenth century.

In addition to artistic representations of the landscape, the discussion also focuses on the landscape itself as art. Picturesque landscapes contained all the elements of a designed, contrived scene in which undesirable elements were erased: 'the views through the windows of the great country houses ... reflected the paintings hanging in their interiors'.[4] In the eighteenth century Humphrey Repton was a strong influence in landscape design and its artistic representation as ordered vision: his landscapes were effectively edited to 'hide the natural defects of every situation ... it must studiously conceal every interference of art ... all objects of mere convenience or comfort, if incapable of being ornamental, or of becoming proper parts of the garden scenery, must be removed or concealed'.[5] David Lowenthal and Hugh Prince suggest that the preferred landscape of the English was the bucolic (anti-urban), the picturesque, the tidy, the deciduous (seasonal), the antiquarian (reflecting the 'grace of antiquity'): 'The English like landscapes compartmentalised into small scenes furnished with belfried church towers, half-timbered thatched cottages, rutted lanes, rookeried elms, lock gates, and stiles ...', that is, landscapes as pictures.[6]

Changing literary and artistic taste in England had direct implications for Ireland, whose élites shared the same cultural milieu.[7] Some contemporaries in nineteenth-century Ireland wrestled with the methodologies of landscape representation and its utility as an accurate reflection of place and scenery: '... as language, unaided by the pencil, is insufficient to convey distinct ideas of visible objects; so the productions of art, unaccompanied by a detailed verbal explanation,

4 W.J. Darby, *Landscape and identity* (Oxford, 2000), p. 29.   **5** H. Repton, *Enquiry into the changes of taste in landscape gardening* (London, 1806) quoted in Bermingham, *Landscape and ideology*, p. 199. For further discussion on history of landscape art, see Mitchell (ed.), *Landscape and power*; Darby, *Landscape and identity*; J. Barrell, *The dark side of the landscape* (Cambridge, 1980).   **6** D. Lowenthal and H. Prince, 'English landscape tastes' in P.W. English and R.C. Mayfield (eds), *Man, space and environment* (New York, 1972), pp 81–114, p. 86; see also Prince, 'Landscape through painting' who catalogues the commonest elements in English landscapes as: humidity (Constable's great coats, misty mornings), rusticity (thatched cottages and cornfields), antiquity (ruins); D. Lowenthal and H. Prince, 'The English landscape' in *Geographical Review*, 54 (3) (1964), pp 309–46.   **7** See L. Gibbons, 'Romanticism, realism and Irish cinema' in K. Rockett et al. (eds), *Cinema and Ireland* (Syracuse NY, 1988).

can communicate little knowledge of a place ...'[8] An early nineteenth-century traveller to Ireland addressed this issue of art and topographic facts. Anne Plumptre commissioned a number of artistic engravings for her *Narrative of a residence in Ireland during the summer of 1814 and that of 1815* and was anxious in her preface to 'reprobate ... the too common practice among artists, of rather aiming at forming a pleasing combination of objects, than delineating the spot such as it really is.' However, it was 'remarkable scenery' she was interested in and all her plates are of Salmon Leap, Giant's Causeway, The Scalp, Pollaphuca waterfall, Blarney Castle and so on: 'Ireland abounds everywhere with noblemen's and gentlemen's seats; but these did not excite my curiosity like the natural beauties and wonders of the country.'[9] In spite of many of these observations, however, there are some rare painted or engraved records which illustrate everyday life and as W.H. Crawford observes, provide detail on the artifacts and craftsmanship which characterised the vernacular world of our ancestors in rural Wicklow or provincial towns.[10]

PAINTED PLACES AND IMAGES OF LANDSCAPE

Until the era of seventeenth-century Dutch painters, landscape painting, like landscape itself, held little aesthetic interest.[11] What became landscape, had simply been land, which had been appraised mainly in terms of its utility for agriculture or its opposite, wild and uncultivated nature. Although landscape was represented fairly realistically in classical Greek and Roman painting and poetry, in medieval pictures landscape was usually depicted in a highly formalised metaphorical mode frequently with classical or biblical allusions. Landscape as property became the driving force which came with the age of merchant capitalism. By the late seventeenth century in England, 'landscape' with its many meanings and manifestations was the antithesis of 'land', which was mainly about material things like farms and agricultural production. Prince has suggested that the work of artists and designers has had an important role in shaping a discourse of landscape: 'for they constantly re-state and re-examine the values by which we make our judgements in the only way they can be stated – visually'.[12] Most artists and painters select what (they deem) is important from the many 'appearances' in a landscape, which led to Charles Baudelaire's claim that the 'majority of our landscape painters are liars'.[13]

8 I. Weld, *Illustrations of the scenery of Killarney and the surrounding country* (London, 1812), p. ii. See A. Bermingham, 'Reading Constable' in S. Pugh (ed.), *Reading landscape: country – city – capital* (Manchester, 1990), pp 97–120. **9** A. Plumptre, *Narrative of a residence in Ireland during the summer of 1814 and that of 1815* (London, 1817), preface and p. 215. **10** See W.H. Crawford, 'The patron or festival of St Kevin at the seven churches' in *Ulster Folklife*, xxxi (1986), pp 37–47; also idem, 'Provincial town life in the early nineteenth century: an artist's impressions' in Kennedy & Gillespie (eds), *Ireland: art into history*, pp 43–59. For a general discussion of this topic, see H. Prince, 'Art and agrarian change, 1710–1815' in Cosgrove & Daniels (eds), *Iconography of landscape*, pp 98–118. **11** Berger, *Ways of seeing*, p. 105. **12** Prince, 'Landscape through painting', p. 16. **13** Quoted in Pugh, *Reading landscape:*

For instance, artistic evidence for an agricultural revolution underway in eighteenth-century England is largely absent from the record.[14]

Artistic texts

'One of the consistent purposes of landscape painting has been to present an image of order and proportioned control, to suppress evidence of tension and conflict between social groups and within human relationships in the environment' which was 'true for the arcadian image of English landscape parks in the Georgian period of rural conflict and transformation'.[15] Gainsborough's painting of 'Mr and Mrs Andrews' which shows them presiding as privileged landowners over 'nature,' over 'their' landscape, has been characterised as the epigrammatic celebration of private ownership of the landscape in the eighteenth century, a pose that was replicated in similar Irish portraiture.[16] Most illustrations of eighteenth-century English and Irish landscapes are emptied of labourers and peasants, showing the power and dominant view of landscape by an élite landowning class; if they are shown, it is usually in the margins, or as John Barrell, expert on history and art of the eighteenth and early nineteenth centuries, characterised it – the dark side of the landscape. Elites dispossessed peasantry and reconstructed parts of landscape for their own pleasure, as one commentator suggested in 1836: 'you cannot *freely* admire a noble landscape, if labourers are digging in the field hard by'.[17] Parks or paintings were frequently filled with classical allusions, which spoke of privilege of class and an education in Oxbridge or on the Grand Tour.

Until the early eighteenth century, visual representations of landscape in Ireland were limited in scope, content and number. This artistic poverty reflected a war-torn undeveloped landscape in which a new colonial class was settling, with limited incentive for artistic patronage. Notions of landscape and aesthetic appreciation of landscape were minimal: land was perceived in strictly utilitarian terms and nature in its wilder places was regarded with hostility. The closest to artistic representations of landscape were the maps and surveys of new estates, often accompanied by primitive sketches of views or buildings, and written descriptions and surveys, represented in such sources as *Pacata Hibernia*, or the drawings of Francis Place or Gabriel Berenger.

By the mid-1700s, the beginnings of what has sometimes been characterised as a 'colonial' art emerged in Ireland to match the growing political and cultural confidence of the Protestant establishment in the country. It was influenced by contemporary movements in aesthetic and intellectual thought in England and on the Continent and nurtured by the Dublin Society which encouraged interest in landscape art and landscape 'improvement' in general.[18] Native Irish art was

country – city – capital, p. 4.   **14** Prince, 'Art and agrarian change, 1710–1815'.   **15** Cosgrove, 'Prospect, perspective and the evolution of the landscape idea' in *TIBG*, 10 (1) (1984) p. 58. **16** See Berger, *Ways of seeing*, p. 108.   **17** R. Emerson quoted in Mitchell (ed.), *Landscape and power*, p. 15. The construction of demesnes especially reflected these attitudes.   **18** See B. Arnold, *A concise history of Irish art* (London, 1969); A. Crookshank and the Knight of Glin,

confined mainly to a rural peasant and folk art which was best represented in song and oral traditions. By the mid-eighteenth century the 'landscape' began to emerge more prominently into the aesthetic horizons of the élite, particularly where it impinged on the Big House. The artistic legacy from the eighteenth century is dominated by the preferences of the privileged in society, produced by artists (or gardeners) working for commissions from wealthy gentry or bourgeois patrons. 'The houses which Richard Castle had designed earlier in the century had merged into the Irish countryside, trees and gardens had matured, and men such as Barrett, Ashford and Roberts were employed to paint pictures of them'.[19]

Such representations generally edited out 'the menacing muddle of peasant life'[20] from the scene. These sources have been subject to the specialised intellectual analysis of fine art historians and have been under-exploited by social historians. Art historians, for instance, have asserted the role of an artist such as James Arthur O'Connor (1792–1841) in painting 'pictures in which the mood and atmosphere, the time of day and the season of the year, the originality of composition and the communication of an event or moment mattered more than the locality and who owned it'[21] – a motivation which might considerably reduce its value to social historians who must rely on more topographical art, which has been characterised by art historian critics as mere 'industry'. To what extent, however, did Irish artists notice the changing landscape in the eighteenth and early nineteenth centuries and the gradual development of enclosure for instance? It may have been too imperceptible to record. It has been suggested that hedgerows did not feature commonly in paintings in England prior to 1910 when post-impressionist ideas discovered beauty in such geometrical patterns.[22] Indeed, hedges and enclosures were not considered sufficiently notable to be included by the early Ordnance

The painters of Ireland, 1660–1920 (London, 1978); idem, *The watercolours of Ireland: works on paper in pencil, pastel and paint, c.1600–1914* (London, 1994); W. Strickland, *A dictionary of Irish artists* (2 vols, Dublin, 1968); P.A. Butler, *Three hundred years of Irish watercolours and drawings* (London, 1990); M. Bourke and S. Bhreathnach-Lynch, *Discover Irish art at the National Gallery of Ireland: a reference book on Irish art* (Dublin, 1999) is a good introduction to the range of works available which includes a list with short notes of the principal artists of the eighteenth, nineteenth and twentieth centuries. J. Hewitt, *Art in Ulster: 1* (Belfast, 1977) is an account of work by 119 visiting artists in the eighteenth century and native Irish artists up to the mid-twentieth century. *Portraits and prospects: British and Irish drawings and watercolours from the collection of the Ulster Museum* (Ulster Museum, Belfast, 1989) is a good introduction to the range of Irish landscape views held by the Museum. W. Laffan (ed.), *Painting Ireland: topographical views from Glin castle* (Tralee, 2006) contains 200 views of houses, townscapes and gardens from the Knight of Glin's collection accompanied by interdisciplinary essays. **19** P. Harbison, H. Potterton and J. Sheehy, *Irish art and architecture from prehistory to the present* (London, 1978); V. Kreilkamp, 'Painting Mayo's landscape: The big house, the pleasure grounds, and the mills' in V. Kreilkamp (ed.), *Éire/Land* (Boston, 2003), pp 71–8 for discussion of James O'Connor's commissioned work. **20** As T.C. Barnard puts it, in 'Chisel the image of the chief' (*Times Literary Supplement*, 23 June 1995). **21** B. Arnold, *A concise history of Irish art* (New York, 1989), p. 95. **22** P. Howard, 'Painters' preferred places' in *Journal of Historical Geography*, 11 (2) (1985), pp 138–54, p. 152.

5.1 Carton House and Park, County Kildare (courtesy of Dr J.K. St Joseph Collection, Cambridge University)

Survey. Not until it reached mid-Monaghan in 1835 did it begin to include all the field enclosures on the face of the six-inch maps.

It is instructive to speculate on the seeming underdevelopment of much of the rural landscape in the seventeenth- and early eighteenth-century artistic representations of landscape in Ireland. Perhaps the comparative emptiness of contemporary maps of landscape matched a lack of interest by landowning élites, whose attention was being lavished on the immediate environs of their mansions and parklands, though as John Andrews notes this is probably more a reflection of cartographic tradition than environmental reality.[23] Parklands and houses became

23 See Andrews, *Plantation acres*, pp 156–8.

the primary objects of attention of architects, surveyors, landscape gardeners, and eventually artists and painters as well. The English commentator on late eighteenth-century rural improvement and development, Arthur Young was taken aback by this disinterest in their domestic localities by Irish gentry – a 'surprising inattention … to the food, clothing, possessions and state of the poor, even in their own neighbourhood; many a question have I put to gentlemen upon these points, which were not answered without having recourse to the next cabbin'.[24]

Patrons, therefore, commissioned painters to represent their properties 'as much like an earthly paradise as possible, and to make this state of affairs look natural … the artists' brief was to bolster the pride and pleasure of the land-owning class'.[25] James Arthur O'Connor (with Thomas Roberts, William Ashford and many others) established a reputation for producing 'portraits of houses' catering to this gentry market which required painters to show off their estate landscapes. Others who contributed to this vogue were George Barrett, Jonathan Fisher, Thomas Roberts, William Ashford, William Sadler, James Malton, Thomas Sautelle Roberts, Joseph Peacock, John Henry Campbell, George Petrie, Francis Danby, Thomas James Mulvany and William Howis. The estate papers of the enormous Downshire estate show it to be an epitome of social and landscape order.[26] An illuminated address from the marquis of Downshire's tenants in 1865 represents an arcadian prospect in marginal illustrations of houses, mills, workshops in harmony with the pastoral rurality of the estate.

To what extent do artistic representations in paintings, prints, sketches and drawings assist in recovering or imagining the past landscapes which environed our ancestors at different periods in the past? Artists were not painting places for historians or geographers to study in times to come, but usually for rich patrons and commissions. In terms of landscape facts, perhaps more obscure artists or sketchers, who were not preoccupied with the market or patrons' wishes, might have more to say to us. However, they are unlikely to represent humbler landscapes, as the widespread popularity of prints and engravings of landscapes which resulted from improved printing techniques in the early nineteenth century simply popularised the upper class romantic taste in landscape.

Topographical facts

Bearing in mind the influence of market and patronage, as well as the dominant discourses of landscape controlled by 'schools' of art, the selectivity in subject matter depicted, as well as the capacity of the artist to 'edit' his portraits, what kind of facts might landscape art provide that would be useful to historians? The framed view

---

24 A. Young, *A tour in Ireland, 1776–1779* (Shannon, 1970), p. 35. F. O'Kane, *Landscape design in eighteenth-century Ireland* (Cork, 2004) explores the passion for landscape design which gripped many of the landowning gentry in Ireland; see also Friel, *Frederick Trench, 1746–1836, and Heywood*. **25** J. Hutchinson, *James Arthur O'Connor* (National Gallery of Ireland, Dublin, 1985), p. 12. **26** W.A. Maguire, *The Downshire estates in Ireland, 1801–1845* (Oxford, 1972) and *Letters of a great Irish landlord*, ed. Maguire.

5.2 Lucan House and demesne, *c.*1770 by Thomas Roberts (photograph courtesy of the National Gallery of Ireland). Full painting and detail.

was a dominant influence on the way the landscape was seen, a device to 'frame nature', composing it like a picture, which was the precursor to the later nineteenth- and twentieth-century camera and postcard construction of the view/scene.

In general, the best recorded and most painted landscapes in the country in the eighteenth and nineteenth centuries are the demesnes and other preferred pictur-esque landscapes of the élite. This is demonstrated in contemporary compilations of prints and engravings, as for instance in Thomas Milton's *Collection of select views from the different seats of the nobility and gentry of Ireland* (Dublin, 1793) and Francis Grose's *Antiquities of Ireland* (London, 179?–95). Mapping the locations of identified views in Ireland in the late eighteenth and early nineteenth centuries shows the popularity of Big Houses and antiquities in most of the paintings.[27] Within the prevailing landscape aesthetics in eighteenth- and nineteenth-century art, there is potential interest for historians of landscape in the topographical detail of many paintings, drawings, prints and what has been characterised as primitive art from the seventeenth to the nineteenth centuries. During the nineteenth century particularly, before the onset of photography, drawings and illustrations which featured in travel journals, newspapers and periodicals were comprehensively topographical in detail, documentary in intention, and often picturesque in presentation. Local texture of roads and fields, architecture of buildings and house types, people's dress, machines and transport, even the 'red and white' (hereford) cows of Nathaniel Hone's paintings of north County Dublin, represent in broad terms, human or social landscapes.

James Malton's Dublin paintings are perhaps the best and most well-known accurate representations of buildings and streetscapes on the eve of the Union, as are his lesser known drawings of country houses.[28] Dublin is best represented in landscape art. Comparisons of the representations of streetscapes in Dublin by Henry and Samuel Frederick Brocas, W.H. Bartlett, Michael Angelo Hayes, James

---

27 See *Illustrated summary catalogue of drawings, watercolours and miniatures [in the NGI]* compiled by A. Le Harivel (Dublin, 1983). The NGI catalogues accompanying exhibitions since the 1980s contain comprehensive introductory essays. R. Elmes and M. Hewson, *Catalogue of Irish topographical prints and original drawings* (NLI, Dublin, 1975) lists *c.*6,000 holdings in National Library of Ireland, which has in addition a collection of 5,000 architectural drawings from the eighteenth and nineteenth centuries. See E.M. Kirwan, 'Prints and drawings in the National Library' in *History Ireland*, 3 (Summer 1995), pp 48–52. The NLI houses many manuscripts. One (NLI 2003TX) consists of 93 pages of sketches dating from 1849–50 – water colour, pencil and pen and ink sketches for west and northern parts. The Irish Architectural Archive, the RIA and TCD have additional extensive collections.   **28** See E. McParland, 'Malton's views of Dublin: too good to be true?' in Kennedy & Gillespie (eds), *Ireland: art into history*, pp 15–25, containing details of all Malton's views in footnotes; also Malton's *A picturesque and descriptive view of the city of Dublin*, (London, 1792–9; Dolmen press edition, 1978); the Irish Heritage series booklet on *The City Hall* which shows a range of drawings of this building (originally the Royal Exchange) from Malton's 1790s picture to Petrie's of 1831. Dublin especially has a wide range of representations of its streetscapes and buildings as befitted the capital city.

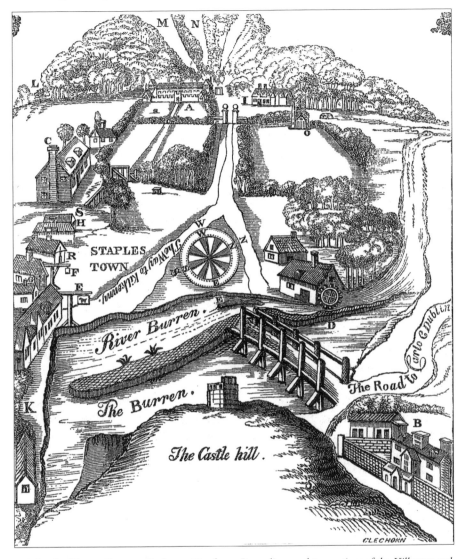

5.3 Staples Town, County Carlow, 1681; from *Proceedings and transactions of the Kilkenny and South-East of Ireland Archaeological Society*, iii (1856–67), p. 44

Wheatley with contemporary written descriptions by Mary Shackleton, show how the busy, lively landscape which she witnessed in the 1820s is absent in Brocas, who concentrated on showing off the architecture and so excluded the 'noise factor' of the populace. 'Architectural' art focussed on the buildings, not the social landscape. Today, one of the problems of photographs of streets in towns and cities is the ever-present intrusion of traffic, obscuring the architectural structure of buildings. This qualification also applies to many representations of rural landscapes where minor details of poorer marginal settlements are excluded from the painted record. However, artists such as Malton, Bartlett, Joseph Tudor, Wheatley or Hayes, provide selective records of human activity in the streetscape, with references to dress, modes of transport, economic activity, poverty, and begging. Rose Barton's late nineteenth-century paintings of Dublin ('Going to the Levee', for instance) have been seen as a paean to the end of Empire/Anglo-Irish gentry in Ireland in a similar way to Elizabeth Bowen's writings.

Thomas Phillips's 1684 series of watercolours were probably the first real topographical views of Irish towns and forts, emphasising the landscape priorities of his time – defence and conquest.[29] Apart from Dublin which is well covered, pictures of provincial towns are comparatively rare for the eighteenth century or earlier: there are no pictures of Ennis between a sketch by Thomas Dineley (or Dingley) in 1680 and a faded photograph from 1867, an extraordinary absence for a county town.[30] Dineley provided rough sketches of buildings in Limerick, Kinsale and Youghal also, as well as some mansion houses, monuments and abbeys in the countryside.[31] Francis Place's Irish drawings constitute an important source for reconstructing the social landscape of the main towns in Leinster at the end of the seventeenth century: he rendered the first and most comprehensive views of Dublin, Waterford, Kilkenny and places en route.[32] His Waterford in 1699 can be usefully compared with William Van der Hagen's famous 1736 view.

Like most artists in the second half of the eighteenth century, Francis Wheatley was preoccupied with acquiring commissions from wealthy landed patrons.[33] Consequently, many of his works fall into the genre of romantic and picturesque landscape representations, emphasising the importance of 'improving' on nature in painting: it had the aim of 'not merely describing; but of adapting the description of natural scenery to the principles of artificial landscape …,'[34] that is, making the view of the landscape like a picture. Much of his work, however, is topographically accurate, providing useful insights into the material world of the later eighteenth century, especially his representations of what were fashionably perceived as 'rustic' scenes of peasantry, beggars and tradespeople, for example in Donnybrook Fair.

29 R. Gillespie, 'Describing Dublin: Francis Place's visit, 1698–99' in Dalsimer (ed.), *Visualizing Ireland*, pp 99–117.   **30** L.M. Cullen, *Six generations: life and work in Ireland from 1790* (Cork, 1970), p. 117; see also his *Life in Ireland*.   **31** See his *Observations in a voyage through the kingdom of Ireland … in the year 1681*, ed. J. Graves (Dublin, 1870); also 'Extracts from the journal of Thomas Dineley. Esq., giving some account of his visit to Ireland in the reign of Charles 11' in *Proceedings and transactions of the Kilkenny and South-East of Ireland Archaeological Society*, i, ii, iii, v (1856–67).   **32** Gillespie, 'Francis Place's visit', p. 102. Van der Hagen's view is held by Waterford Corporation. See R. Loeber, 'An unpublished view of Dublin in 1698 by Francis Place, in *Quarterly Bulletin of the Irish Georgian Society*, 21 (1978), pp 7–15.   **33** See J. Kelly, 'Francis Wheatley: his Irish paintings, 1779–1783' in Dalsimer (ed.), *Visualizing Ireland*, pp 145–64.   **34** W. Gilpin, quoted in B.P. Kennedy, 'The traditional Irish thatched house: image and reality, 1793–1993' in Dalsimer (ed.), *Visualizing Ireland*, p. 165.

Like Wheatley, Joseph Peacock painted Donnybrook fair and his work has strains of realism.[35] W. H. Crawford has shown how Peacock's detailed panoramic crowd scene at the 'Pattern of Glendalough' in 1813 may be read by social historians.[36] Breaking it down into its component parts, Crawford shows how the accuracy of Peacock's observation may be used to illuminate social and economic life in early nineteenth-century Wicklow. For instance, several forms of vehicles can be distinguished:

> Examining this range of vehicles, we become more aware of the continuing great importance to early nineteenth-century society of the horse as the major means of transport. Because of the great improvements in the Irish road network over the previous half-century, the wheel car had become the commonest vehicle for transporting goods throughout much of the country … Many people still travelled on horseback. In the party arriving at the fair, just behind the entertainment tent, there are two women riding their horses side-saddle in the contemporary style.[37]

He also identifies local utensils and footwear. It is an exemplary commentary on the documentary evidence available in a painting. Geraldine Stout demonstrates very well the use which can be made of many late eighteenth- and early nineteenth-century paintings in local studies. Drawings and pictures by Beranger, Tudor, du Noyer, Wakeman and others provide useful information on houses and landscapes in the Boyne valley.[38]

In spite of the presence of ruinous, tumble-down cottages with happy, healthy, hard-working peasantry as often fictional picturesque landscape settings, paintings can provide indirect depictions of buildings, poverty and country life in a landscape context.[39] Indeed Kevin O'Neill has suggested that 'these images are our only real record of certain aspects of architecture, dress, technology, food ways, and other aspects of daily life.'[40] Wheatley's portrait *The Marquess and Marchioness of Antrim* (1782), in the National Gallery of Ireland, is a typical representation of the wealth and importance of nobility with their material possessions on display. The landscape context of these portraits is sometimes believed to be largely a studio-based fiction,

35 See S. Ó Maitiú, 'Changing images of Donnybrook fair' in D.A. Cronin, J. Gilligan and K. Holton (eds), *Irish fairs and markets: studies in local history* (Dublin, 2000), pp 164–79. **36** Crawford, 'The patron, or festival of St Kevin'; idem, 'Provincial life in the early nineteenth century: an artist's impressions'; idem, 'The linen industry portrayed in the Hincks prints of 1783' in Crawford, *The impact of the domestic linen industry in Ulster* (Belfast, 2005), pp 49–57. **37** Crawford, 'The patron, or festival of St Kevin', p. 44. **38** Stout, *Newgrange and the bend of the Boyne*, pp 37, 41, 42, 54, 73, 85 91, 103, 119, 153–4, 190–204. **39** See Barrell, *The dark side of the landscape*; Bermingham, *Landscape and ideology: the English rustic tradition, 1740–1860*. **40** K. O'Neill, 'Looking at the pictures: art and artfulness in colonial Ireland' in Dalsimer (ed.), *Visualizing Ireland*, p. 60. See also V. Kreilkamp, 'Painting Mayo's landscape: the big house, the pleasure grounds, and the mills' in Kreilkamp (ed.), *Éire | Land*, pp 71–8.

though Wheatley is known to have visited Glenarm on the Antrim estate, and his painting is topographically authentic.

In the later nineteenth and twentieth centuries landscapes of the west of Ireland came to be seen by artists and writers as representative of an 'authentic' (largely mythical) past. The rugged environment of remote islands and mountains, with a still vibrant traditional culture, captured the eastern urban imagination. 'The heroic peasants of Synge's texts and Yeats's images populate [Paul Henry's] early pictures, and the men and women digging potatoes, cutting turf, and fishing are observed with a striking dignity.'[41] These views helped to shape popular conceptions of an idyllic, happy and wholesome countryside which matched the populist political constructions of de Valera and the Catholic church in the new independent state. A range of artists depicted the landscape and society of the Aran islands in this mode, for example, from the antiquarian and romantic perspectives of George Petrie, W.F. Wakeman and Frederick William Burton to the realism of Jack Yeats, the Celtic revivalism of William Orpen and the cultural nationalism of Seán Keating, Charles Lamb, Maurice MacGonigal and Paul Henry.[42] Ordinary people came to feature more naturally and prominently in their landscapes. Henry's 'grim realism' contrasted with the romantic landscapes of late eighteenth-century and nineteenth-century renditions. Many of his landscapes convey 'a pervasive sense of humanity – of land that has been "camped on before", in Seamus Heaney's phrase; they express the timelessness of our relationship to the land that supports us'.[43] His iconographic western landscapes of expansive skies, islands and seas, brown bogs, blue mountains, windblown trees, turf stacks and thatched houses became emblematic of the new Free State's cultural identity; indeed his work was also commissioned by the new Northern Ireland tourism agency.[44] The landscapes Henry painted have now completely disappeared and in this sense he has captured the atmosphere and sense of place of a rapidly vanishing landscape almost at the point of disappearance.

Antiquarian landscapes

The antiquarian movement from the early eighteenth century, though it had an esoteric focus on relict and ruined landscapes, was the most frequent source of sketches, drawings and engravings which often included more panoramic and extensive views of landscapes as contexts of particular sites. In terms of understanding our legacy of archaeological and built environment, these early antiquarian descriptions and illustrations are important records of the state of the monuments, some of which have disappeared from the landscape.[45] Sponsored by the Royal

---

41 S.B. Kennedy, *Paul Henry* (NGI, Dublin, 2003), p. 27.   **42** See A. Korff, 'The artist's eye' in J. Feehan et al. (eds), *The book of Aran: the Aran Islands, Co. Galway* (Kinvara, 1994), pp 269–88.   **43** Kennedy, *Paul Henry*, pp 14, 64.   **44** See B.P. Kennedy, 'The traditional Irish thatched house' in Kennedy & Gillespie (eds), *Ireland: art into history*, p. 174; M. Bourke, 'Yeats, Henry and the western idyll' in *History Ireland*, 2, no. 2 (Summer 2003), pp 28–33. **45** M. de Paor, 'Irish antiquarian artists' in Dalsimer (ed.), *Visualizing Ireland*, pp 119–32; see also Crookshank and the Knight of Glin, *The watercolours of Ireland*, which contains important samples of work which might be of use to local historians.

Irish Academy, which was the driving force behind scholarship in the arts and sciences from 1785, interest in antiquities in Ireland grew out of a European interest in classical antiquity generated by the Grand Tour experiences of travellers like James Caulfield, first earl of Charlemont (1728–99).[46]

The works of Gabriel Beranger (*c.*1730–1817) provide 'an insight into the state of historic monuments in the eighteenth century and, even more significantly, his watercolours include the only visual records we have of some of them which have since disappeared almost without trace', such as Castle Blaney in County Monaghan.[47] Many of his drawings were done in *situ*, others were copied from contemporary artists such as Jonathan Fisher, William Ashford and Thomas Roberts. Most of them date from the 1770s. In general, they focus on the buildings and ruins in which he was interested: like most antiquarian artists he was attracted by 'the melancholy pleasure of ruins as much as the colourful figures of an arcadian peasantry.'[48] There are incidental glimpses of local landscape contexts such as cultivation ridges, though is the absence of roadside hedges, as for instance in the view of Trim with livestock free to wander, an artistic license to display the main objects of his studies, or does it reflect the reality? His drawings of the Boyne valley were described by anti-quarian Sir William Wilde as being 'stiff' but 'most faithful'. Some of the views, such as those of Ardfinnan Castle in Tipperary or Leighlin Bridge in County Carlow, show a very bare and unenclosed background landscape which may not be realistic, although the background hills to Carlow ('Graig') Castle does show a network of small fields. In general, however, Berenger and others interested in antiquities, by-passed ordinary workaday landscapes. His literary descriptions of some the landscapes he passed through supplement the information in the pictures: in June 1779, for instance, he travelled from Kells in County Meath by Bailieborough, County Cavan, to Clones in Monaghan county (a route which was off the tourist and artists' trail at the time), through countrysides which 'looked poor, the land coarse, the cabins as if going to ruin, half-thatched, several bogs close to the road and digging turf going on almost everywhere'. His chaise broke down, forcing him to walk to Clones, where he spent the day sketching the old church and the market cross.[49] While in Sligo (June 1779) he arrived at the shore of a lake to find

> a great crowd … a dance for a cake … gentlemen and ladies, on horseback and on foot, being mixed with the country people, forming a triple ring round the dancers, whilst a fellow standing on some bench or barrel, held up

46 M. Gibbons and M. Gibbons, 'Charlemont on the Grand Tour' in *History Ireland*, 13, no. 2 (Mar./Apr. 2005), pp 21-27. Also Earl of Roden (ed.), 'The diaries of Lord Limerick's Grand Tour 1716 to 1723' in *Journal of the County Louth Archaeological and Historical Society* (hereinafter *Louth Arch. Soc. Jn.*), xxv (3) (2003), pp 302–35. **47** P. Harbison, *Beranger's antique buildings of Ireland* (Dublin, 1998), pp 21–2, 155. *Beranger's views of Ireland*, ed. P. Harbison (RIA, Dublin, 1991) are based on original mss drawings in the Academy and NLI. **48** De Paor, 'Irish antiquarian artists', p. 119. **49** Sir W. Wilde, *Memoir of Gabriel Beranger, and his labours in the cause of Irish art and antiquities from 1760 to 1780* (Dublin, 1880), p. 36.

a pole, at the end of which the cake was hung in a clean napkin, adorned with ribbands, to be given as a prize to the best performers.

Wilde's nostalgic comment, from his vantage point a century later, reflects on the changing social landscape, remembering the same dances and tunes, which were all but broken up, he said, by the dance houses being turned into Ribbon lodges and the outrages hatched therein: then came the Peelers and the mutual distrust between the upper and peasant classes.[50]

Francis Grose's *Antiquities of Ireland* included drawings by Edward Ledwich, James George O'Brien (alias Oben), Jonathan Fisher and others. Many of his 260 engravings are accompanied by ancillary details of neighouring houses and cabins, as, for example, in Dunamase and Carnew castles. Some of these antiquarian artists also recorded buildings of their own time, especially mansions. William Frederick Wakeman (whose large series of watercolours are in the Royal Irish Academy), who worked with George Petrie in the Ordnance Survey, was also responsible for numerous illustrations for guide books and other publications.[51]

Private publications such as guidebooks and the increasing numbers of tours and traveller accounts required engravings by Irish artists from the early nineteenth century. Mr and Mrs Hall commissioned a team of artists including Andrew Nicholl to do illustrations for *Ireland, its scenery and character* (London, 1841–3). Like many other artists of the nineteenth century, Nicholl drew accurate and useful pictures: his 'View of Belfast' in *The parliamentary gazetteer of Ireland*, vol. 1 (London, 1846) provides accurate foreground detail on a cornfield being harvested in Knockbreda.[52] W.H. Bartlett provided the 114 illustrations comprising mainly antiquities, town views and natural scenes for J. Stirling Coyne's *Scenery and antiquities of Ireland* (London, 1842). The Royal Irish Academy, Ordnance Survey and Geological Survey also afforded opportunities for artistic illustrations of aspects of the Irish landscape in the early decades of the nineteenth century. George Petrie, Andrew Nicholl, Francis Danby, George du Noyer, W.F. Wakeman were among a coterie of artists who were associated with the work of the topographical division of the Ordnance Survey in the 1830s and 40s. Petrie's *Ecclesiastical architecture of Ireland* was published in 1845, featuring his principal interest in the Irish landscape and he illustrated a wide range of publications in pre-famine Ireland.[53] Du Noyer illustrated the Ordnance Survey's first (and last) published memoir of Templemore in County Londonderry. His panoramic landscapes are full of interest and accurate observations, depicting open sun-drenched countrysides: 'His Wicklow landscapes contain conventional Romantic elements, yet they are restrained and the scenes

50 Wilde, *Beranger*, p. 63.   **51** See P. Murray, *George Petrie (1790–1866): the rediscovery of Ireland's past* (Cork, 2004), pp 53–81 for discussion of the popularity of engravings and prints in guidebooks and accounts of tours in the early nineteenth century. Carlo Bianconi started his career in Ireland selling prints from door to door.   **52** Reprinted in B. Walker, *County Down: a topographical dictionary by Samuel Lewis* (Belfast, 2003), p. 5.   **53** See Murray, *George Petrie*. A large collection of Petrie's watercolours repose in the RIA. Francis Danby's watercolours are in the Ulster Museum.

remain plausible.'[54] While in the field for the Geological Survey of Ireland he was able to produce drawings and paintings of a large number of castles, crannógs, churches, cathedrals and crosses.

Prints and drawings

With technical advances in engraving in the 1820s and 30s, prints and drawings became popular sources of illustration available for mass publications in tourism guidebooks, newspapers and periodicals which until the development of photography provided an important outlet for the talents of artists. *Punch*, the *Lady's Newspaper*, the *Pictorial Times* and the *Illustrated London News* all commissioned artists to picture the traumatic events of the famine which had inevitably an enormous impact on landscape. *The Illustrated London News* (commencing in 1842) is an important source for factual details of settlement landscapes, for example.[55] Even in the most appalling circumstances artists could not escape the conventions of the picturesque, in many cases providing accurate renditions of buildings and scenes which understated the poverty and distress of the local population. In February 1847 James Mahony, the Cork artist, was commissioned to go out to record events in Skibbereen. He sketched the town and locality, providing stark images of dereliction and poverty. One of the advantages of the print media was that many artists like Mahony were able to accompany their sketches with heart-rending commentaries which lent effectiveness to the illustrations.

Inclusion of these written commentaries with published prints in the nineteenth century adds utility to the pictures for today's historian. The *Dublin Penny Journal* in August 1832 accompanied a sketch of Kilmallock (on the 'artists trail' from Limerick to Cork featuring in numbers of paintings and drawings) with the comment that '... some wretched peasants had indeed here and there taken up their residence in the corner of a tower or mansion, which, like a solitary figure in a mountain scene, only added to the effect of sadness and desolation ...'[56] John George Mulvany's view of the town *c.*1820 is full of incidental activity by the inhabitants, with a group waiting on the stagecoach which has just entered the street. The abiding impression of the town, however, is the ruinous condition of its range of three-storied buildings, focussed on the sixteenth-century King's Castle.[57] Isaac Weld, in an earlier illustration of Kilmallock, attributed its 'misery' to 'the total want of manufactures, and to the land of the surrounding country being almost

54 J. Archer, 'Geological artistry: the drawings and watercolors of George Victor du Noyer in the Archives of the Geological Survey of Ireland' in Dalsimer (ed.), *Visualizing Ireland*, p. 142. His drawings and watercolours are now in the GSI, RIA and RSAI. See National Gallery of Ireland, *George Victor du Noyer, 1817–1869: hidden landscapes* (Dublin, 1995) and P. Coffey, 'George Victor du Noyer, 1817–1869: artist, geologist and antiquary' in *JRSAI*, 123 (1993), pp 102–19. **55** M. Crawford, 'The great Irish famine, 1845–9: image versus reality' in Kennedy & Gillespie (eds), *Ireland: art into history*, pp 75–88. **56** *Dublin Penny Journal*, 25 Aug. 1832, p. 65. The *DPJ* ran from 1832 to 1835. **57** Mulvany's view of Kilmallock is in the National Gallery of Ireland, no. 991.

5.4 West of Ireland house, 1880; *The Graphic*

wholly devoted to grazing bullocks. The peasantry are few, and their condition abject ... Throughout this district, man seems to derive less benefit from the bountiful gifts of nature, than the beasts which repose in the luxuriant meadows.'[58]

A *Dublin Penny Journal* sketch of 1824 shows the last half-timbered house in Drogheda, reputedly erected *c.*1570, which may have been typical of an earlier period in other towns in the Pale. It was built by Nicholas Bathe of Athcarne in County Meath and consisted of three floors over a basement, with the upper floor projecting over the others: '... having been for many years suspected of harbouring rats, reprobates, and typhus fever, was at length condemned to annihilation by the corporation, and disappeared for ever in the year 1824; the present handsome modern brick buildings were erected on its site'.[59] Illustrations in the *Journal* consist mostly of antiquities, castles, gentry residences or romantic scenes (as well as portraits of animals in Dublin's new Zoological Gardens). There is a detailed drawing of The Lady's Island, County Wexford, showing the island, with ridges, field networks, a windmill, castle, 'a Roman Catholic chapel, a school-house and eight or ten tolerably comfortable cottages.'[60] The timber bridge at Cappoquin, County Waterford, was described as 'a favourite excursion for summer parties ... The scenery around is highly picturesque, and the town is much superior in point of cleanliness to many Irish towns of the same size. The bridge existed prior to the

58 Weld, *Illustrations of the scenery of Killarney*, p. 245.   **59** *DPJ*, i (12), 15 Sept. 1832, p. 90. **60** *DPJ*, i (30), Jan. 1833, pp 233–4.

time of Charles the Second, as an act was passed during his reign for its repair. It is now exceedingly crazy; the passage of a single individual caused it to tremble from one end to the other.'[61]

Book cover designs have recently been examined as a source for landscape research.[62] Books especially on tours and travels through regional landscapes have invited distinctively themed engraved covers, as have posters by tourism boards and transport companies, many of which exhibit idyllic renditions of rural landscapes for example. Artists like Paul Henry were commissioned by the Ulster Tourism Board, the Irish Tourism Authority, Great Northern Railway or An Gúm, the state publishing agency established in 1925. Posters and postcards illustrating the Irish landscape for the past century have all participated in what might be characterised as a 'lie of landscape' in which a largely fabricated discourse of landscape has been projected. Brian Kennedy has examined book covers incorporating 'Celtic' motifs, as well as iconographic representations of landscape in such media as postage stamps, postcards, tourism posters, paper currency notes, and new monuments in the capital's streets. Even collectable cards by cigarette, chocolate and confectionary producers have purveyed images of Ireland.[63]

PHOTOGRAPHED LANDSCAPE

Landscape photography often followed the traditions of painters, producing images and selecting subject matter which grew out of the earlier artistic vision, although landscape came late as a subject, with earliest attention being focussed on people, often in incidental landscape contexts. However, photography has been especially useful in recording buildings in the nineteenth century. It is difficult for us to appreciate the details of housing, for example, in the nineteenth (and earlier) centuries. Our living conditions and economic circumstances are worlds apart from the landscapes of nineteenth-century reports, and images often provide the most effective witness to this. The unique colour photographs taken by two Parisian women, Mmes Mespoulet and Mignon, as recently as 1913 are striking images of impoverished living conditions in the west of Ireland, with grass growing on roofs and dunghills in situations difficult to imagine today.[64]

61 *DPJ*, ii (93), Apr. 1834, p. 325.   **62** See C. Brace, 'Publishing and publishers: towards an historical geography of countryside writing, c.1930–1950' in *Area*, 33, no. 3 (Sept. 2001), pp 287–96; idem, 'Envisioning England: the visual in countryside writing in the 1930s and 1940s' in *Landscape Research*, 28 (4) (2003), pp 365–82 where she looks at the publications of Batsford.   **63** See 2004 exhibition of *An Gúm* covers, John J. Burns Library of Boston College, www.bc.edu/libraries/centers/burns/; B.P. Kennedy, 'The Irish Free State 1922–49: a visual perspective' in Kennedy & Gillespie (eds), *Ireland: art into history*, pp 132–52; B. Share, 'Pasteboard perceptions: European images of Ireland, 1870s–1940s' in *History Ireland*, 10, no. 2 (2002), pp 26–30.   **64** Part of the project sponsored by Albert Kahn to make a photographic archive of many parts of the world in the process of change, available in the Albert Kahn Museum in Paris, featured in RTÉ's 'Townlands' series on 18 Aug. 2004. See

Photographs can be powerful sources for local history, and this is reflected in their widespread use in local historical publications.[65] Though photographs suggest an authentic reality in each scene, as with paintings, photographs are social/artistic constructions, and posing a picture was important. In addition technical restrictions such as the need to have still subjects or bright light conditions lead to impressions of towns, for example, which are always sunny or devoid of life and movement. For this reason, they are especially valuable sources for urban streetscapes with details on architecture, street furniture, advertising, shopfronts, as well as conditions of street surfaces and the basic morphology and rooflines of buildings in a time before traffic. The shape and structure of most towns and villages today are obscured by traffic and parked cars. Early photographs show the towns as they were meant to be seen.

The postcard market generated a plethora of idyllic rural scenes especially, which collectively lead to erroneous assumptions or impressions of these places in the past. Postcards were usually published to respond to the 'tourist gaze', so that the general romanticism of an earlier period has permeated down to our present day way of seeing landscape. John Hinde, who was a prodigious producer of postcard images of rural Irish scenes in the 1960s, is credited with inventing for the tourist market an Ireland that did not exist: his photographs were retouched, his sunsets intensified and his scenes frequently enhanced to produce an idyllic landscape.[66] However, it has been pointed out that the earlier William Lawrence Collection of photographs also presented an idealised picture of Ireland and yet are highly valued today as records of earlier periods and places. As with paintings and drawings, however, unknown amateur photographers have produced important records of scenes and places which have been radically transformed in modern times. For this reason, photographic sources are particularly appropriate for the historian interested in the local and ordinary day-to-day happenings and places.

The Dublin Photographic Society was founded in 1854 and by the late nineteenth century commercial photography was mainly concerned with taking views which could be sold in the postcard market. The Lawrence collection of *c.*40,000 glass plate negatives in the National Photographic Archive in Meeting House Square in Dublin is one of the most extensive and mainly catered for this market from the 1870s (http://www.nli.ie/ca_java.htm). Apart from some personal/journalistic interests of the photographer, the postcard market generally dictated the kind of scenes photographed. In 1990–91 The Lawrence Project saw the re-photographing of 1000 Lawrence scenes to illustrate the rate of change and

also G. Neville, 'A la recherche de l'Irlande perdue: two French photographers in Ireland in 1913' in *Études Irlandaises*, xvi (2) (1991), pp 75–89.   **65** See M. Hill and V. Pollack, 'Images of the past: photographs as historical evidence' in *History Ireland*, 2, no. 1 (Spring 1994), pp 9–14 in which the large photographic collections such as Lawrence, Welch, Green, Hogg, Rose Shaw, Alice Young etc. are discussed. Many institutions hold substantial archives with local topographic value.   **66** See L. Gibbons on Hinde in *Transformations in Irish culture* (Cork, 1996), pp 37–43.

5.5 The Square, Caher, c.1900 (courtesy of the National Library of Ireland)

continuity through the twentieth century and these are available in the National Library of Ireland.

The National Library's Photographic Archive houses the Lawrence, Eason, Valentine, Poole and Wynne collections which incorporate thousands of photographs, most of them for postcards. Other collections in the National Library are parts of estate paper archives, essentially gentry family albums, such as the Clonbrock collection from the Dillons of Ahascragh in County Galway. The Congested Districts Board collection (1892–1914) and the Connemara album (1892) are important illustrations of impoverished marginal landscapes in western parts of counties Donegal, Mayo and Galway especially.[67] There are valuable Irish collections also in the Ulster Museum, the RDS, the Victoria and Albert Museum and the Hulton Getty archive in London. The photographic section of National Monuments (Department of Environment, Heritage and Local Government) has an extensive array of photographs of monuments and buildings, as have many of the county libraries for their local areas.[68] The Irish Architectural Archive, as well as the British Architectural Library, Drawings Collection, contain photographs of Irish buildings most notably Great Houses (www.artguide.org/uk/). Other important repositories of photograph collections are: The Dublin Civic Museum, South William Street; Royal Society of Antiquaries of Ireland, Merrion Square; Royal Irish Academy, Dawson Street; Ordnance Survey of Ireland; Geological Survey of Ireland; DoE, Northern Ireland, Monuments and Buildings Branch (for the St Joseph collection and McCutcheon archive of industrial archaeology); Ulster Folk and Transport Museum.[69]

In 1942 the Irish Tourist Association embarked on an extensive topographical survey of scenery in Ireland. Thirty-three officers were commissioned by the association to undertake a parish-by-parish survey of antiquities, castles and Big Houses, sporting facilities, accommodation, historic sites, houses and spas, as well as details on towns and villages. By February 1943, for example, a total of thirty-one parishes in County Kerry alone had been photographed and surveyed. A wealth of information on local areas was amassed which would repay investigation in local studies.[70] This enormous catalogue is now with Bord Fáilte, Dublin and also in most county libraries.

Unlike most photograph collections (and paintings and sketches from earlier periods) which are often static posed representations of views and buildings, the Fr

67 See *On the verge of want*, ed. Morrissey.   **68** S. Rouse, *Into the light: an illustrated guide to the photographic collections in the National Library of Ireland* (Dublin, 1998); J. Scarry, *Monuments in the past: photographs, 1870–1936* (Dublin, 1991) is a selection from the OPW's photographic archive. The provenance of the collections is discussed in the foreword. The photographs are important records of the state of the monuments in the later nineteenth century.   **69** http://www.dublintourist.com/details/dublin_civic_museum.shtml; http://www.rsai.ie/; http://www.ria.ie/; http://www.osi.ie/; http://www.gsi.ie/; http://www.doeni.gov.uk/; http://www.uftm.org.uk/   **70** See I. Furlong, 'The state promotion of tourism in independent Ireland, 1925–1955' (unpublished PhD thesis, NUIM), pp 162–3; http://www.waterfordcountylibrary.ie/library/web.

Frank Browne SJ, collection is marked by its high artistic qualities.[71] Many of Browne's photographs can be used to evoke a sense of place in Ireland of the 1920s and 30s, full of atmosphere, with people in the act of moving through time/space, stepping off a footpath, almost transmitting the sounds of lost local worlds. In this sense, they can be compared to the photography of famous French photographers Henri Cartier-Bresson, Willy Ronis or Robert Doisneau. Such high artistic qualities are not necessary in a data source about past landscapes – but they do add to the enjoyment of the study! In all this collection contains over 40,000 negatives covering unique views of industrial, agricultural, commercial and social life in post-independence Ireland.[72]

Large numbers of collections have been published independently, the unifying theme usually being locality or place. Friar's Bush Press in Belfast has published selections from many of these photographs. For example, *In the days of the Clogher Valley* shows the range of sources which might be used in a local study: apart from collections in Armagh County Museum, PRONI, the Ulster Museum (Welch and Hogg collections), Ulster Folk and Transport Museum (Green and Rose Shaw collections), it also used a wide range of private photograph collections covering the railway landscapes, towns and villages, rural life, industry and the Big House.[73] Roger Weatherup includes some characteristic early twentieth-century streetscapes in Armagh, uncluttered by traffic, illustrating an impressive range of modes of transport in the town in the late nineteenth and early twentieth century.[74] Theo McMahon has published street scenes in Monaghan from as early as 1860 and 70s, showing military marching and imperial bunting.[75] *The Beckett country* (Dublin, 1986) is a good example of how literature and photography can be integrated into a study of landscapes. The photographs and extracts of Samuel Beckett's writing successfully evoke early twentieth-century suburban Dublin.[76] Searches will always uncover other useful collections relating to particular areas. For example, an album of prints and negatives of landscapes prior to the 1940 flooding of Poulaphuca

---

71 The Fr Brown photographic collection is now preserved and catalogued on a computerised database in Ark Life, Burlington road, Dublin.   **72** Some have been published, for instance, *Fr Browne's Ireland: remarkable images of people and places* compiled by E.E. O'Donnell (Dublin, 1989).   **73** J. Johnston, *In the days of the Clogher Valley: photographs of the Clogher Valley and its railway, 1887–1942* (Belfast, 1987).   **74** R. Weatherup, *Armagh: historic photographs of the primatial city* (Belfast, n.d.), based on the Allison Studio collection in PRONI, Lawrence collection in NLI, and Welch collection in the Ulster Museum; also J.E.M. Crosbie, *A tour of mid- and south Down 1910–1935: historic photographs from the W.A. Green collection at the Ulster Folk and Transport Museum* (Belfast, 1992); H. Lanigan Wood, *Enniskillen: historic images of an island town* (Belfast, 1990) publishes many from the Fermanagh County Museum and District Council Archives. W.A. Maguire, *Heydays, fairdays and not-so-good old days* (Belfast, 1986) contains photographic records of the Tempo estate in Co. Fermanagh from 1890 to 1918.   **75** T. McMahon, *Old Monaghan, 1785–1995* (Monaghan, 1995); see also *Photographic memories: a pictorial history of Castleblayney* (Castleblayney, 1999) in which there are effective juxtapositions of streetscapes in the early twentieth century with the same streets at the close of the century.   **76** E. O'Brien, *The Beckett country* (Dublin, 1986).

reservoir taken by Liam Price's sister, Kathleen, are deposited in the Placenames Branch of the Ordnance Survey in the Phoenix Park. Pictures of Dublin during the civil war taken by the *Manchester Guardian* were recently discovered.[77]

Aerial photography is obviously of immense value in landscape studies. As an historical record, it came later in the twentieth century, but it can provide unparalleled insight into local landscape history, where the researcher familiar with the local landscape can greatly extend the utility of this sophisticated resource. Aerial photographs clearly are capable of covering wide swathes of rural landscape and can highlight features invisible to field workers on the ground. The St Joseph collection, which focuses mainly on archaeological sites in the 1960s, is an important source, as is the Morgan (Aerophotos) collection from 1950s, and collections by Leo Swan, Daphne Pochin Mould, Gillian Barrett, Geological and Ordnance Surveys. More recent aerial photography has uncovered a great many formerly unknown inscriptions of early settlement.[78]

MAPPING LANDSCAPES

Jacinta Prunty's *Maps and map-making in local history* (Dublin, 2004) has examined in detail the history and scope of map surveys in Ireland. The following section will look more generally at themes relating to landscape representation in maps. Maps are probably the most appropriate and promising sources that provide readable spatial representations of the landscape. They use the same language of distance, direction and elevation (that is, three-dimensional scaled-down renditions) as the landscape itself. Like most texts they can be very powerful though partial constructions, selective in their representation of certain landscape features and, as with artistic depictions, shaping the ways of seeing the landscape.[79] Tim Robinson has produced detailed maps of the Burren, Aran islands and Connemara which

77 See *The Liam Price notebooks*, ed. Corlett and Weaver, i, xxiv; 'Darkroom yields up dramatic momentoes of the Civil War' in *History Ireland*, 9, no. 1 (Spring 2001), pp 32–5.   78 See E.R. Norman and J.K.S. St Joseph, *The early development of Irish society: the evidence of aerial photography* (Cambridge, 1969). The St Joseph negatives are indexed in the National Museum and Monuments and Building, DoE Belfast. T. Condit and C. Corlett (eds), *Above and beyond: essays in memory of Leo Swan* (Dublin, 2005); G.F. Barrett, 'Aerial photography and the study of early settlement structures in Ireland' in *Aerial Archaeology*, 6 (1980), pp 27–38; idem, 'The reconstruction of protohistoric landscapes using aerial photographs: case studies in Co. Louth' in *Louth Arch. Soc. Jn.*, 20 (3) (1983), pp 215–36; idem, 'Recovering the hidden archaeology of Ireland: the impact of aerial survey in the River Barrow valley, 1989–91' in *Forschungen zur Archaologie im Land Brandenburg*, 3 (1995), pp 45–60; idem, 'Flights of discovery: archaeological air survey in Ireland 1989–2000' in *Journal of Irish Archaeology*, XI (2002), pp 1–29; P. Lenihan, 'Aerial photography: a window on the past' in *History Ireland*, 1, no. 2 (Summer 1993), pp 9–13.   79 See J.B. Harley, 'Maps, knowledge, and power' in Cosgrove & Daniels (eds), *Iconography of landscape*, pp 277–312; M.S. Monmonier, *How to lie with maps* (Chicago, 1991); G. Hooper, 'Planning control: cartouches, maps and the Irish landscape, 1770–1840' in G. Hooper (ed), *Landscape and empire, 1770–2000* (Aldershot, 2005), pp 17–44

express a personal and artistic sensitivity in depicting local places. He has mapped Connemara in all weathers, in many ways reflecting the sentiments of a *pleine air* artist, transmitting Connemara's sense of place, its hard resistant reality, and its loneliness to the drawing of the final map.[80]

> Sometimes old maps disclose the altered course of a river or the displacement of the sea-shore; but oftener they have preserved ancient facts of human geography for us: forests now destroyed, marshes turned into grazing or tilling lands, antiquated thoroughfares, previous sites of a village or a town.[81]

Using maps as empirical sources of information about past landscapes is the most popular approach to these records, seeing 'old maps' as innocent sources which contain facts/ data that help to elucidate the past. Another perspective sees them very much as being part of a constructed narrative of past landscapes, surveyed and mapped with a specific military or economic or cultural objective, as for instance in the Down Survey (1650s) which was designed to facilitate dispossession and re-settlement. Many of the markers of the dispossessed, for example, were systemati-cally edited out of such landscapes: attempts (unsuccessful in the main) to erase and replace native placenames are a classic example of this process. Whatever about Brian Friel's imaginary reconstruction of the Ordnance Survey experience in the Donegal landscape in his play *Translations*, maps and cartography of the Irish landscape have been ineluctably involved with colonial conquest from the outset in the sixteenth century.

The early history of maps in Ireland is essentially a colonial one. Pre-Tudor Ireland had no worthwhile mapping tradition. Medieval English Ireland relied largely on written inventories of the landscape. Gaelic lordships maintained a strong topographical knowledge in traditions of *dinnseanchas*, narrative constructions of place steeped in lore and legend which grounded local septs' genealogies. The colonial maps of the later sixteenth and seventeenth centuries had no such connectivities, being essentially surface inventories of facts of landscape: economic geography in many ways superseded cultural genealogy. In terms of historical depiction of the Irish landscape, maps fall broadly into three general phases: in the sixteenth and seventeenth century as instruments of colonial conquest; in the eighteenth century, especially, as mechanisms of colonial (estate) development and improvement; and in the nineteenth century as expressions of state administration and surveillance.

Maps were in the first place critically important tools of Tudor colonial enter-prise in Ireland so this purpose to a great extent shaped the nature of information contained in them. The battle of Kinsale (1601) as represented in *Pacata Hibernia* (London, 1633, reprinted London, 1821) is principally military in function with little useful landscape detail beyond occasional groups of woods. The map of the

---

80 T. Robinson, 'A Connemara fractal' in *Technology Ireland*, 23, no. 3 (June 1991), pp 32–7.
81 Goblet (ed.), *A topographical index of the parishes and townlands of Ireland*, p. v.

fort on the Blackwater in 1587 for instance shows the fort in detail with its towers and bastions and some ancillary local information on hills and trees.[82] Some maps of battlefields, however, show incidental details such as house types, churches, castles and towns, villages, or settlement clusters with sometimes suggestive details on cornfields, woodlands, or forest. Sixteenth-century maps by English map-makers usually had a military sub-text, showing bogs, mountains and forests as obstacles to movement, as well as passes and routeways through them. A great deal of attention was paid to forts and defensible structures such as castles or earthworks and stockades, bridges, town walls and towers, as well as harbours, ports and coastlands. Many contain rather impressionistic views of the contemporary landscapes.[83]

Maps with mostly military functions were also accompanied by general topographical maps illustrating what might be characterised as the economic potential of regions as reflected in existing infrastructures of buildings, communications, natural assets such as lakes and rivers, streams and woodland, occasionally with reference to land-use potential, and many also including details on local proprietors of land and some aspects of settlement such as crannógs. The map of the barony of Oneiland in north Armagh on the eve of the Ulster Plantation in 1610 identifies some of the territorial divisions, including churchlands and townlands, bogs, lakes and rivers. A similar map of Loughtee in Cavan shows hills, lakes, bogs and streams, as well as some of the territorial divisions.[84] Plantation schemes commencing in the Midlands in the 1550s, Munster in 1580s and Ulster in 1610 saw the emergence of maps concerned particularly to identify territorial boundaries, where possible including the names of existing Gaelic proprietors. One of the most striking maps from this early-modern period which reflects the dynamism of England's colonial interest in Ireland is the Laois-Offaly map from 1560–2. It shows nine Gaelic

82 Reproduced in R. Loeber, *The geography and practice of English colonisation in Ireland from 1534 to 1609* (Dublin, 1991), p. 44 and Swift, *Historical maps of Ireland*, p. 42; Hayes-McCoy, *Ulster and other Irish maps*, p. 14. For discussion of early-modern maps and the Gaelic world, see W.J. Smyth, *Map-making, landscapes and memory: a geography of colonial and early modern Ireland, c.1530–1750* (Cork, 2006). **83** For a selection of reasonably well-reproduced early maps, see Swift, *Historical maps of Ireland* based on the British National Archives collection of Irish maps. See also Hayes McCoy, *Ulster and other Irish maps*. For exemplary scholarship on map history, see Andrews, *Plantation acres* and *Shapes of Ireland: maps and their makers, 1564–1839* (Dublin, 1997) which examine a wide range of maps undertaken by government and especially private surveyors before the Ordnance Survey. See also his comprehensive unpublished 'Catalogue of Irish maps before 1630' which may be consulted in the Library, NUIM; idem, 'Sir Richard Bingham and the mapping of western Ireland' in *PRIA*, x, sect. C, 3 (2003), pp 3–95; idem, 'Geography and government in Elizabethan Ireland' in Stephens & Glasscock (eds), *Irish geographical studies*, pp 178–91; idem, 'The mapping of Ireland's cultural landscape, 1550–1630' in Duffy et al. (eds), *Gaelic Ireland*, pp 153–80; idem, 'The Irish surveys of Robert Lythe'. Also *Dictionary of land surveyors and local mapmakers of Great Britain and Ireland, 1530–1850*, 2nd edn, by S. Bendall (2 vols, London, 1997). **84** See J.H. Andrews, 'The maps of the escheated counties of Ulster, 1609–10' in *PRIA*, lxxiv, sect. C (1974), pp 133–70; Swift, *Historical maps of Ireland*, pp 60, 62.

territories or *tuatha*, together with a detailed overview of passes through extensive woodlands which divided up the territory, along with fortified planter houses and settlements.[85] Robert Lythe's 1569 map of the barony of Idrone in Carlow is notable for its representation of village settlements.[86] Inadequate surveys carried out in Munster in 1585 hampered the successful implementation of the plantation project, so that when the Ulster Plantation was mooted twenty-five years later, more rigorous reconnaissance was undertaken by surveyors such as Josias Bodley, Richard Bartlett, Francis Jobson, and Robert Lythe. Although inaccurate and largely impressionistic, Bodley's preparatory survey successfully represented the intricate pattern of townland networks.[87] The Ulster Plantation was accompanied by follow-up surveys by Nicholas Pynnar and Thomas Raven, for example, who mapped the progress and development of the new settlement. Maps of the new towns were produced showing streets of half-timbered houses, market squares with their crosses and accompanying yards and enclosures. Charlemont in County Armagh is depicted with streets and cabins, houses and inns, including a maypole, a symbol of an emergent community.[88]

The dominant theme in maps of the Irish landscape in the seventeenth century is the geography of territorial land divisions, as one would expect in a century which witnessed extensive dispossession and transfer of land. One of the more successful local examples was the survey of the earl of Essex's barony of Farney carried out in 1634 by Thomas Raven, who at this stage would have been very familiar with these features of the Ulster landscape. The aim of most surveyors would have been to map the Gaelic structure of ballybetaghs and smaller divisions which eventually came to be called townlands (see chapter three). Raven mapped the intricate geometry of the tates (townlands) of Farney in groups of three and four on each parchment sheet to form an atlas of the barony which is presently in the Library of Longleat House in Wiltshire.[89] He also showed some of the internal contents of each unit, including lakes and woods, cabins and houses. Sir William Petty's Down Survey ambitiously attempted to capture this territorial structure for the whole island, producing barony and parish maps with internal boundaries outlined, and occasional details on infrastructure of roads and settlement.[90] Petty's

85 J.H. Andrews and R. Loeber, 'An Elizabethan map of Leix and Offaly: cartography, topography and architecture' in W. Nolan and T.P. O'Neill (eds), *Offaly: history and society. Interdisciplinary essays on the history of an Irish county* (Dublin, 1998), pp 243–85. The map (B.L. Cotton: Augustus I, ii, 40) is reproduced as a frontispiece in Smyth's *Celtic Leinster*. **86** Swift, *Historical maps of Ireland*, p. 35. **87** Ibid.; D.A. Chart (ed.), *Londonderry and the companies, 1609–1629* (HMSO, Belfast, 1928). See V. Treadwell, 'The survey of Armagh and Tyrone, 1622' in *UJA*, 27 (1964), pp 140–54. **88** Hayes-McCoy, *Ulster and other Irish maps*, p. 7. **89** P.J. Duffy, 'Farney in 1634 – an examination of Thomas Raven's survey of the Essex estate' in *Clogher Rec.*, 11 (1983), pp 245–56. **90** Andrews, *Plantation acres*, 63–75. *Hiberniae Delineatio* was published in 1685 as a county atlas of Ireland compiled from the earlier Down Survey (reprinted Newcastle upon Tyne, 1968). See T.A. Larcom, *History of the survey of Ireland commonly called the Down Survey, by Sir Wm Petty ad 1665–66* (Dublin, 1851). For studies of individual surveys, see for example, P. O'Flanagan, 'Rural change south of the

maps continued as the cadastral benchmarks for territorial divisions down through the eighteenth century. Early estate maps perpetuated Petty's preoccupation with property boundaries, making only limited reference to internal content.[91]

The eighteenth century was marked by the consolidation and stabilisation of landed estates in Ireland. The age of the landed ascendancy witnessed the development and improvement of their estate properties which increasingly called for the implementation of estate surveys. Although varying greatly in quality and detail, the main objective of these private land surveys was to produce accurate cartographic representations of the internal content of each townland on the estate, including details on leases, farmholdings and in some cases houses.[92] In many cases also, improving landlords employed surveyors to lay out remodelled field patterns on their estates. A great variety of plans of estates, farms, towns and villages, roads, canals and harbours were produced: 'the overall impression of the new landscape depicted in such maps is one dominated by geometric patterns seen in field boundaries, rectangular-shaped building plots in towns and villages and straight roads and lanes'.[93]

The maps of John Rocque and Bernard Scalé broke with the tradition of empty landscapes concentrating only on boundaries. They showed the full topographical variety of the landscape. Indeed as John Andrews noted, 'the maps he [Rocque] inspired must have seemed so vivid as to eliminate the need for first-hand knowledge, a kind of absentees' charter declaring that all the grass was green, all the houses freshly painted, all the roads smooth, all the water blue, and all the rentpayers happy'.[94]

Rocque's maps of the earl of Kildare's estates come closest to artistic portraits of the landscape.[95] They were unprecedented in the manner in which the landscapes of fields and hedges, houses, gardens and villages were portrayed, including colour-coding to denote land use and ownership of individual fields. The quality of the artistic display in the maps and their margins sets them apart from anything produced either before or after. Rocque employed a number of assistant surveyors and engravers in his Dublin establishment, such as Bernard Scalé (his brother-in-law), and Matthew Wren and Hugh Douglas Hamilton, who were responsible for many of the landscape views incorporated in elaborate cartouches.[96]

river Bride in counties Cork and Waterford: the surveyors' evidence, 1716–1851' in *Ir. Geography*, 15 (1982), pp 51–69; H. O'Sullivan, 'Two eighteenth-century maps of the Clanbrassil estate, Dundalk' in *Louth Arch. Soc. Jn.*, xv (1) (1961), pp 39–87.   **91** See Refaussé & Clark, *A catalogue of the maps of the estates of the archbishops of Dublin, 1654–1850*. Reeves microfilms of Down Survey are in the NLI.   **92** See Andrews, *Plantation acres* and entries on Irish estates by J.H. Andrews in *Dictionary of land surveyors and local map-makers of Great Britain and Ireland, 1550–1850*.   **93** D.G. Lockhart, 'The land surveyor in Northern Ireland before the coming of the Ordnance Survey c.1840' in *Ir. Geography*, 11 (1978), pp 102–9 examines advertisements by surveyors in the *Belfast News Letter* from c.1760, six of which are discussed in this paper.   **94** Andrews, *Plantation acres*, p.172.   **95** Ibid., pp 161–74.   **96** See J.H. Andrews, 'The French school of Dublin land surveyors' in *Ir. Geography*, 5 (1967), pp 275–92; John Varley, 'John Rocque: engraver, surveyor, cartographer and map-seller' in

Scalé's 1777 map of the Bath estate in Monaghan was one of a number of estate surveys undertaken by him. Rocque and Scalé were pioneers in the convention of representing buildings in plan form instead of the earlier tradition of pictorial representations, though a great many of the private map surveys of the eighteenth century were crudely executed local surveys. The nineteenth century saw an increasing intervention by the state as part of a growth and modernisation in government bureaucracy and an escalation in information gathering to answer the need for national and local surveys and maps. In many cases these mirrored similar exercises in other landscapes of the British Empire, such as India.[97] The Bogs Commission was established to survey the bogs as a potentially important natural resource and produced detailed maps of many of the lowland bogs in the country.[98] The Geological Survey initiated extensive surveys of the physical landscape, producing maps at half-inch and one-inch scale, accompanied by artist sketches notably by George Victor du Noyer. The Ordnance Survey (OS) produced maps to match those national surveys underway in France and the United States. Its six-inch maps and memoir project were instigated in the 1830s.[99] The maps produced a comprehensive and systematic record of all elements of the Irish landscape, including details on nearly all its visible features with selective information on the cultural landscape.[1] In many ways it brought closure to three hundred years of endeavour in mapping the Irish landscape.[2]

The accuracy and utility of the OS 1:2500 large scale maps, completed in the second half of the nineteenth century and exhibiting remarkable detail, has been underused in local studies.[3] In conjunction with aerial photography, they have been used in studying structures such as ring forts, mottes and baileys, as well as sand dune and coastal erosion. During the second world war, both the German and

Imago Mundi, 5 (1948), pp 89–91; P.J. Duffy, 'Eighteenth-century estate maps' in *History Ireland*, 5, no. 1 (Spring 1997), pp 20–24; A. Horner, 'Cartouches and vignettes on the Kildare estate maps of John Rocque' in *Quarterly Bulletin of the Irish Georgian Society*, 14 (1971), pp 57–76. **97** M.H. Edney, *Mapping an empire: the geographical construction of British India, 1765–1843* (London, 1997), p. 28. **98** See A. Horner, reprint series of maps of the Bogs Commission, note 15, chapter 2. **99** On history of Ordnance Survey see Andrews, *A paper landscape*; Prunty, *Maps and map-making in local history*; T.E. Jordan, *An imaginative empiricist: Thomas Aiskew Larcom, 1801–1879 and Victorian Ireland* (Lampeter, 2002); S. Ó Cadhla, 'Mapping a discourse: Irish Gnossus and the OS 1821–44' in *Irish Journal of Anthropology*, iv (1999), pp 84–109. **1** On the history of production of OS maps see J.H. Andrews, 'Medium and message in early six-inch Irish Ordnance maps: the case of Dublin' in *Ir. Geography*, 5 (1973), pp 579–93. **2** P. Ferguson, *Irish map history: a select bibliography of secondary works, 1850-1983, on the history of cartography in Ireland* (Dublin, 1983). Much of the research on Irish mapping consists of one-off publications of case studies in local historical journals by researchers who move on to other topics. There is a need to compile this diverse material. Ferguson attempts this in this booklet which lists *c.*280 separate papers. However, there is still value to be gained by trawling through local journals, especially for material published since 1983. **3** See M. Stout, 'Plans from plans: an analysis of the 1:2500 OS series as a source for ringfort morphology' in *PRIA*, 92, sect. C (1992), pp 37–53.

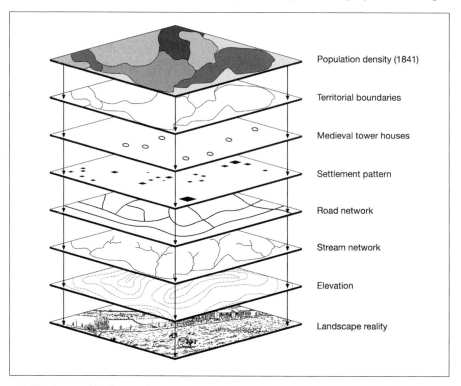

Population density (1841)

Territorial boundaries

Medieval tower houses

Settlement pattern

Road network

Stream network

Elevation

Landscape reality

5.6 GIS, layers of landscape data

British authorities made strategic use of Irish OS maps, producing for instance composites of the one-inch and a 1:25 000 composite of the six-inch survey.[4] Today digital technology can access a range of detailed OS maps including an archive commencing with the first edition in the 1830s.

In a project which might be replicated in Ireland, the British Countryside Commission has produced maps of the countryside character of England based on indicators such as geology and soils, topography and drainage, ecological associations, land use, historical and cultural associations, population density and so on. Each of these is subdivided into secondary attributes and some sixty-eight significant attributes emerged in a pilot study used in a national project.

Atlases attempt to compile a broader more general overview, as with the early example of Petty's *Hiberniae Delineatio* of 1685. More modern atlases attempt to represent a range of themes, as in the *Atlas of the Irish rural landscape* (Cork, 1997) and *The Irish Historic Towns Atlas* (Dublin, 1981–); L.D. Stamp, *An agricultural atlas of Ireland* (London, 1931) and S. Lafferty et al., *Irish agriculture in transition: a census atlas*

4 *An illustrated record of the Ordnance Survey in Ireland* (OSi Dublin & OSni Belfast, 1991), p. 46.

of agriculture in the Republic of Ireland (Maynooth, 1999). A.A. Horner, J.A. Walsh and V.P. Harrington produced *Population in Ireland: a census atlas* (Dublin, 1987) and, using GIS techniques, Donegal County Development Board published a *Donegal County Atlas* in 2001. Local atlases have attempted to profile specific territories, as in P.J. Duffy, *Landscapes of south Ulster: a parish atlas of the diocese of Clogher* (Belfast, 1993) or J. Crowley et al., *Atlas of Cork City* (Cork, 2005) which is a comprehensive profile of the historical and geographical character of the city of Cork.

PARK LANDSCAPES

> The ideal was to surround the mansions with wide expanses of smooth, open turf dotted with clumps of noble trees, secluded from the outside world by plantation belts and perimeter walls … a diversity of circuit walks and rides orchestrated a succession of pastoral Arcadian scenes, featuring hillocks and winding streams, glinting lakes that mirrored the sky, woodlands that dissolved into sunlit glades, and flocks and herds placidly grazing in the shadow of classical temples and ruins.[5]

In keeping with a broader British perspective into the nineteenth century, the Irish landowning class was keenly interested in construction of idyllic demesnes and parks. There was a close relationship between the design of landscapes and their artistic representations from the seventeenth and especially the eighteenth centuries. Designers/gardeners intervened in nature to modify or improve it, usually in accordance with classical or picturesque artistic conventions.[6] The standard works on the history of landscape design in Ireland, such as *Lost demesnes* or *Irish gardens and demesnes from 1830* and others all rely strongly on contemporary artistic evidence in their studies which contain a wide range of well interpreted, informative reproductions of paintings and drawings.[7]

As with artistic portrayals of landscape, designs of the actual landscape itself were shaped by the ideology of the élite landowning class from the later seventeenth

5 Reeves-Smyth, 'Demesnes', p. 201. **6** See S. Daniels and S. Seymour, 'Landscape design and the idea of improvement, 1730–1900' in Dodgshon & Butlin (eds), *An historical geography of England and Wales*, pp 487–520; L.J. Proudfoot, 'Placing the imaginary: Gosford Castle and the Gosford estate, ca.1820–1900' in Hughes & Nolan (eds), *Armagh: history and society*, pp 881–916; idem, 'Place and *mentalité*: the "big house" and its locality in County Tyrone'; idem, 'Landscaped demesnes in pre-famine Ireland: a regional case study' in A. Verhoeve and A.J. Vervloet (eds), *The transformation of the European rural landscape: methodological issues and agrarian change, 1770–1914* (Brussels, 1992), pp 230–37. **7** E. Malins and the Knight of Glin, *Lost demesnes: Irish landscape gardening, 1660–1845* (London, 1976); E. Malins and P. Bowe, *Irish gardens and demesnes from 1830* (London, 1980); T. Reeves-Smyth, *Irish gardens and gardening before Cromwell* (Kinsale, 1999); idem, 'The natural history of demesnes' in Wilson Foster (ed.), *Nature in Ireland*, pp 549–72; O'Kane, *Landscape design in eighteenth-century Ireland*; Earl of Roden, *Tollymore: the story of an Irish demesne* (Belfast, 2005).

century, particularly with reference to gardens and parklands. In Ireland many of the attitudes to landscape and its development from the eighteenth century reflected the exigencies of a largely colonial élite, though it has also been suggested that their investment in landscape improvement, parks and mansions was an expression of an emerging place-based Irish identity. In general, however, the houses, demesnes and gardens of this class reflect perspectives which are repeated across the British Empire where colonial society attempted to control and shape the landscapes they encountered in the image of a European design aesthetic asserting power over nature and over neighbours.[8] The more economic priorities of medieval demesnes were superseded from the late seventeenth century by designs incorporating French Baroque and, from the mid-eighteenth century, a more informal pastoral aesthetic of pleasure gardens. In Ireland as in England many estates surrounded their demesnes and gardens with high walls and perimeter trees to block access and sight of neighbouring workaday landscapes, enclosing commons and introducing agricultural improvements. Indeed service tunnels and sunken paths were part of garden designs, where servants 'knew their place' and were kept out of sight of their superiors in much the same way as they were painted out of their pictures. Improving on nature was seen very much in terms of a morality of landscape by the English designer Humphrey Repton whose ideas were influential in Ireland also – imposing order and civilisation on chaos: 'He connected the aesthetics of landscape gardening more to a benevolent morality of estate management. [His] ideal of landscape improvement had its basis in a conservative respect for landed property and its attendant duties.'[9]

The influence of the English garden designer (Lancelot) 'Capability' Brown may also be seen in many 'Brownian' Irish parklands and gardens in the eighteenth century. Carton park at Maynooth is attributable to Emily Lennox, daughter of the second duke of Richmond, who was at the forefront of parkland design in early eighteenth-century England. Thomas Dawson employed the garden designer Nathaniel Richmond (one of Capability Brown's assistants) to lay out Cremorne Gardens for him in Chelsea and probably his park at Dawson Grove in Monaghan. Frequently, landlords and agents removed or controlled the development of unsightly houses and farms, hedges and ditches, of the older farm landscape from the neighbourhood of their demesnes and diverted roads afterwards to create a private world for themselves.[10] This was a well-established practice in England also,

8 See Muir, *Approaches to landscape*, p. 212.   9 S. Daniels, 'The political landscape' in G.Carter et al. (eds), *Humphrey Repton landscape gardener, 1752–1818* (Norwich, 1982), p. 118, quoted in Butlin, *Historical geography: through the gates of space and time*, p. 139. Markree castle and demesne was the appropriate setting for Cecil Frances Alexander's hymn, 'All things bright and beautiful'. See T. Dunne, '"A gentleman's estate should be a moral school": Edgeworthstown in fact and fiction' in Gillespie & Moran (eds), *Longford: essays in county history*, pp 95–121.   10 See A. Horner, 'Carton, Co Kildare: a case study in the making of an Irish demesne' in *Bulletin of the Irish Georgian Society*, xxviii (1975), pp 62–71.

where much eviction took place along with obliteration of roads and rights of way to accommodate new parks, facts often forgotten about in nationalist renditions of Irish gentry landscapes.[11] Peter Connell refers to one landlord in 1825 bemoaning this fashion for 'the English, or picturesque, style of gardening' which tended 'to seclude the wealthy proprietor more than formerly from his industrious and humbler neighbours'.[12] Because of the developing interest in pastoral, 'natural' landscapes with emphasis on water, river valleys were favoured locations for houses and demesnes in the later eighteenth century: the Boyne and Liffey valleys, for instance, the Slaney and Barrow, Lee and Suir, where the parklandscapes were laid out with a southerly aspect from the house whose rooms, like their walled fruit and vegetable gardens, were heated by the sun.

Approximately 6 per cent of the land of Ireland was developed as demesnes and parks, over 7,000 of them comprised of ten acres or more. There were 3,500 in excess of 50 acres, though many were enormous, like Carton's 1,200 acres. The most extensive parks were located in Leinster and Munster.

Mary Delany's description of the early stages of planning a house and demesne near Clough in County Down in 1751 alludes to all the elements of pioneering improvement which characterised the age:

> Within four miles of Mount Panther we met Mrs Annesley and Lady Anne Annesley on horseback, going to dine under a tent on cold meat about a mile from that place, where they are going to build. They say it is a fine situation, has much of the majestic about it – as mountains, wild rocks, woods, and an extensive view of the main ocean; ... they have walled in, and planted with oak, three hundred and fifty acres of ground, for a park. Near them is a large bleach-yard, and Mr Annesley is going to *build a town* ...

Dangan Castle in Meath in 1732 was 'very large, handsome, and convenient, the situation not very pleasant, the country being flat about it, and great want of trees. Mr Wesley is making great improvements of planting trees and making canals.' Many of the improvements initiated by Wesley exhibited a contemporary taste in ornamentation, with groves, temple and statues to Vesta, Apollo, Neptune, Proserpine, and Diana, invoking the classical culture of his class.[13] Studies of the making of these landscapes have been undertaken by Arnold Horner, who outlines the construction of Carton's parkland, and Finola O'Kane, who has comprehensively documented the history of the landscapes in Breckdenston, Castletown, Carton and Frascati.[14]

11 See R. Muir, *The* New *reading the landscape* (Exeter, 2002), pp 133–40. 12 Connell, *The land and people of county Meath*, p. 49 quoting Pratt papers (NLI MS 13326). 13 *Letters from Georgian Ireland: the correspondence of Mary Delany, 1731–68*, ed. A. Day (Belfast, 1991), pp 214–15, 122; see also Friel, *Frederick Trench, 1746–1836*, and Heywood, p. 65, where he 'moved hills, dammed rivers and created lakes ... delicately highlighted by his carefully considered placing of rational, classical-inspired elements.' 14 Horner, 'Carton, Co. Kildare',

The contribution of the Anglo-Irish gentry endures as an important element in the Irish landscape. A 1940s recollection still holds true:

> Their houses could be spotted with ease because the woods, fields and gardens around them, known collectively as the 'demesne', were almost always surrounded by a stone wall eight to ten feet high, often stretching for several miles along the road. It sounds impressive but seldom was, since the walls were inevitably covered with ivy and usually falling down … inside the houses were stone-flagged corridors long enough to bicycle along, and endless staircases and hiding places ideal for games of catch and hide-and-seek or midnight feasts.[15]

More modern designed landscapes from the twentieth century are worth taking account of in local studies as well. Many of these might be characterised as landscapes of sport and leisure such as sportsfields, tennis courts, cricket grounds, racecourses, and golf courses, all of which have had a significant impact on local landscapes. Croke Park (and Hill 16), for example, has iconic significance for the GAA as would other provincial parks like Thurles for hurling, or Thomond or Lansdowne Road for rugby. Golfing societies were established throughout the country in Victorian times by the growing urban middle class. Golf clubs were fairly exclusive associations which were instrumental in designing and laying out significant local micro-landscapes. They usually have individual histories and photographic and written records which might repay investigation.

SYMBOLIC LANDSCAPES

Many landscapes or parts of landscapes have been deliberately constructed as symbols of power, order, national or cultural identity. Colonial authorities provide especially good examples of such landscape design embracing material and cultural manifestations of hegemony. These places have often provoked alternative contested symbolic meanings. Religion has also had an important role in the construction of symbolic landscapes, especially differentiating sacred and secular/profane space. Urban morphologies, architectures or monuments are particularly important settings for displays of authority, with the imposition of geometric symmetry and order on the landscape in most cases obliterating earlier unsanitary, overcrowded lanes and streets, which were often seen as representing an older, unwholesome, disordered society. Paris is the ultimate expression and model of this trend historically and its boulevards, squares and formal spaces, ornamental buildings, parks, and its multiplicity of monuments have influenced urban design throughout the world.

pp 45–104; O'Kane, *Landscape design*.   **15** M. Girouard, *Town and country* (New Haven & London, 1992), pp 104–5.

A recent theme in post-colonial urban studies is the symbolic meanings encoded in the urban landscapes, reflected in Ireland, for example, in the iconography of street plans, placenaming, erection of monuments and public buildings.[16] The symbolism of colonial, nationalist, unionist or imperial inscriptions on the landscape has been a source of conflict, especially since the post-famine period. Street-naming for instance was an important marker of cultural dominance, a signifier of colonial or imperial authority which was replaced by a later nineteenth-century Catholic nationalism. There was also a nationalist re-invention of Dublin after independence, with debate about siting a new parliament, commemorating the 1916–21 period, and erasing the iconographies and memorials of imperial glories. Townscapes throughout Ireland experienced similar symbolic marking of space and place, sanctifying sites of significance within the towns. Dublin's Phoenix Park, for instance, was remodelled in the mid-nineteenth century as a significant space containing the Wellington monument (erected in 1814), the Vice-regal Lodge and the Chief Secretary's residence. The re-design was projected as a celebration of Empire and was based on earlier designs in St James Park, Hyde Park and Regents Park in London.[17] War memorials, especially to the Great War, became important statements for unionism in Northern Ireland in the inter-war years. The National War Memorial at Islandbridge in Dublin, laid out in classical mode by Sir Edwin Lutyens to commemorate the Irish dead of the first world war, was erected in the 1930s and was originally intended to link across the Liffey with the Phoenix Park. It was an urban space, however, that like the veterans of the Great War itself was largely forgotten in the new Free State which sought instead to memorialise 1916 and the war of independence.

Townscapes have also been laid out as important settings for display, performance and exhibition. Streets and squares (and other classical variants of diamonds,

16 Y. Whelan, *Reinventing modern Dublin* (Dublin, 2003); B.S. Yeoh, 'Street-naming and nation-building: toponymic inscriptions of nationhood in Singapore' in *Area*, 28, no. 3 (1996), pp 298–307.   **17** See Y. Whelan, 'Monuments, power and contested space – the iconography of Sackville Street (O'Connell Street) before independence (1922)' in *Ir. Geography*, 34 (1) (2001), pp 11–33; idem, 'Symbolising the state – the iconography of O'Connell Street after independence (1922)' in *Ir. Geography*, 34 (2) (2001), pp 135–56; idem, 'Written in space and stone: aspects of the iconography of Dublin after independence' in Clarke et al. (eds), *Surveying Ireland's past*, pp 585–612; G. Owens, 'Nationalist monuments in Ireland, *c.*1870–1814: symbolism and ritual' in Kennedy & Gillespie (eds), *Ireland: art into history*, 103–17. See also J. Hall, 'Reputations: nineteenth-century monuments in Limerick' in *History Ireland*, 5, no. 4 (Winter 1997), pp 44–8; D. Arnold, 'Distorting mirrors: Phoenix Park, Dublin, 1832–1849, and the ambiguities of Empire' in M. Dorrian and G. Rose (eds), *Deterritorialisations ... revisioning landscapes and politics* (London, 2003), pp 142–51; P.J. Duffy, 'The town of Monaghan: a place inscribed in street and square' in E. Conlon (ed.), *Later on: the Monaghan bombing memorial anthology* (Cork, 2004), pp 14–32; N. Johnson, 'Sculpting heroic histories: celebrating the centenary of the 1798 rebellion in Ireland' in *TIBG*, 19 (1994), pp 78–93; idem, 'Cast in stone: monuments, geography and nationalism' in *Environment and planning D: Society and Space*, 13 (1995), pp 51–65; B.P. Kennedy, 'The Irish Free State, 1922–49: a visual perspective' in Kennedy & Gillespie (eds), *Ireland: art into history*, pp 132–52.

octagons, malls, boulevards and so on) were for shop-window display, for more formal ceremonial parades and processions and for promenading to see and be seen, in the mode of the *flaneurs* of the nineteenth century. Many footpaths, elegant residential buildings, street furniture like railings, lamp standards and monuments, represented civic order and the passing parades of power, control and celebration. As in many county towns, Monaghan's municipal spaces, for example, were used for symbolic communal occasions over the past two centuries and more – for public spectacles, marching bands, flags and bunting, military display, demonstrating support for party, creed or ideology. Landowning gentry connections in England, Europe and Empire had impact back home in terms of transfer of ideas on aesthetic taste in urban design. County Grand Juries also provided an incentive for inscriptions of status and privilege on the face of the towns where their formal assemblies took place. The county town, like the capital city, was a stage for the public expression of colonial authority in the nineteenth century, especially in statues and memorials to overseas imperial endeavours or local landlord authority. The same spaces and buildings were witnesses to contrasting nationalist demonstrations and decorations from the 1920s. The past couple of decades has seen the conservation and rehabilitation of many buildings and monuments from the age of ascendancy and Empire, as they have become an acceptable part of the vocabulary of Irish townscapes.

At a broader level, some landscapes have acquired symbolic status as icono-graphic reflections of power or ideology. In the early twentieth century, nationalism in many parts of the world sought to combine nation and nature in landscapes in attempts to find the iconic English/French/German garden with native plants.[18] In Ireland in many ways, Connemara and the West of Ireland emerged as the landscape expression of a national identity with rural, pastoral and ancient Celtic overtones, articulated in art and cultural nationalism. The artist Paul Henry believed that the West of Ireland, 'a remote place of wild beauty, rugged mountains, flat bog-land and coastal fields, represented the 'real soul of Ireland', and this deeply held conviction is central in his response to the people and landscape of the region.'[19] J. M. Synge, W.B. Yeats, and film-makers like Robert O'Flaherty (*Man of Aran*) or John Ford (*The Quiet Man*), as well as Padraig Pearse and Eamon de Valera shared a similar conception of the West of Ireland's landscape.

Northern Ireland is a region shared by two communities whose diverging interpretations of their past have frequently found expression in contested narratives of landscape.[20] Apart from the obvious examples of marching and marking sectarian landscapes in town and country, attempts to represent the 'common ground' of an Ulster heritage have frequently been troubled, as reflected in Henry Glassie's work in Fermanagh, John Hewitt's poetry, and other readings of folklife and folklore. The

18 See Schama, *Landscape and memory*, pp 117–19.   **19** S.B. Kennedy, *Paul Henry* (NGI, Dublin, 2003), p. 27; K. Rockett, L. Gibbons and J. Hill, *Cinema in Ireland* (Syracuse, 1988). **20** B.J. Graham, 'The contested interpretation of heritage landscapes in NI' in G.J. Ashworth and P.J. Larkham (eds), *Building a new heritage: tourism, culture and identity in the New Europe* (London, 1994), pp 10–22.

campaign in Northern Ireland to restore townland postal addresses, has been used as a bridging project between the two communities and is an example of a degree of cross-community agreement on one aspect of cultural heritage. The Ulster Folk and Transport Museum (UFTM) and the Ulster American Folk Park (UAFP) have also been conscious attempts to address issues of contested identities by using the material landscape as a bridge between divided communities. The UFTM, which largely reflected Estyn Evans's ideas on Irish heritages, aimed to represent the distinctiveness of Ulster's material legacy as a part of Ireland's, but with a well-established regional identity. Its exhibits of houses, churches, villages, mills and intervening landscapes of walls and hedges, reflect the diversity of Ulster culture. The UAFP was constructed to represent the links between Ulster and America in terms of migration and colonisation. However, in both instances, the founding ideologies informing these readings of Ulster landscapes were firmly based in a Protestant, unionist heritage which downplayed Irish connections. In both cases, the Catholic community in Northern Ireland tended to be excluded, though in recent years concerted efforts have been made to re-define the scope and objectives in both exhibits in a more inclusive Irish context, reflected for instance in the establishment of a centre for migration studies in the UAFP.

Religion has played an important role in designating sacred space in the landscape. As archaeology moves increasingly to adopt a broader landscape perspective (as opposed to a singular site preoccupation), there is a willingness among some to address the notion of ritual or ceremonial landscapes, perhaps prehistoric sacred places whose symbolism may elude us today. These are classically exemplified in Neolithic, Bronze and Iron Age sites at Brú na Bóinne and Newgrange, Cruachan in Roscommon, or Sliabh na gCalliagh in Meath, which possessed a cosmological religious significance for early societies (associated perhaps with burials and other ceremonies, assemblies and games) that is inaccessible to us today.[21] Holy mountains, wells and other features in the natural environment which have characterised indigenous religions across the world were sanctified by Christianity for prayer or worship in Ireland from Patrician times. Church buildings were constructed in elegant or imposing architecture of steeples and towers, or accompanied by monuments or shrines to mark the significance of hallowed place. More traditional sacred landscapes and sites have been the focus of pilgrimage for Christian – especially Catholic – communities for centuries. The most notable examples in Ireland are Lough Derg in Donegal and Croagh Patrick in Mayo, both penitential sites of pilgrimage to which people have journeyed for more than a thousand years.[22] Maméan in west Galway, Lady's Island in Wexford and the innumerable holy wells and springs, with their traditional 'pattern' (patron) day on

---

21 See Aalen et al. (eds), *Atlas of the Irish rural landscape*; Stout, *Newgrange and the bend of the Boyne* and idem, 'Embanked enclosures of the Boyne region' in *PRIA*, 91, sect. C, 9 (1991), pp 245–84.   **22** See J.S. Donnelly, jnr., 'Lough Derg: the making of the modern pilgrimage' in Nolan et al. (eds), *Donegal: history and society*, pp 491–508.

the saint's feast are other examples of sacred places in local landscapes. Many of these were officially abandoned by the Catholic church in the nineteenth century as a consequence of the revelry and rioting which marked the patterns.

In contrast to urban landscapes, the open countryside was a more workaday and less symbolic landscape. The most notable exceptions were the parklands and demesnes favoured by the landowning gentry of the eighteenth and nineteenth centuries which incorporated much symbolism in their design as already discussed. Apart from an overall expression of civilised taste and what might be called 'anglican' order and improvement, surrounding walls, tree-planting enclosing vistas, water features and ornamental buildings were all symbols of power and privilege. These private demesnes were the only parts of the rural landscape which were marked with an overt monumental symbolism. Classical statuary and follies such as obelisks, pillars and columns were located throughout these landscapes; Gothic 'monastic ruins' such as those at Killua Castle in County Westmeath, or the 'Jealous Wall' at Belvedere represented a fabricated romantic antiquity reflecting the cultural priorities of their owners.

CONCLUSION

That every picture tells a story is undoubtedly true of landscape. This chapter has discussed a range of visual images of past landscapes. How places, buildings and scenes were represented in paintings, drawings and other pictorial records is an important source of knowledge about landscapes at other points in time. The places we observe today – including the landmarks, prospects, horizons, vegetation and the arrangement of settlements and buildings – are fundamental parts of our tangible world. What such places looked like in the past is of immediate use in local studies. Antiquarian drawings or topographical art, for example, can allow reconstructions of buildings and streetscapes, or measure rates of change. Drawings and paintings collectively also reflect the kinds of places which were of interest in the past, throwing light on earlier discourses of landscape which continue to shape popular taste today. Catalogues in the National Gallery, National Library, Office of Public Works, Royal Irish Academy, Geological Survey, Irish Architectural Archive, Ulster Museum, Crawford Gallery, and other repositories mentioned in the foregoing discussion, including private collections in many estate houses, are worth exploring for material of use in local studies. Local museums and libraries are probably the best starting points for local landscape pictorial images. The local landscape itself, which we inhabit and move through, is the ultimate visual artefact, parts of which demonstrate historical sequences in its ordering, improvement and re-arrangement – and this is especially true of parklands and monumental landscapes.

CHAPTER 6

Writing landscapes

'Our poetry, our fiction, our drama is itself a mapping of the world, wide-ranging, highlighted in some parts, dark in others, always changing in space and time. A very large part of our writing is a story of its roots in a place: a landscape, region, village, city, nation or continent.'[1] This chapter mainly focuses on real and imagined landscapes, observed and represented in writings. All of them, whether first-hand descriptions, accounts of places in tour or travel journals, or fictive places of the imagination, reflect individual, class or other ideological contexts and ways of seeing the landscape by the artist/writer, audience/society. Imagined landscapes are valid perspectives in that fictive reality can often contain more truth than everyday reality; '"fact" and "fiction" can also be seen as inextricably mixed or confused, with "histories" and "novels" containing elements of both'.[2]

We can talk about sources of precision and sources of impression in writings on landscape, which are respectively 'quantitative' or 'qualitative' in nature. In the first place are those which are topographically or materially 'accurate' or factual, which can be used to reconstruct elements of the material or social landscape in the past, sources which have been referred to frequently in earlier chapters. Maps and census data, for instance, as well as being descriptive accounts of a place in time would generally be considered to be empirically precise in their usefulness. In the second place are sources in which the place or landscape is represented visually or verbally in a poem, text or painting. These sources are more impressionistic, containing opinions, reflecting attitudes and reporting feelings or are more broadly imaginative, even fictional works, where a place/landscape invented by the creative skill of the writer may have a powerful and persuasive reality. 'Ballybeg' is a metaphorical place in Brian Friel's plays which has the substance of an actual village or parish in Ireland. Sources such as written accounts, in the same way as paintings or postcards, may also be either location-specific (as with accounts of nineteenth-century Connemara, Achill or individual parishes or townlands) or can refer more generically to the character of a broader region, as in diffuse descriptions of Mayo, West of Ireland or Ulster landscapes.

Paintings and creative literature are both mimetic approaches to landscape and environment, serving to represent it in various imitative ways. Literature traditionally had a role to represent nature and landscape in what has been called literary

---

1 M. Bradbury (ed.), *The atlas of literature* (London, 1998), p. 7.   2 See D.C.D. Pocock, 'Place and the novelist' in *TIBG*, 6 (1981), p. 15; Dunne, ' "A gentleman's estate should be a moral school" ', p. 96.

pictorialism. One of the distinguishing features of eighteenth- and nineteenth-century literature is the detailed description of nature, for example, weather and storms, as well as the physical landscape, especially in its wilder state. Apart from contemporary aesthetic interests in wild nature, this is also an important reflection of the reality for most people living at the time and up until rural electrification in the middle of the twentieth century, whose work or journeys made them more directly aware of nature and the elements, weather and the physical environment: the letters of John O'Donovan and others walking or travelling in the Ireland of 1830s reflect this. Many of these literary descriptions can be useful as sources for understanding aspects of particular places at particular times in the past. At one level, therefore, literature can be of assistance to historical studies not just as embellishment or decoration but for its factual insights: for this reason the following chapter contains several extended excerpts from written texts/literature as illustrations of the nature of the sources, to give a sense of the value of this source in local studies of landscape. Charles Dickens was especially good at imbricating his work with material and social details. But accuracy of such detail was not really the intention or function of fictional works of literature, which were more concerned with the human experience of the landscape at the time.

Of course words and language are endowed with different meanings at different times and writers/poets are individuals who write about very particular, personal representations of a landscape or place. Some landscapes resist language, especially well exemplified in the New World when the (largely imperial) gaze of travellers in the nineteenth century was confronted with unfamiliar scenes: artists in Africa frequently had to resort to re-arranging their landscapes in a more familiar picturesque mode, with its exotic trees, or other elements like houses or wagons framing the picture. 'How are we to read the African landscape? ... Is it readable only through African eyes, writeable only in an African language?'[3] Many travellers to Ireland in the seventeenth century and later were similarly confronted with an unfamiliar place in their terms. For this reason it is interesting for us to see how they represented these places in the past. An additional consideration relating to landscape and literature is the manner in which language is endowed with power to influence meaning and discourse. The printed word has been especially influential historically in this sense – the English language for instance has been responsible for power-laden representations of the colonial world: stereotyping the inferior races, the lazy, the cunning, the barbaric and uncivilised people on the outposts of Empire. This dimension to writings is noteworthy in the way Ireland and its regions were depicted in reports in the culturally dominant English language from the seventeenth century onwards.[4]

---

3 J.M. Coetzee, *White writing: on the culture of letters in South Africa* (New Haven, 1988), p. 62.
4 See C. Kaplan, 'White, black and green: racialising Irishness in Victorian England' in P. Gray (ed.), *Victoria's Ireland: Irishness and Britishness, 1837–1901* (Dublin, 2004), pp 51–68; K. Kenny (ed.), *Ireland and the British Empire* (Oxford, 2004).

LITERARY LANDSCAPES

Writers have long been recognised as witnesses to our world, possessing important qualities of insight which help us understand society and place. Society honours its writers and poets who are seen as interpreters of national culture, gifted with a talent to articulate and represent the experience of the times and spaces we live in. The extent to which our views of reality in Ireland today and in the past century have been shaped by the literary and artistic imagination is a reflection of the power of the writer as witness and is demonstrated by the manner in which W.B. Yeats, Seamus Heaney or Paul Durcan are quoted approvingly in particular instances to represent a state of mind about the Ireland or Irelands we live in.

'Poets make the best topographers' according to W.G. Hoskins in the opening sentence of *The making of the English landscape*. Literary landscapes, while obviously growing out of an author's experience of particular places, also represent imagined consciously-created landscapes that do not exist except in the mind of the writer. This writing captures the spirit of place and is designed to imprint an image in the mind of the reader which was important before the revolution in visual imagery that came with photography and film. Good writing on landscape, locality or place uses the power of language to summon up images of the texture of place, evoking an atmosphere and sense of place, reflected perhaps in the sounds or light of the landscape, reflected in noisiness, wetness, coldness or dampness, darkness or sunlight. Powerful descriptive writing as in Dickens's *Bleak House* can add a further dimension of meaning to a bland assembly of landscape facts. He uses words with 'marvellous precision and subtlety ... not being limited by the need to describe the landscape, but ... choosing certain images and details, sounds and pictures, to bring it before us.'[5] Creative literature can be used as a source of data and landscape facts, as in the genre of literary pictorialism, for example in eighteenth- and nineteenth-century writing, with some of the classic topographical descriptions in Charles Dickens or Thomas Hardy. Seán O'Casey has described a Dublin tenement landscape with strong imagery that is Dickensian in its impact:

> He could see the street stretching along outside, its roughly cobbled roadway beset with empty match-boxes, tattered straws, tattered papers, scattered mounds of horse-dung, and sprinkled deep with slumbering dust waiting for an idle wind to come and raise it to irritating life again. Lean-looking gas-lamps stood at regular intervals on the footpaths, many of them deformed from the play of swinging children ... There were the houses, too – a long, lurching row of discontented incurables, smirched with the age-long marks of ague, fevers, cancer, and consumption, soured tears of little children, and the sighs of disappointed newly-married girls ...[6]

5 J.R. Watson, 'Literature and landscape: some relationships and problems' in J. Appleton, *The aesthetics of landscape* (Didcot, 1980), p. 29.   **6** From *Inishfallen, fare thee well* (New York, 1949), pp 57–8.

Literature can also be used to provide environmental or cultural contexts, as reflected in the genre of regional novels. The manner in which the home places of novelists inhabit their writing is an important facet and has been grasped by the marketing wizards in tourism as a means of packaging and commodifying these landscapes as, for instance, in Yeats Country, Kavanagh Country, and Goldsmith Country.[7] This 'narrative creation of place' is best exemplified in the writing of Yeats (and others) about the West of Ireland, where landscape and place, like Yeats's Lake Isle of Inishfree, have acquired more reality than the material geographies of the landscape.[8] In general, therefore, there is scope for recognising the value of creative literature as a valid source in itself for understanding landscape in the past. Writers are valuable interpreters of our worlds in the past and the present; their work adds the flesh of meaning to what are often the bald facts of place.

The Irish landscape in various guises features in the works of many Irish writers. Oliver Goldsmith's *Deserted Village* has been seen as a lament for the replacement of older cleared village countrysides with new, rational, enclosed landscapes in the eighteenth century. It is a narrative of depopulation of the peasantry to be replaced with a more silent landscape of picturesque mansions and parklands.[9] William Carleton and Patrick Kavanagh are two writers whose works are imbued with the spirit and reality of the south Ulster landscape in the early nineteenth and twentieth centuries. Carleton has been described as 'a mirror of his folk and the country out of which they were sprung ... he was the Walter Scott of the humble peasant', expressing the 'sheer vitality and density of human life'.[10] Both writers were sons

---

7 See Gibbons, *Transformations in Irish culture* and J. Leerssen, 'The western mirage: on the Celtic chronotype in the European imagination' in Collins (ed.), *Decoding the landscape*, pp 1–11; also P.J. Duffy, 'Landscapes and Irish literature' in G.L. Anagnostopoulos (ed.), *Art and landscape* (Athens, 2001), pp 650–62 and idem, 'Writing Ireland: literature and art in the representation of Irish place' in B.J. Graham (ed.), *In search of Ireland* (London, 1997), pp 64–83; idem, 'Writing Ireland: literary reflections on Irish migration in the nineteenth and twentieth centuries' in R. King, J. Connell and P. White (eds), *Writing across worlds: literature and migration* (London, 1995), pp 20–38. R. Loeber and M. Loeber, *A guide to Irish fiction, 1650–1900* (Dublin, 2006) highlights an extensive range of forgotten writing which reflects on the life and culture of Ireland in the past.   8 See P. Sheeran, 'The narrative creation of place: the example of Yeats' in Collins (ed.), *Decoding the landscape*, pp 149–64; idem, '*Genius Fabulae*: the Irish sense of place' in *Irish University Review*, 18 (1988), pp 191–206.   9 His *Deserted Village* undoubtedly reflects some experiences of his Longford homeland: '... The man of wealth and pride/ Takes up a space that many poor supplied;/ Space for his lake, his park's extended bounds/ Space for his horses, equipage and hounds/ ... His seat, where solitary sports are seen,/ Indignant spurns the cottage from the green/... While scourged by famine from the smiling land,/ The mournful peasant leads his humble band;/ And while he sinks, without one arm to save,/ The country blooms – a garden and a grave ... If to some common's fenceless limits strayed,/ He drives his flock to pick the scanty blade,/ Those fenceless fields the sons of wealth divide,/ And even the bare-worn common is denied.'   10 S. Leslie, foreword, in R. Shaw, *Carleton's Country* (Dublin, 1930), p. 9; M. Harmon, 'Aspects of the peasantry in Anglo-Irish literature from 1800–1916' in *Studia Hib.*, 15 (1975), pp 105–27, p. 119; also B. Hayley, *Carleton's Traits and Stories and the nineteenth-century Anglo-Irish tradition* (Gerrards Cross, 1983).

of the soil in this small-farm, hilly region and the natural and human landscapes inevitably seeped into their writings. Though each left his homeland in adulthood, these were the landscapes of first and formative memory which to a great extent inspired their literary work.

Carleton's writing reflects the landscape of the landlord, the agent, the struggling, impoverished tenant farmer: 'the soil covered with pauper occupants, one huddling under another in a series that diminished from bad to worse in everything but numbers'.[11] His stories also record the busy countrysides of his early experience, abuzz with people crowding kitchens, barns, chapels or road-side altars, or the fields and gardens, the lanes and boreens to market, holy well or pilgrimage.[12] In his *Autobiography*, the landscape forms a constant backdrop whose localities were scenes of intense activity – dances and visiting, schools opening and closing in barns and outbuildings within half a mile of his home.[13] Writing for a largely English readership in the mid-nineteenth century, Carleton's depictions of landscape adhered to fashionable conventions of the picturesque and pastoral. His descriptions of local landscapes in a time of famine are authentic, where the wet turf in the hearths smouldered, emitting 'long black masses of smoke which trailed slowly over the whole country ... In some parts the grain was beaten down by the rain – in airier situations it lay cut but unsaved, and scattered over the fields ... the groves and hedges were silent, for the very birds had ceased to sing.'[14] His recollection of travelling through the countryside reflected the footsore experience of the thousands who similarly walked these landscapes in the time before motorcars and tarmac:

> These roads are generally paved with round stones, laid curiously together in longitudinal rows like the buttons on a schoolboy's jacket. Owing to the infrequency of travellers on them, they are quite overgrown with grass, except in one stripe along the middle, which is kept naked by the hoofs of the horses and the tread of foot passengers.[15]

Carleton's description of the landscape setting of the pattern or pilgrimage and the tents and social activity prevailing might be a useful complementary written text to Joseph Peacock's painting of a similar theme in 1813:

> The highways, the fields, and the boreens, or bridle-roads, were filled with living streams of people pressing forward to this great scene of fun and religion. The devotees could in general be distinguished from the country folks by their pharisaical and penitential visages, as well as by their not wearing shoes, for the stations to such places were formerly made with bare

---

11 W. Carleton, *The Black Prophet: a tale of Irish famine* (London, 1865), p. 259. **12** See 'The Party fight and funeral' and 'The Midnight Mass' in his *Traits and stories* i, 180–235, 325–80; also 'Tubber Derg' in ibid., ii, 363–414. **13** *The autobiography of William Carleton* (London, 1968). **14** Carleton, *The Black Prophet*, pp 16–17. **15** 'The Lough Derg pilgrim' in Carleton, *Traits and stories*, i, 244.

feet – most people, however, content themselves with stripping off their shoes and stockings on coming within the precincts of the holy ground ... In the glen were constructed a number of tents, where whisky and refreshments might be had in abundance. Every tent had a fiddler or a piper; many two of them. From the top of a pole that ran up from the roof of each tent was suspended the symbol by which the owner of it was known by his friends and acquaintances. Here swung a salt herring or turf, there a shillelah, in a third place a shoe, in a fourth place a wisp of hay, in a fifth an old hat.[16]

Carleton's stories attempted to establish an Irish tradition of writing and representing Ireland, its landscapes and people, though his work is probably more heavily involved in people, behaviour and manners than with the landscapes that accommodated them. Like Maria Edgeworth, Gerald Griffin and others, he was writing largely for an English market and for English publishers and some of his descriptions would fall into the more romantic pastorals of an English readership which did not rest comfortably with impressions of a densely populated, pre-famine south Ulster landscape.[17]

Much of Carleton's world would have been familiar to Patrick Kavanagh. Indeed though separated by a hundred years, there are uncanny continuities. In many ways the rural landscape had changed little in the pre-electric age: Kavanagh noted that 'notwithstanding the arrival of the tractor and the combined harvester, the spirit I found here had not changed in a hundred and fifty years. This was the society to which Carleton gave a voice.'[18] The material landscapes of fields and lanes, houses and outbuildings, the tools and household appliances were in many cases those of Carleton's time. 'From Cavan and from Leitrim and from Mayo/ From all the thin-faced parishes where hills/ Are perished noses running peaty water': Kavanagh was particularly adept at evoking landscapes in their natural and social manifestations, in this instance reflecting on the dripping drumlin landscapes of hills and streams, lakes and marsh in the opening lines of his poem 'Lough Derg.' The hill country and small fields and farms of south Monaghan are summoned up in images that mirror the experience of one who laboured in this landscape, reflecting the texture of local micro landscapes with a sharp eye for the details that Carleton also noticed at times. Kavanagh is especially important as a poet of the local landscape and community who, like Carleton, also represented a busy, well-peopled countryside, in spite of the emigration which had emptied many houses and farms since Carleton's time. His landscapes are full of the sounds of people and animals, cans clattering, cart-wheels rattling along roads, calves bawling, dogs

16 Carleton, 'Phelim O'Toole's Courtship' in *Traits and stories*, ii, 192.   **17** P.J. Duffy, 'Carleton, Kavanagh and the south Ulster landscape, *c.*1800–1950' in *Ir. Geography*, 18 (1985), pp 25–36.   **18** *November haggard: uncollected prose and verse of Patrick Kavanagh*, ed. P. Kavanagh (New York, 1973), pp 69–70. See interview with Kavanagh ('Meet Mr. Patrick Kavanagh') in *The Bell*, xvi (1948), pp 5–11 in which he claimed that he was 'the only man who has written in our time about rural Ireland from the inside.'

barking, people calling to each other over fields, intimate representations of a small-farm countryside in a pre-mechanised age.[19]

Seamus Heaney's remembered Ulster landscape has the same texture about some of its description: Mossbawn was

> the land of haycock and corn-stook, of fence and gate, milk-cans at the end of lanes and auction notices on gate pillars. Dogs barked from farm to farm. Sheds gaped at the roadside, bulging with fodder ... In the names of its fields and townlands, in their mixture of Scots and Irish and English etymologies, this side of the country was redolent of the histories of its owners. Broagh, The Long Rigs, Bell's Hill; Brian's Field, the Round Meadow, the Demesne; each name was a kind of love made to each acre.[20]

Kavanagh's sense of landscape is well exemplified in the manner in which he also invoked the names of local places and townlands which recur throughout his poetry and prose, markers of locality and identity: placenames used, says Heaney, as 'posts to fence out a personal landscape.'[21] Heaney, Benedict Kiely, John Montague and John Hewitt have the same affinity with the placename rhythms of the landscapes of their early memories. Montague's recitation of names in Tyrone: 'Beragh, Carrickmore,/ Pomeroy, Fintona –/ placenames that sigh/ like a pressed melodeon' mirrors Kavanagh's 'Mullahinsha, Drummeril, Black Shanco,'[22] or the musicality of John Hewitt's 'Drumbo, Dungannon, or Annalong.'[23]

Much of twentieth-century writing outside Ireland is about the urban landscape of the city. Indeed, Seán O'Faoláin and many twentieth-century writers rebelled against Irish parochialism focussed on rural culture and rural life and out of tune with mainstream European culture. Many like James Joyce, Samuel Beckett, Seán O'Casey, John McGahern and others escaped what Kavanagh called the 'grip of irregular fields'. Joyce's great modernist project *Ulysses* was written so that 'if the city one day suddenly disappeared from the earth it could be reconstructed out of my book.' Although possibly overcome by the exuberance of writing *Ulysses*, this indicates his intention to represent accurately his remembered landscapes of Dublin. Joyce's reconstructions of Dublin were based on meticulous preparatory research. The topographical content of much of his writing is supremely 'visual' and his *Dubliners* has been read in conjunction with Bartholomew's 1900 map of

19 See for example, P. Kavanagh, *Tarry Flynn* (New York, 1949), p. 80.   **20** Heaney, 'Mossbawn' in *Preoccupations*, pp 18–20.   **21** Heaney, 'Sense of place' in *Preoccupations*, p. 141. See P.J. Duffy, 'Patrick Kavanagh's rural landscape' in *Éire–Ireland*, xxi (1986), pp 105–18; idem, 'Carleton, Kavanagh and the south Ulster landscape'; idem, 'Change and renewal in issues of place, identity and the local' in J. Hourihane (ed.), *Engaging spaces: people, place and space from an Irish perspective* (Dublin, 2003), pp 13–29.   **22** J. Montague, 'Last journey' in *Selected poems* (Oldcastle, 1995), p. 171; P. Kavanagh, 'Stoney grey soil' in *The complete poems of Patrick Kavanagh*, ed. P. Kavanagh (New York, 1972), pp 73–4.   **23** J. Hewitt, 'Ulster names' in *The collected poems of John Hewitt* (Belfast, 1991).

Dublin. He 'makes much of tram routes, the names of the streets, the 'street furniture', the hotels and bars, the realistic texture of turn-of-the-century Dublin.'[24]

In contrast to writings about past places written in contemporary time, some creative historical writing is also valuable as retrospective imaginings of past worlds, with the added benefits of hindsight and the insights of scholarship. Many can be important and useful illuminators of past landscapes. Examples of such writers today include John Banville (*Birchwood* and *The Newton Letter*), James Plunkett (*Strumpet City*) and Brian Friel (*Translations*, *The Home Place*), representing landscapes of gentry decline, urban poverty, emigration, and colonial appropriation. J.G. Farrell's trilogy on the end of Empire in three different places at three different times (*Siege of Krishnapoor*, *The Singapore Grip* and *Troubles*) are good examples of this mode.

Topographical poetry, largely in the Anglo-Irish tradition of writing through the eighteenth century in particular, matched the fashionable aesthetic of the picturesque which prevailed in England and took its cues from new-found interest in landscape art, especially Italian art, in wild nature, as well as the science of surveying and mapping from the late seventeenth century. Topographical poetry provided pictorial, metaphorical reflections of harmony and order in society and nature, or wild nature in the later eighteenth century. Ireland, with its extensive wild landscapes, provided suitable locations for this poetry, and into the nineteenth century more and more of such topographical poetry described in detail different locations within Ireland, in increasingly scientific surveying terms, 'until their poems resembled versified Ordnance Survey maps.'[25]

This has been considered as distinct from Gaelic topographical traditions, a higher Gaelic art form which had lost its patrons in seventeenth-century plantations. In the eighteenth century Gaelic poetic tradition was mainly replaced by a folk art that was socially inaccessible to the Anglo-Irish literary world. Katherine Simms, in an examination of Gaelic perceptions of landscape from the thirteenth to the seventeenth centuries, suggests that poets and their patrons considered an extensive landscape aesthetically pleasing.[26] Some writing in the Gaelic tradition by the late eighteenth century was also taking its cues from a wider European aesthetic, however, and is reflected for instance in the opening passages of Merriman's Cúirt an Mheán Oíche, in which the landscape is imagined in classic terms. Amhlaoibh Ó Súilleabháin's Diary also reflects evidence of this tradition:

> Thángamar abhaile go socair sámh d'éis braoinín uisce beatha d'ól ag tigh
> ósta an Phaoraigh. Bhí an lá uile, agus an tráthnóna go háirithe, ró-aoibhinn.
> Ag cora Mhuilleann an Bhrianaigh tá eas agus linn bhreá, inis saileog ar an
> taobh theas den linn, agus oileán go cranna giúise ar an taobh thuaidh.

---

24 D. Pierce, *James Joyce's Ireland* (New Haven, 1992), p. 83. St John Ervine wrote about early twentieth-century industrial and Presbyterian Belfast in contrast to the ruralism of Catholic writers. **25** J. Wilson Foster, *Colonial consequences: essays in Irish literature and culture* (Dublin, 1991), pp 9–29, p. 23. **26** 'References to landscape and economy in Irish bardic poetry' in Clarke et al. (eds), *Surveying Ireland's past*, pp 145–68.

Sheasaigh an ainnear álainn idir mé and an t-eas, ag amhrán, agus an t-eas ag crónan, agus na crainn ag canrán. Sheasaigh sí mar bhean sí I gceo an easa. Bhí greidhn ar mo chroí. Bhíodar scamaill chraorag ina luí ar Sliabh na mBan. D'iontaíodar ó chraorag go buí, ó bhuí go glas, gorm, dubh, ciardhubh. Do stad an ainnirín.

[trans.] We came home at our ease having had a drop of whiskey at Power's inn. The entire day, and the evening in particular, was delightful. At the weir of O'Brien's Mill there is a waterfall, and a lovely pool with a field of willows bordering its south side and an island with pine trees on the north side. The young woman stood between me and the waterfall, singing, against the boom of the waterfall and the murmur of the trees. She stood like a fairy woman in the midst of the fall. I was enraptured. Crimson clouds capped Slievnamon. They turned from crimson to gold, from gold to grey, dark blue, black, jet-black. The maiden ceased.[27]

As with painted landscapes, there is a large body of writing encompassing the theme of the Big House and estate landscapes. Indeed, the gentry manor house is frequently the centre piece of many works of historical fiction.[28] A great deal of Elizabeth Bowen's writing is based on her experience of gentry Ireland, with *The Last September* being characterised as an 'elegy' on the 'twilight world of the Anglo-Irish whose tone and atmosphere throughout is coloured by the mood of valediction'.[29]

As with many of the Anglo-Irish gentry, Bowen's landscape and its visuality and sense of place were more emblematic than its community. Her's is a slightly detached 'outsider' observation (including an aerial perspective) of the detailed texture and geography of the countryside in the 1930s which would contrast with the more insider local view of Kavanagh's *Green Fool*, for example. Her Cork landscape

---

27 From B. Ó Madagáin, 'The picturesque in the Gaelic tradition' in Collins (ed.), *Decoding the landscape*, pp 48–59, pp 53–4. **28** See, for example, Maria Edgeworth, the progenitor of the genre in *Castle Rackrent* (London, *c*.1964); Anthony Trollope, *Castle Richmond* (London, 1994) and *The MacDermots of Ballycloran* (London, 1991); Elizabeth Bowen, *The Last September, Mulberry Tree* and her memoir *Bowen's Court*; Somerville and Ross, *The Real Charlotte, In Mr Knox's country, Irish RM*. George Moore, *A drama in muslin*; S. Leslie, *Doomsland* and later replications of these themes by D. Thomson, *Woodbrook* (London, 1988), J. Banville, *Birchwood* (London, 1973), J.G. Farrell, *Troubles* (London, 1970), and B. Friel, *The home place* (Oldcastle, 2005). For commentaries on this genre and its historical context, see V. Kreilkamp, *The Anglo-Irish novel and the big house* (Syracuse, 1998); Somerville Large, *The Irish country house*; M. Bence-Jones, *Life in an Irish country house* (London, 1996); D.G. Boyce, 'Lever among the landlords: Charles Lever (1806–1872) and the search for a rural order' in Collins, Ollerenshaw and Parkhill (eds), *Industry, trade and people in Ireland, 1650–1950*, pp 173–91. **29** G. Cronin, 'The Big House and the Irish landscape in the work of Elizabeth Bowen' in J. Genet (ed.), *The Big House in Ireland* (Dingle, 1991), pp 143–62, p. 145.

is not as empty as it appears. Roads and boreens between high hedges, sunk rivers, farms deep in squares of sheltering trees all combine by their disappearance to trick the eye. Only mountainy farmhouses, gleaming white on their fields reclaimed from the bog, and facades of chapels on hills or hillocks, show. The country conceals its pattern of life, which can only wholly be seen from an aeroplane. This is really country to fly over – its apparent empty smoothness is full of dips and creases. From the air you discover unknown reaches of river, chapels, schools, bridges, forlorn graveyards, interknit by a complex of untravelled roads.[30]

Bowen also represented the Irish countryside ('the unloving country') as a sometimes silent place of menace in contrast to the peace and order of the Big House and demesne which purported to rule over the resentful countryside. The denouement in *The Last September* is the burning of the house against a dark, foreboding surrounding landscape. These expressions of a social and landscape divide in Ireland at the end of the nineteenth century are also invoked in George Moore's *A Drama in Muslin* where the world of the Irish landlord was doomed, with each Big House 'surrounded by a hundred small ones, all working to keep it in sloth and luxury.'[31]

David Thomson's *Woodbrook*, Molly Keane's *Good behaviour* (London, 1982), William Trevor's *Fools of Fortune* (London, 1983), John Banville's *Birchwood*, J.G. Farrell's *Troubles*, latterly Brian Friel's *The Home Place* might be categorised with the works of Elizabeth Bowen as commentaries on the eclipse and decline of Anglo-Irish landscapes. Together with *Bowen's Court*, *Woodbrook* weaves a narrative of the Anglo-Irish Big House with glimpses of the historical development of Ireland and its colonial settlement.

Poetry and other creative literatures, therefore, can add an important dimension to many studies of landscape that are inaccessible to map, survey or census. The insights of creative artists are important primary sources in not only describing the world, but helping to shape it; their imaginations help make real the landscape.[32] Obviously literary reflections will lack precision, but will contain important reflections of the placeness and metaphorical significance of the landscape. Montague's remembered Tyrone landscape, according to one commentator, 'is a cacophany of loss, its untidy topography ... spelling out the remnants of a mislaid, and an overlaid, culture. Most conspicuous by their absence are the people themselves: "Like shards/ Of a lost culture, the slopes/ Are strewn with cabins, deserted/ In my lifetime."'[33]

Using literature and art as a research tool in historical studies has pitfalls in explanation and understanding that need to considered too. For example, Brian

---

30 *Bowen's Court* (London, 1942), p. 2.   **31** *A Drama in Muslin* (London, 1886), p. 68 quoted by V. Kreilkamp, '*Going to the levée* as ascendancy spectacle: alternative narratives in an Irish painting' in Dalsimer (ed.), *Visualizing Ireland*, pp 37–54, p. 50.   **32** See D.W. Meinig, 'Geography as art' in *TIBG*, new series, 8 (1983), pp 314–28, p. 317.   **33** J. Montague's *The Rough Field* (Dublin, 1972) discussed by Wilson Foster in *Colonial consequences* which also examines the work of Yeats, Heaney, Hewitt and Kavanagh.

Friel's *Translations* is an enigmatic rendition of Ireland's place in Empire, 'concerned with cartography as metaphor, not as practice'.[34] Measuring and naming the land, even though as historians have shown undertaken with scholarly integrity, are ultimately far-from-innocent political impositions of knowledge and power on the landscape. However, the historical geographer John Andrews is concerned about the use of fiction as history.[35] Friel has used his artist's prerogative in imagining the local operation of the Ordnance Survey as it mapped the Irish landscape, interlocking perhaps with a discourse of imperial appropriation. The problem for Andrews, author of *A paper landscape: the Ordnance Survey in nineteenth-century Ireland* (Oxford, 1975), is that many people accepted Friel's account as historically plausible. Many of the practices detailed in the play, particularly the process of 'naming' the Irish landscape which was central to the play's theme, are unsubstantiated by all the historical evidence: the OS was rigorous in its approach to placenames, using the authority and expertise of a range of distinguished Irish scholars.[36]

FOLKORE AND ORAL NARRATIVES OF PLACES

Folk memory is an important repository of stories or narratives of landscape and its constituent places (as in *dinnseanchas*) and the bonding of community and landscape, especially traditional community. The role of the Folklore Commission, established in 1935, for example, has been significant, building on an earlier antiquarian tradition. Collectors have been working away, quietly collecting stories, customs, and folklore.[37] Collections on folklore and folklife are increasingly valuable in an age of very rapid change which has resulted in a form of landscape amnesia in many parts of Ireland. There is an increasing disjuncture between local communities in many places and the landscapes they inhabit, reflected in a County Down instance where one old man could name 156 townlands in his locality, while a middle-aged man identified thirteen and his teenage son could only name the townland in which he lived.[38] Introduction of road names and post codes in

---

34 C. Connolly, 'The turn to the map: cartographic fictions in Irish culture' in Kreilkamp (ed.), *Éire/Land*, pp 27–33, p. 32.   **35** J.H. Andrews, 'Notes for a future edition of Brian Friel's *Translations*' in the *Irish Review*, 13 (Winter 1992–3), pp 93–106; see also '*Translations* and *A paper landscape*: between fiction and history' in the *Crane Bag*, vii (1983), pp 118–24; on the symbolism of cartography in the Irish past, see Hooper's 'Planning Control: cartouches, maps and the Irish landscape'.   **36** See G. Smith, '"An eye on the Survey": perceptions of the Ordnance Survey in Ireland 1824–1842' in *History Ireland*, 9, no. 2 (Summer 2001), pp 37–41. Dispute also centred on Friel's reference to soldiers being armed, though curiously, there is a painting of Royal Sappers and miners surveying in 1837 in which the soldiers are clearly under arms: see *An illustrated record of the Ordnance Survey in Ireland*, p. 19.   **37** The main collection, the 1938 Schools Collection and the Irish famine questionnaire undertaken in 1945 comprise the National Folklore Collection deposited in the Department of Irish Folklore in University College Dublin.   **38** See P.J. Duffy, 'Townlands: territorial signatures of landholding and identity' in B.S. Turner (ed.), *The heart's townland: marking boundaries in Ulster* (Belfast, 2004), pp 18–38, p. 23.

Northern Ireland has helped this memory loss, though a growing development all over Ireland of roadside name stones carved with local townland names is reflection of renewed local interest.

Folklore consisting of songs and stories, often mythic in tone, reflect the voices of the ordinary community which are quite distinct from the official narratives of state or the more literate and rationalist narratives of élites. Care must be taken in assessing folk material, however, where chronologies and histories are frequently transposed in the folk memory, and placenames, for instance, can be misrepresented. Local perspectives on bigger processes and events can be different. Glassie's work in south Fermanagh, however, in the view of one historical geographer, 'is a remarkable fusion of scholarship, artistry, and emotion. An unknown people in an obscure place are given an intensely real vitality. The ordinary lives and landscapes of individuals and of a whole community are portrayed and analysed with breathtaking skill in search for the meaning of it all'.[39] On the other hand, the histories and narratives which he records need to be carefully deconstructed.

Many of these sources, such as songs and ballads, are especially evocative of life and landscape during famine and periods of mass emigration. But as with more formal literary sources which have influenced popular discourses of the past, folk memory (in the texts of song or story) has also been instrumental in shaping popular understanding of past experiences of landlords, famine, or emigration. In west Mayo, for instance, a local belief that the village clusters and their intermingled fields were deviously planned by 'Lord Rundale' was more real and attractive than orthodox historical explanations. In south Monaghan, schoolchildren in 1938 believed that the local landlord was a 'bad landlord' because he evicted people for keeping goats.[40] Memories of the night of the Big Wind in 1839, for instance, recorded a hundred years later, focus on its extraordinary impact on local landscapes. In the parish of Muckno in Monaghan it was recalled:

> The Big Wind of 1839 did a lot of damage in this district. It blew all the thatch off the houses and blew down hay stacks. It blew the fish out of the river and the roof was blown off J Hughes' house in Tomacrow. The slates are still to be seen in the meadow a distance of three fields. The people wrapped their grown up children in blankets and tied them to the roots of trees to keep them from being blown away.[41]

The concept of 'vernacular landscape' is valuable in focussing not only on the material landscape, but also on the cultural memory embodied in the relationship between local communities and their landscapes. There are differences between the

39 D. Meinig, 'Geography as an art' in *TIBG*, 8 (1983), p. 323 reviewing Glassie, *Passing the time*   **40** Westport story told to author. The Monaghan memory from the NFC schools collection probably related to regulations on the Shirley estate in the 1830s to prevent the young whitethorn quicks from being eaten by goats.   **41** In the National Folklore Schools Collection, 1939.

geographical concept of material space and the cultural sense of place expressed through oral and written narratives. Exploring folklore records from the 1930s, Guy Beiner uncovers several hundred sources relating to memories of 'The Year of the French' in the West of Ireland in which the landscape was marked with marching routes of the French, battlefield sites, sites of execution and burial:

> The map of *Bliain na bhFrancach* in folk memory went beyond the footsteps of the Rebel army and also charted sites of popular agitation and local uprisings, routes Irish recruits took on their way to join the French, local skirmishes between smaller forces separated from the main body of the army, the flight of fugitives after the defeat at Ballinamuck, guerilla warfare and outlaw activities after the French surrender, and the punitive activities of the military and yeomen terror in repressing the local population. These geographical delineations may not always conform with studies of military historians yet, for the people of Connacht the French invasion and its aftermath, as it was remembered in social memory, was an integral part of their vernacular landscape. In fact, the a-historicity of traditions relating to commemorative landscape is of lesser relevance to understanding than the influence they maintained in popular imagination.[42]

Elizabeth FitzPatrick has studied the lore relating to Gaelic inauguration and assembly sites which survived in local memory down to the nineteenth century, when some communities tried to organise Repeal meetings at these historic sites.[43] Indeed Raymond Gillespie has examined earlier usage of folkloric narratives in 'origin legends' surrounding County Down plantation settlements or medieval Dublin. A late seventeenth century story referred to the building of the Tholsel in Dublin probably in the late fifteenth century: 'Local legends such as these were validated by the very landscape and buildings to which they became attached.'[44]

Local buildings in the landscape are sometimes recalled vividly, like Lisaroo chapel in Devenish parish, County Fermanagh, built in the early nineteenth century by the local landlord:

> a wee thatched house ... when I went to it first, the altar was in the middle and the railings around it. The choir was boarded up with a couple of steps up to it. I mind all they had for an organ was a flute ... And the townspeople

42 G. Beiner, 'Mapping the "Year of the French": the vernacular landscape of folk memory' in E. Caldicott and A. Fuchs (eds), *Cultural memory: essays on European literature and history* (Oxford, 2003), pp 191–208, p. 198.   **43** E. FitzPatrick, 'An Tulach Tinóil: gathering sites and meeting-culture in Gaelic lordships' in *History Ireland*, 9, no. 1 (Spring 2001), pp 22–6; idem, *Royal inauguration in Gaelic Ireland, c.1100–1600: a cultural landscape study* (Woodbridge, 2004).   **44** R. Gillespie, 'Robert Ware's telling tales: a medieval Dublin story and its significance' in S. Duffy (ed.), *Medieval Dublin V* (Dublin, 2004), pp 291–301, p. 301. See also idem, 'Seventeenth-century migration myths: some Ulster stories' in B. S. Turner (ed.), *Migration and myth: Ulster's revolving door* (Downpatrick, 2006), pp 9–21.

and up-to-date people had forms of their own round the walls. The floor was clay and when a big flood came, the water came in ... The police got a form for themselves. The rest of us had to kneel where we like ... The priest got straight forms put across the chapel. Then they got a sacristy built. Then they put a gallery up. And they wrought on with this till they got a new Chapel built in 1910 in Irvinestown.[45]

John O'Donovan in his researches for the Ordnance Survey in the 1830s was aware of the value of folk memory, especially in understanding local placenames, though he was also alert to its eccentricities. In Clontibret parish in Monaghan, for instance, he met an old man who told him that

> gentlemen know nothing about Irish names of townlands – that they wish to harden, shorten and make them like English names – and as this work is going on since the reign of Oliver Cromwell it is now most difficult to come at the oult names, for even the farmers are now forgetting the names which their grandmothers used to call these lands and adopting the hard and shortened names which they hear with their landlords.[46]

Field names are often a sensitive indicator of when Irish was a living language in the rural community: many field names recorded in the NFC in 1938 in Farney in south Monaghan, for instance, reflect the survival of the Irish language well into the nineteenth century. Similarly today many field names recorded around Westport are in Irish.[47]

The song and ballad tradition is sometimes a valuable source of information. Pre-famine landscapes of labour were important themes in local memories both in story and song: hiring fairs, and seasonal labour migration. 'Tá mo mhéire stiofálta le búaint an fhóghmhair' / 'My fingers are stiffened from reaping the harvest': songs and poetry from north Meath recall the spáilpíni or wandering labourers' annual migration south from the Ulster hills and the social tensions which frequently accompanied it.[48] There is a rich ballad tradition about local places which frequently catalogues aspects of their topography. Dancing, sporting, hunting and

---

45 IFC, 559, 320, remembered in 1938 by a 92-year-old woman. There are also memories of porridge houses and soup kitchens during the Great Famine. 46 RIA, *Letters containing information relative to the antiquities of the counties of Armagh and Monaghan*, reproduced under the direction of Revd Michael Ó Flanagan (Bray, 1927), p. 37 typescript (manuscript p.72). 47 Duffy, 'Unwritten landscapes'. 48 S. MacGabhann, 'A people's art: the great songs of Meath and Oriel' in *Ríocht na Midhe*, ix (1998), pp 103–20; see also P. Ní Uallacháin, *A hidden Ulster: people, songs and traditions of Oriel* (Dublin, 2003) and E. Estyn Evans, *Mourne Country* (Dundalk, 1951), pp 211–14 for ballads from south Down; K. Whelan, 'The bases of regionalism' in P. Ó Drisceoil (ed.), *Culture in Ireland: regions, identity and power* (Belfast, 1992), pp 5–62. Thomas Moore popularised Irish identity and place for the rising urban and rural middle class in nineteenth-century Ireland with iconic lyrics in his ten-volume *Irish Melodies*.

other activities were situated in a background of a richly named landscape. Songs about hunts are particularly resonant of landscape which usually features as the dramatic backdrop to the progress and adventure of the hunt, whether it was foot hunting (beagling in south Ulster) or the more elaborate mounted hunts of Munster and the Midlands, and contain litanies of placenames as markers of landscape. 'Tally ho' celebrates one such hunt in Galloon parish in County Fermanagh:

> It being in October the year of sixty eight,
> We had a fine hunt in Col. Madden's estate,
> There were sportsmen from Newtown and from Lough na Rye,
> We all met on Donagh Hill our hounds for to try…
> When the hare she was started she ran round Drumcoff,
> She headed for Screevagh and then for Moorlough,
> When she ran round Moorlough she turned back again,
> Into Drumsastra and on through Drumrain
> Tally-ho hark away, tally-ho hark away …[49]

MEMOIRS, LETTERS AND DIARIES

The genre of records of real landscapes includes all the writing on reminiscences and reconstructions of images of past places as well as journals and diaries recorded in real time. There is an enormous output and great range in quality.[50] Some have become classics such as Paddy the Cope Gallagher's *My story* (London, 1939) – his recollections on hiring days in Donegal, working in Scotland, establishing a cooperative in Gweedore in the late nineteenth century; Mici MacGabhan's *Rotha Mór an tSaoil* (Dublin, 1959)[51] in similar vein; Tomás O Croimhthain's *An tOileánach* (Dublin, 1929), Muiris O Súileabhain's *Fiche Bliain ag fás* (London, 1933), and Peig Sayer's *A scéal féin* (Dublin, 1939). A great many recall West of Ireland places, remoter poorer landscapes, reflecting the innate story-telling talent of these same communities as well as the popular interest in these presumed authentic native places.[52]

John McKenna's more recent reconstruction of one year in the history of Castledermot in County Kildare is based on solid empirical data, leavened with a modicum of imagined recollection: in the later winter/ spring

---

49 From NFC, S946, 328. Apart from the Folklore Collections in UCD, much useful folk material on landscapes and places can also be obtained in the Ulster Folk and Transport Museum, Ulster American Folk Park, journals such as *Ulster Folklife*, *Béaloideas* and the many local historical society journals.   **50** See, for example, W.K. Parke, *A Fermanagh childhood* (Belfast, 1988); A. Taylor, *To school through the fields* (Dingle, 1988).   **51** Translated by V. Iremonger as *The hard road to Klondyke* (London, 1962).   **52** See R. Flower, *The Western Island or The Great Blasket* (Oxford, 1944) and G. Thomson, *Island home: the Blasket heritage* (Dingle, 1988).

in the fields and on the farms around Castledermot the pace of life was increasing. At Cope's mill in Prumplestown farmers were arriving to collect sacks of seed oats and barley. Their carts and traps and trailers travelled from Graney and Kilkea and Levitstown to collect the crop seeds, meeting on the tight bend at the Mill Pond. At the Mill itself work went busily on. The huge wooden wheel turned, dripping the waters of the Lerr as it powered the machinery inside. Pulleys raised and lowered the hundredweight sacks. Trailers were loaded and driven to Maganey for the up and down train. And, in the slowly brightening evenings, men cycled home from the mill to begin work on tilling their own gardens.[53]

Elizabeth Bowen's memoir of the neighbourhood of her ancestral home at Bowenscourt is a portait of a lived-in landscape:

> On Sundays you get an idea of the population: everybody appears. The roads converging on chapels teem with people going to mass. Horses and traps turn out of impossibly narrow lanes; cyclists freewheel with a whirring rattle down from mountainy farms. Dark Sundayfied figures balance on stepping-stones, take tracks through plantations, leg it over stiles. After midday mass the streets of the villages give out a static hum. On holy days and on fair days the scene also becomes living and dark; race days, big matches or *feishes* bring all the hired cars out, and people out on the banks to watch the cars. At funerals the *corteges* are very, very long. Early on weekday mornings the roads rattle with ass carts taking milk cans up to the creameries. And from dusk on young men gather at the crossroads and bridges and stay talking, faceless, well into the dark. Sometimes they light fires. On fine summer nights there is dancing, twice a week, on boards put down at crossroads or outside the villages. Lights burn late in cottages near the dancing, and the music gives the darkness a pulse. When the music stops, the country rustles with movement of people going home …[54]

In an age before film and telephone, letters were much more descriptive of life and landscape, frequently passing on to the addressee many details of changes that had taken place. For ordinary people, not many letters have survived, unless those to and from emigrants. Letters to emigrants in particular frequently responded to requests for details of the home area and its families, just as the letters from emigrants give little pen pictures of the new world.[55] Letters were an important form of communication for élites in the eighteenth and nineteenth centuries and, in view of their education and literacy, offer important perspectives.

53 J. McKenna, *The lost village: portrait of an Irish village in 1925* (Dublin, 1995), p. 13. **54** Bowen, *Bowen's Court*, p. 2. **55** See D. Fitzpatrick, *Oceans of consolations* (Cork, 1994); C.J. Houston and W.J. Smyth, *Irish emigration and Canadian settlement: patterns, links and letters* (Belfast, 1990); T. Parkhill, '"With a little help from their friends": assisted emigration schemes, 1700–1845' in Duffy (ed.), *To and from Ireland*, pp 57–78.

Ascendancy women, especially, had time on their hands and were remarkably productive writers of letters and memoirs which are worth exploring for the light they cast on changes and developments in their properties and those of their neighbours. The letters (1690–1723) between Robert Molesworth of Breckdenston, Swords and his wife, as well as those between the duke of Richmond's daughters in Kildare – Louisa Conolly and Emily FitzGerald – are classic reflections of changing tastes in garden and parkland design from late seventeenth to the mid-eighteenth century, containing much information on planting and designing gardens and demesnes. In 1762 Lady Emily was involved in the development of the parkland in Carton, in which the planting of mature trees was undertaken from the outset:

> The new river is beautiful. One turn of it is a masterpiece in the art of laying out … I had great pleasure in seeing ten men thickening up … the plantation between the Dublin and Nine Mile Stone Gate with good, tall, shewy-looking trees, elm and ash; but there are still quantities of holes not fill'd, and I suspect that to satisfy our impatience last autumn Jacob Smith dug more than he will get trees to fill this winter.[56]

For many of the gentry in the eighteenth and nineteenth centuries, hunting was one of their most popular pursuits and there is a strong sense of the Irish landscape and its inhabitants being picturesquely represented from the vantage point of the saddles of the West Carbury Hunt in the case of Edith Somerville and Violet Martin.[57] Hunting was tolerated as a spectacle by the peasantry, with the gentry galloping noisily and arrogantly across the workaday landscape of farmers and tenantry. Somerville and Ross describe hills and hollows, marshes, fences, hedges, gaps, boreens and bog roads, 'good' and 'bad' places – landscapes of obstacles and boundaries, though the hunt generally ignored property boundaries in an era of estates when the landowning gentry owned the land. The hunt was used as a vehicle of resistance during the Land League protests in 1881 and '82 when groups noisily marched through the countryside to disturb any hidden foxes. Somerville and Ross's evocation of hunting was castigated by one writer of the Irish literary revival in 1919 as 'inflicting a lasting hurt upon the character of their country'.[58] However, Julie Ann Stevens has revisited their writing and suggests that their representation of the Irish landscape at the close of the nineteenth century parodied

56 *Correspondence of Emily, duchess of Leinster*, ed. B. FitzGerald (London, 1949); see also for accounts of parkland design, his *Lady Louisa Conolly* (London, 1957). Molesworth correspondence in PRONI and NLI, cited in E. Malins and the Knight of Glin, *Lost demesnes* (London, 1976) and O'Kane, *Landscape design in eighteenth-century Ireland*. See also *Letters from Georgian Ireland*, ed. Day.   **57** *The selected letters of Somerville and Ross*, ed. Lewis; see also Somerville and Ross, *Some experiences of an Irish RM* (1898), *Further experiences of an Irish RM* (1908) and *In Mr Knox's Country* (1915).   **58** Susan Mitchell quoted in Hilary Pyle, *Red-headed rebel: Susan L. Mitchell, poet and mystic of the Irish cultural renaissance* (Dublin, 1998), p. 191.

a landscape of Protestant gentry myths, especially in its portrayal of the hunt. They were both interested in art and landscape and Stevens suggests they 'employed parody to reveal what might lurk behind the picture frames enclosing the romantic scenery or venerable portraiture of nineteenth-century Ireland.'[59]

Their report of the hunt vividly portrays the face of the landscape with the local populace as extras, viewing and encouraging the performance:

> at last after about half an hour, we heard very faint shrieks the far side of the hill to the west. We belted round and found the fox had broke here [map and drawing] and the whole pack got away a mile ahead of old Beamish ... we could see no sign of anything, but little fringes of country fellows along the hills waved to us the way. It was a horrid country – rotten fences and very high stone gaps. Our horses went splendidly, over horrible ground, till we came to a boreen with a low wall across it, on the other side a stream full of huge stones, and a sort of bank – Sorcerer jumped it in the most able way, but the mare wouldn't have it ... Just then on a hill about a mile away to the north – going like blazes, we saw the hounds and Mr Beamish. Between us and them was a big turf bog with no sort of passage so A and I made a sort of hurried guess by the look of things at the way he was running, and set off as hard as we could lick round the bog, on a bog road ...[60]

The lively correspondence of John O'Donovan (and his assistant Thomas O'Connor) as they travelled the roads of Ireland for the Ordnance Survey have an immediacy about local conditions in the 1830s. West Donegal was a land of few roads where horse traps had to be dismantled to cross rivers. 'We are sometimes detained for hours under a bush or the shelter of a rock to avoid the sudden showers that rush down the glens of this district'.[61]

Diaries are occasionally useful records of landscape at particular times in the past. Generally, however, they are more concerned with life than landscape, as changes in the former lend themselves to a daily chronicle whereas, apart from seasonal rhythms, landscape offers less for the diarist. The exception is the nature diary which emerged in late eighteenth-century England as an expression of burgeoning interest in the landscape's natural history. *Cinn Lae Amhlaoibh Uí Shúileabháin* probably falls into this genre in Ireland.[62] A schoolmaster in Kilkenny from 1827 to 1836, he describes a landscape very similar to the pre-war landscape of the 1930s.

Diaries written by Irish people are relatively uncommon. In most cases there is more in the way of travel journals, accounts or memoirs by visitors such as Asenath

59 J.A. Stevens, 'Picturing the past: reaction to popular representation of the nation in Somerville and Ross's Irish RM stories' in *Journal of the Cork Historical and Archaeological Society*, 105 (2000), pp 175–90, p. 177.   **60** *The selected letters of Somerville and Ross*, ed. Lewis, p. 125.   **61** OS Letters, Co. Donegal, typescript p. 86 (typescript), 161 (manuscript). **62** *The diary of Humphrey O'Sullivan. Part 1 containing the diary from 1st January 1827 to the end of August 1828*, ed. M. McGrath (Irish Texts Society, London, 1936). See B. Ó Madagáin, *An dialann dúlra/ the nature diary* (Dublin, 1978).

Nicholson during the famine.[63] And being often concerned with personal impressions their use as sources for examining landscapes in the past needs careful balancing.[64] A noteworthy exception is Elizabeth Smith, whose diaries and memoirs are an important source for her small estate in County Wicklow.[65] She moved to her husband's Irish estate in 1830 and recorded in considerable detail the management problems on the estate up to and during the famine, which with supplementary data from the census and Griffith's Valuation provides an invaluable picture of landscape, settlement and society on a small Irish estate. She was taken aback by the manner in which her tenants married and set up house without any reference to the landlord. During the progress of the 1841 census, when everyone was warned to record residents on the night of 6 June, Smith noted in her diary: '… the poor people here are all terrified that they were to have been kidnapped or pressed or murdered on the night of the 6th. Half of them were not to go to bed and had barricaded their doors.'[66] During the famine, she noted,

> I went up the hill again first calling on the Widow Quinn, who being left some years ago on her husband's death insolvent with a very large and very young family and she an ailing woman, the Colonel relieved her of her land, forgave her seven years' rent, gave her the stock and crop to dispose of and left her the house and garden for her life. I put mother and daughter on the souplist, times being so hard … the daughter [married] … a sickly labouring lad who is often laid up, but to whom she has brought seven children. They live in the mother's cowhouse where she had no right to put them and thus settle a whole family of beggars upon us … It is the most wretched abode imaginable, without window or fireplace, mud for the floor, neither water or weather-tight, nor scarce a door, all black with smoke, no furniture scarcely …[67]

William Steuart Trench was a prolific writer of letters and commentaries on the various estates he managed as agent. His memoir on his experiences as a land agent classically represents the perspective of the landowning class on the state of mid-nineteenth-century rural land and society in Ireland.[68] In spite of Trench's some-

63 See M. Lenox-Conyngham (ed.), *Diaries of Ireland: an anthology, 1590–1987* (Dublin, 1998). **64** *Retrospections of Dorothea Herbert, 1770–1806*, with foreword by L.M. Cullen (Dublin, 2004) is a mainly introspective record, with limited local references to gentry life. **65** *The Highland lady in Ireland: journals, 1840–50*, ed. P. Kelly and A. Tod (Edinburgh, 1991); J.K. TeBrake, 'Personal narratives as historical sources: the journal of Elizabeth Smith, 1840–1850' in *History Ireland*, 3, no. 1 (Spring 1995), pp 51–5; *The Irish journals of Elizabeth Smith, 1840–1850: a selection*, ed. D. Thomson and M. McGusty (Oxford, 1980); D. James and S. Ó Maitiú (eds), *The Wicklow world of Elizabeth Smith, 1840–1850* (Dublin, 1996). **66** *The Highland lady* quoted in M. Stout, 'The geography and implications of post-famine population decline in Baltyboys, County Wicklow' in C. Morash and R. Hayes (eds), *Fearful realities: new perspectives on the famine* (Dublin, 1996), pp 15–34, p. 18. **67** Stout, 'Post-famine population decline in Baltyboys', p. 24. **68** Trench, *Realities of Irish life*. See Duffy, 'Management problems on a large estate in mid-nineteenth Ireland: William Steuart Trench's

times controversial opinions and practices, especially in relation to his assisted emigration schemes, his work as an agent provided him with extensive insights into the condition of land and landholding on estates in Kerry, Monaghan and Laois.

ACCOUNTS OF TRAVELLERS AND SURVEYORS

Accounts of travels and tours in Ireland are important sources because they are overtly concerned with observation and description, essentially the outsider views of visitors recording their passing impressions. Apart from the occasional unreliability of such fleeting descriptions seen from horseback or through stagecoach or carriage windows, they have the advantage of being contemporary as opposed to retrospective accounts, and being first-hand descriptions of places experienced. They are important also because they take notice of many things overlooked or taken for granted by local reporters. For students of history, akin to travellers back in time, this is a rich and important source, though it may be insufficient for detailed case studies of local landscapes. All of the published accounts were usually aimed at an English readership and in many cases address English preconceptions about Ireland.

The numbers and comprehensiveness of accounts of tours by travellers (mainly British) increases steadily from the seventeenth century, when visitors were largely interested explicitly in the colonial potential of the land. William Brereton's 1635 account of his travels in Wicklow and Wexford provides insights into the kind of changes that were occurring to the Irish landscape during this early phase of settlement by planter pioneers and entrepreneurial investors:

> Two miles hence in Carnue, the town wherein Mr Chambers his castle is erected, and which is a neat, rough-cast, and well-contrived, convenient house … Here is now Mr Odell, who doth commend and magnify beyond all measure the park belonging to this house, which is about seven miles in compass, and wherein are both fallow and red deer good store … Not far hence, about a quarter of a mile, he hath erected an iron-work … Herein the sows of iron [pig-iron] which are brought from Bristow are melted into iron bars … In the way to Ennescorffie, about two miles thence on the other side of the Slane, I went to survey (over the river) the manor of the Ollort, in the county of Wexford, in the parish and diocese of Fernes and Loghlein, which is to be sold … This land lies upon the bank of the Slane, which is plentifully furnished with salmon and trouts; down this river abundance of timber is conveyed down to Wexford, so to be transported by sea. Upon this river bank many pleasant convenient seats for houses or towns may be found out … Our host, Mr Plummer (who lives in Ennerscoffie, and is a Scotchman; his

report on the Shirley estate in 1843'; idem, '"Disencumbering our crowded places": theory and practice of estate migration in the nineteenth century' in Duffy (ed.), *To and from Ireland*, pp 79–104; Lyne, *The Lansdowne estate in Kerry*.

wife an Englishwoman), affirmed that the third part of the corn (for so the Irish tenants sow their landlords' grounds, and allow them the third sheaf, and take two sheaves for their pains) which grew last year upon that ground was sold for 120L. There is meadow land and bog, which being guttered, ditched, and drained ... will be good and rich meadow.[69]

This passage, which is part of a continuum of investigation from Petty's surveys of the seventeenth century to the Physico-Historical Society's efforts in the mid-eighteenth century, fits well into the discourse of travel and exploration where the colonial potential of the newly-appropriated land, laid out before the gaze of the traveller, is classified and surveyed in terms of the richness of its soils, the abundance of its game and fish and the economic opportunities afforded by its environmental resources.[70]

By the eighteenth century, tours by writers or artists tended to follow well-trodden trails or mail-coach roads through the country, with a preference for Leinster, east Ulster and Munster. Tours usually commenced in Dublin, then followed the road to Carlow, branching towards Wexford, Waterford or Cork via Clonmel; or continued to Cashel, Limerick and Killarney; or to Drogheda, Newry, Belfast and the Giant's Causeway. Visits to Connacht or west Ulster were rare until the mid-nineteenth century; in any case travel here was restricted by poor or non-existent roads, not to mention the absence of creature comforts in good inns. Tour writers were predominantly members of landed or literary élites with leisure to indulge antiquarian or natural history interests, as well as the exotic world of customs and manners. Many of the tours in the British Isles (and Europe) arose from a burgeoning interest among the educated élite in the aesthetics of sublime, picturesque and romantic landscapes, so the places visited from the later eighteenth century mirrored these interests, being wild, mostly uninhabited natural landscapes.

In addition many tours featured the parklands and houses of the landed gentry (who provided hospitality and entertainment) and they usually incorporated accounts of improvements and estate management policy, though Arthur Young in the 1780s was taken aback by the arrogance of the landowning gentry in Ireland during his tours:

> It must strike the most careless traveller to see whole strings of carts whipped into a ditch by a gentleman's footman to make way for his carriage; if they are overturned or broken in pieces, no matter, it is taken in patience; were they to complain they would perhaps be horsewhipped. The execution of the laws lies very much in the hands of justices of the peace, many of whom are drawn from the most illiberal class in the kingdom.[71]

69 'Travels of Sir William Brereton in Ireland 1635'.   **70** See M.L. Pratt, *Imperial eyes: travel writing and transculturation* (New York, 1992). For a comprehensive survey of traveller's accounts of nineteenth and twentieth-century Ireland, see G. Hooper, *Travel writing and Ireland* (Basingstoke, 2005).   **71** A. Young, *A tour in Ireland 1776–1779* (London, 1892), p. 54. See also I. Leister, 'Orchards in County Tipperary' in *Ir. Geography*, 4 (1962), pp 292–301.

By the second half of the eighteenth century and continuing into the nineteenth, élite tourism, by English vistors especially, was preoccupied with scenery, wilderness and the picturesque. These 'pleasure tours' often provide detailed descriptions of the appearance of the land and the landscape, of the people and the agricultural economy which shaped the land. Scotland was more favoured than Ireland by English tourists of the pre-famine period. Irish landscapes were not as 'picturesque' or 'romantic' as their Scottish counterparts. Images of Scotland were largely empty of people, or people were situated at a 'romantic' distance whereas Ireland was usually represented with its clamouring and unruly millions. Many of the artist tourists, however, were drawn to wild and empty landscapes. Commentaries accompanying drawings by George Petrie, Andrew Nicholl and Henry O'Neill in the 1840s show where the artist 'poetically harmonizes' with the scene to 'excite sentiments of solemnity and grandeur' and (on Gougane Barra) 'A sense of desolation – the feeling of a total severance from mankind – of utter abandonment, now forces itself on the imagination. Escape seems impossible.'[72] The Glen of the Downs in County Wicklow, painted by O'Neill, sums up the contemporary attitude to landscape. The drawing includes an apparently accurate depiction of a thatched house on the roadside: 'In the foreground is a genuine Irish cabin, an object to the artist, of picturesque, to the philanthropist, of melancholy interest; adding beauty, by contrast, to the face of nature, but detracting most sadly from the prospect of national improvement'. The Halls in 1843, though commenting extensively on social and economic conditions, were mainly impressed with the opportunities the West of Ireland afforded the painter, with its 'lines of mountains … passes rugged … rivers rapid … broadest lakes … Nature abundant.'[73] John Wesley on the other hand cared little for such wild 'natural' scenery, but liked nature tamed and improved: Clonmel was 'the pleasantest town, beyond all comparison, which I have yet seen in Ireland. It has four broad streets of well-built houses, which cross each other in the centre of the town. Close to the walls, on the south side, runs a broad clear river. Beyond this rises a green and fruitful mountain, and hangs over the town: the vale runs many miles both east and west, and is well cultivated throughout.'[74]

To many English gazes, however, the ordinary people of Ireland, especially the beggars and poor in the decades before the famine, had an unfortunate tendency to get in the way of the view. Thomas Carlyle and others were repelled by the

72 From commentaries on *Illustrations of the landscape and coast scenery of Ireland from drawings by George Petrie, Andrew Nicholl and Henry O'Neill* (Dublin, 1843). For a classic combination of illustrator (W.H. Bartlett) and commentator, see J. Stirling Coyne, *The scenery and antiquities of Ireland* (London, 1842). See S. Nenadic, 'Land, the landed and the relationship with England: literature and perception, 1760 to 1830' in R.J. Morris et al. (eds), *Conflict, identity and economic development: Ireland and Scotland, 1600–1939* (Edinburgh, 1995).   **73** Mr and Mrs S.C. Hall, *Ireland: its scenery and character* (3 vols, London, 1841–3), iii, 392. See E. Slater, 'Contested terrain: differing interpretations of Co. Wicklow's landscape' in *Irish Journal of Sociology*, 3 (1993), pp 23–55.   **74** From *Journals of the Rev John Wesley*, 4 vols, Everyman edition, quoted in T.W. Freeman, 'John Wesley in Ireland' in *Ir. Geography*, 8 (1975), pp 86–96.

hordes of beggars who besieged their coaches. Looming demographic and economic crisis generated more commentary on social problems and their resolution
in the early nineteenth century.[75] This was accelerated particularly with the onset
of the Great Famine when large numbers of visitors published increasingly
prescriptive accounts armed at solving those problems.[76]

Although there is a wide range of travel accounts, a great deal of effort can be
put into trawling through them for quite limited returns. A large number are
unpublished and catalogues of tour reports often do not adequately indicate
contents.[77] Christopher Woods has catalogued more than 700 traveller accounts
from the late seventeenth century onwards with short summaries of their main
themes.[78] Local journals, especially the older ones, frequently contain reprints of
traveller accounts which are worth exploring, such as Thomas Monk's account of
Kildare in 1682 which may have been part of William Molyneux's or William
Petty's project for regional topographies of Ireland. He describes the Curragh of
Kildare as 'thronged with flocks [of sheep] all the yeare round … to which the
nobility and gentry have recourse for hunting and racing'. The county is divided in
two by the River Liffey, on its course to the sea 'drenchinge severall noble
gentlemens seates.'[79]

The tour by the French diplomat Marc Bombelles in 1784 is, in many ways, a
classic.[80] In Woods's report,

75 T. Carlyle, *Reminiscences of my Irish journey* (London, 1882). For some pre-famine examples
see C. Bowden, *A tour thro' Ireland* (Dublin, 1791); J. Fisher, *Scenery of Ireland* (London, 1795);
R. Colt Hoare, *Journal of a tour in Ireland AD 1806* (London, 1807); H. Inglis, *A journey
throughout Ireland* (London, 1834); J. Barrow, *Tour around Ireland* (London, 1836); Lady
Chatterton, *Rambles in the south of Ireland during the year 1838* (London, 1839). **76** See, for
instance, W.M. Thackeray, *The Irish sketchbook* (London, 1842) which features more
observations about the people than the landscape. T. Colville Scott, *Connemara after the
famine: journal of a survey of the Martin estate, 1853*, ed. with introduction by T. Robinson
(Dublin, 1995) contains sketches of housing conditions and local landscapes on this 196,000
acre property which went on sale in 1849; see also E. Bourke, ' "The Irishman is no
lazzarone': German travel writers in Ireland 1828–1850' in *History Ireland*, 5, no. 3 (Autumn
1997), pp 21–5; *Narrative of a journey from Oxford to Skibbereen during the year of the Irish
Famine. By Lord Dufferin and the Hon. G.F. Boyle* (Oxford, 1847). **77** See C.J. Woods,
'Review article: Irish travel writings as source material' in *IHS*, xxviii, no. 110 (1992), pp
171–83 which contains many references to sources of traveller accounts, such as D. Dickson's
'bibliography' in T.W. Moody and W.E. Vaughan (eds), *A new history of Ireland, iv: eighteenth-
century Ireland* (Oxford, 1986), pp 738–43. For convenient reprints of travel accounts, see M.
Ryle, *Journeys in Ireland* (Aldershot, 1999) with examples from the mid-nineteenth century;
J.P. Harrington, *The English traveller in Ireland* (Dublin, 1991) which looks at travellers over
500 years. M. Fewer, *A walk in Ireland: an anthology of walking literature* (Cork, 2001) is a
collection of forty extracts from accounts of travel in Ireland from the eighteenth, but
mainly the twentieth century. G. Hooper, *The tourist's gaze: travellers to Ireland, 1800–2000*
(Cork, 2001) contains good introductory discussions for seventy-two accounts, many of
them classics. **78** Available in the Russell Library, Maynooth. **79** 'A descriptive account
of the county of Kildare in 1682 by Thomas Monk' in *Journal of Kildare Archaeological Society*,
6 (1909–11), p. 341; see also *The journal of John Stevans, 1689–91*, ed. R.H. Murray (Oxford,
1912). **80** *Journal de voyage en Grande Bretagne et en Irlande, 1784*, ed. J. Gury (Oxford, 1989).

He landed at Donaghadee [22 October] from Scotland, spending an evening in Belfast before going on to Dublin via Lisburn, Newry, Dundalk and Drogheda, the route taken by numerous other travellers, noticing, like so many of them, how poverty was more common the further south one left the linen districts behind and, strangely for the season, that the mountains and much of the countryside near Newry were covered in snow. Dublin captivated him. In size and beauty it ranked high – after Paris, London and Naples, he thought at first ... Thanks to an introduction to the Duke of Leinster, he three times visited Carton. The young Lord Edward Fitzgerald drove him over to Castletown ('the finest house in Ireland') and to the salmon-leap at Leixlip ... He was also impressed by the manufacturing industry introduced to Maynooth and Leixlip by the duke and to Celbridge by Conolly ... [he] also visited Robert Brooke's cotton factory at Prosperous and the newly completed Liffey aqueduct of the Grand Canal near Sallins.

Another French visitor in 1835 was Alexis de Tocqueville,[81] who while more interested in the political state of the country does have some descriptions of living conditions, housing and landscape. Rolf Loeber and Magda Stouthamer-Loeber have examined twenty guide books for travellers which contain short descriptions of places and gentry houses on a variety of routes in Ireland.[82] The most innovative was Taylor and Skinner's *Maps of the roads of Ireland* first published in 1778 and their *Post-chaise companion* published in 1784. The Ordnance Survey Memoir project from 1835 also contains important descriptions of town and country landscapes in the north of Ireland, frequently coloured by the class and ethnic prejudices of the officer reporters. Although they vary according to the commitment of the writers, some provide detailed material on the buildings and infrastructure such as roads and drainage.

Newspapers were especially prominent in commissioning visitors to report on the Irish countryside, especially during and after the famine. Alexander Somerville's reports for the *Manchester Examiner*, contain useful general accounts of conditions in various parts of the country during his three-month visit, when he especially focussed on the inequities of the land system. Like most tour accounts, they consist of general observations recorded as he passed through various districts, supplemented by data from local contacts. His description of the landscape of Kildare in late January 1847 from the newly constructed railway is typically informative:

Two-thirds of that country is lying in grass. It feeds cattle and sheep, and furnishes hay for Dublin. The farms are nearly all of an acreage, to be counted by the hundred, and not by units of acres as in other parts of Ireland ... The

81 *Alexis de Tocqueville's journey in Ireland, July-August 1835*, ed. F. Larkin (Washington, 1990). **82** R. Loeber and M. Stouthamer-Loeber, 'The documentation of architecture and sites in Irish gazeteers and road books, 1647–1875' in Clarke et al. (eds), *Surveying Ireland's past*, pp 329–51.

meadows, even at this advanced period of winter, have a rough herbage on them. Some of them are partially flooded. The enclosures, fenced by ill conditioned thorn hedges, seem to range in measurement between six and ten acres. Several elegant villas and mansions are seen, and a good many humble dwelling-places; but not so many of the latter as to give one the idea of a dense population ... This Irish South Western, or Dublin and Cashel line, now opened as far as Carlow, fifty-six miles, is the smoothest line of rails I ever travelled on ... the station building at Dublin promises to be almost regal in magnificence.[83]

A half century later, the *Manchester Guardian* commissioned John Millington Synge (with Jack Yeats as artist) to report on Connemara during a local crisis in June 1905. Much of Synge's experience, besides inspiring his later dramatic renditions of the west, echoed earlier nineteenth- and indeed eighteenth-century accounts: the landscape had changed little in terms of its economic capacity to support its population. The road through

the lower western end of Gorumna led through hilly districts that became more and more white with stone, though one saw here and there a few brown masses of bog or an oblong lake with many islands and rocks. In most places, if one looked round the hills a little distance from the road, one could see the yellow and white gables of cottages scattered everywhere through this waste of rock; and on the ridge of every hill one could see the red dresses of women who were gathering turf or looking for their sheep or calves. Near the villages where we stopped things are somewhat better, and a few fields of grass and potatoes were to be seen, and a certain number of small cattle grazing among the rocks ...'[84]

The nineteenth century saw a big increase in tourism visitors to Ireland and a large number of travel guides were produced, many by visitors interested in recording their impressions for newcomers.[85] Into the twentieth century the newly independent Free State was an attractive destination for many encouraged by an embryonic tourism industry. The American, Harold Speakman, who journeyed up the West of Ireland on a donkey cart, reflects on the damaged infrastructure in Munster following the civil war and the artist in him records impressions of the slowly unfolding landscapes.[86] H.V. Morton, who popularised tourism by car, continues the tradition of the outsider recording passing impressions of Irish

83 Somerville, *Letters from Ireland during the famine of 1847*, ed. Snell, p. 32. His description of the coach journey through Carlow and Kilkenny contains graphic accounts of the roadside settlement. 84 J.M. Synge, *Collected works: prose* (Gerrards Cross, 1982), compilations of reports to *the Manchester Guardian* quoted in Dalsimer, ' "The Irish peasant" ', p. 208. 85 See J. McVeagh, *A bibliography of Irish travel writing* (Dublin, 1996). 86 H. Speakman, *Here's Ireland* (New York, 1931).

6.1 Paul Henry Railway poster (courtesy of Science and Society Picture Library, London)

landscapes in the 30s, sharing many of the sentiments of earlier English visitors to this exotic and different part of what had been part of the United Kingdom a hundred years earlier or even before the Union. For example, in Wicklow,

> I smell for the first time the incense of Ireland, the smoke of turf fires, and here for the first time I see the face of the Irish countryside ... It is not an easy, comfortable countryside like that of England. It has not the same settled confidence. It has a strange and foreign look. I feel at times that I am in France. No half-timbered cottages stand rooted in the soil wearing thatches like old hats; no cosy inns call themselves 'The Nag's Head' or 'The Fox and Hounds'. There are instead small one-story houses of stone, white-washed so that they hurt the eyes as they shine in the sun. Some are so small that a child might think them the houses of fairies.[87]

The exotic still densely populated landscapes of the West captivated this English visitor:

> Seven thousand people, connected to Ireland by a narrow bridge, live on the Isle of Achill in the shadow of blue mountains and in the gloom of brown peat bogs ... Their little white cabins cluster incredibly on rock ledges; their small potato patches are scratched with heroic industry in the hard rock. They love dancing and music. The sound of their fiddles is like the twittering of sparrows ... The whole island lives on credit. It is in debt from harvest to harvest. In the spring every able-bodied man, and many a sturdy girl, leaves Achill for England or Scotland, where they sell their strong arms to foreign farmers ... Special boats put in from Glasgow and Liverpool. The male population troops down to the sea, waves good-bye to its women-folk, and depart overseas on its gold rush.[88]

At the same time Seán O'Faoláin was recording his impressions as an Irishman more sensitive to the rhythms of his landscape. He saw his Rathkeale home place as a microcosm of Ireland in the 1930s, in Joycean imagery: '... it was the same silent night for miles about, far beyond the town, in the cabins glimmering among the moist fields, always the same for mile after mile through the whole length and breadth of Ireland, a gentle, dim night where only the small sounds murmured in the grass and the dark and oncoming sleep muffled human speech.'[89] His description of Cork city has resonances of a soundscape in its depiction of its rickety infrastructure during the season of winter gales:

87 H.V. Morton, *In search of Ireland* (London, 1930), pp 42–3. **88** Ibid., p. 219. **89** S. O'Faoláin, *A nest of simple folk* (London, 1934) quoted in O'Connor, *All Ireland is in and about Rathkeale*, p. 6.

Then the floods rise, the streets are sometimes submerged, and the winds from the ocean tear into the cup of the valley of the town. Then the age of the place, so well hidden under its rouge of paint (like a French seaport), is shamelessly exposed in the rattling and shaking and shivering and banging of all its poor decrepit parts. All that weather-slating you see in Cork is not for nothing. In these gales it flies in slivers through the air and, on mornings after gales, the streets where there are such houses are likely to be strewn with slates. The winters are hard here, and lashing rains, gutters spilling, pavements rippled with flood-water, hoardings flapping, and the news, passing from mouth to mouth like the gossip in a Dutch town, that the river is rising, all give a great sense of nearness to the elements. Cork, in its old meaning of *marsh*, is never far from its origins in that way – sleepy in summer, wet in winter.[90]

CONCLUSION

Literature in its many forms is a worthwhile source of evidence about local landscapes in the past. Writing which had topographical or descriptive intentions, in the genre of tour accounts (classically exemplified by Arthur Young, for example) or the county surveys of the Royal Dublin Society have obviously provided useful material for historical geographies of landscapes. But other literatures including imaginative, creative and fictional writing can also provide valid perspectives on places in the past. Writing as art can put flesh on bald facts and enliven bare statistics. Seamus Heaney's poetry, like Patrick Kavanagh's, while having universal appeal, takes its landscape cues principally from Derry or Monaghan. Just as our cognitive understanding of landscape today is based on personal perception of surroundings, or feelings and emotional connections with place, so too such insights into past landscapes are valid sources of knowledge. Local libraries make the best starting points for writings on local places which mainstream historians would normally by-pass. Local historians might re-visit such imaginative reconstructions of the sense of place of local landscapes.

90 S. O'Faoláin, *An Irish journey* (London, 1940), pp 85–6.

CHAPTER 7

Population and landscape dynamics

Population, demography and landscape are inextricably connected. The common theme throughout this book is the fact that the majority of the landscapes which we have inherited have been produced by people interacting with their local environments through time. The most emblematic reflection of rural depopulation, for example, is the abandoned landscapes of overgrown fields, house clusters and lanes in many of the remoter uplands of Ireland. Conversely, many of our suburban landscapes in the fringes of towns and cities comprise landscapes of re-population and growth. At a superficial level in rural landscapes, much of the distinctive colour (of buildings and crops, for instance) and sounds (human voices, dogs barking, livestock) are part of our humanised landscapes, which are also inevitably distinguished by topographies of families linked by kinship, marriage and experience of the same place, lives *taking place* within the farmscapes and townlands of the landscape. Rural landscapes reflect the unceasing labour which was involved historically in 'making' landscapes, the large investments of time and energy by earlier inhabitants in constructing, reclaiming and 'taming' the landscape for subsequent generations; even more so with the material infrastructure of streets, pavements and drainage systems of urban landscapes. Later generations inherit a largely completed infrastructure which usually only requires maintenance or minor modification. This is a universal aspect of all narratives of landscape evolution.

It has been suggested that the focus on 'ways of seeing' in landscape studies (via representation, metaphor and ideology) and away from material landscape has led cultural geographers and historians to concentrate on 'remarkable' and 'élite' landscapes such as demesnes and parklands.[1] By directing attention to landscapes of practice (or 'experienced landscapes'), social historians and geographers can return to everyday, unexceptional, domestic landscapes. So in nineteenth-century Ireland, we can begin to look at the fields, laneways, bog-edges and marginal landscapes instead of the exclusive 'valued' landscapes of the élites which tend to dominate discussion. The ordinary inhabitants of the landscape were obviously the most important makers and builders of landscape. There is no doubt that the hedges and houses of the Irish countryside owe more to the routine exertions of its ordinary inhabitants in the past than any number of grand conceptualisations about agents of change. Certainly the disorderly and unregimented nature of many landscape modifications, like the amorphous farm clusters of the west and the irregular field patterns in many places, all attest the results of individual enterprise unguided by

---

1 Cresswell, 'Landscape and the obliteration of practice', p. 280.

any over-arching controlling hand. The following chapter therefore focuses attention on the dynamics in the relationship between landscape and people mainly during
the past three centuries when most of the material landscape was constructed.

THE MAKING AND MAINTENANCE OF THE LANDSCAPE

One can appreciate the association between the landscape and population dynamics
by examining population trends in familiar spaces over a century. Ireland, Scotland
and England, for instance, are of approximately the same order of size – 33m, 20m
and 50m hectares respectively. But considering that the population of England at
50m inhabitants is ten times that of Ireland (Scotland is the same at 5m), one would
expect the resultant landscape impacts would reflect these differences, even before
one takes into account matters of rural density, urban population size and the
contrasting economic and industrial histories of Great Britain and Ireland. When
one considers the historical demography of both islands, clearly population size and
dynamics have been significant drivers of landscape change in the past couple of
centuries. Ireland had twice as many people in 1841 as today, and indeed in 1800
its population was approximately the same as England's (6–10m). Both islands'
demographic experiences diverged substantially from the mid-nineteenth century
– England's exploded and urbanised significantly, Ireland's declined and stagnated.
There were direct consequences for the urban and rural landscapes of both
countries. Accompanying the increased population in England in the nineteenth
century, the Industrial Revolution in its northern regions had direct impacts on
landscape that were absent in Ireland. Half the population of the 'first industrial
nation' was urban in 1850 and the countrysides of the Black Country, the Potteries
and Lancashire were scarred with mines, spoil heaps, mills and factories and criss-
crossed with canals, railways, new roads, bridges and viaducts. Dickensian
descriptions of traumatised urban and industrial landscapes teeming with people
and dirt and smoke would have been out of place in Ireland, though on his return
to England following his tour of famine-stricken Ireland, Carlyle thanked heaven
for the sight of real human industry in the English landscape.[2]

The eight millions who lived in Ireland in its most crowded period were
overwhelmingly rural. In the century before the Great Famine there were
historically unprecedented assaults on the Irish countryside. In many high-density
regions, such as Connacht and south Ulster, the landscape was stripped bare of
timber and wood, picked over by an impoverished rural population, attested by
recurring references to the 'nakedness' of the land. Walls around many landlord
demesnes were designed not just as property markers but defences against the
poaching of trees and game by desperately poor people: only the better-off farmers
could afford to invest in tree planting. Reclamation of wasteland was encouraged

---

2 The modern rural landscape of Britain, however, is better protected and managed than that
of Ireland precisely as a consequence of its large urban-industrial population.

by landowners as settlement and population were pushed to unprecedented limits. Wasteland reclamation continued apace in the western counties till the end of the nineteenth century, with local districts showing population growth up to the 1901 census.[3]

During the 1840s Ireland lost 282,000 houses and in the half century after the famine, there was a further decline of at least 200,000, in both cases mostly cabins of the poorest classes. There was a net emigration of almost three-quarters of a million people from the twenty-six counties between 1926 and 1956 which further emptied much of the countryside. Settlement landscapes from the mid-nineteenth to the mid-twentieth century, therefore, were mostly characterised by the consequences of contraction and withdrawal which are still in evidence in the fossil potato ridges and house ruins at the very margins of existence on mountainsides of the west and remote and impoverished localities elsewhere. Large numbers of people, who created the familiar lattice of lanes, fields and fences, lived in clustered or dispersed cottages or cabins. Huge swathes of countrysides lost over half their populations in the last decades of the nineteenth century: counties Clare, Mayo, Galway and Monaghan, for instance, lost over one quarter of their populations in the 1840s alone.[4]

In the early 1840s Shirley's 27,000-acre estate in County Monaghan had an enormous population, with an average density of almost one person per acre. It had a huge burden of cottiers and a great number of its houses and cabins were dark, damp and miserable structures, many having neither windows, bedsteads, tables nor chairs in 1843. In an 1814 survey it was described as a bleak and bare landscape. In the early 1840s much of its countryside, today so well clothed in seemingly immemorial hedgerows, was largely hedgeless, treeless, and worn out.[5] Cabins in many densely populated regions of Ireland were mired in dunghills located outside the door. Were wells, from which water was drawn, polluted? Were there chronic diseases in some locations, in an age when washing and hygiene were very rudimentary? In general in 1841, however, waste and refuse was of local provenance and organic in nature. One-roomed 4th class houses in the nineteenth century were very biodegradable and quickly melted back into landscape when they were

3 See S.H. Cousens, 'Regional variations in population changes in Ireland, 1861–1891' in *TIBG*, 33 (1963), pp 145–62; idem, 'Population trends in Ireland at the turn of the century' in *Ir. Geography*, v (1964–8), 387–401; K.H. Connell, 'The colonisation of waste land in Ireland, 1780–1845' in *Economic History Review* (hereinafter *Econ. Hist. Rev.*), 2nd series, iii (1950), pp 44–71; idem, 'Land and population in Ireland, 1780–1845' in D.V. Glass and D.E.C. Eversley (eds), *Population in history: essays in historical demography* (London, 1965), pp 423–33; see also J. Feehan, 'Threat and conservation: attitudes to nature in Ireland' in Wilson Foster (ed.), *Nature in Ireland*, pp 573–96. **4** See, for example, P.J. Duffy, 'The famine in County Monaghan' in C. Kinealy and T. Parkhill (eds), *The famine in Ulster* (Belfast, 1997), pp 169–96. **5** Trench's 1843 survey: see Duffy, 'Management problems on a large estate in mid-nineteenth Ireland: William Steuart Trench's report on the Shirley estate in 1843'; for the 1814 survey: see P.J. Duffy, 'Remarks on viewing the estate of John Shirley' in *Clogher Rec.*, 12 (1987), pp 300–5.

7.1 Tirmoghan Commons, County Kildare (1838)

abandoned. The siting of much rural housing in the past contrasts with present-day conditions. In the mid-nineteenth century, for instance, shelter was paramount, with siting in hollows and in the lee of hills. For most farming households, the 'view' was unimportant: only the élites of the eighteenth century and a slowly rising bourgeoisie in the nineteenth century appreciated landscape as a scenic phenomenon. Many nineteenth-century estate policies on farm subdivision and inheritance, tenant marriage and assisted emigration, were aimed at addressing what was perceived by a large number of landowners and agents as a malthusian crisis that threatened the future sustainability of the landscape, its farms, peatland, woodland and other resources.[6]

The claiming and taming of the land by farmers is a fundamental part of understanding the rural landscape in a technical, economic and social context. Digging, ploughing, clearing, reclamation with human and animal energy has ultimately shaped the relationship between society and landscape and brings to bear a whole range of contextual considerations about the nature of the landscape heritage. In 1841 there were 685,000 farms in Ireland which fell to 514,000 by 1900. In 1961 there were 210,000 farmers in Ireland and today there are 87,000

6 See Duffy, ' "Disencumbering our crowded places" '.

with a projection of *c.*40,000 full-time farmers in the next twenty years. This will have significant landscape consequences especially in the West of Ireland where much marginal land will be abandoned as farming practices change. The replacement of manual farming (spade/scythe) by draught horses (ploughs and other machinery) through the nineteenth century, subsequently displaced by tractors from the mid-twentieth century, had significant roles to play also in making and shaping the rural landscape. Apart from its manual nature, the form of agriculture in the nineteenth century was a 'mixed farming' economy, so a broad range of crops and livestock were produced, all with varying environmental ramifications quite different to the monocultural industrial agriculture of the modern age. In contrast to the pervasive impact of mechanisation today, the low-technology impact of man and animal was different also. Large numbers of livestock, in particular draught horses and ponies, had a huge requirement for fodder crops which played an important role in preventing the regeneration of scrubland. Goats were especially voracious consumers of plants and a threat in the early stages of hedge-planting. There were over half a million horses in Ireland at the close of the nineteenth century.

Table 1. Changes in livestock numbers in Ireland, 1855–1950[7]

Livestock	1855	1900	1950	1970	1990
Cattle/cows	5.2m	6.1m	6.8m	9.4m	10.9m
Sheep/ewes	5.3m	6.2m	4.3m	7.3m	16.5m
Goats	284,000	306,000	59,000	n/a	n/a
Horses/ponies	556,00	567,000	442,00	n/a	69,000
Mules/asses	172,000	273,000	124,000	n/a	n/a

Source: Farming since the famine: Irish farm statistics, 1847–1996 (CSO: Dublin, 1997)

The post-famine abandonment of many areas, decline in farm numbers, fall in population, the quite sudden reduction in mixed farming, the increase in tractors as well as the steady drop in the numbers of draught horses, asses and goats after World War Two combined to result in a rapidly changing rural landscape. The increased cattle and sheep numbers from the 1970s reflect intensification of farming following membership of the European Community and have had different environmental impacts on uplands and grasslands. Although a description of Clontibret parish in County Monaghan during the progress of the rural electrification scheme in 1954, written in the mode of nineteenth-century surveys, continues to have echoes of an intensively worked landscape, electricity was a portent of further change:

7 Data for 1950–90 is for the Republic of Ireland and Northern Ireland combined: see *Farming since the famine: Irish farm statistics, 1847–1996* (CSO: Dublin, 1997).

The area is intensively tilled, the main crops being potatoes, oats, flax and root crops. Every aspect of mixed farming is to be seen and pigs, poultry and cattle are universal. Part of the income comes from milk which is handled by two sub-creameries. The main cash crop has always and traditionally been flax, followed by pigs, poultry ... Flax prices the previous year (1952) had collapsed and the crop had been almost entirely abandoned as a source of income in the current year.[8]

In terms of the landscape-population nexus, we can talk of macro, meso and micro levels of analysis of population and landscape. At macro level are the published generalised data for county, Rural District and Electoral Division from which details on population density, inhabited houses and population change can help interpretation of landscape change over comparatively extensive areas.[9] At meso level, townland and parish data on population and housing is available from census and valuation records, supplemented with information from six-inch Ordnance Survey maps of the 1830s and 40s. Micro-level analysis is possible with unpublished household data, particularly from the 1901 and 1911 manuscript household schedules, as well as small amounts of salvaged manuscript material from nineteenth-century censuses.[10]

In studying the regional impact of nineteenth-century population, T.W. Freeman's maps of population in 1841 represent an important contextual source. His maps of population density by parish in 1841 have never been surpassed in terms of detail.[11] He made systematic use of many nineteenth-century sources on social and economic landscapes which had been largely ignored by historians. He used the 1841 census in conjunction with the first edition of the OS maps and the Railway Commission report of 1838, lending accuracy to his maps by excluding unin-habited mountains and boglands, demesnes and rough pastures.

8 Inspector's report, 26 Mar. 1954 (ESB Archives, Harold's Cross, Dublin).   **9** Extensive population data is available in the nineteenth-century censuses, especially from 1841: see Crawford, *Counting the people*. For earlier periods, see B. Gurrin, *Pre-census sources for Irish demography*. Maynooth Research Guides for Irish Local History series (Dublin, 2002); W.J. Smyth, 'Wrestling with Petty's ghost: the origins, nature and relevance of the so-called "1659 census"' in Pender (ed.), *A census of Ireland circa 1659* (2002 edn.), pp v–lxii; S.T. Carleton, *Head and hearths: the hearth money rolls and poll tax returns for County Antrim, 1660–69* (Belfast, 1991). An incomplete 1766 census directed by parliament is available in transcripts in the National Archives, Bishop Street, Dublin. See also *Census of Elphin, 1749*, ed. M-L. Legg (IMC: Dublin, 2004) and T. Graham, 'Whitelaw's 1798 census of Dublin' in *History Ireland*, 2, no. 3 (Autumn 1994), pp 10–15.   **10** See, for example, fragments from Meath and Cavan in Connell, *The land and people of County Meath*, p. 95; K. O'Neill, *Family and farm in pre-famine Ireland: the parish of Killashandra* (Madison, 1984).   **11** T.W. Freeman, *Pre-famine Ireland: a study in historical geography* (Manchester, 1957). The following regions were mapped: Dublin, Meath, Louth, Kildare; King's Co., Westmeath and Longford; Southeast Ireland; Waterford, Kilkenny, Tipperary, Queen's Co.; Clare and Limerick; Cork and Kerry; Sligo and Leitrim; east Connaught; west Connaught; east Ulster; Derry and Tyrone; Donegal; Fermanagh, Cavan and Monaghan.

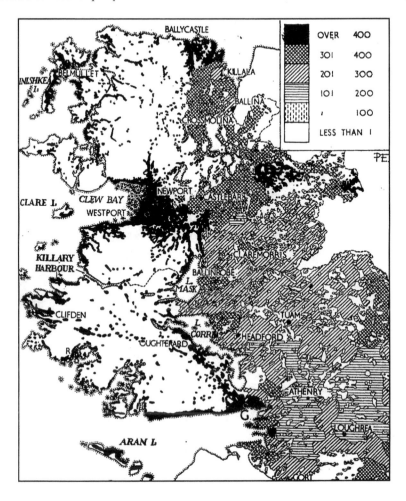

7.2 Population density per square mile, west of Ireland, 1841; from T. W. Freeman, *Pre-famine Ireland* (Manchester, 1957), p. 265

In his studies of mid-twentieth-century Ireland, Freeman included similar detailed maps of population from the 1961 census.[12] In past decades these have been supplemented with a range of maps of nineteenth-and early twentieth-century population density by townland for counties and parts of counties, showing the intricate detail of population-land ratios.[13] Only in recent years has it been possible to match the detail of Freeman's maps. Historians and geographers now have an opportunity to exploit digital mapping technology in using the enormous

---

12 T. W. Freeman, *Ireland a regional geography* (4th edn, London, 1969), pp 253–499. **13** These are mostly in unpublished theses. See P. J. Duffy, 'Irish landholding structures and population in the mid-nineteenth century' in *Maynooth Review*, 3 (2) (1977), pp 3–27.

databases on population, housing and landholding for the nineteenth century. Townland base maps which are now available digitally, can produce extremely detailed representations of the human landscape up to two centuries ago.[14]

Tabulating data on population and housing at townland and parish level in 1841 or 1901 and the present, is instructive where today's inhabitants can best appreciate the implications of the numbers for their surrounding landscape. Thousands of townlands which each today accommodate a couple of dozen people or less, contained a couple of hundred over a century ago. The parish of Pettigo in Donegal, for instance, contained 4,800 people in 1841 and *c.*770 in 1990. The following table shows the numbers of inhabited houses in the nineteenth and twentieth century in parts of two parishes in south Ulster where population numbers have fallen continuously:[15]

Table 2. Inhabited houses 1841, 1901, 1990

Donacavey Parish (Co. Tyrone)				*Ematris Parish (Co. Monaghan)*			
Townland	*1841*	*1901*	*1990*	*Townland*	*1841*	*1901*	*1990*
Blackfort	13	10	4	Drumgole	25	5	6
Corrashesk	14	7	2	Drummulla	35	5	4
Dungoran	19	14	6	Edergole	22	8	2
Freughmore	21	15	8	Kinduff	29	10	3
Gargrim	21	10	4	Lisnaveane	39	11	8
Kilgort	28	16	11	Maghernaharney	37	13	8
Lisconrea	17	8	5	Unshinagh	20	6	1

Peter Connell aptly describes the extensive variability in local landscape impacts in pre-famine Meath: 'For the half century before the Famine generations of Meath people crowded straggling townlands between the great fields of grass, settled along

14 All nineteenth-century censuses from 1841 contain data on population and housing by townland, parish and electoral division which can be digitally mapped. The ESRC's online historical population project contains data from nineteenth-century census reports for the UK: www.data-archive.ac.uk. Griffith's Valuation is by townland, parish, poor law union and barony. N. Kissane's *The Irish famine: a documentary history* (Dublin, 1995) presents a wide range of documents, maps and illustrations relating to Ireland's population and landscapes, including maps showing the density of 4th class housing in 1841. *Mapping the Great Irish Famine* by L. Kennedy, P. Ell, E.M. Crawford and L.A. Clarkson (Dublin, 1999) also presents an array of maps on population density, decline, mortality as well as agricultural holdings and land use. B. MacDonald's '"A time of desolation": Clones Poor law Union 1845–50' in *Clogher Rec.*, xvii (2000), pp 5–145 is based on the Relief Commission and Distress Papers corresponding to the area of the diocese of Clogher. The archive is published in volume xvii of the *Clogher Record* for 2000 (pp 147–400) and 2001 (pp 401–655). **15** Table 2 is based on census of population data and the 1990 Clogher diocesan census, published in the *Clogher Record*. Small area housing data for recent decades is also available from the CSO. Many townlands in parts of west Mayo and west Donegal only reached their peak population in the late nineteenth century: see, for example, Cousens, 'Regional variations in population changes in Ireland, 1881–1891'.

7.3 Changes in houses and farms (a) in nineteenth and (b) twentieth centuries in two Monaghan townlands

roadsides and villages, filled the lanes of the county's towns ...' while elsewhere in the county were areas that were 'little better than vast deserts ... of green grass on which there are no inhabitants of the human species, the magnificent fertility being given over to flocks and herds'.[16] Matthew Stout has reconstructed a nineteenth-century Wicklow landscape by combining data from the 1841, 1851 and 1881 censuses, the Tithe Applotment Books, Griffith's Valuation and subsequent valuation lists, and the diaries of Elizabeth Smith. He has mapped farm households by size and household depletion in the townland of Baltyboys in County Wicklow. Surviving remnants of the manuscript census in 1821 allow similar exercises to be replicated for a few areas.[17]

Similar methods based on the 1901 and 1911 manuscript census schedules have been used to map house and farm changes and demographic contraction in County Monaghan for selected townlands in the nineteenth and twentieth centuries.[18] The first edition of the Ordnance Survey (for the 1830s in Monaghan), Griffith's Valuation (1840s–50s) and its accompanying maps, and census data on inhabited houses enable a reconstruction of houses and farms for the mid-nineteenth century and a longitudinal study of the desertion of houses and the consolidation of farms through post-famine decades (7.3).

By combining field work with analysis of early twentieth-century censuses, it is possible, for instance, to reconstruct the demographic landscapes of a rundale village in west Mayo and a rural parish in Monaghan and by reconstituting the households from the 1901 and 1911 enumeration schedules to carry out a longitudinal study of household and landscape change. Not enough use has been made of these sources in the past twenty years when significant cohorts of survivors from the early twentieth century were still alive. People born in the second and perhaps third decade of the twentieth century who have continued to live in the area will still recall the households listed for 1911. In Loughloon in west Mayo, for example, based on the enumerator's list, one witness was able to recollect virtually every family and the individuals in them.[19] He could remember old men and women from the list, their nicknames, their homes, their idiosyncrasies. He was also able to recall the migration experience of the households. The census summaries for each

16 Connell, *The land and people of County Meath*, p. 247, and quoting *Drogheda Independent* from James Gilligan, *Graziers and grasslands: portrait of a rural Meath community, 1854–1914* (Dublin, 1998).   **17** Stout, 'The geography and implications of post-famine population decline in Baltyboys, County Wicklow'; Connell, *The land and people of County Meath*, p. 95; O'Neill, *Killashandra*. The 1821 manuscript census for Navan can be compared with data from the 1749 and 1766 censuses in Meath Diocesan Archives. J. Grenham, *Tracing your Irish ancestors* (Dublin, 1999) lists areas for which fragments of the 1821 census remain.   **18** Duffy, 'Irish landholding structures', pp 3–27. See S.A. Royle, 'Irish manuscript census records: a neglected source of information' in *Ir. Geography*, 11 (1978), pp 110–25 which examines manuscript relics of all the nineteenth-century censuses from 1813, 1901 and 1911. See also Crawford & Foy (eds), *Townlands in Ulster*.   **19** Based on interviews with the late John McGreal, Westport in 1988. See also F. Coll and J. Bell, 'An account of life in Machaire Gathláin (Magheragallen), north-west Donegal, early this century' in *Ulster Folklife*, 36 (1990), pp 80–5.

townland also enumerate the numbers and conditions of all buildings. Loughloon contains approximately five households today in contrast to 25 farm households in 1901. In 1851 there were 50 and in 1841 there were as many as 70 inhabited houses in the village. Like many landscapes in rural Ireland the population experience of this community is inscribed in its landscape. The recollection of the populated landscape in the early decades of the last century was vivid: the hill, now a ferny wilderness, was 'black' with potatoes, 'teeming' with men and boys cultivating the ridges with spades. A similar reconstruction of the experience of seventy-five farms and families in rural Monaghan was based on the 1911 census, valuation records and field work. For urban landscapes, the census schedules and valuation House Books allow a reconstruction of households and land use street-by-street as well as analysis of the structure and condition of buildings.

Apart from the labour, sweat and tears which was invested by families in the making of much of the farmed landscape (commemorated in John B. Keane's *The Field*, for example), there were other painful episodes in the construction of our heritage of roads and buildings. During times of distress, in the eighteenth but especially in the nineteenth century, relief work involved hundreds literally making the roads which we take for granted today. Near Skibbereen at daybreak in mid-December 1846 a reporter

> saw a gang of about 150, composed principally of old men, women and little boys, going out to work on one of the roads near the town. At the time the ground was covered in snow, and there was also a very severe frost; seeing they were miserably clad, I remarked to a bystander that it was a miracle that the cold did not kill them ... In the course of the day I went out to visit this gang, who were opening a drain inside the fence on the Marsh road, and such a scene I hope I may never again be called upon to witness. The women and children were crying out from the severity of the cold, and were unable to hold the implements with which they were at work...[20]

In the summer of 1905 history repeated itself in a Connemara landscape:

> We drove many miles, with Costello and Carraroe behind us, along a bog-road of curious formation built up on a turf embankment, with broad grassy sods at either side – perhaps to make a possible way for the barefooted people – then two spaces of rough broken stones where the wheel ruts are usually worn and in the centre a track of gritty earth for the horses. Then, at a turn, of the road, we came in sight of a dozen or more men and women working hurriedly and doggedly improving a further portion of this road, with a ganger swaggering among them and directing their work. Some of the people were cutting out sods from grassy patches near the road, others were

---

20 Quoted in Cormac Ó Gráda, *Black 47 and beyond* (Princeton, 1999), p. 68.

carrying down bags of earth in slow, inert procession, a few were breaking stones, and three or four women were scraping out a sort of sandpit at a little distance. As we drove quickly by we could see that every man and woman was working with a sort of hang-dog dejection that would be enough to make any casual passer mistake them for a band of convicts.[21]

MIGRATION AND LANDSCAPE

Migration into, out of and within Ireland has been one of the most formative landscape experiences. Seventeenth-century immigration of settlers from Great Britain coincided with the onset of landscape modernisation. While most of the in-migrants settled into pre-existing parameters of settlement landscapes in Leinster and Munster (townlands for instance), as illustrated in the Civil and Down Surveys of the 1650s, a great deal of the country's infrastructure was in ruins. Immigration, actively encouraged by government, gave a necessary spurt to economic development. Seventeenth-century wars, destruction, dispossession and the emigration of many of the Gaelic and Old English Catholic élites led to traumatic upheaval in the material fabric and social context of large sections of the Irish landscape. The settlement of Ulster led to the most extensive changes to the face of the landscape, with the plantation scheme representing an early version of urban and regional planning based on a system of land grants and settler in-migration.[22] Lowland Scots farmers whose diligent husbandry would encourage rural development and landscape reclamation, were favoured by planters, although for a generation or more, many simply adopted the older Gaelic ways of pastoral farming. Significant Scottish immigration continued in the late seventeenth and early eighteenth century. By the late seventeenth century, Ulster was transformed from its predominantly rural state of the early seventeenth century.

In the eighteenth century there were trickles of immigrants such as the Huguenots, Quakers and Palatines who made significant contributions at local level: Foster's Collon in County Louth, French's Monivea in Galway and in the late eighteenth century Brooke's Prosperous in Kildare were all the result of planned in-migrations, encouraged by landlords. In 1709 more than 800 Palatine families arrived from the German Rhineland, nearly half of whom were settled in Limerick and Wexford. The Limerick Palatines established a thriving, industrious farming community in the neighbourhoods of Rathkeale and Adare which, though sharing the footloose migration history of many other colonists to Ireland, retained a strong cultural self-consciousness into the twentieth century.[23] There were smaller

21 J.M. Synge's report for the *Manchester Guardian* quoted in Dalsimer ' "The Irish peasant"', p. 213. 22 Robinson, *The plantation of Ulster*; M. Percival-Maxwell, *The Scottish migration to Ulster in the reign of James 1* (London, 1973); G. Camblin, *The town in Ulster* (Belfast, 1951); Gillespie, *Transformation of the Irish economy*; L.M. Cullen, *The emergence of modern Ireland, 1600–1900* (London, 1981). 23 See P.J. O'Connor, *People make places: the story of the Irish*

revivalist groups who settled in the West of Ireland in the nineteenth century, endeavouring to introduce more productive farming conditions (as well as prose-lytising the local populations), many of which have left settlement legacies in west Mayo and Galway. Members of the settler communities in parts of Ulster emigrated in the eighteenth century: the agent on the Barrett-Lennard estate in Clones, for instance, reported that a hundred families had passed through the town in March 1718 on their way to New England, leaving up to fifty townlands waste.[24]

Two generic types of migration had important landscape repercussions in the nineteenth century. Firstly assisted migration by landlords and other agencies involved a degree of social engineering in removing whole households (often following eviction) of impoverished small tenant families to free up farms for consolidation/improvement. Many of these schemes were accompanied by the 'throwing down' of vacated houses or cabins to prevent the return of the migrants.[25] The intention of such schemes was to facilitate a re-fashioning of the landscape into larger more sustainable holdings with a squaring of fields and re-location of houses.

The second form of out-migration, which characterised much of rural Ireland up until 1960s, was individual voluntary migration where farms and households were depleted in a geographically and demographically more unpredictable fashion. In this case the repercussions were more long-term and haphazard, adding social to landscape malaise. There was usually a time lag between migration and its reper-cussions on landscape in terms of abandonment of houses and other aspects of settlement. Lanes and roads, the marks of a long settled, busy landscape which originally served scores of houses, came to link an attenuated random pattern of residual households. In many cases, especially in remoter areas, farm households endured as young people emigrated, leading ultimately to the landscape becoming run down as the older generation died out – marked by abandoned houses, overgrown lanes, boreens and fields reverting to a limbo of rushes and briars, often planted by forestry.

The decades after 1911 saw the gradual abandonment of many of the upland fields in Loughloon in west Mayo as its young people emigrated to America: out of a total of 74 children and young people listed from 15 families in 1911, 46 later went to America and ten went to England. Of those who stayed in the village and

Palatines (Newcastle West, 1989). **24** Edmond Kaine to Dacres Barrett, 1718 (PRONI, Barrett-Lennard papers, T. 2529/6 c.37 310). See Turner, *Migration and myth: Ulster's revolving door*; P.J. Duffy (ed.), *To and from Ireland: planned migration schemes* (Dublin, 2004). **25** See Power, 'The Palmerston estate in County Sligo'; Lyne, *The Lansdowne estate in Kerry*. On nineteenth-century emigration from Ireland, see Cousens, 'Regional variations in emigration'; idem, 'The regional impact of emigration during the great Irish famine, 1846–51' in *TIBG*, 28 (1960), pp 119–34; idem, 'Emigration and demographic change in Ireland, 1851–1861' in *Econ. Hist. Rev.*, 14 (1961), pp 275–88; idem, 'The regional variations in population change in Ireland, 1861–81' in *Econ. Hist. Rev.*, 17 (1964), pp 301–21; idem, 'Population trends in Ireland'.

had families subsequently, most of their children also emigrated in following decades. In the 1940s and 50s a number of families were 'migrated' by the Irish Land Commission to County Meath. This was a recognition by the state of the congested and probably unviable nature of agriculture in the area and an attempt to rationalise its farm structure. In its most extreme form this was demonstrated in the abandonment of their home landscapes by many remoter island communities in the first half of the twentieth century: the small populations on the Inishkeas in Mayo and the Blaskets in Kerry were assisted by the state to remove to farms on the adjacent mainland.[26] In 1925 Harold Speakman on his journey by donkey cart in the west described with a touch of drama this process in west Mayo: he called into a

> shabby two-roomed cabin ... There were eleven people in the living room – an old woman, a young couple and their eight children, seven of whom were boys. The oldest child, I found, was eight years. The children had all come singly, except the two youngest who were twins a month old, lying ... side by side in a large soap box ... Little boys of assorted sizes, resting themselves first on one leg and then on the other, stood against the walls. They seemed to be waiting for something. As I shared my raisin bread with them, there came to my mind the bizarre notion that they were waiting to grow up and go to America.[27]

The surname geographies of most counties in Ireland reflect the impact of past migrations, whether in the late medieval or early-modern periods and the repercussions of local community interactions.[28] In Fermanagh, the results of the Ulster Plantation are reflected in landscapes of surnames, with plantation names concentrating on the right bank of Lough Erne. Maguires and their associated Gaelic families (McManus, McCaffrey and Gilleece) dominate the county. Following the plantation, the names Armstrong, Elliot, Foster, Nixon and Noble can be traced – names from a particular part of the Anglo-Scottish border.[29]

A further aspect of the dynamics of population and rural landscape is the association between the territorial structure and the spatial organisation of the community producing landscapes of cohesive social networks which integrated households, population and farms. Community life and behaviour took place within the template of the built and humanised environment of fields, farms and houses. Traditional communities up to and over a century ago interacted intensively

26 See Dornan, *Mayo's lost islands* and Keogh, 'Leaving the Blaskets, 1953'; Aalen and Brody, *Gola*.   **27** H. Speakman, *Here's Ireland*, p. 163   **28** W.J. Smyth, 'Excavating, mapping and interrogating ancestral terrains: towards a cultural geography of first names and second names in Ireland' in Clarke et al. (eds), *Surveying Ireland's past*, pp 243–80; idem, 'Continuity and change in the territorial organisation of Irish rural communities' in *Maynooth Review*, 1 (1975), pp 51–78   **29** G.B. Adams, 'Surname landscapes' in *Bulletin of Ulster Place-names*, series 2 (1) (1978), pp 27–43; idem, 'Surnames landscapes in Fermanagh' in *Bulletin of Ulster Place-names*, series 2 (3) (1980–1), pp 56–68; B. Turner, *Surname landscapes in the county of Fermanagh* (Downpatrick, 2002).

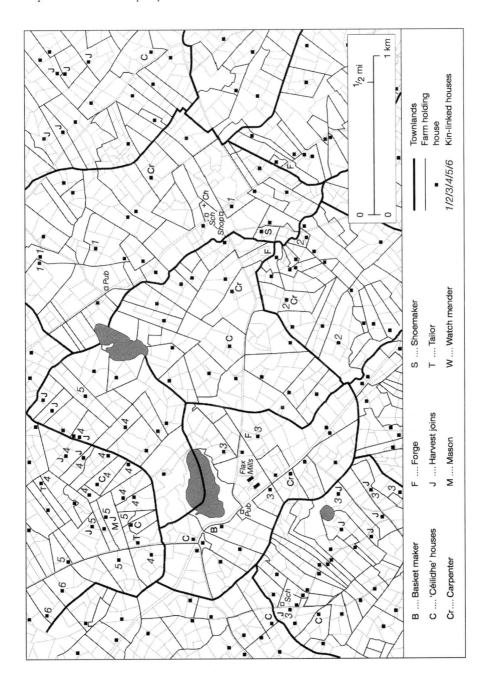

7.4 A social landscape *c.*1900

with their local landscape. Mobility was largely restricted to the parish and its immediate neighbours. Such local interaction was reflected in marriage fields and kinship networks, for instance, with marriage distances (between brides, and grooms' households) being restricted to the locality.[30] Family names and surnames are an important feature of the cultural landscape and the clustering of names within rural localities illustrates the importance of kinship patterns evolving over several generations.

Much of the territorial social organisation was reflected in a social landscape evolving within the spatial parameters of parish, townland, farm and household. This was discernible in such practices as kin-linkages between households in the parish, which were expressed in local family nick-naming patterns to identify branches of families. Mutual aid arrangements (or patterns of 'joins', 'swaps', or 'cooring') developed between neighbouring farm households which were activated at harvest time, with the farms and their named fields being worked in succession by the *meitheall*. Much of the social activity of the community mirrored these other relationships in the landscape: selected *céilidhe* (or rambling) houses were regular meeting places for neighbours and with house dances, flux/harvest parties and station masses were focal points which bolstered territorial identities within the community. Weekly assemblies in the chapel often saw families occupy distinctive places or pews, and funerals were public demonstrations of kin and neighbourly links in the community. Overlying these sites of activity were patterns of movement between farms and fields, to the bog, to the fair day in the town perhaps with its 'calling houses' of shops and public houses which had associations with the parish: many of the farms in the community had ties of debt with selected merchants which were paid off after the November fairs. Processes of change and modernisation by the mid-twentieth century gradually eliminated these intra-rural connections in the social landscape. Widening mobility with the car led to urban centres penetrating the rural hinterland and incorporating larger swathes of landscape and communities in expanding urban fields.

WALKING THE LANDSCAPE: FIELDWORK

Documentary records are the preferred sources for historical research although in most cases such records are partial and selective. As much of this book has shown, the landscape itself is the ultimate record of the experience of past generations. Field work is about observing and 'reading' the landscape and making contact with the place and the people in it. There is the visible landscape we encounter first by looking and the more intangible landscape we engage with in field work and discussion with the local population. A mark of many good local historians is the clear evidence that they know the places they talk about. For those undertaking placename research, for instance, the following advice is worthwhile:

30 See Smyth, 'Nephews, dowries, sons and mothers'.

Although fieldwork forms an integral part of place-name research, it is difficult for a library researcher to acquire the familiarity with an area that the local inhabitants have. Local people can walk the bounds of their townlands, or compare boundary features with those of the early 6-inch maps. Written or tape-recorded collections of local names (especially those of smaller features such as fields, rocks, streams, houses, bridges etc.), where exactly they are to be found, how written and pronounced, and any stories about them or the people who lived there, would be a valuable resource for the future.[31]

Local archaeological exploration provides an opportunity to explore the worlds of the largely silent majority, the voiceless, powerless subaltern classes who left no documents and few traces beyond their folklore and songs. The cottier class in nineteenth-century Ireland left little evidence of their existence. Archaeology, however, can shed 'new light on the social conditions of cottier life just before, during, and after the Famine. Broken ceramic dishes, discarded smoking pipes, fragmented bottles, and lost buttons help to tell the personal side of the Great Famine.'[32] Many historical geographers have looked to field evidence for inspiration if not for facts about the past. The work of Estyn Evans was largely driven by extensive field work in many parts of Ireland and his interest in vernacular landscapes has been largely reliant on field exploration. He emphasised the importance of participation in the landscape and its activities as a key to reading the Irish rural landscape: 'the French agrarian historian, Marc Bloch, wrote his classic books as a farmer who could plough, who knew the feel of the land and the smell of hay and manure. He was able to look beyond the legal and institutional framework of agrarian systems, interpreting them on the ground and in the intimacy of small regions.'[33] The English landscape historian, W.G. Hoskins, believed in the importance of walking over the ground, stout boots and a good bicycle being essential tools of research. He established a strong school of local history based on the evidence of landscape 'written in a kind of code'.[34]

Field work will usually be preceded by desk research. Maps are a *sine qua non* for landscape research, ranging from the various editions of the six-inch survey, through the obsolete one-inch and half-inch series. Topographical maps, such as the successive editions of the six-inch or 25-inch surveys are important for recording field evidence on landscape change. Although digital versions of townlands can be

31 Kay Muhr, General introduction in Fiachra Mac Gabhann, *Place-names of Northern Ireland*, vol. 7, County Antrim (Belfast, 1997), p. xvii. **32** Directed by C.E. Orser jnr, the Archaeology of Rural Life in Ireland Project commenced in 1994 and has undertaken research on three tenant villages in Co. Roscommon and on the Coopershill estate of the O'Hara's in Co. Sligo. On one he has uncovered 1,309 artifacts. See also C.E. Orser, jr., 'Can there be an archaeology of the great famine?' in Morash & Hayes (eds), *'Fearful realities': new perspectives on the famine*, pp 77–89 and 'Archaeology and nineteenth-century rural life in County Roscommon' in *Archaeology Ireland*, ii (1997), pp 14–7. **33** Estyn Evans, *The personality of Ireland*, p. 6. **34** Hoskins, *English landscapes*, p. 5.

obtained today, the old townland index map is still a most useful tool for the local researcher. It can be used to produce base maps of townlands or parishes as starting points for mapping data (such as population) or the location of features in the settlement landscape.

CONCLUSION

One of the most important driving forces for historical change in landscapes is the changing nature of the relationship between the local population and its habitat and environment: demographic growth and decline, migration of population from place to place, changing local economic and social conditions in the past are reflected in expansion or contraction of settlement, buildings and fields patterns, as well as changes in local social relationships in the landscape. Although some evidence may be resurrected for the seventeenth century as demonstrated in William Smyth's *Map-making, landscapes and memory* (Cork, 2006), the nineteenth century saw the assembly of comprehensive ranges of data on population and landscape change, fortuitously during a time of great changes in both. Censuses of population, land valuations, Ordnance Survey maps and a plethora of parliamentary reports provide a wealth of evidence on the interaction between landscape and population. Field work including interviews with local people, examination of records such as school rolls, parish records, Irish folklore material, local newspapers and so on can also help to cast light on how the lineaments of landscape have been modified by changing trends in demography and economy.

Researching landscape heritages

So all-pervasive is the landscape in our lives that this short book has only been able to scratch the surface as it were. Broad suggestions have been made about the variety of landscape elements which might be studied and ways of interpreting them. This book is based on the fact that the heritage of landscape is a constant and important part of our lives. We see it day by day, year by year. It is a fundamental part of our identities. Knowing a place and landscape is part of the human experience of growing up and belonging.

One of the recurring themes throughout this discussion has been the fact that the landscape is more than a random assembly of constituents. It is the product of constant change in the relationship between it and the community which has occupied it in the past. It is a time-specific legacy of the generations who have passed through before us and have inscribed their surroundings with the marks of their presence, in fields, farms, houses, places of worship, villages and towns, roads and lanes, even an infrastructure of drains. And not only in such material artefacts, but also for the past three or four centuries especially, they have left records and descriptions, images, stories, folklore, even songs relating in various ways to their contemporary environments, allowing historians, geographers and others to reconstruct them and to understand what the landscape meant to them. David Lowenthal's assertion that there 'are few blanks on the map of England; almost everywhere is a *place*, with a meaning and a character of its own' could equally be applied to Ireland.[1] Understanding these places encourages respect, which in turn drives the protection and conservation of the legacy as a significant part of existence for future generations.

There has been a fundamental change in our understanding and appreciation of landscape heritage from the 1950s when interest in Dublin's Georgian heritage was dismissed as a whimsy of 'belted earls' and 'left-wing intellectuals'. Nowadays, official, scholarly and popular interest in the rudiments of our surrounding rural and urban landscapes has increased substantially. The National Heritage Council which was set up in 1988, leading eventually to the statutory establishment of The Heritage Council (An Comhairle Oidhreachta) in 1995, reflects official govern-ment commitment to research, conservation and protection of the broad ranging heritage of Ireland, a great deal of which relates to the landscape. The National Trust for Northern Ireland which has been in existence since 1936 is caretaker of

1 D. Lowenthal and H. Prince, 'The English landscape' in *Geographical Review*, 54 (3) (1964), pp 309–46, p. 310.

selected countrysides, mansion houses and industrial buildings. The Irish Heritage Trust which was established by the government in 2006 is aimed at acquiring and preserving properties with significant heritage value. An Taisce which was founded in 1948 is a voluntary organisation with a wide remit to protect and manage our contemporary environment for future generations. Much of its interest over the years has been in conserving aspects of our environmental heritage in buildings and landscape. The Irish Georgian Society was founded in 1958 with the aim of protecting important heritage buildings in Ireland. In recent years there has been a growth in local organisations (often reacting to radical impacts on local landscapes), reflecting an upsurge of interest in all aspects of landscape heritage. Local landscape has becomes a touchstone for bolstering local identities in a globalising increasingly placeless world: connecting with the local landscape and its material present is a key to connecting with a community's past.

Disciplines such as history, archaeology and historical geography have distinctive approaches to studying the landscape, with varying emphases on documentary or field evidence, for instance.[2] Local history offers the best opportunity for inter-disciplinary approaches where landscape is principally geographical in essence with a focus on local space and the evolution of its morphologies through time.[3] An important consideration for local studies which is often forgotten in researching the particular, is that local landscapes are part of a broader picture. This book has tried to place the local in a regional and national context, suggesting that what happened at local level is normally one expression of a universal experience.[4]

In studying local landscape history a number of approaches can be followed. If the objective is to explain the origin and evolution of the modern landscape legacy, it may be best to select aspects of the morphology of the existing landscape (such as settlement or field systems, for example) and examine their development over time. This will suggest the nature of sources required to explain how the modern landscape emerged. Another approach, usually dictated by the existence of useful sources for particular periods, is to take cross-sections of a case study area at selected points in the past: for example, *c*.1650, 1750, 1850 and perhaps mid-twentieth century. Sources approximating to these time periods are then assembled to

2 There are a great many exemplary local historical and geographical studies published in recent years: see, for instance, Gillespie & Hill (eds), *Doing local Irish history*; Gillespie (ed.), *Cavan: essays on the history of an Irish county* and the County: history and society series published by Geography Publications. See also F.H.A. Aalen (ed.), *Landscape study and management* (Dublin, 1996) and idem, *The future of the Irish rural landscape* (Dublin, 1985). **3** For examples, see P.J. Duffy, 'Locality and changing landscape: geography and local history' in Gillespie & Hill (eds), *Doing local Irish history*, pp 24–46; idem, 'Change and renewal in issues of place, identity and the local' in Hourihane (ed.), *Engaging places: people, place and space from an Irish perspective*, pp 13–29; idem, 'Heritage and history: exploring landscape and place in Co. Meath' in *Ríocht na Midhe*, xi (2000), pp 187–218; idem, 'The territorial identity of Kildare's landscapes' in W. Nolan and T. McGrath (eds), *Kildare: history and society. Interdisciplinary essays on the history of a county* (Dublin, 2006), pp 1–25.   **4** See, for example, J. Lynch, 'The comparative aspect in local studies' in Gillespie & Hill, *Doing local Irish history*, pp 128–47.

reconstruct the landscape as it appeared at each period. A third perspective focuses on the ways the case study landscape was represented in earlier periods by contemporary witnesses, either in maps or other images, or in written accounts or stories. Different methods of studying the landscape usually call for a different range of sources.

Continuity and change are important themes in most historical and broader socio-cultural studies, which are of considerable importance in studies of landscape history. The normal processes of change are slow and incremental, measured often in human lifetimes. Contemporary social and economic needs frequently conflict with the material legacies of the past, so there should be a balance between processes of change and the patterns which endure from one period to another. From historical, geographical and landscape perspectives, Estyn Evans's summary is most apposite where he speaks of the landscape 'stage' and the drama of history as a series of acts where 'the stage is never cleared for the next act' and our 'choice of action at any point in time is restricted by actions previously taken'.[5]

In terms of projects which might be worth studying, it is hoped that earlier chapters will prompt readers to follow themes that interest them.[6] The following are examples of some projects which might be explored:

- Territorial history: field and farm, townland, parish and barony comprise the landscape parameters which are of ultimate importance to local studies where textures of ownership, cultural identity, economic development and territorial organisation all intersect
- Histories of settlement landscapes: rundale and field systems, the relationship between field and farm size, changes in enclosures and settlement patterns in the nineteenth and twentieth centuries, road networks, other topics as illustrated in *The Atlas of the Irish rural landscape* and engaging with different editions of the Ordnance Survey, estate records, CDB and ILC records, field work and interviews
- The relationship between the natural and cultural landscapes, the evolution of land reclamation and improvement using such sources as soil maps, maps of peatlands, and details on tree plantations from the Tree Registry in the National Archives
- Designed landscapes as demonstrated by Finola O'Kane's *Landscape design in the eighteenth century* and Patricia Friel's *Frederick Trench and Heywood*. This is one of the most rewarding case studies in the sense that the parkland legacy is often substantially intact and forms a significant locally distinctive landmark. In addition, in most cases, its historical development is more likely to be supported by documentary estate records than more ordinary workaday countrysides

---

5 E. Estyn Evans, *The personality of Ireland* (Cambridge, 1973), p. 68.   **6** See, for example, A. Simms, 'A perspective on Irish settlement studies' in Barry (ed.), *A history of settlement in Ireland*, pp 228–47; P. Coones, 'Geographical approaches to landscape study' in Aalen (ed.), *Landscape study and management*, pp 15–37.

- As cities and towns represent the most intensive contribution to landscape change (as opposed to the more extensive and diffuse nature of rural change), cities have more comprehensive records, especially from the eighteenth century. The historical development of buildings and streetscapes of cities and towns can be more easily recovered from documentary and field evidence and it is possible to construct individual building genealogies.[7]
- More systematic analysis might be made of sources such as the Down Survey, Civil Survey or Books of Survey and Distribution, Griffith's Valuation and OS maps as demonstrated in Crawford and Foy (eds), *Townlands in Ulster* (Belfast, 1998). In this case it has been possible to profile individual townlands in an exemplary fashion by using a range of data sources from the seventeenth century to the twentieth century, from photographs and field work, with Griffith's Valuation and the OS maps as centrepieces. Similar methods have been used in Ó Dálaigh et al. (eds), *Irish townlands* (Dublin, 1998)
- Longitudinal studies of changing family and farm structures are worthwhile, involving reconstruction of rural family, farm and settlement history from the 1901 and 1911 census enumerator schedules available in the National Archives and for 1901 only in PRONI. This source contains a wealth of local data (see chapters four and seven) which in conjunction with field work and interviews can provide rewarding insights into local social landscapes where farms and families were linked by kin and marriage for generations
- In general, local case studies should make more use of field research strategies to reconstruct the dynamics of population-landscape interactions. Many of the techniques, if not the queries, of the Irish Folklore Commission's 1938 schools survey might be replicated in order to recover evidence on rural landscapes which are in process of disappearing and being forgotten. This includes tangible material such as placenames, fieldnames and other minor names along the lines of Eamon Lankford's placenames project in Munster (see chapter three) or material on traditions/*dinnseanchas* about local places as shown in Henry Glassie's work in Fermanagh
- There is more scope also to replicate recent research by Raymond Gillespie on the use of stories and folktales from the medieval and early-modern period as records of changing environments and landscapes (see chapter six). Although in terms of chronological reliability they must be treated with caution, they provide valuable evidence which it may be possible to match with other sources: the late seventeenth-century Montgomery manuscripts, for example, contain stories about the early Ulster plantation which might be fleshed out with Thomas Raven's maps of the emerging new settlements
- GIS and computer technology presents new and expanding possibilities for revisiting, re-working and re-presenting old historical landscape or topographical

---

7 See Nolan & Simms (eds), *Irish towns: a guide to sources*; Christine Casey, *Dublin* (New Haven, 2005); see also http://www.eneclann.ie/house-history.htm

evidence. The plethora of numerical data from the nineteenth century, for example, can now be processed rapidly for analysis and more conveniently presented in digitized maps. The Ordnance Survey of Ireland's Historic Maps Archive allows on-line searches to be undertaken for a limited range of settlement data on the nineteenth-century maps. These techniques will be increasingly applied to earlier data from the seventeenth century for instance. The townland as a territorial entity for which comprehensive quantitative information exists, affords endless possibilities to local historians to reconstruct past landscapes in considerable detail

Leabharlanna Fhine Gall

Select bibliography

Aalen, F.H.A. (ed.), *The future of the Irish rural landscape* (Dublin, 1985)

Aalen, F.H.A., K.Whelan, and M. Stout (eds), *Atlas of the Irish rural landscape* (Cork, 1997)

Andrews, J.H., *Plantation acres: an historical study of the Irish land surveyor and his maps* (Belfast, 1985)

— and A. Simms (eds), *Irish country towns* (Cork, 1994)

— and A. Simms (eds), *More Irish country towns* (Cork, 1995)

— *A paper landscape: the Ordnance Survey in nineteenth-century Ireland* (Oxford, 1975)

Simms, A., H.B. Clarke, R. Gillespie, and K.M. Davies, *Irish Historic Towns Atlas*, vols 1 and 2 (Dublin, 2002)

Bellamy, D., *The wild boglands* (Dublin, 1986)

Buchanan, R.H., E. Jones, and D. McCourt (eds), *Man and his habitat: essays presented to E. Estyn Evans* (London, 1971)

Canavan, T. (ed.), *Every stoney acre has a name: a celebration of the townland in Ulster* (Belfast, 1991)

Casey, C. and A. Rowan, *The buildings of Ireland: north Leinster* (London, 1993)

Clarke, H.B., J. Prunty, and M. Hennessy (eds), *Surveying Ireland's past: multidisciplinary essays in honour of Anngret Simms* (Dublin, 2004)

Collins, T. (ed.), *Decoding the landscape* (Galway, 1994)

Connell, P., D.A. Cronin, and B. Ó Dalaigh (eds), *Irish townlands: studies in local history* (Dublin, 1998)

Crawford, W.H. and R.H. Foy (eds), *Townlands in Ulster* (Belfast, 1998)

Dalsimer, A.M. (ed.), *Visualizing Ireland: national identity and the pictorial tradition* (Boston, 1993)

Delany, R., *A celebration of 250 years of Ireland's inland waterways* (Belfast, 1986)

Doherty, G.M., *The Irish Ordnance Survey: history, culture and memory* (Dublin, 2004)

Duffy, P.J., 'The changing rural landscape: pictorial evidence 1750–1850' in B. Kennedy and R. Gillespie (eds), *Art into history* (Dublin, 1994), pp 26–42

—, 'The town of Monaghan: a place inscribed in street and square' in E. Conlon (ed.), *Later on: the Monaghan bombing memorial anthology* (Dingle, 2004), pp 14–32

—, 'Trends in nineteenth- and twentieth-century settlement' in T. Barry (ed.), *A history of settlement in Ireland* (Oxford, 1999), pp 213–15

—, 'Townlands: territorial signatures of landholding and identity' in B.S. Turner (ed.), *The heart's townland: marking boundaries in Ulster* (Belfast, 2004), pp 18–38

—, 'Unwritten landscapes: reflections on minor place-names and sense of place in the Irish countryside' in Clarke et al. (eds), *Surveying Ireland's past*, pp 689–712

—, D. Edwards, and E. FitzPatrick (eds), *Gaelic Ireland: land, lordship and settlement, c.1250–c.1650* (Dublin, 2001)

—, *Landscapes of south Ulster: a parish atlas of the diocese of Clogher* (Belfast, 1993)

Evans, E. Estyn, *Mourne Country: landscape and life in south Down* (Dundalk, 1951 2nd edn, 1967)

—, *Irish heritage: the landscape, the people and their work* (Dundalk, 1942)

—, *The personality of Ireland – habitat, heritage and history* (Cambridge, 1973)

Feehan, J. and G. O'Donovan, *The bogs of Ireland: an introduction to the natural, cultural and industrial heritage of Irish peatlands* (Dublin, 1996)

Feehan, J., *Farming in Ireland: history, heritage, environment* (Dublin, 2003)

Freeman, T.W., *Pre-famine Ireland: a study in historical geography* (Manchester, 1957)

Gillmor, D. (ed.), *The Irish countryside: landscape, wildlife, history, people* (Dublin, 1989)

Glassie, H., *Passing the time: folklore and history of an Ulster community* (Dublin, 1982)

Graham, B.J. and L.J. Proudfoot, *Urban improvement in provincial Ireland, 1700–1840* (Dublin, 1994)

Harbison, P., *Guide to the national monuments in the Republic of Ireland: including a selection of other monuments not in state care* (Dublin, 1975)

Herries-Davies, G.L. *Sheets of many colours: the mapping of Ireland's rocks, 1750–1890* (Dublin, 1983

Horner, A. (ed.), *Iveragh Co. Kerry in 1811* (Dublin, 2002)

—, *Kenmare River in 1812* (Dublin 2003)

—, *Wicklow and Dublin mountains in 1812* (Dublin, 2004)

Hourihane, J. (ed.), *Engaging spaces: people, place and space from an Irish perspective* (Dublin, 2003)

Malins, E. and the Knight of Glin, *Lost demesnes: Irish landscape gardening, 1660–1845* (London, 1976)

McCracken, E., *The Irish woods since Tudor times: their distribution and exploitation* (Newton Abbot, 1971)

McErlean, T., 'The Irish townland system of landscape organisation' in T. Reeves-Smyth and F. Hammond (eds), *Landscape archaeology in Ireland* (Oxford, 1983)

Mac Gabhann, F. (ed.), *Place-names of Northern Ireland* (8 vols, Belfast, 1993, 1995, 1996, 1997, 2004), vol. 7 (1997)

Mitchell, F. and M. Ryan, *Reading the Irish landscape* (Dublin, 1997)

O'Brien, J. and D. Guinness, *Great Irish houses and castles* (London, 1992)

O'Connor, K., *Ironing the land: the coming of the railways to Ireland* (Dublin, 1999)

O'Connor, P.J., *Atlas of Irish place-names* (Newcastle West, 2001)

O'Kane, F., *Landscape design in eighteenth-century Ireland* (Cork, 2004)

Proudfoot, L.J., *Property ownership and urban and village improvement in provincial Ireland, c.1700–1845* (London, 1997)

Reeves-Smyth, T., 'The natural history of demesnes' in J. Wilson Foster (ed.), *Nature in Ireland: a scientific and cultural history* (Dublin, 1997), pp 549–72

Rothery, S., *Everyday buildings of Ireland* (Dublin, 1975)

Rowan, A.J. (ed.), *The building of Ireland: North west Ulster* (London, 1979)

Shaffrey, P. and M. Shaffrey, *Irish countryside buildings: everyday architecture in the rural landscape* (Dublin, 1985)

Smyth, W.J., *Map-making, landscapes and memory: a geography of colonial and early-modern Ireland c.1530–1750* (Cork, 2006)

Villiers-Tuthill, K., *Alexander Nimmo & the western district: emerging infrastructure in pre-famine Ireland* (Clifden, 2006)

Index